STRATEGIC MARKETING MANAGEMENT

STRATEGIC MARKETING MANAGEMENT

S. SOUNDAIAN

MJP Publishers

MJP PUBLISHERS

© Publishers, 2024   New No. 5, Muthu Kalathy Street
All rights reserved   Triplicane
                         Chennai 600 005

To

My Dear Grandson

Rithek Sankar

PREFACE

A customer is the one who has the power to customise not only the strategies of the organisation but also the organisation's objectives. Customers are not ordinary humans. As Gandhiji said, they are special people and the organisation depends on them; they do not depend on the organisation. These words of Gandhiji which were said many decades ago hold true even today and it will continue to do so.

In those days, selling was the primary objective of business. Those were the days when most of the products were sold in a seller's market. But things changed as the race for customers intensified. The customer became knowledgeable, thanks to the consumer movements around the world. Even though the consumer movement in India started at Ahmedabad long back, it could not pervade the entire country because there were few sponsors to take the idea to the grass roots, viz., the customers. As Indian literacy rate increased steadily barring a few states, the product awareness increased because of globalisation which brought to the fore the existence of organisations like the ISO as far as India is concerned. Now Indian customers know much better about the ISO, thanks to the propaganda made by companies in their advertisements. Today's Indian consumers are very well aware of their value in the market and have started demanding things like better quality and lower price for their product. Thus the concept of marketing slowly replaced the concept of selling in India. Business in India has become comparable to that of developed countries because it is the Indian middle class that makes the chunk of the consumers in the country. The consumers in the low-income group of the country are not serious on their purchases, barring a handful of knowledgeable people among them.

Marketing implied production of goods as per the desires of the customers. It studies the pulse of the consumers, and the companies react accordingly. Those companies which were able to do this process effectively grew fast and the image of such companies in the minds of the buyers reached Himalayan heights. The other companies which failed to study the minds of the customers could not grow fast and they still relied on the concept of selling. Therefore they lagged much behind, struggling for their very survival. This made them realise their mistakes, and now most of the Indian companies are pursuing policies based on total quality, and recognition of the value of a customer. Thus things changed in India too.

The entry of multinational corporations into India and the entry of Indian companies in the global market have made a sea change in the domestic as well as international business scenario. The companies, be it Indian or foreign, have to follow the dictums of the customer. They found it not only from their experience but also from researches conducted by various experts and organisations like McKinsey, CII, and BCG. The global market is becoming nearer and nearer to all, be it consumer, seller, supplier, or a channel member. The IT revolution has converted Mother Earth into a global village. Today's customer places orders via Internet and is able to get the goods needed within a very short period of time. Companies are also keeping up their promises by despatching the goods reliably to the unknown customers. The customers have begun placing trust on the companies as they receive the goods as per their instructions from the sellers.

All these things have resulted in a battle among the manufacturers to bring the customers into their fold. This battle has made the customer more prominent. Now the customer is occupying the centre stage while the sellers act as the audience who study the behaviour of the players on the stage. The race among the companies forced them to think better ways of marketing their products and finally they came to the conclusion that customers must be given more prominence in their approaches towards them. This was realised long back in the developed countries like the U.S., and the result was *strategic marketing management.* American companies were the first to recognise the need for approaching the market from strategic management point of view.

What is strategic marketing management? Strategic marketing management stresses strategic approaches to the challenge of marketing. The term *strategy* implies a long-term look on policies and objectives of the organisation. The past, present, and future environments play a vital role in the formulation of marketing strategies suitable for an organisation. By *reading* the environment, the companies are able to study the market more effectively, and thus, they are able to take proactive measures to win the minds of the customers. Take for example, a channel of distribution. Previously (in India even now, many companies are following the old ways only), channel members were selected on the basis of some criteria. Strategic marketing management suggests that the internal and external environment be considered first, and only those people who fit into the environments are selected as members of the supply chain. If a person's policies are incompatible with the mission and vision of the organisation, then that person does not deserve to become a member of the supply chain. Thus strategic marketing management stresses the need for giving a fresh look at the marketing strategies of the organisation this way.

In India, some of the companies have already started adopting the concept of strategic marketing and many others are yet to follow the new idea. However, very soon they will also realise the need for adopting the concept of strategic marketing. The market is becoming more and more complex, and marketers find it more difficult than ever before to study buyers' behaviour. In this environment, the concept of strategic marketing ought to be a valuable tool with the marketer.

This book studies the concept of strategic marketing in a succinct manner so that even a beginner will be able to understand the idea of strategic marketing easily. This book offers useful information to students of management and marketers from companies of all sizes.

S. Soundaian

CONTENTS

7. Market Segmentation and Product Positioning   135

8. Strategic Product Pricing   157

9. The Distribution Strategy   171

1

ESSENTIALS OF STRATEGIC MARKETING MANAGEMENT

After reading this chapter, you will be able to

- *understand the concept of strategic management,*
- *recognise the connection between marketing management and strategic marketing management,*
- *know about the scope of strategic marketing management,*
- *become knowledgeable about the key terms used in strategic marketing management, and*
- *understand the role of information technology in strategic marketing management.*

KEY TERMS

- Selling
- Marketing
- Strategic marketing
- Strategic marketing plan
- Buyer behaviour
- Environmental analysis
- Marketing mix
- Policies

- Product life cycle
- Strategic brand management
- Marketing communications strategy
- Salesforce management
- New product planning
- Objectives

- Mission
- Vision
- Strategy
- Unique resources
- Core competencies
- Strategic control
- *SWOT* analysis
- Information technology

INTRODUCTION

There was a businessman who was sensitive to the market environment and who was shrewd enough to cope with the changes not only in his line of trade but also with the general business trends. He purchased goods from the nearby city and sold them to his customers in the town. When he started his business, he purchased for his requirements in small quantities because he could not judge the sales level in his business. But after learning that there was good demand for the goods, he started buying more and more to satisfy the customers. He was happy that he could sell goods which suited the needs of his customers. His customers were also happy that they got the required goods at the right price. As he became knowledgeable about his customers' requirements, he kept with him the right quantity of specific goods in ready stock. Since he never said *no* to any customer, his business became famous around the area. *This way of identifying customer needs and buying or manufacturing and selling goods to satisfy their needs is known as marketing management.*

The first-generation businessmen were primarily concerned with just *disposing* of the goods manufactured and they were very much interested in seeing that their warehouses did not hold more than the desired level of stock. They took all the steps to *push* their goods in the market, by whatever means available. They knew nothing about the customers' desires and thus they were ignorant of what was really required by the customer. They produced what they could and they sold them by following traditional selling methods. This is the old concept of *selling*. Then came marketing. Marketing started to rule the business world for several decades until the new concept of strategic marketing found its way in today's business. Marketing management was brought into the picture by the entrepreneurs to make their business a market leader and gain in the market by way of attracting a large number of customers to their fold. We may say that they did that in order to survive in the market in the *long run* and to keep in their fold a good number of loyal customers. Therefore, we can say that it is the competition and the customer preference for new things, which made the difference between *selling* and *marketing*.

Even now, we find marketing management as the core subject of study in most of the B-Schools of today. Nevertheless, *marketing management* contains basic concepts which form the basic of the new field of *strategic marketing management*.

The marketing manager of yesteryears was very much concerned with identification of customers' needs and supplying them with goods capable of satisfying these needs. Later, the same marketing manager went a step forward and created new needs for the new products found by the organisation. Marketing management contains strategies which can be used in the ordinary course of business of confronting the competitors and knowledgeable customers.

WHAT IS STRATEGIC MARKETING MANAGEMENT

When marketing management becomes vigorous and aggressive in tackling the competitors and satisfying the customers using human knowledge power not only in the short run but also in the long run, it becomes *strategic marketing management.* Strategic marketing management applies human skills fully in marketing the goods and it sees that no vacuum is created in this endeavour. Leo Lingham says that a strategic marketing approach attempts to determine ways of offering superior value to the more profitable segments without damaging individual customer relationships.[1] The strategic marketing manager, therefore, aims at identification of profitable market segments and he then tries to offer superior or special value to the customers of that segment in order to obtain the best business. Strategic marketing management may be defined as the process of application of superior skills in selected market segments keeping in mind the long run and environmental needs of the marketing organisation and offering the best product to the consumers belonging to those segments in order to improve their satisfaction levels, enabling the creation of a loyal customer base.

The marketer considers the short-term as well as the long-term requirements in formulating the strategies in finding customers for his goods. A strategic marketing manager is one who

- is aware of value of brands of goods.
- makes a scientific study of environment in which he acts and reacts to customers' behaviour and competitors' strategies.
- looks for a high degree of probability of success in his plans, both short and long term.
- leaves no room for any malfunctioning of the marketing system of his organisation.

Marketing is the core of the business. To outperform the competition, solid marketing knowledge and precision in marketing decision-making are required. The positioning of an organisation and its products and services depend on the formulation and implementation of intelligent and aggressive strategic marketing plans. This is what strategic marketing management purports to do. Strategic marketing is, therefore, both a philosophy and a set of techniques which address such matters as research, product design and development, pricing, packaging, sales and sales promotion, advertising, public relations, distribution and after-sales service.[2]

Table 1.1 shows the comparison between the concepts of selling,, marketing and strategic marketing.

Table 1.1 A comparison between the concepts of selling, marketing, and strategic marketing

Variable	Selling	Marketing	Strategic marketing
Period under consideration	Immediate	Short-run and near future	Present, near, and distant future
Objective	Current profit	Profit during current period and immediate future	Profit at all times
Stress	On selling	On satisfying customer needs	On satisfying customer needs and on positive approach
Means	Any means	Any means that wouldn't damage the firm's reputation	Means acceptable to ethics as well as to customers
End product	Profit	Profit and customer satisfaction	Profit, customer satisfaction, and strong brand name

Exhibit 1.1 Transition from selling to strategic marketing

The Connection between Strategic Management and Strategic Marketing Management

Discourse in the field of strategic marketing has drawn heavily on ideas and concepts from strategic management. As both fields of study are concerned with issues affecting the relationship between the organisation and its environment, strategic management provides a context for the marketing process.[3] The connection between strategic management and strategic marketing management is akin to the connection between general management and functional areas of management, viz., production management, marketing management, financial management, and human resource management. We consider general management principles wherever necessary in the functional areas of management.

By strategic management, we denote the set of approaches to be followed by management in the long run, say 10 years, which goes hand in hand with long-term plans and objectives. In strategic management, the stress is the longer period. It does not mean that the short term, i.e., the present is ignored. Of course this includes the immediate future, and near future as well. Strategic management takes care of the entire future including today, tomorrow, and the day after, i.e., present, near future, and the distant future. The second point is that strategic management emphasises best practices and strategies which will never fail the organisation if executed correctly. Similar is the case in strategic marketing management. All this is possible with a team of highly skilled managerial personnel which is the core of strategic management. Strategic management recognises the quality of manpower in determining the courses of action the management must pursue in its efforts to make its organisation world-class. The specific contribution of marketing in the organisation lies in the formulation of strategies to choose the right customer, build relationships of trust with them and create a competitive advantage. [4]

The business organisation operates in a dynamic market place. This dynamism must be responded with a greater degree of dynamism from the management. The organisation will succeed in today's competitive environment which includes a well-educated lot of customers, only if it makes a concerted effort to fight back and overtake the competitors with better strategies and products packed with quality and fair price. This is possible with a mature team of strategic marketing managers who repulse any attack from the competitors with a heavy blow to them. Look what Walmart is doing! It offers an excellent mixture of what the customer needs: quality, service before, during, and after the sale, fair prices, and pleasing counter service. What else you need to succeed? It is all concerned with strategic marketing management! Knowingly or unknowingly they are following it. When they can, why not you? If you want to beat Walmart, you need the will for it. You have to earn the brand name first. Is it that easy? You need a grand and effective plan for it. That is the strategic marketing plan.

Resource-based View of Strategic Marketing

The resource-based view of the firm is one of the latest strategic management concepts to be enthusiastically embraced by marketing scholars. This view holds much promise as a framework for understanding strategic marketing issues but cautions that, before it is adopted, it needs to be fully understood. Organisations are endowed with different amounts and types of resources and capabilities, which allow them to compete in different ways. Organisations which are better endowed have lower average costs than competitors and can provide products and services at lower cost or provide greater customer value. These resources are difficult to transfer among organisations because of transaction costs and because the assets may contain tacit knowledge.[5] Such resources and core capabilities of the organisation, particularly those which involve collective learning and are knowledge-based, are enhanced as they are applied.[6]

Fahy and Smithee[7] too possess a similar view and stress for the need to adopt a resource-based approach to strategic marketing. They state: "Over the past decade or so, there have been a large and diverse collection of contributions in the areas of economics and strategic management that seek to either refine the concept of the Resource-based view or uses it as a framework for tackling conceptual and empirical questions. Consequently, the basic propositions of the RBV have become increasingly well delineated. In short, the principal contribution of the resource-based view of the firm to date has been as a theory of competitive advantage. Its basic logic is a relatively simple one. It starts with the assumption that the desired outcome of managerial effort within the firm is a sustainable competitive advantage (SCA). Achieving a SCA allows the firm to earn economic rents or above-average returns. In turn, this focuses attention on how firms achieve and sustain advantages."

The organisation possesses certain capabilities, the glue that binds the organisation's assets together and enables them to be used to advantage.[8] Capabilities are so deeply embedded in the organisation's routines and practices that they cannot easily be traded or imitated.[9] The organisation's competitive advantages are derived, therefore, from the nature of its products, markets, technological orientation, resources and knowledge. The essential elements of the resource-based view of the firm are, the firm's key resources and the role of management in converting these resources into positions of sustainable competitive advantage leading to superior performance in the marketplace.[10]

Characteristics of strategic marketing management

Strategic marketing management has some unique characteristics. Let us examine them briefly.

1. ***Derivative in character***   Strategic marketing management is not an independent field of study. It can be originally found in *strategic management.* It has been taken from there for the purpose of giving a special impetus to marketing which is a key function in any business.

2. ***Strategies subject to change***   The marketing strategies suggested in the area of strategic marketing management are only suggestive in nature. These strategies are subject to change. This requires detailed analysis of the situation under consideration. Therefore a good degree of flexibility is needed while applying the strategy in a specific situation. It requires special skills to determine the right strategy for the situation.

3. ***Requires coordination from the top management***   Marketing executives require constant feedback and coordination from the top management. Sometimes,

broad policy statements are issued to them in the form of marketing objectives and the marketing executives will have to work according to these guidelines.

4. *Straightforward task* Once marketing objectives are formulated and handed over to the marketing vice president, the responsibility of carrying out the defined assignment is to be shouldered by the marketing executives. The marketing executives must see that the target is achieved within accepted policy statements of the organisation. Therefore, it becomes a straightforward task to the marketing executives.

5. *Greater expectations from peers and stakeholders* The peers in other departments are eager to see the performance of the marketing department. Not only the peers but also every stakeholder of the organisation is eager to find out the performance of the marketing department that too when new concepts are being adopted in the department. Therefore, the marketing department which is adopting the strategic marketing management concepts is being closely watched by all concerned.

The Strategic Marketing Plan

Strategic planning is concerned about the overall direction of the business. It is concerned with all the functional areas of the business including marketing, of course. The objective of a strategic plan is *to set the direction of a business and create its shape so that the products and services it provides meet the overall business objectives.* Marketing has a key role to play in strategic planning, because it is the job of marketing management to understand and manage the links between the business and the "environment".

What is a Strategic Marketing Plan? A strategic marketing plan consists of a broad outline of specifications of what should be done to accomplish specific marketing objectives during a specified future period which is normally a ten-year period. It is in tune with the organisation's stated vision and mission statements and the stated corporate objectives in the overall long-term strategy of the organisation. The strategic marketing plan is a part of the overall strategic plan of the organisation.

The strategic marketing plan specifically contains strategies that the organisation must adopt with regard to the four P's, viz., product, price, promotion, and place (distribution). In addition, it contains strategies to beat the competitors, and to effectively manage the salesforce.

The following questions are very relevant for any strategic market planning process.

- Where are we now?
- How did we get there?
- Where are we heading?
- Where would we like to be?

- ❋ How do we get there?
- ❋ Are we on the right track?

A very important aspect of the strategic marketing plan is its flexibility. After all, no plan can remain fixed for an indefinite period. As changes occur in the environment, suitable changes must be necessarily made in the marketing plan. The marketing personnel must take corrective steps to match new conditions in the environment. Obviously, they have to take measures to counter competitors' moves.

It is worth noting the observation of Tim Calkins.[11] According to him, a marketing plan should be built around three things: goals and objectives, strategic initiatives, and tactics (GOST). A good marketing plan should always begin with the goals and objectives. At the same time, a marketing plan cannot have too many goals; this dilutes focus and leads to confusion. The heart of a marketing plan is the strategic initiatives. These are the most important moves. Identifying the strategic initiatives, answers the question: What are we going to do in order to deliver the objectives? Strategic initiatives are actions. They are what the organisation will actually do in order to drive the business. The tactics of a marketing plan provide the details. This lays out in detail what will happen against each of the initiatives. This might include advertising campaigns, new product launches and product improvements.

A detailed discussion on strategic marketing plan will be taken up in Chapter 2.

Scope of Strategic Marketing Management

The scope of strategic marketing management is limited to its functions. Therefore, the scope of the subject has to be studied from the angle of the topics covered by the discipline. Let us dwell at some length on the scope of strategic marketing management.

Analysing buyer behaviour The first function of strategic marketing management is to analyse the behaviour of the buyers. An important aspect of the marketing management is to find out why a customer takes so much of care while making a purchase. Some people take lot of care in making their purchase and some others don't. Without this knowledge, businesses would find it difficult to respond to the customer's needs and wants. This buyer behaviour has been traditionally split into two broad groups for analysis: i) individual buyers and ii) industrial buyers. *Individual buyers* are those who purchase goods for their personal or family consumption. *Industrial buyers* are those who purchase goods on behalf of their organisation. Businesses try to find out answers to the following questions:

- ❋ Who buys?
- ❋ How do they buy?

* When do they buy?
* Where do they buy?
* Why do they buy?

At the outset, the answers for these questions may look to be simple. But in reality it is not the fact. Each customer has his preferences for buying. Therefore, the marketing executive must find out the category to which his customers belong.

Environmental analysis   As the study of environment of business is a prerequisite for strategic management, this becomes logical for strategic marketing management also to follow suit. Business environment is i) internal, and ii) external. By internal environment, we mean a study of the firm's resources and capabilities through *SWOT* analysis. By external environment, we mean the external factors like product market, and aspects of external environment having a bearing upon marketing matters including competition. A study of business environment shows the direction the strategic marketing plan must take in order to achieve marketing goals.

Strategic marketing plan   As we discussed earlier, the strategic marketing plan is derived from out of the firm's *strategic plan*. The strategic marketing plan consists of a broad outline of specifications of what should be done to accomplish specific marketing objectives during a specified future period which is normally a ten-year period. This plan must be drafted by a committee consisting of the Chief Executive Officer (CEO), the Chief Marketing Officer (CMO), and a few other senior executives. This plan is the starting point for the CMO. He formulates derivative plans in consultation with his senior colleagues.

Managing marketing mix and product life cycles   Managing the marketing mix continues to be one of the key challenges facing organisations today. The major marketing management decisions can be classified into one of the these four categories: i) product, ii) price, iii) promotion, and iv) place (distribution). These variables are known as *marketing mix* or the *4 P's* of marketing.

Product refers to the service or tangible good that satisfies the target customer's needs—it is obviously first essential that a real target market is identified, quantified and justified. *Price* consists of the policies regarding competitive upgrades, reseller pricing, discounts, list price, distributor and street price (the actual selling price). *Promotion* includes advertising, public relations, event marketing, online marketing, direct marketing, personal selling, channel marketing, and alliances. *Place* refers to placement (usually managed by sales manager), such as having the product available where and when targeted customers want to buy it.

Product life cycle management is the employment of suitable strategies by management as a product goes through its life cycle. Like any living being, a product also passes through several stages from introduction till withdrawal from the market. The conditions in which a product is sold change over time and must be managed as it moves through its succession of stages.

Strategic brand management   Branding seeks to distinguish a firm, product or service from the competition and create a lasting impression in the prospect's mind. According to the American Marketing Association (AMA), brand is a "name, term, sign, symbol, or design, or a combination of them, intended to identify the goods and services of one seller or group of sellers and to differentiate them from those of competition." Brand management is consciously providing a product with an identity that is understood on all levels. Good branding begins with knowing what makes the product special and exploiting its advantages. Branding may be for a specific product or could cover an entire corporate image. It plays a key role in shaping the future of an organisation. However, it must be noted that brand name minus product traits will be of no value. *Brands that do not offer its traditional features will slowly disappear from the market.* Therefore brand management is an important task to be looked after with care.

Communications strategy   Marketing communications is the process of informing, reminding, and persuading the consumers about a particular product or service. The various promotional tools involved in product promotion comprise the communications mix of an organisation. Marketing communications is instrumental in influencing the purchase decision of the consumer.

Marketing communications strategies relate to the process of communicating the consumer as well as the stakeholders of the developments taking place in the firm in regard to the new products of the firm. It is necessary to integrate marketing communications to more precisely defined segments of "empowered" customers and consumers as they relate to the firm's products and services.

The marketing communications strategy process usually begins with creating a strategy that determines the consistent theme or fundamental selling message that will be used in all marketing materials. Another important task of marketing communications is to create the positioning statement. This positioning statement is critical to making all of the other parts of the marketing communications strategy work well.

Salesforce management strategies   An effective salesforce strategy is critical to achieving sales targets and aligning the salesforce with the strategic direction of the firm. Sales managers must be able to craft strategy and communicate it to the sales team in order to win the right kind of business and achieve growth targets for the business. Developing a salesforce strategy explores the key success factors involved in creating an effective salesforce and communicating the strategy to salespeople. It helps managers develop a comprehensive, prioritised business plan, including required strategic and tactical elements.

Managing the salesforce involves a number of key areas including, performance measurement, selection and training of sales people, and motivational methods. Sales force management also includes decision on salesforce organisation. Salesforce organisation refers to the type and size of the salesforce. The type determines the degree of controllability while the size has profit implications. If the salesforce is large, the organisation has to decide about the kind of specialisation and coordination to use.

New product planning strategies　New product planning and development is the term used to describe the complete process of bringing a new product or service to market. There are two parallel paths involved in this process: one involves the idea generation, product design, and detail engineering; the other involves market research and marketing analysis. Ideas for new products can be obtained from basic research using a *SWOT* analysis, market and consumer trends, firm's research and development department, competitors, focus groups, employees, sales people, corporate spies, and trade shows.

It is important to plan and execute overall growth through a well-managed portfolio by addressing current and long-term needs in the firm's new product planning and strategic alliance systems. In fact, this is one of the purposes of strategic marketing management.

Service and relationship strategies　Customer relationships are the keys to the marketing strategy. Relationship marketing recognises the long-term value to the firm of keeping customers. Relationship marketing refers to a long-term and mutually beneficial arrangement wherein both the buyer and seller focus on value enhancement with the goal of providing a more satisfying exchange. This approach attempts to transcend the simple purchase-exchange process with customer to make more meaningful and richer contact by providing a more holistic, personalised purchase, and use the consumption experience to create stronger ties.

Customer service is one of the most important ingredients of the marketing mix for products and services. High quality customer service helps to create customer loyalty. Customers today are not only interested in the product they are being offered but also in all the additional elements of service that they get, starting from the greeting they receive when they enter a retail outlet till the refund or replacement and help that they receive when they have a complaint about a faulty product for which they already paid their money.

Key Terms Revisited

Strategic marketing management makes use of key terms used in strategic management. Therefore it becomes imperative to look at them again in order to understand them in the correct perspective. They are: mission, vision, strategy, unique resources and core competencies, strategic control, *SWOT*, policies and objectives.

Mission   In the Mission Statement Book by Jeffrey Abrahams, *TRINOVA* Corporation defines a *mission statement* in the following way: "A mission statement is an enduring statement of purpose for an organisation that identifies the scope of its operations in product and market terms, and reflects its values and priorities." Stone (1996) gives another definition extracted from 'Say and Live it: The 50 Corporate Mission Statements That Hit the Mark': "Corporate mission statements … are the operational, ethical and financial guiding lights of companies. They are not simply mottoes or slogans, they articulate the goals, dreams, behaviour, culture and strategies of companies." Basically, a mission statement is designed to say exactly what the organisation anticipates it will achieve.

Vision   Corporate vision is a short, succinct, and inspiring statement of what the organisation intends to become and to achieve at some point in the future, often stated in competitive terms. Vision refers to the category of intentions that are broad, all-inclusive and broad thinking. It is the image that a business must have of its goals before it sets out to reach them. It describes aspirations for the future, without specifying the means that will be used to achieve those broad desired ends.

Strategy   A *strategy* is the direction of the firm in the long run. The strategist draws plans to accomplish the final goals of the organisation. It is more or less expressed in broad statements of the route the firm should take in the course of its functioning.

Unique resources **and** *core competencies*   These are the special plus points enjoyed by the organisation over the others. They may also be called as competitive advantages.

Strategic control   This is the constant monitoring of the direction in which the organisation is moving. A good amount of vigilance and alert is needed to maintain strategic control over the organisation.

SWOT   *SWOT* is the abbreviation used in management to mean strengths, weaknesses, opportunities, and threats. This model is the basic commandment for all organisations of today. If this model is applied perfectly, the firm will mostly not face any irresolvable challenge in its lifetime.

Policies   These are the means by which the objectives, either short-term or long-term are achieved. Policies include guidelines, rules, and procedures established to support efforts to achieve the objectives.

Objectives   Objectives are the milestones that organisations must achieve to reach objectives of short-term or long-term. Objectives should be measurable, quantitative, challenging, realistic, consistent, and prioritised.

INFORMATION TECHNOLOGY AND STRATEGIC MARKETING MANAGEMENT

Information systems are the foundation for conducting business in today's globalised market. In many organisations, survival and even existence without extensive use of information technology is beyond imagination and it plays a very critical role in increasing productivity. Although information technology has become more of a commodity in organisation and management, it can provide the foundation for new products, services, and ways of conducting business that provide firms with a strategic advantage. Information technology in larger organisations tends to strongly influence its development, use, and application in various spheres of activity.

Information technology can be used by organisations to more effectively pursue strategic marketing, by further enabling:

* Analysis of existing business drivers of profitability
* Assessment of customer base for cross selling
* Development of new products and features on a profitable basis
* Determination of cost structures for products, customers and products
* Evaluation of producer profitability and growth opportunities
* Assessment of the value of customer service and online support service
* Evaluation of competitive pricing trends and levels needed for targeted profitability.

There has to be an evaluation of what specific information and analysis are needed to fulfil the complete strategic marketing requirements. Once this information is provided to the information technology professionals, they will be able to devise systems and methods to resolve strategy-based marketing issues. It is also important to evaluate the cost/benefit to meet those needs. Typically, an information technology solution that will meet 80–90% of the strategic marketing need is sufficient to make effective decisions.

Todorka Kovacheva has provided a list of information technology services and solutions which can be used for strategic management. This list[12] will be very useful for strategic marketing management as well.

i.   Knowledge management systems
ii. Ontology generation systems
iii. Expert systems for different knowledge domains

    iv. Business intelligence systems

    v. Knowledge map systems

    vi. Innovation support tools

    vii. Competitive intelligence tools

    viii. Knowledge portals and web services

    ix. Knowledge collaboration systems

    x. Knowledge exchange systems

    xi. Knowledge-based support systems

Strategic marketing management for whom?   Many entrepreneurs think that strategic marketing management is meant for big organisations only and small organisations cannot afford to have an exclusive department for strategic marketing management. This is a wrong notion. Organisations of any size can make use of strategic marketing management. What is required is a good understanding of the concept of strategic marketing management.

Earlier in this chapter, we studied how strategic marketing emerged from the function of selling. The concept of selling has been replaced by the concept of marketing. Similarly the concept of marketing is being replaced with strategic marketing. It is no wonder that strategic marketing will reach an ordinary Many entrepreneurs soon.

SUMMARY

* The marketing manager of yesteryears was very much concerned with identification of customers' needs and supplying them with goods capable of satisfying these needs. Later the same marketing managers went a step ahead and new markets were created by them for the new products found by their organisation. Marketing management contains strategies which can be used in the ordinary course of business of confronting the competitors and knowledgeable customers.

* When marketing management becomes vigorous and aggressive in tackling the competitors and satisfying the customers using human knowledge power not only in the short run but also in the long run, it becomes *strategic marketing management.* Strategic marketing management applies human skills fully in marketing the goods and it sees that no vacuum is created in this endeavour. The marketer considers the short run as well as the long run in formulating the strategies in finding customers for their goods.

* The connection between strategic management and strategic marketing management is akin to the connection between general management and

functional areas of management, viz., production management, marketing management, financial management and human resource management.

* A strategic marketing plan consists of a broad outline of specifications of what should be done to accomplish specific marketing objectives during a specified future period which is normally a ten-year period. It is in tune with the organisation's stated vision and mission statements and the stated corporate objectives in the overall long-term strategy of the organisation. The strategic marketing plan is a part of the overall strategic plan of the organisation.

* The characteristics of strategic marketing management are: i) Derivative in character, ii) Strategies subject to change, iii) Requires coordination from the top management, iv) Straightforward task, and v) Greater expectations from peers and stakeholders.

* The scope of strategic marketing management is limited to its functions. Therefore, the scope of the subject has to be studied from the angle of the topics covered by the discipline.

* Strategic marketing management makes use of key terms used in strategic management. Therefore it becomes imperative to look at them again in order to understand them in the correct perspective. They are: mission, vision, strategy, unique resources and core competencies, strategic control, *SWOT,* policies and objectives.

* Information systems are the foundation for conducting business today in a globalised market. In many organisations, survival and even existence without extensive use of information technology is beyond imagination and it plays a critical role in increasing productivity. Although information technology has become more of a commodity in organisation and management, it can provide the foundation for new products, services, and ways of conducting business that provide firms with a strategic advantage.

* Organisations of any size can make use of strategic marketing management. What is required is a good understanding of the concept of strategic marketing management.

REVIEW QUESTIONS

1. What is strategic marketing management?
2. "The marketing manager of yesteryears was very much concerned with identification of customers' needs and supplying them with goods capable of satisfying these needs." Explain the role of today's marketer in the new business setting.

3. Discuss the connection between strategic management and strategic marketing management.

4. Leo Lingham says that a strategic marketing approach attempts to determine ways of offering superior value to the more profitable segments without damaging individual customer relationships. Do you agree with him? Give valid points for your stand.

5. "Discourse in the field of strategic marketing has drawn heavily on ideas and concepts from strategic management." List out the concepts of strategic management that have been absorbed by strategic marketing.

6. What is the resource-based view of strategic marketing?

7. "The principal contribution of the resource-based view of the firm to date has been as a theory of competitive advantage." Explain the theory of competitive advantage.

8. Explain the process of accomplishing sustainable competitive advantage by making a study of competitive advantages.

9. Explain the strategic marketing plan.

10. "A very important aspect of the strategic marketing plan is its flexibility." Explain why we stress flexibility in a strategic marketing plan.

11. According to Tim Calkins, a marketing plan should be built around three things: goals and objectives, strategic initiatives and tactics. Explain the rationale behind the observation of Tim Calkins.

12. State the characteristics of strategic marketing management.

13. Analyse the scope of strategic marketing management.

14. "Some people take lot of care in making their purchase and some others don't." Explain the reasons for their behaviour.

15. Explain the key terms used in strategic management.

16. Explore the connection between information technology and strategic marketing management.

REFERENCES

1. Leo Lingham, on Strategic Marketing in the website http://en.allexperts.com/q/Marketing-1090/Strategic-marketing.htm

2. *Ibid.*

3. Brownlie, Douglas T. (1989). "The migration of ideas from strategic management to marketing on the subject of competition." *European Journal of Marketing.* pp. 7–20.

4. Doyle, Peter (2000). "Valuing marketing's contribution." *European Management Journal.* **18**(3): 235.

5. Teece, D. J., Pisano, G. and Shuen, A. (1996). *Dynamic Capabilities and Strategic Management,* Working Paper, 53. University of California Press, Berkeley, CA p. 15.

6. Prahalad, C. K. and Hamel, G. (1990). "The core competence of the corporation." *Harvard Business Review.* **68**: 79–91.

7. Fahy, John and Smithee, Alan. (1999). "Strategic marketing and the resource based view of the firm." *Academy of Marketing Science Review.* 10: 9.

8. *Ibid.*

9. Day, George. (1994). "The capabilities of market-driven organisations." *Journal of Marketing.* **58**: 38.

10. Dierickx, I. and Cool, K. (1989). "Asset stock accumulation and sustainability of competitive advantage." *Management Science.* 35: 1504–11.

11. Calkins, Tim. (2009). *A Marketing Plan for Turbulent Times,* IVEY Business Journal.

12. These information technology tools are available in a paper published by Todorka Kovacheva titled *Information Technologies for Strategic Management* which was presented in the *Sixth International Conference on Information Research and Applications – i.Tech 2008, Varna, Bulgaria, June–July 2008.*

2

THE PROCESS OF STRATEGIC MARKETING MANAGEMENT[1]

After reading this chapter, you will be able to

- *understand the meaning and definition of strategic marketing management,*
- *learn the steps involved in strategic marketing management,*
- *learn the strategies to be used during the boom period, recession, decline, and business recovery,*
- *learn the process of marketing strategy implementation,*
- *understand fully the challenge of strategy implementation,*
- *know about the obstacles to strategy execution, and the ways to overcome them,*
- *know about the features of strategic marketing decisions, and*
- *learn the steps in performance evaluation, review and control*

KEY TERMS

Environmental scanning	Peak/Boom	Competencies
Situation analysis	Action plan	Resource constraints
Marketing strategy	Authority delegation	Unique advantages
Business cycles	Commands	Management commitment
Recession	Strategy execution	Strategic market position
Recovery	Organisational culture	PERCP
Decline	Competitive advantage	PERC cycle

INTRODUCTION

Strategic marketing management is the process of specifying an organisation's marketing objectives in the long run, developing policies, and strategies to achieve these objectives, formulating the strategic marketing plan, allocating resources judiciously and executing the strategic marketing plan effectively. It is the highest level of marketing activity. It is not a task, but rather a set of marketing skills that ought to be exerted throughout the marketing organisation. The strategic marketing management process is a way for businesses to build marketing strategies that help the company respond quickly to new challenges. Strategic marketing management is very essential for the marketing organisation which is operating in an environment of uncertain future. Nobody in the organisation might know how the close competitor is going to act. Nobody knows what is in store for the firm in future. Nobody knows whether there will be a good monsoon during the next year in the country. Strategic marketing management process prepares the marketing executive to confront all these challenges with confidence.

The process of strategic marketing management involves matching the firm's strategic marketing advantages to the business environment. One objective of an overall marketing strategy is to put the marketing organisation in a position to carry out its mission effectively. A good marketing strategy should integrate an organisation's goals, policies, and tactics into a cohesive whole, and must be based on business realities. Business enterprises can fail despite "excellent" strategy because the world changes in a way which the business enterprise fails to understand. Marketing strategies must connect with vision, purpose, and likely future trends. A marketing strategy consists of an internally integrated but externally focused set of choices about how the organisation addresses its customers in the context of a competitive environment.

The following steps are essential in the strategic marketing management process:

1.   Marketing Strategy Planning/Formulation
2.   Marketing Strategy Implementation
3.   Marketing Strategy Evaluation, Review, and Control

These steps are given clearly in Exhibit 2.1. Let us make an analysis of these components of strategic marketing management process.

MARKETING STRATEGY PLANNING/FORMULATION

Marketing strategy planning is the process of determining appropriate courses of action for achieving the marketing organisation's objectives. It is the process that determines the future direction of the marketing organisation and what organisational structure will be needed. This process identifies business opportunities and resources that are required to convert opportunity into success. The marketing strategy formulated by the management should reflect environmental analysis, lead to fulfilment of its organisational mission, and result in reaching organisational objectives. Special tools it can use to assist the marketing executive in formulating strategies include environmental scanning, *SWOT* analysis, Porter's model for industry analysis, and resource-based model. These four strategy development tools are related but distinct. The marketing executive should use a single tool or combination of tools that is most appropriate for the organisation and the environment in which it operates.

In today's highly competitive business environment, forecast-based planning methods are not adequate for large companies to prosper in the short as well as long run. The firm must engage itself with strategic planning that clearly defines objectives and assesses both the internal and external situation to formulate the marketing strategy, evaluate the progress and make necessary adjustments to stay on the track.

Exhibit 2.1   Strategic marketing management process

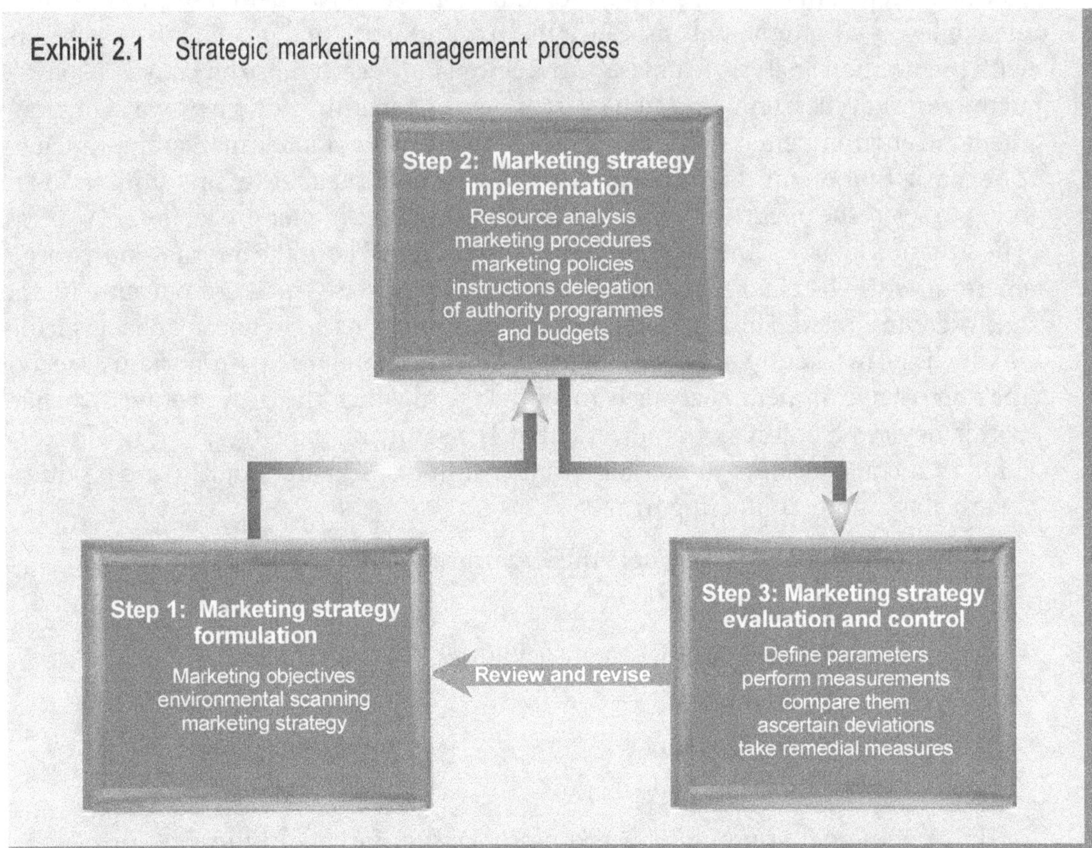

Developing a focused marketing strategy and an implementation plan is far more effective than leaving the future to chances. An effective marketing strategy formulation process will create higher levels of motivation, commitment and fuel continuously higher levels of achievement from everyone within the marketing organisation. The strategy formulation process provides a format for developing specific strategies, converts those strategies into a marketing planning process, and establishes specific, measurable, and attainable goals. It is a process that involves not only determining where a firm wants and needs to go, but also, how it is going to get there.

Marketing strategy formulation involves i) doing a situation analysis—both internal and external ii) setting marketing objectives and iii) planning. This three-step marketing strategy formulation process is sometimes described as determining where you are now, where you want to go, and then how to get there. These are the essence of marketing strategy planning.

ENVIRONMENTAL SCANNING

The next step in marketing strategy formulation is environmental scanning. This is also called as situation analysis. Once the firm has specified its objectives, it begins with its situation analysis to devise a strategic plan to reach those objectives. Changes in the external environment often present new opportunities and new ways to attain them. An environmental scan is performed to identify the suitable marketing strategies. The marketing organisation must also know its own capabilities and limitations in order to select the opportunities that it can pursue with a higher probability of success. The situation analysis, therefore, involves an analysis of both the internal and external environment. The external environment has two aspects—macro-environment and micro-environment. The macro-environment mostly consists of uncontrollable factors to which the marketing organisation must tune its strategies. An important aspect of the micro-environment analysis is the industry in which the firm operates. Michael Porter devised a 5 forces framework that is useful for industry analysis. Porter's 5 forces include barriers to market entry, customers, suppliers, substitute products, and rivalry among competing firms.

The internal analysis considers the situation within the firm itself, such as

- Key staff
- Operational efficiency/capabilities
- Brand power
- Financial resources
- Patents and trade marks

Environmental scanning is a process of gathering, analysing, and dispensing information for tactical or strategic purposes. The environmental scanning process entails obtaining both factual and subjective information on the business environments in which a marketing organisation is operating or considering entering. Coates identified the following objectives of an environmental scanning system:

- detecting scientific, technical, economic, social, political trends and events important to the marketing organisation,

- defining the potential threats, opportunities, or changes implied by those trends and events,

- promoting a future orientation in the thinking of management and staff, and

- alerting management and staff to trends that are converging, diverging, speeding up, slowing down, or interacting.

MARKETING STRATEGY

A strategy has five elements which deals with the following:

1. where the organisation plans to be active,
2. how it will get there,
3. how it will succeed in the marketplace,
4. what the speed and sequence of moves will be, and
5. how the organisation will obtain profits.[2]

The marketing executive who formulates marketing strategies identifies the segments in which he/she wants to be active, chalks out a plan as to how to get there, determines the action plan containing smaller activities, formulates the exact strategy of executing the action plan and selects the right people who would do the execution with razor precision. Successful marketing strategies create a desire for the product. Therefore the strategy that a marketer formulates must inspire the customer toward making a favourable product purchase decision.

The concept of strategy has been borrowed from the military and adapted for use in business. Strategy is the broad outline drawn to defeat the enemy in the battle field. Troops are rightly positioned and instructions are issued as and when necessary. It is used in business for winning the game of business. A firm, especially its marketing wing, operates in a war-like situation. If it does not notice the changes occurring around it, the business is bound to lose the game. The right marketing strategy is determined by executives using their talents effectively and knowledge about the market and its environment. The marketing strategy involves i) the formulation of the goals for immediate, near and distant future and ii) preparation of a blue print that contains the action plan of the marketing organisation.

A marketing strategy may be defined as a specific business approach that contains a detailed action plan for the achievement of marketing objectives in the long run in the light of internal and external forces operating in the marketing environment. It paves the way for effective management of any unforeseen events which are common in the doing of business as future is uncertain. The management of the organisation possesses in its stock all the weapons to confront the unforeseen enemy. The enemy may appear in the scene any time and in any form. The weapons in the arsenal of the organisation are:

    i.   competitive advantages

    ii.   think-tank

    iii.   a team of well-empowered executives

    iv.   the abiding members of the organisation and

    v.   loyal customers.

Marketing strategies are considered from several angles by experts. But all these variations basically have the same idea in mind. Only the names differ. For example, marketing strategies are divided as customer-oriented strategies, competitor-oriented strategies, and specific or situational strategies. Michael Porter[3] has his own classification. He calls them as generic strategies. His generic strategies are 1) cost leadership strategy, 2) differentiation strategy and 3) focus strategy. Under a cost leadership strategy, the firm sells its products either at average industry prices to earn a profit higher than that of rivals, or below the average industry prices to gain market share. A differentiation strategy calls for the development of a product or service that offers unique attributes that are valued by customers and that customers perceive to be better than or different from the products of the competition. The focus strategy concentrates on a narrow segment and within that segment attempts to achieve either a cost advantage or differentiation. The premise is that the needs of the group can be better serviced by focusing entirely on it.

Marketing Strategies Based on Business Cycles

In this book, marketing strategies are looked from the angle of a business cycle. They may be

- boom period strategies,
- declining market strategies,
- recession strategies and
- business recovery strategies.

The firm has to select the strategy that fits it. Strategies need to be formulated whenever the situation in the environment warrants. The management must be alert to these changing conditions. Exhibit 2.2 deals with strategy formulation in a new situation.

Exhibit 2.2   Marketing strategy formulation in a new situation

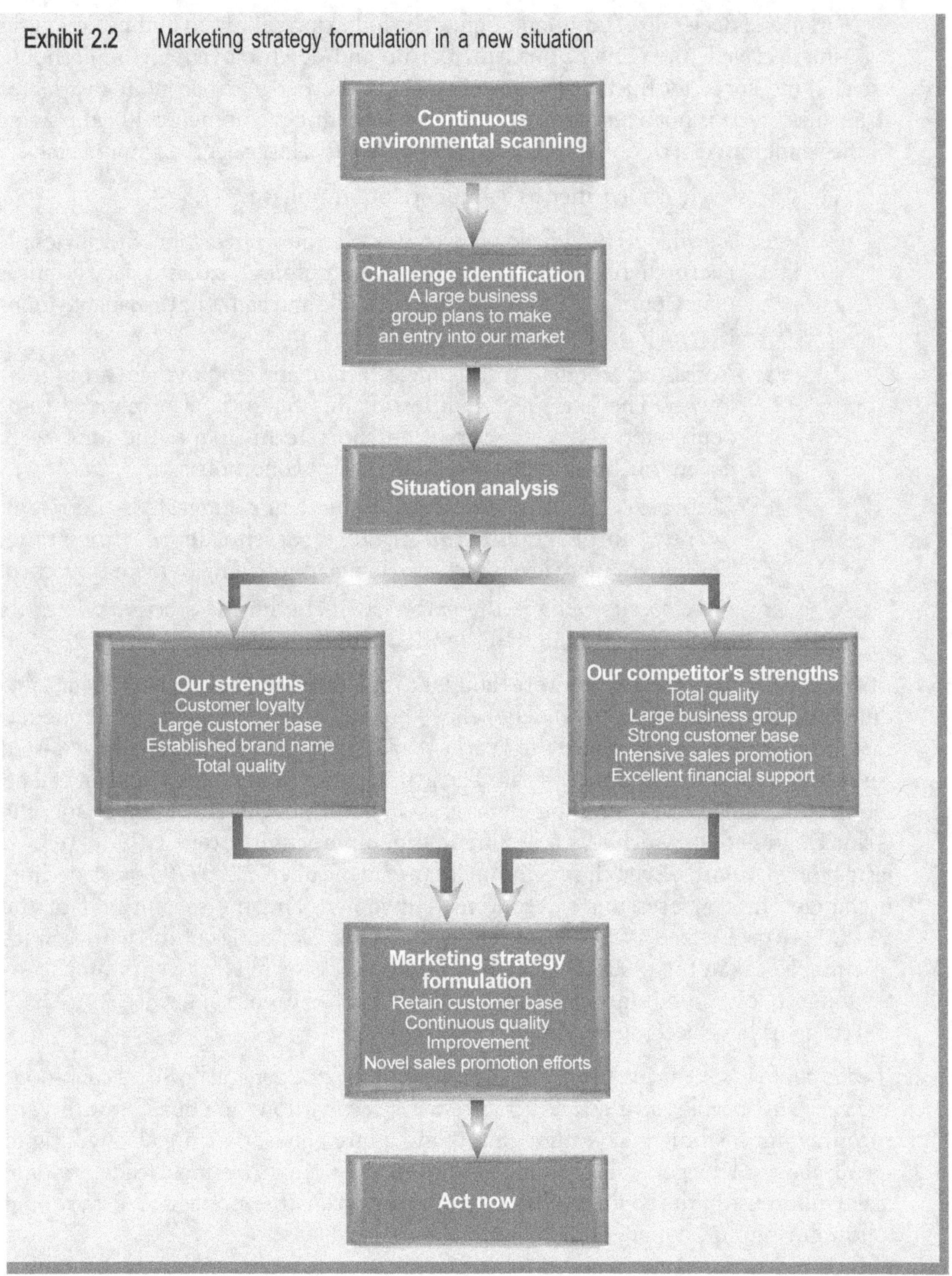

Parkin and Bade's text "Economics" gives the following definition for business cycle: a *business cycle* is the periodic but irregular up-and-down movements in economic activity, measured by fluctuations in real GDP and other macroeconomic variables. A business cycle is not a regular, predictable, or repeating phenomenon like the swing of the pendulum of a clock. Its timing is random and to a large degree, unpredictable.

A business cycle is identified as a sequence of four phases:

- *Decline*   The slowdown becomes a serious contraction. Surpluses are everywhere: product inventories are bulging, excess capacity causes newly purchased equipment to turn idle and banks have loanable funds that no project justifies.

- *Recession/trough*   At this stage, output and employment are at their lowest. The extreme condition of this phase is also referred to as depression. This stage may be short-term or may be long-term depending on circumstances and market conditions.

- *Recovery*   The recovery stage, as the name suggests is the rise in output, employment and trade after the depression stage. The employment levels increase till maximum employment is reached.

- *Peak/boom*   This is the stage when the business activity is at its maximum, although this level of activity is temporary.

At one time, business cycles were thought to be extremely regular, with predictable durations, but today they are widely believed to be irregular, varying in frequency, magnitude and duration. Since the World War II, most business cycles have lasted three to five years from peak to peak. The average duration of an expansion is 44.8 months and the average duration of a recession is 11 months. As a comparison, the Great Depression—which saw a decline in economic activity from 1929 to 1933—lasted for 43 months. Even the beginning of the financial year 2007–08 saw a decline; it changed into a recession or economic slowdown, and the second half of the FY 2009–10 witnessed a slow recovery for the major economies of the world. Since reaching a peak in July 2007, the Leading Economic Index fell for twenty months—the longest downtrend since the mid-1970s—but it has been rising since April 2009 and its gains have become very widespread.

Boom period strategies   During the peak of a business cycle, the general business conditions are very favourable; all the markets are active; conditions for business are very encouraging; customers have enough money to buy goods; they are also willing to spend; above all the general economic conditions are positive. Business leaders should make fullest use of the boom conditions. Let us now study the strategies a firm should follow during the boom period.

1. *Exploit the market fully*   The firm must make the fullest use of this opportunity. The marketplace must be flooded with goods because the customers are willing to buy goods without any reservations. Therefore the plant has to work to its full capacity. Detailed plans for distribution of goods to the market should be drafted in order that at no place the goods are held for lack of transport facilities.

2. *Accumulate cash reserves*   Boom is the right time to accumulate firm's cash reserves. It is the time when the firm must plan for ways of adding reserves to its treasury. Any let up in this process will be a big mistake for which the firm will have to feel at a later stage.

3. *Reduce overall spending*   Spending must be at its lowest level. Only essential expenditures should be sanctioned. Expenditure on ads, discount offers and other expenditure on sales promotion must be reduced. They must be maintained at a low level; but this must be done very carefully. The firm should not distance itself from the customers and other stakeholders. Therefore a strategy that would sustain the market contact should be developed. The stakeholders should not feel the punch; in such a way the strategy should be designed.

4. *Introduce new products*   Boom is the time you have to introduce new products in the market. The customers will buy them without any second thought. If your product is really worthy, they will occupy a good place in the hearts of the customers. Therefore see that your products are really good and deserves a permanent place in the market. When your product is good in quality and packaging, reasonably priced, and introduced through proper ads and outlets, there would be no reason for its failure. Therefore ensure that your product satisfies all these requirements.

5. *Try new channels*   If your present channels need a change, do it at this period. But, see that the new channel will not snatch away the sales volume and the new channel must give a reasonable addition to the sales.

Declining market strategies   Boom is not a permanent state of the economy. Sometimes it may be a lengthy one; at other times boom may end quickly. Research is unable to cite any particular reason for this phenomenon. The firm must adopt suitable strategies in order to sustain its market share during market decline phase. Market declines are often caused by external events such as the creation of competing technology, a shift in customer tastes and needs, and a shift in government policy. Let us discuss a few suitable strategies for the declining market.

1. *Make your market presence visible*   You must take steps to see that you are in the market and your products are much better than ever before. The customers must be reminded of the plus points of your product and you must add new plus points in your product.

2. *Spend more to thwart competition*   You have to spend more sales promotional measures in order that the competitors find it difficult to stay in the market. Don't spend excessively. Have a budget. Create effective advertisements. Introduce attractive packages.

3. *Cover new segments*   Take steps to enter the new segments in the market. Go for niche marketing. Attract new customers through attractive advertisements.

4. *Create a dominant brand*   You must create a good brand. See that you are creating a power-packed brand so that the customer is made to purchase. Dominant brands are very effective in consolidating the firm's position in the market.

5. *Purchase competitor's business*   If you have accumulated sufficient reserves during the boom period, you can go for purchasing the competitor's business. It will be a prudent step. But be careful while doing it. It should not become as an anticlimax. Think well before proceeding to buy your competitor's brand.

6. *Reduce operating expenses*   You must reduce operating expenses considerably. You can reduce the incentive rates. You can sanction only a limited pay rise to your employees. The point is that you must take all the possible steps to reduce your expenditure.

7. *Reduce prices slightly*   Frequently slight reduction may help you very much to sustain sales levels. Sometimes it may even make wonders. Consider the degree of price reduction carefully. It should not erode your profit levels too much.

Recession strategies   A recession just slows everything down. Clients act more slowly, fewer projects enter the pipeline, and we are left with a little extra time. Rather than fill this time with insecurity, we should use it to differentiate ourselves and build our own personal brands as more actionable, affordable and innovative. Recession is a phenomenon of decreasing demand for raw materials, products and services. Technically, its beginning, progress, and ending depend on the operational measures used by different researchers and government agencies. Whichever the case, recession requires marketing managers to modify their marketing strategy and action in order to stay both profitable and consumer-responsive. This generally means adapting the marketing mix and/or changing the target markets. In a recession, consumers become value-oriented, distributors are concerned about cash, and employees worry about their jobs.

Recessionary economic conditions have forced not only European companies but also multinational companies to downsize, to layoff managers and employees. This was almost unheard of prior to the mid-1990s because the government laws were required to be strictly adhered and huge compensation had to be paid to the employees who were out of work. But companies started thinking that compensating the retrenched employees was less costly than retaining them in the firm.

Let us now study some of the important strategies to be followed by an organisation during recession.

1. ***Consult your customers***   Your customers will tell you how to beat recession. Only thing is that you have to ask them. So when customers start tightening their purse, you can do that too. Also they will tell you how much they can pay you. Listen to that and do it. Offering payment plans has worked very well in case of small businesses, and it can work very well for you too.

2. ***Research the consumer***   Instead of cutting the market research budget, you need to know more than ever how consumers are redefining value and responding to the recession. Price elasticity curves are changing. Trusted brands are especially valued and they can still launch new products successfully, but interest in new brands and new categories fades. Conspicuous consumption becomes less prevalent.

3. ***Start re-engaging with your past customers***   Now is a great opportunity to re-engage and strengthen your network. Spend some time fixing up your address book, go through that pile of business cards and enter them into your computer, and start connecting them on who you want to follow-up with.

4. ***Take extra care of your existing customers***   Your existing clients are what keep your business running during lean times. You will need to take special care of them, since your competitors will no doubt have their eyes on your clients. Remember, they are also facing rough economic weather as well. Tell them how you appreciate their support over such a trying period without mentioning the word 'recession.' You can also reward them by offering them special discounts or gifts as a token of your appreciation. Let them know that you appreciate their business and their loyalty.

5. ***Increase your level of service***   In times when competitors are trying to undercut each other on price, let your service level be a notch higher than the others. Satisfied clients are sure to bring in new clients for your business. During recession time it is really important to realise that the customer is truly the King.

6. ***Avoid cutting down marketing budget***   This is not the time to cut advertising. It is well documented that brands that increase advertising during a recession, when competitors are cutting back, can improve market share and return on investment at lower cost than during good economic times. Uncertain consumers need the reassurance of known brands. Don't cheapen your advertising by trying to save on creative or production costs. Your customers will notice and worry about quality. This is a time to stress quality and value.

7. ***Adjust product portfolios***   Marketers must re-forecast demand for each item in their product lines as consumers trade down to models that stress good value, such as cars with fewer options. Tough times favour multi-purpose goods over specialised products and weaker items in product lines should be pruned. New products, especially

those that address the new consumer reality and thereby put pressure on competitors, should still be introduced; but advertising should also play its role.

8. *Support distributors* In uncertain times, no one wants to tie-up working capital in excess inventories. Early-buy allowances, extended financing and generous return policies motivate distributors to stock your full product line. This is particularly true with unproven new products. However, now may be the time to drop your weaker distributors and upgrade your salesforce by recruiting those sacked by other companies.

9. **Emphasise core values** Although most companies are making employees redundant, chief executives can cement the loyalty of those who remain by assuring employees that the firm has survived difficult times before, maintaining quality rather than cutting corners, and servicing existing customers rather than trying to be all things to all people. CEOs must spend more time with customers and employees. Successful companies do not abandon their marketing strategies in a recession; they adapt them.

10. *Prepare your team for business recovery* A very important point is to recognise the fact that the onset of market recovery is very near and while trying to manage the recessionary conditions, you should not fail to take into account this fact. It is sure that market will recover sooner or later and you must prepare your team side by side to look into this aspect also. You may need to introduce new products on the onset of the recovery of the economy and you can keep in store ready a few dominant new products. You must enter into the market with the new products at the right time. Study the market thoroughly and enter the market with your new products. But you must understand the fact that this is not an easy job because you might have all your attention turned on the management of recession. However a *prudent* businessman will surely prepare for the future.

Business recovery strategies Recovering the lost business is a delicate process and it requires concerted efforts on the part of management. Let us now see the probable impacts of recession which has the capability to devastate even big businesses.

- Customer relationships would have been under stress at the time of recession because the firm would have been strict in its approach to them. No one is to blame for this situation. Therefore rebuilding the customer relations has to be given top priority in its agenda.

- The second priority is to be given for the state of finance in the business. There would have been expenditure from unexpected quarters at the time of recession. These expenditures might have been necessary at the time; but they would have brought no return to the organisation. In small and medium organisations, the problem would be still worse and even sometimes beyond the control of the management. Contacts with the fund providers must be re-established and a detailed report must be prepared to fix fund requirements.

* Another group of sufferers is the employees. The employees' morale would be at a low and it might require honest assurances from management to the workers on the future of their employment. Sometimes, the retrenched employees may have to be recalled to fill the gap. A fresh manpower plan may be required to determine manpower requirements for future.

* Next, the firm will have to turn its attention to the vendors who supplied materials and other requirements to the firm. A new relationship will have to be built with them. Of course nobody is going to find fault with the organisation, as recession is a common problem to all the stakeholders.

And, many more dislocations in the business will have to be set right before approaching the market with new vigour and enthusiasm. Let us now discuss important strategies for business recovery.

1. *Enlist customer support* The first and foremost step to be taken by the firm is to see that the customers are retained. Had the firm been in the good books of the customers, the firm may not need strenuous efforts to enroll their support. Just a phone call will do. If the case is otherwise, the firm would have to start its work from scratch to gain the support of the customers. In the latter case, the firm may have to spend lots of money to woo the customers. Big meetings with special arrangements to look after the hospitality of the customers will be required. It would require lot of money and time management.

2. *Assure better services* You will have to promise better quality products with reasonable price. It is a must because the business has returned. The competitors will also return to their business. Therefore, there will be tough fight in the marketplace to woo the customers. The competitors may try to snatch your customers forcefully. They may get down into the market and play even a *rough* game. You should also be prepared to confront it. Any way it is customer loyalty that is going to win. But you cannot sit quietly watching the television channels. Even though your customers are loyal to you, you should reciprocate it by meeting them frequently. You would have done this in the peak of the recession itself.

3. *Alter your marketing strategies to suit the new situation* The firm, in its new environment, may be under compulsion to alter its marketing strategies such as pricing, segmentation, distribution, salesforce management, research and development, new product planning, and marketing research. The marketing manager in consultation with superior officers must chart out suitable marketing strategies.

4. *Meet your distributors* You must arrange gala gatherings for your distributors who are the people between you and your customers. The distributors can turn the tides in your favour. Therefore don't forget to enlist their support fully. Of course it is the quality of your product, your pricing policy, your packaging style, your mind-catching ads, your homely approach, and above all your reputation in the market, which will be deciding. However, the distributors and other channel members have their role also to play. Therefore never forget to *honour* them; but you must possess that kind of reputation in the market that the distributors and others come to your doorsteps on their own, i.e., without your invitation.

5. *Advertise heavily*   In the initial stages of the recovery phase, needless to say, you will have to spend heavily on ads. You must take the messages to the market and you must take an all-out effort to persuade the customers about the plus points of your organisation and its products.

6. *Make fullest use of internet*   The Internet is ushering in a new wave of business dynamics. No longer is it enough for companies to put up simple websites for customers and employees. To take the full advantage of the internet, companies need to change the way they distribute goods, deal with suppliers, attract customers and serve customers. Internet can help you in a big way to recuperate your organisation with bulk orders. The Internet eliminates the geographic protection/monopoly of local businesses. Basically, companies need to re-invent the way they do business to take full advantage of Internet.

THE PROCESS OF MARKETING STRATEGY IMPLEMENTATION

Look at what Theodore Levitt[4] said for making the strategy successful:

"To be successful a strategy must also be simple, clear and expressible in only a few written lines. If it is elaborate and complex, and takes a lot of space or time to communicate, few people will understand it or march to its tune. Complexity tends usually to mask a vague or unsubstantial sense of the realities that face the enterprise. The most dramatic and visible realities that so obviously destroy companies are usually fiscal: insufficient cash flow to finance debt and interest payments, to pay vendors, and the like. These usually make the headlines, because they lead so often and so obviously to bankruptcy. Often they are due to wrong decisions about purely financial affairs. Most commonly such wrong decisions are based on miscalculations or plain dumb assumptions about the marketplace—that sales would be sufficiently good, prices sufficiently high, accounts receivable sufficiently low and short-term. Hence, fiscal failure originates in the marketplace."

According to Robertson and Gatignon,[5] obtaining the *support of senior management* has been recognised in a vast array of organisational and management fields as an essential component in successful strategy implementation efforts. Similarly, in the marketing strategy implementation context, it is expected that a higher level of perceived senior management support will be associated with higher levels of strategy commitment among managers with implementation responsibilities.[6]

Marketing strategy implementation involves several steps. Exhibit 2.3 gives these steps in a summarised form. The task of accomplishing the marketing objectives can be done by successful execution of the strategy. While the cooperation of the marketing personnel directly concerned in this process is very essential at this stage, the implementation should be carried out under the supervision of the team consisting of the Marketing Vice President or the CMO (Chief Marketing Officer) and the senior marketing officers.

Step 1 *Educate managers*   The marketing personnel are responsible for the execution of the marketing strategy. Therefore, they must know what is what regarding the strategy implementation programme. The Marketing Vice President/CMO must, first, call a meeting of the marketing personnel and tell them everything about the programme. He must clarify all the points raised by them. The managers may also be called as strategic marketing managers. These strategic marketing managers play a vital role in the marketing strategy implementation process. The CMO must explain to them the benefits of successful implementation of the strategy to the organisation as well as to the individual strategic managers. He must create awareness among the strategic managers and call for their unconditional cooperation in this task. The CMO must, at the same time, explain the consequences of the failure of the programme. He must make the individual strategic managers accountable for the tasks assigned to them in the process of execution of the programme.

Step 2 *Formulate action plans*   The team under the leadership of the CMO is responsible for formulating necessary tactical plans for each marketing function. These plans include preparation of programmes, projects, budgets, set of instructions and guidelines, outline of the report to be submitted at the weekend, and so on. The strategic marketing managers must call for meetings of their subordinates in their respective sections and they must explain the idea and call for their cooperation. These action plans must contain fine details or steps that have to be taken by the strategic managers. The detailed plans prepared by them must be placed before the team for approval. The team must go through every detail in the plans, discuss their pros and cons and finalise them after making necessary alterations in these plans.

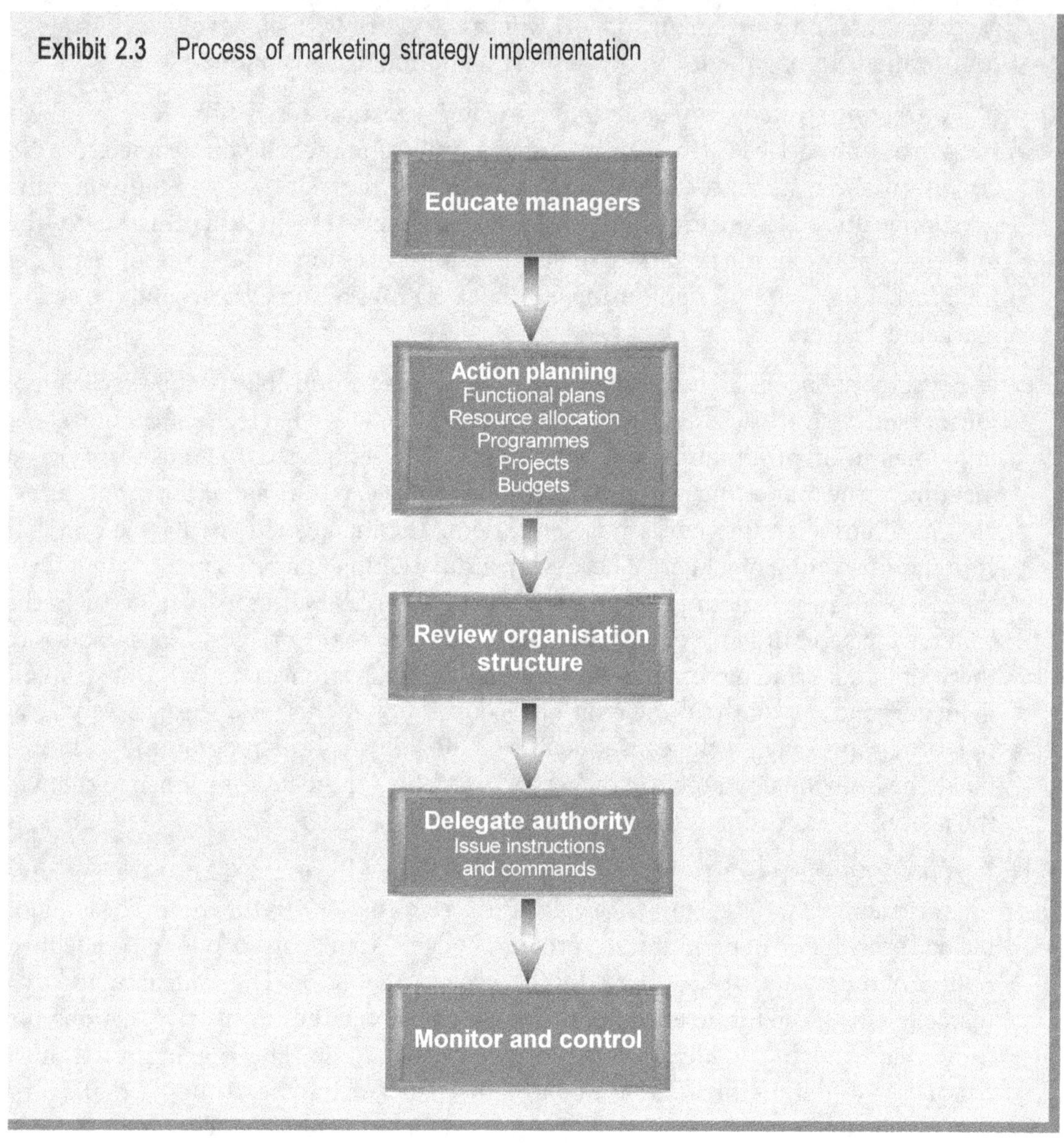

Exhibit 2.3   Process of marketing strategy implementation

Step 3 *Review organisation structure*   Here, the management should make a thorough overhaul of the marketing organisation structure. A study must be made with regard to the suitability of the existing organisation structure to the new marketing programme. Duplication of authority should be avoided. The study on delegation of authority is essential. If need be, necessary changes must be made so as to make the authority relationships meaningful and suitable to the new environment. This and every other part of the programme should be carried out with enough care and precision.

Step 4 *Delegate authority, issue guidelines and commands*   The actual process of executing the marketing strategy begins here. The review of the marketing organisation structure made already will help carry out this step easily. Written instructions must be given to the strategic marketing managers and, in turn, they must do the same to their subordinates. Now the marketing organisation is ready for the task and once the instructions and commands are issued by the strategic managers, the marketing strategy implementation phase may be presumed as started.

Step 5 *Monitor, review and control*   The strategic marketing managers have to prepare weekend reports and submit them to the team headed by the CMO and the team must meet at the end of the week, review the performance, discuss the results, identify the areas of concern and suggest steps to rectify the deviations, if any. The team should again meet in the middle of the week and discuss the efficacy of its previous suggestions and if there is any need, further changes may be made. The strategy execution is not a one-time work. It is a continuous process and in the course of time, it will become an inseparable part of the marketing organisation. When things move in the right direction, the results will be tangible and to the satisfaction of everyone concerned.

THE CHALLENGE OF STRATEGY IMPLEMENTATION

What is a strategy? Is it necessary? What is the aim of strategy? Who decides it? Who executes it? What are the basic requirements for its execution? What is the role of managers? What are the steps? What are the obstacles? How can these obstacles be overcome? What is the cost of its failure? These are all relevant questions. These questions must be answered before a CEO proposes to implement a Strategic Management Programme in his organisation. It is not a child's play. Neither is it a gentleman's job. It requires dedicated and talented people, good organisational environment, strategic leadership, necessary resources, and many more. All these are inputs and when these inputs are put in the right proportion, the outcome will be a perfect product. Two things are important: i) determining the suitable strategy and ii) executing it perfectly. This needs talent as well as dedication on the part of managers who are directly connected to the job. Connecting the strategic plan to the real-time operations is to be perfect and without any deviation.

Is strategic management necessary?   Strategic management is relatively a newer concept, may be a few decades old. The reason why strategic management came in the scene is important to analyse. The common reason for bringing and implementing new concepts and methods is merely to *excel* in whatever programme the management plans to execute. Strategic management is yet another but powerful concept. This way came strategic management. Whether it is strategic management or any other management, what is required is effectiveness in whatever we do. The difference between strategic management and conventional management is that in the former a strong impetus is given to the attainment of the corporate objectives whereas in the latter case some of the executives may miss the *stress*. Awareness is created by the strategic management.

Strategic management focuses on both immediate and long-term objectives. It is not a static plan. The strategy gets altered as and when sure changes are forecast in the environment. Strategic management puts the firm in the state of alert. One of the important techniques that come handy to the strategic manager is the *SWOT* analysis. This technique is a guide that shows him the direction in which the organisation should direct its activities. When the manager acts promptly, the organisation becomes the winner. The manager is able to get through the obstacles as he knows where the organisation stands and what its strengths and weaknesses are. Strategic management creates awareness in the organisation. It also creates accountability. The competencies of the people are revealed, and they are rewarded suitably by the management. Thus, strategic management motivates the people who excel in their jobs. Core competencies of the human resources of the organisation become the essence of strategic management as people with talents prove their mettle. Therefore, strategic management has become a necessary tool in the hands of an able executive.

Who decides the strategy ?   A strategy is the basic approach that a firm has to follow in order to achieve its objectives in the short-run and its mission in the long-run. Therefore the responsibility to decide the corporate strategy rests with the top management. The top management decides the strategy in consultation with experts in the field. Strategy is derived from the corporate objectives; objectives from the mission and in turn, the mission comes from the vision. Whoever recommends the strategy, it is the sole responsibility of the top people in the administration who decide the vision, mission, objectives and then, the strategy.

Who executes it ?   The responsibility of implementing the strategy rests with the line managers. They are the strategic managers. A team under the leadership of the CEO oversees the implementation of strategies. This team consists of various functional heads of the organisation apart from the CEO. The team discusses weekly reports received from different departments on the first day of the next week. Unfavourable deviations, if any, are analysed by the team and appropriate measures are recommended by the team. Then a middle-of-the-week meeting is arranged to see how far the system is responding to the implementation of the suggestions. In this way the performance of the system is closely monitored and suitable remedial measures are taken then and there.

What are the basic requirements for strategy execution?   Let us now see the essential requirements for strategy execution. In the first place, the firm should be capable of it.

Rigid policies won't help. At the same time, highly flexible attitudes of management will also take the firm nowhere. A high degree of reasoning and rationale should be there for any decision or action. Moreover, the management should commit itself to the implementation. Management commitment is basic in this game plan. Strategy is akin to the plan to win the battle. Withdrawing in the middle will lead to negative consequences which will be difficult to reverse. Secondly, the unconditional and whole-hearted support of the managers who are going to play the main game to the efforts of management is essential. This would be possible where an excellent organisational culture and climate prevail. A rich organisational culture is one which makes the members contribute voluntarily their best for the welfare of the organisation. Thirdly, the management must be able to allocate sufficient resources, financial and non-financial, to the critical areas of the organisation. A resources analysis would help to determine which department requires how much and at what point of time. An organisation without the necessary financial background is difficult to achieve the strategic objectives. Fourthly, the firm should install the best methods and practices in the departments. This would help to enlist the support of the specific departments to the plan. For example, the production department should adopt production processes that are best and cost-effective and that will minimise defective parts. The shut-down time of the plant and machinery should be minimum resulting in best utilisation of resources.

The next requirement is the establishment of a good reward structure in the organisation. No member with worthy or even small contribution in the accomplishment of the task should be left out. Whatever you say in words and through testimonials will not work like money. Words coupled with deeds alone will be effective in making men work. Therefore, the management should draw a good incentive plan to all the members of the organisation. The incentive plan you draw should perfectly fit organisational needs. Of course, a cost-benefit analysis at this stage is also important. However, it will be difficult to assess the benefits because the benefits will have a long-term implication. The benefits may be in cash as well as an invisible appreciation in the value of the enterprise. Another important requirement is an assertive leadership which will act boldly at times of any unforeseen crises in view of changing environment that the organisation may have to face in its work. Even though risks are inherent in business, the management must be prepared to tackle any kind of enemy that may appear in the scene. An adequate cushion of resources must be available withthe firm.

What is the role of managers?   The managers play the key role in the implementation of a strategic management programme. It is the line managers who must play an active role in this process. They must first understand the concept. Then they must offer full cooperation by supervising the process of implementation and reporting the deviations, if any, to their functional heads. A detailed discussion on this topic will be taken up in the next section of this chapter.

Obstacles to strategy execution Like any other programmes, a strategy execution programme also has its own obstacles. Of course there are also ways to overcome them. First let us see these obstacles.

1. *The 'yes' managers* The first obstacle is the problem of an 'yes' manager. The 'yes' managers don't think in the right perspective, they don't apply their minds to the problems surrounding them, they always say 'yes' to their superiors; and they are the biggest obstacles to the strategy implementation task. They don't have initiative, new ideas and a sense of good imagination.

2. *Inability to understand the concept* A few strategic managers don't possess the ability to understand the concept. And, they always disturb their superiors asking clarifications every now and then.

3. *Wrong choice of the consultant* This is a real obstacle. The entire programme stands on the strength of the consultant. If he/she is not worthy of the job, then how can we expect success?

4. *Unsuitable organisational culture* The organisational culture may not be in a condition to implement such a plan like strategic management. A culture that does not fit will lead to nowhere. Mere anxiety on the part of management won't do the magic.

5. *Inadequate resources* People start strategic management execution with the hope that they would be able to raise resources as and when required. This idea is suicidal. Resources are not that easy to procure for many organisations.

Ways to overcome the obstacles These obstacles can be easily overcome by a smart management. The case of 'yes' managers can be tackled by identifying them. When doing this, it is important that *Halo* effect will not come in the way. These managers should not be given important responsibilities. In the case of second obstacle, similar action may be taken. While choosing the consultant for implementation of the strategic management programme, sufficient enquiry regarding his/her calibre and the past record of the consultant with other organisations should be found out. The organisational culture has to be improved by taking all the necessary steps. The cooperation of the members of the organisation is essential for creating a favourable atmosphere which would help improve its culture. An assessment of organisational resources must be made before carrying out the programme of strategic management.

STRATEGIC MARKETING DECISIONS

In the course of studying about strategic marketing management, it is necessary to learn about strategic marketing decisions and strategic market position. Strategic marketing decisions are the marketing strategies being followed by the organisation. The strategic decisions must possess the characteristics given in Exhibit 2.4.

The characteristics of marketing strategy or strategic marketing decisions may be stated as follows:

1. *Long-term decision*   Marketing strategy is concerned with the long-term decision of the organisation. The strategic marketing decision provides a direction in which the marketing organisation must move. It incurs least cost and time. In such a situation productivity will be high.

2. *Competitive advantage*   Strategic marketing decisions normally lead to competitive advantages. It is also about acting, before competitors do it. Since strategic decisions provide competitive advantage to the firm over the competitors, they would find it difficult to adapt their technologies and policies to our direction.

3. *Resources and environment*   Strategic marketing decisions help matching of the resources with the organisational environment and activities. It is important that organisation's resources are sufficient enough to take up and execute the strategic marketing decision which has to be implemented in the organisation's internal as well as external environment.

4. *Competencies and strategies*   Strategies, most of the times, cash in on the organisational competencies available. Therefore strategic marketing decisions have to do a lot with organisational competencies. In this regard, it is necessary that the marketing organisation is conscious of its competencies as well as weak points. A thorough *SWOT* analysis can help achieve this. *SWOT analysis is the biggest and most useful technique available to the strategic marketing manager.* A correct use of this technique can do wonders for the organisation.

5. *Resource constraints and strategic decisions*   The *SWOT* analysis will be able to identify the organisation's resource constraints as well. This comes under '*W*,' i.e., weaknesses. In the case of resource constraints, the market planning should ascertain wherefrom the resources can be arranged. The firm should be prepared to face any eventuality in this matter too.

6. *Organisational culture*   Organisational culture is very much linked to the strategic plan implementation. If the culture is such that the members of the organisation always exhibit a hostile attitude towards the organisation, then there is little use in planning for strategic management. Therefore the members of the organisation should be cooperative to the efforts of the organisation in determining strategic plans.

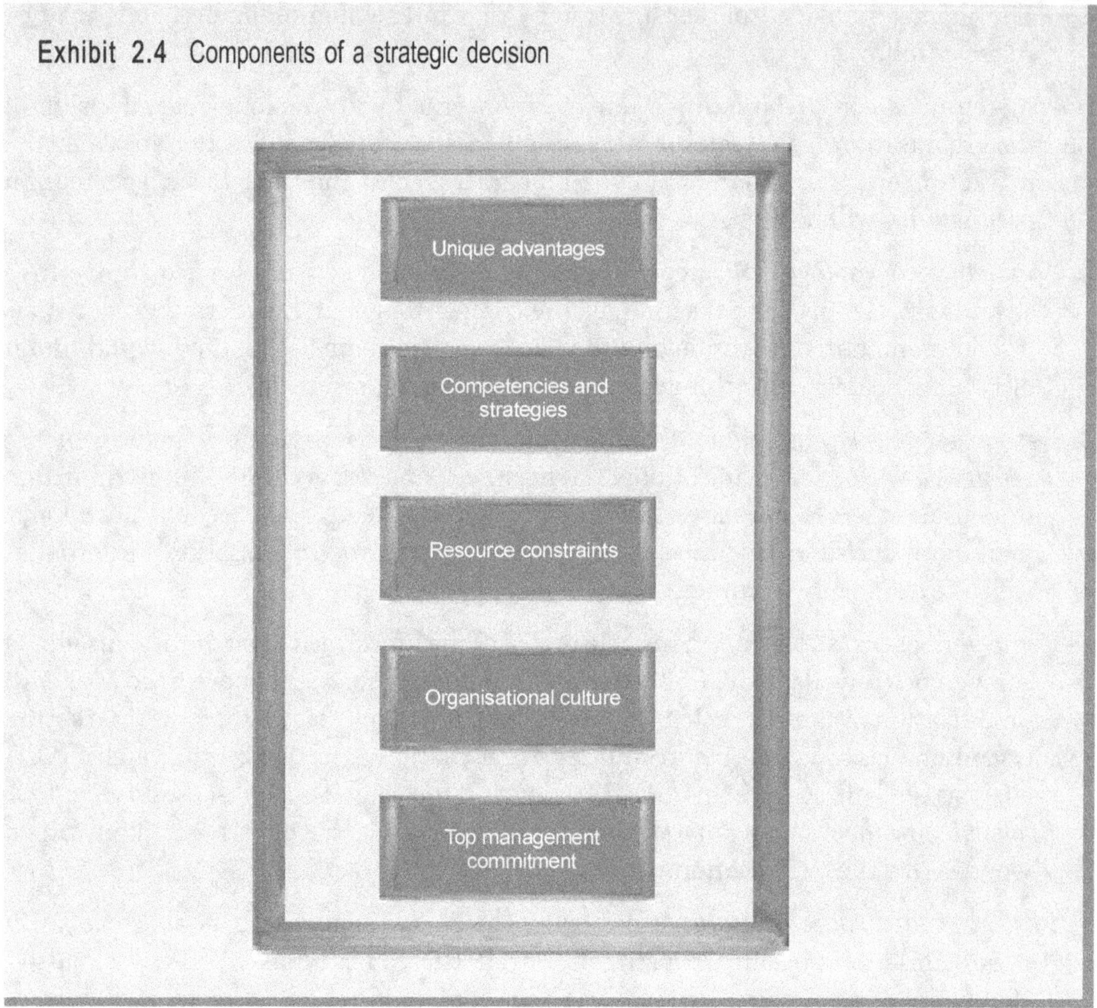

Exhibit 2.4 Components of a strategic decision

7. *The role of the top management* The commitment of the top management to the implementation of the strategic marketing decision is very essential. The management should not be half-hearted in making strategic decisions. It must fully understand the issue and extend its fullest support to the team which is entrusted the job of strategic decision implementation.

However, there are many other factors that may come in the way of strategic marketing decision execution. During such interruptions, it is necessary to follow situational management techniques and overcome the problems as and when they appear. The concept of situational management requires a thorough understanding of the situation and a timely action by the concerned managers before it is too late.

STRATEGIC MARKET POSITION

Strategic market positioning is the placing of an organisation in its due place in the market. It includes the decision on the desired future market position of the organisation on the basis of the present and foreseeable developments and the making of plans to realise that positioning. The strategic market positioning aims at ensuring the continuity of the organisation. "Strategic position is the face of the business strategy, specifies how the business aspires to be perceived relative to its competitors and market. Strategic initiatives and communication programmes are driven by strategic position and it is the guiding beacon for organisational culture and values. For all of these reasons, it is crucial to get the strategic position right."[7]

Marketing executives need to frame a marketing strategy statement for a marketing organisation which may include its strategic position in the market scenario. By doing so, it is creating awareness among the stakeholders about the future plans without revealing its specific strategies. A strategic marketing position statement is a kind of statement for the company that tells about the company's intent. The strategic marketing managers explain in this statement how they view their market and how they view it within the rest of their marketplace.

The reason for understanding the strategic marketing position is to form a view of the key influences on the present and future well-being of the organisation and what opportunities and threats are created by the environment, the competencies of the organisation and expectations of the stakeholders. Various questions have to be asked with strategic positioning here: how does the future look like? how could the organisation be roughly positioned in the market? how are the things in the organisation at present? how can opportunities be seized and how can threats be met? and how can this be put into practice in a systematic way? All these questions and many others have to be answered in order to capture a strategic market position in the industry.

PERFORMANCE EVALUATION, REVIEW AND CONTROL

Richard Rumelt's four criteria[8] for evaluating strategy may be applied to find out the efficacy of marketing strategies. They are: 1) consistency; 2) consonance; 3) feasibility; and 4) advantage. These criteria have to be satisfied, if a strategy is to be a good one. Therefore we can call them as qualities or characteristics of successful strategies. However, Rumelt did not give the steps for evaluating, reviewing and controlling strategies. Therefore we are now going in for the steps which would help the evaluators in doing their job. The following are these steps:

Step 1   Consider desired results.

Step 2   Collect actual results.

Step 3   Organise evaluation sessions.

Step 4   Take stock of initial and end of period competencies.

Step 5   Find deviations: favourable or adverse, if any.

Step 6   Analyse causes of deviations.

Step 7   Decide on remedial actions.

Step 8   Execute them.

Exhibit 2.5 provides us a model for Performance Evaluation, Review and Control (PERC). *PERC is the most important step in strategic management.* Because it is here where we make an analytical study of what we have done so far in the issue of strategy formulation and strategy implementation. It is here where we understand the pitfalls and our efficiencies in the field of strategic management. Sir Winston Churchill said, "Continuous effort—not strength or intelligence—is the key to unlocking our potential". Therefore as in Total Quality Management, continuous development of targets, continuous strategic planning and continuous evaluation are very essential for the success of the organisation. We are living in the age of hyper-dynamic and hyper-competitive businesses. Therefore, continuous and untiring effort on our part will bring sure success to our organisation. Let us now dwell into the practical steps in the PERC. *A Panel to oversee the process of programme evaluation review and control must be appointed. The members of this Panel may consist of an external business consultant and senior marketing executives. This Panel will hereafter be referred to as PERCP.*

Step 1 *Consider desired results*   In the beginning of the period under consideration, the strategists determine the targets or desired results for each of the four functional areas of management. Under the PERC, the first step is this: Go through thoroughly the desired-result statements prepared at the end of the previous period, for the next period. Perhaps every strategist will have it in finger tips. However records alone speak. Therefore,   the PERC Panel (PERCP) should possess the statements of desired results for each department and each section of the organisation. This has to be kept by the PERCP for reference purposes.

Step 2 *Collect actual results*   Secondly, the Performance Evaluation, Review, and Control Panel (PERCP) should collect documents showing actual results accomplished during the period from all the departments concerned. This is a very important step in the sense that this is what has been achieved during the period under review through the implementation of strategic plans. Therefore, actual data, without any window dressing, should be supplied to the PERCP by all the departments. It is the responsibility of the department heads to see that everything goes on perfectly as per the strategic plan not only during the period under study but also during the future periods. If there is any obvious adverse variation, the department head and others responsible for implementing the strategic plan would have to explain the reasons to the management.

Step 3 *Organise evaluation sessions* Meetings of PERCP, viz., senior marketing managers and an external business consultant will generally be conducted as many times as necessary. The leader of the Panel explains the purpose of the session to the other members in order to make them understand the need for such sessions. These sessions should be arranged at regular intervals so that the Panel can evaluate continuously the performance of the strategic plans.

Step 4 *Take stock of initial and end-of-period competencies* It is a very crucial step. The Panel studies the competencies and competitive advantages possessed by the marketing organisation in the beginning of the period. Nowadays the market has become hyper-dynamic, hyper-sensitive and hyper-competitive. Therefore, it is necessary to study whether there is any improvement in the core competencies of managers and in the competitive advantages enjoyed by the organisation at the end of the study period. Chances are there that anything might happen to these variables. But the organisation always prefers an improvement in the core competencies and the competitive advantages enjoyed by it. But what is the reality? Thomas Henry Huxley aptly said, "The rung of a ladder was never meant to rest upon, but only to hold a man's foot long enough to enable him to put the other somewhat higher". Here the ladder may be compared to that of a strategic marketing plan. Like the ladder rests upon the floor with nobody to climb on it, what is the use of the ladder? The purpose of the ladder is to take the person to a higher level. It must be achieved by the manager who has been entrusted with the task of executing the strategic plan successfully.

Step 5 *Find deviations: favourable or adverse, if any* The primary aim of the PERCP is to come out with its finding whether the results are favourable or adverse during the period under consideration. This is a very important step. As brilliant students (our managers are experts in their fields) want to obtain a very high score in their final examination in order that they can enter a good course of study in a good institution, good managers also anticipate a favourable result in this process. They are happy, if they have achieved it. Since they know it already whether they have accomplished the target or not, they know their fate. But in case of adverse performance, they are very much worried, and their explanation should be reasonable and acceptable. If it is beyond the control of the manager concerned, it is alright and the panel would not find fault with them. At the same time, if the causes are within the control of the managers they are sure to receive some kind of punishment because the organisation has made huge investments in the hope that the managers will perform more effectively.

Step 6 *Analyse causes of deviations*   The PERCP has to analyse causes of both favourable and adverse results. One, the executives' performance must have exceeded the target. Or, two, their performance must be below the target. Either of these two things would have happened. The PERCP should discuss in detail the causes of both *favourable* and *adverse deviations*. To study the cause of adverse reactions is more important than studying the causes of favourable deviations.

Possible causes of adverse performance

1. *Over-estimation of the core competencies*   The strategists and other senior managers might have been overambitious about the capabilities of the firm's core competencies. This might have happened because the managers of the organisation might have created a very good impression about their competencies in the past. This might have led to wrong conclusions in the present time about the competencies of managers. General H.Norman Schwarzkopt rightly said; *"The truth of the matter is that you always know the right thing to do. The hard part is doing it."* Therefore the manager might have suggested very good things, but he/she might not have possessed the capability to implement them successfully.

2. *Under-estimation of our competitors' competencies*   Once we decide to make a strategic plan, we have to study the capabilities and competencies of our competitors also. Here the assessment of the talents and resources of the competitors is very important. Henry Ford said, "If there is any great secret of success in life, it lies in the ability to put yourself in the other person's place and to see things from his point of view—as well as your own." Ford's words are very relevant here. Strategy is something concerned with winning over the enemy, the competitor. We have to put ourselves in their place and see things from their point of view as well as from our point of view. Attitude is very important in the executive. Raymond Chandler rightly said, *"Ability is what you are capable of doing. Motivation determines what you do. Attitude determines how well you do it."*

3. *Unfavourable market trends*   It may be another important cause for the poor show of the firm with regard to its strategic marketing plan. See what is happening today! The present global slow-down has been doing havocs not only to the business world but also to the millions of talented employees. *It proves the oft-said business jargon: the future is becoming more and more uncertain.* Managers who are very alert and sensitive to the changing market trends alone can succeed in this hyper-competitive world. The management should watch carefully what is going on in the market. If anything goes wrong in the market, immediate counter-action becomes

necessary. If the manager is lethargic and slow, then the competitors would certainly overtake us. Jim Rohn said, "Success is neither magical nor mysterious. Success is the natural consequence of consistently applying the fundamentals." The single truth is that failure to watch the changing market is a grave error committed by the managers because it is a fundamental lesson that market trends should be closely observed by the manager concerned.

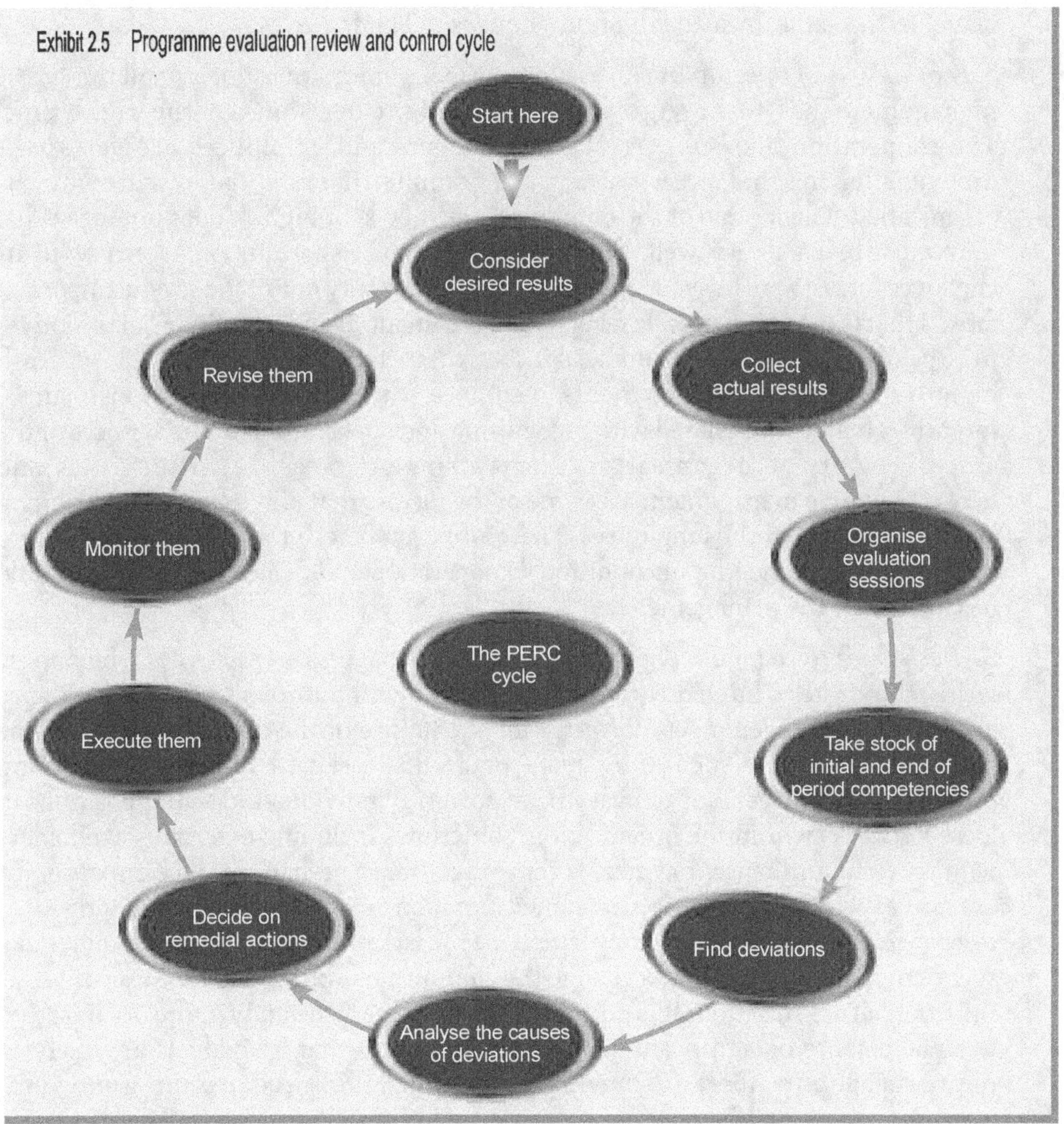

Exhibit 2.5 Programme evaluation review and control cycle

4. *Unfavourable changes in the environment*   Environment is a silent player in the game. This player must be closely followed by an efficient manager. But many times, it is difficult to change the route, the environment takes. Suppose that the government announces a major policy change suddenly regarding our product. Nothing could be done in this case. Similarly when floods come inside the plant like the ones that happened in Mumbai, what can one do? If the lightning strikes a major powerhouse in a factory, what can one do? That is why the environment is a big and important player in the game. In such situations, none is to blame.

5. *Poor morale of the employees*   Running an organisation is not a small thing. The management has to be vigilant and take right decisions at the right time. The cooperation and support of the managers and employees are very basic prerequisites for the success of any programme that is to be executed by the organisation. The morale of the employees must be kept high. It does not mean that they must be paid very well. That is, the firm must share its prosperity with its employees at least to a lesser degree. Compensation is only one of the several important factors that lead to high morale level. There are financial and non-financial incentives to be paid to the employees. Financial incentives include reasonable wage levels, cash incentive schemes, bonus payments, insurance schemes and others. Non-financial incentives mainly are related with recognition and appreciation of the services of the employees of the organisation. Very stringent measures, rigid rules and non-cooperative management are some of the factors that play a big role in bringing down the morale of the employees. Therefore even before the firm is stepping into any new programme, the unconditional cooperation and dedication to work should be ensured by the management.

6. *Resistance to change*   There may be some managers or employees who oppose tacitly the strategy implementation process. They might not show their resistance openly. But, they would act indirectly for the failure of the programme. It may be necessary to remove such individuals, or groups resistant to strategic planning programme. These persons can vary from powerful individuals in senior positions to loose networks within the organisation, sometimes including external stakeholders with powerful influence, to whole layers of resistance perhaps in the form of senior executives who may be in a threatened function or service. In overcoming such resistance, the major problem may simply be the lack of power to be able to undertake such activity. It is one thing to change the commitment of a few senior executives at the top of an organisation. It is quite another to convert the body of the organisation to an acceptance of significant change. The danger is that individuals are likely to regard change as temporary; something with which they need to comply only until the next change comes along.

7. *Competitors' role*   It is possible that competitors may, sometimes, play a devastating role in hampering the execution of our organisation's strategic management process. In the fear that our organisation may further excel, if the strategic planning is executed, some competitors may play the villain's role to thwart our attempt to further strengthen our organisation's competencies. These competitors may possess competencies which are much lower than our organisation's. If there is any such thing, the management may secretly order a probe so that we can find out the culprit within organisation who is working for the competitors.

Possible causes of favourable deviations   Now, let us study the possible causes of favourable deviation. Favourable deviation also is an important aspect of strategic planning. Just because we have reached a point far beyond the target, the organisation cannot ignore this. There may be genuine reasons for a favourable deviation. Let us now analyse the possible causes of favourable deviations.

1. *Under-estimation of our competencies*   The management of our organisation or the strategist might have underestimated the competencies of our organisation's executives. This may be due to the fear that their estimation may fail, if the target is not achieved. This may have resulted in a favourable deviation.

2. *Over-estimation of our competitors' competencies*   Out of an extra cautiousness, our team of strategists might have overestimated the efficiency of our competitors. In fact the competitors' competencies might be much below the competencies of our executives. Perhaps, this would, on one hand, help to understand the efficiency of our competitors; and, on the other hand, this would help in our strategic planning for the next period. But, remember that competencies of any organisation do not remain constant. They may change as new people are inducted into the organisations.

3. *Highly favourable market trends*   There might be a sudden spurt in the demand for our products. This may be due to so many reasons; there might be a labour problem in the competitors' units which might have resulted in short supply of their output; there may be a sudden tilt in favour of our products due to change in customers' tastes and preferences; and so on.

4. *Highly favourable changes in the environment*   The environmental conditions might have become highly favourable to our products and the organisation. These environmental changes are highly unpredictable. Therefore, these are beyond our control.

5. *High morale of employees*   When the members of the organisation offer their whole-hearted cooperation to the strategic planning programme, the programme is bound to succeed beyond our imagination. A survey must be conducted to find out whether employees' morale really contributed to the success of the strategic planning

process. If it is proved that employees' morale contributed considerably to the success of the programme, they must be suitably rewarded.

Step 7 *Decide on remedial actions*   Now that we have analysed the causes for deviation in the results of our strategic management programme, the next step is to set right the unfavourable deviations. We have studied that the deviations may be of two types: 1) favourable deviations and 2) adverse deviations. Whatever the type of deviations, we have to take necessary remedial measures so that in our next strategic plan, we can do the job more effectively. We can do this by making a function-wise analysis, viz., production/operations management, marketing management, finance management and human resource management.

Step 8 *Execute them*   The final step in the PERC programme is to execute the remedial measures or suggestions made by the PERCP. The top management should take the responsibility to undertake this task. The task should be entrusted to the managers who are committed to the welfare of the organisation. The top management should closely monitor the steps taken by these executives so that any approach in the wrong direction can be set right.

Step 9 *Monitor them*   It is essential to have a monitoring mechanism to see what is happening to the remedies which are being implemented in the organisation.

SUMMARY

* Strategic marketing management is *the process of specifying an organisation's marketing objectives in the long run, developing policies and strategies to achieve these objectives, formulating the strategic marketing plan, allocating resources judiciously, and executing the strategic marketing plan effectively.*

* The essential steps followed in the strategic management process are: i) marketing strategy planning/formulation, ii) marketing strategy implementation, and iii) marketing strategy evaluation, review, and control.

* Marketing strategy planning is *the process of determining appropriate courses of action for achieving the marketing organisation's objectives.* It is the process that determines the future direction of the marketing organisation and what organisational structure will be needed.

* An environmental scan is performed to identify the suitable marketing strategies. The marketing organisation must also know its own capabilities and limitations in order to select the opportunities that it can pursue with a higher probability of success. The situation analysis, therefore, involves an analysis of both the internal and external environment.

❋ Marketing strategy implementation involves several steps. The task of accomplishing the marketing objectives can be done by successful execution of the strategy. While the cooperation of the marketing personnel directly concerned in this process is very essential at this stage, the implementation should be carried out under the supervision of the team consisting of the Marketing Vice President or the CMO (Chief Marketing Officer) and the senior marketing officers.

❋ Richard Rumelt's four criteria for evaluating strategy may be applied to find out the efficacy of marketing strategies. They are: 1) consistency; 2) consonance; 3) feasibility; and 4) advantage. These criteria have to be satisfied, if a strategy is to be effective.

❋ The steps in the process of performance evaluation, review, and control are: i) consider desired results, ii) collect actual results, iii) organise evaluation sessions, iv) take stock of initial and end of period competencies, v) find deviations: favourable or adverse, if any, vi) analyse causes of deviations, vii) decide on remedial actions, and viii) execute them.

REVIEW QUESTIONS

1. Explain the steps in the process of strategic marketing management.

2. "The process of strategic marketing management involves matching the firm's strategic marketing advantages to the business environment."Explain how, as a marketer, you will do this matching.

3. How do you formulate a marketing strategy?

4. "In today's highly competitive business environment, forecast-based planning methods are not adequate for large companies to prosper in the short as well as long run." Do you agree? Give valid reasons for your answer.

5. What is environmental scanning?

6. "The management of the organisation possesses in its stock all the weapons to confront the unforeseen enemy." In the light of this statement, state who is the enemy and what the weapons are in the stock of the organisation to defeat the enemy.

7. Explain the marketing strategies based on business cycles.

8. Do you think that business cycles can be irregular? If so, state the reasons for your answer.

9. Explain the boom period marketing strategies.

10. Explain the marketing strategies to be used during recessionary periods.

11. "Don't 'cheapen' your advertising by trying to save on creative or production costs. Your customers will notice and worry about quality." Is it true? Substantiate your answer with suitable arguments.

12. Explain the marketing strategies to be used during the business recovery stage.

13. Explain the marketing strategies to be used during market decline period.

14. Explain the process of marketing strategy implementation.

15. What are the hurdles to be faced at the time of strategy execution?

16. What are the basic requirements for strategy execution?

17. "A higher level of perceived senior management support will be associated with higher levels of strategy commitment among managers with implementation responsibilities." Prove or disprove the statement.

18. What are the impending obstacles in the process of strategy execution?

19. What are the features of strategic marketing decisions?

20. What is strategic market position?

21. Explore the steps involved in performance evaluation, review and control.

REFERENCES

1. Soundaian, S. (2011). *New Dimensions in Management.* MJP Publishers, Chennai.

2. Hambrick, C. Donald and Fredrickson, W. James. (2001). "Are you sure you have a strategy." *Academy of Management Executive.* 15 (4): 50.

3. Generic strategies were used initially in the early 1980s, and seem to be even more popular today. They outline the three main strategic options open to the organisation that wishes to achieve a sustainable competitive advantage. Generic strategies were first presented in two books by Professor Michael Porter of the Harvard Business School (Porter, 1980, 1985). Later many experts began using Porter's views on marketing strategies. Even today, many organisations use the term "generic strategies" freely.

4. Levitt, Theodore, *The Marketing Imagination* (Excerpt), p. 3 of 8. Theodore (Ted) Levitt was the Edward W. Carter Professor of Business Administration Emeritus at the Harvard Business School and former Editor of the Harvard Business Review. He was one of the most widely read and respected authorities in management and marketing. Professor Levitt is the author of *The Marketing Imagination*, the acclaimed best-seller now in eleven languages. He is also

author of numerous articles on economic, political, management, and marketing subjects.

5.   Robertson, T. and Gatignon, H. (1986) "Competitive effects on technology diffusion." *Journal of Marketing.* 50 (3): 1–12.

6.   Noble, C. and Mokwa, M. (1999). "Implementing marketing strategies: developing and testing a managerial theory." *Journal of Marketing.* 63(4): 57–73.

7.   Aaker, D. A. (2001). *Strategic Market Management,* 6th edn. Wiley and Sons, New York. p. 192.

8.   Rumelt, R. (1991). "How much does industry matter?" *Strategic Management Journal.* 12: 167–185.

3

ANALYSING BUYER BEHAVIOUR

After reading this chapter, you will be able to

- *understand the importance of studying the buyer behaviour,*
- *learn the consumer buying process,*
- *learn the business customer's buying process,*
- *know the factors influencing the buyer behaviour, and*
- *know about the use of research on buyer behaviour.*

KEY TERMS

- Stimulus–response model
- Law of effect
- Law of readiness
- Law of exercise
- Straight rebuy
- Modified rebuy
- Professional buyers
- Individualism
- Collectivism
- Power distance
- Reference groups
- Perception
- Attitude
- Personality
- Traits

INTRODUCTION

Carola Burnett is a resident of South London. She visits the retail outlets at Fulham Road, South Kensington for her bi-monthly purchases. She enjoys shopping there. She visits *Donovan Design Studio, Secrets of the Boudoir, Brompton Cross,* and *Jacobs* for her requirements. She believes that her favourite stores offer her high quality goods at reasonable prices even though she is rich enough to ignore pricing.

Sudharshan is a middle-aged and well-educated man with just above average financial background, viz., middle-income class. However he is particular in having a good amount of savings in a nationalised bank. He is working with a government undertaking in Pune. He purchases his requirements on a monthly basis in the second week of each month as he thought that the market would remain congested during the first weeks. He owns a medium car that can carry his family comfortably. He makes consumer durable goods purchases at the time of Diwali when firms give offers which would save him a few thousands of rupees. Even his car was purchased at the time of Diwali. He saved about ₹ 30,000 on his car purchase. He looks for quality, brand and the price. He is a man who gathers information via the internet and decides his purchase schedule like many others, in the city of Pune do. He considers after-sales service important while making purchases. He knows very well that most of the Indian business owners receive them well in their showrooms whenever he was there to make a purchase. But thereafter the kind of hospitality extended by them is beyond one's imagination. They do not oblige and instead they give explanation after explanation; the customer feels helpless and nothing concrete materialises for his visit after his purchase. Even though he is very well aware of this seller *behaviour,* he is left with no other alternative because in most of the cases all the business owners behave in the same way, of course with a few exceptions.

Lily Mary Albert of Chicago visits WalMart whenever she finds spare time to make her purchase and if she goes there once, she will see to it that she would not have to visit again for the next fifteen days. This way she makes all her purchases there. She says that she is overwhelmed by the way the salespersons speak to her and the way they behave while she is there. She is not worried about quality or price because she believes that whatever sold by WalMart will be good. She is of staunch belief that WalMart never commits mistakes and even if they do, they admit it politely and compensate for it. Committing mistakes too brings name and fame to an organisation!

All the above stories tell us a few lessons about why and how the people buy a product. Each customer has a story for the seller. The seller's job is to find out what the buyers look for when they make a purchase. Research abounds on buyer behaviour. A few researchers suggest fitting a micro camera in the spectacle of the buyer.

They claim that the buyers' movements can be observed as they move around a store. Is it not highly ridiculous? What is the guarantee that the customer will not condition their behaviour for the expectations of the seller or researcher?

WHAT IS BUYER BEHAVIOUR

Buyer behaviour may be defined as a series of response patterns of an individual or organisation that occur in his/its search for products or services that are capable of satisfying his/its conscious and subconscious needs. Blackwell, Miniard, and Engel[1] define consumer behaviour as "activities people undertake when obtaining, consuming, and disposing products and services."

Assessing buying behaviour is never simple, yet understanding it is the essential task of marketing management. Large companies make research on consumer behaviour to have answer to important research questions—what consumers buy, where they buy, when they buy, how much they buy and why they buy. Marketers can study actual consumer purchasers to find out what they buy, where, when and how much. But learning about the *whys* of consumer behaviour is not so easy—the answers are often locked deep within the consumer's head. "Consumers are goal-oriented, and their purchase decisions are often (but not always certain) carefully calculated to provide the greatest amount of benefits received for the money spent."[2]

The study of consumer behaviour is done in an effort to explain the overall process involved in any purchasing decision. And not just to describe it: we must also get to predict and ultimately control it. This task includes three levels of study:

* the individual consumer perspective, needs, perceptions, attitudes, etc.,

* the interpersonal level, which considers the importance of groups, opinion leaders, etc., in their decisions, and

* socio-cultural level interprets the influence of social class, culture and lifestyle on consumer behaviour.[3]

A well-developed and tested model of buyer behaviour is known as the *stimulus–response* model.

Marketing stimuli consist of the marketing mix, viz., product, price, place and promotion and other stimuli which include other forces in the buyer's environment—economic, technological, political and cultural. All these inputs enter the buyer's brain, where they are turned into a set of observable buyer responses, i.e., product choice, brand choice, dealer choice, purchase timing and purchase amount.

How the stimuli change into responses inside the consumer's brain? Two points must be considered: i) buyer characteristics, and ii) buyer decision process. The buyer's characteristics influence how he or she perceives and reacts to the stimuli, and the buyer's decision process itself affects his buying behaviour (Exhibit 3.1).

Thorndike's stimulus-response theory of learning[4] proposes that all learning consists primarily of the strengthening of the relationship between the stimulus and the response. In developing this theory, Thorndike proposed three laws: the law of effect, the law of exercise, and the law of readiness.

1. *Law of effect*   If the response in a connection is followed by a satisfying state of affairs, the strength of the connection is considerably increased whereas if followed by an annoying state of affairs, then the strength of the connection is marginally decreased.

2. *Law of exercise*   We learn by doing. We forget by not doing, although to a small extent only. The lessons: i) connections between a stimulus and a response are strengthened as they are used, and ii) connections between a stimulus and a response are weakened as they are not used.

3. *Law of readiness*   Interference with goal-directed behaviour causes frustration, and causing someone to do something they do not want to do is also frustrating.

The lessons: i) when someone is ready to perform some act, to do so is satisfying, ii) when someone is ready to perform some act, not to do so is annoying, and iii) when someone is not ready to perform some act and is forced to do so, it is annoying.

Several factors influence the extent to which stimuli will be noticed. One obvious issue is *relevance*. Consumers, when they have a choice, are also more likely to attend to *pleasant* stimuli (but when the consumer cannot escape, very unpleasant stimuli are also likely to get attention—thus, various very irritating advertisements are remarkably effective). One of the most important factors, however, is repetition. Consumers often do not give much attention to a stimulus—particularly a low priority one such as an advertisement—at any one time, but if it is seen over and over again, the cumulative impact will be greater.

Surprising stimuli are likely to get more attention—survival instinct requires us to give more attention to something unknown that may require action. A greater contrast (difference between the stimulus and its surroundings) as well as greater prominence (e.g., greater size, centre placement) also tend to increase likelihood of processing.

It is very relevant to remember here some of the personal influences of the buyer while making buying decisions listed out by Kurt Lewin's "black-box model." They are

1. Inner needs
2. Thoughts
3. Beliefs
4. Attitudes
5. Values
6. Motives
7. Perceptions
8. External environmental forces

The essence of the black-box model is that consumers will respond in particular ways to different stimuli after they have 'processed' those stimuli in their minds. In more detail, the model suggests that factors external to the consumer will act as a stimulus for behaviour, but that the consumer's personal characteristics and decision-making process will interact with the stimulus before a particular behavioural response is generated.

It is called the black-box model because we still know so little about how the human mind works. We cannot *see* what goes on in the mind and we don't really *know* much about what goes on in there, so it is like a black box. As far as consumer behaviour goes, we know enough to be able to identify major internal influences and the major steps in the decision-making process which consumers use, but we don't really know how consumers transform all these data, together with the stimuli, to generate particular responses.

CONSUMER BUYING PROCESS

There are many models of consumer buying behaviour, but the steps below are fairly common to most of them.

Step I Need Identification

The buyers identify the product to be bought through some method. They might have come across with the product accidentally like noticing a big sign board glittering at night while passing through a city road. They might have read about the same product in a magazine or newspaper. Or, a friend would have spoken very high of the product.

Step II Gathering Information

In the next step, the buyers start information search looking at the internet or other sources. They might visit the store and look at the information printed on its package. They would check whether the manufacturer is reliable and reputed for quality. They collect information about competing products or substitutes. If the buyers are

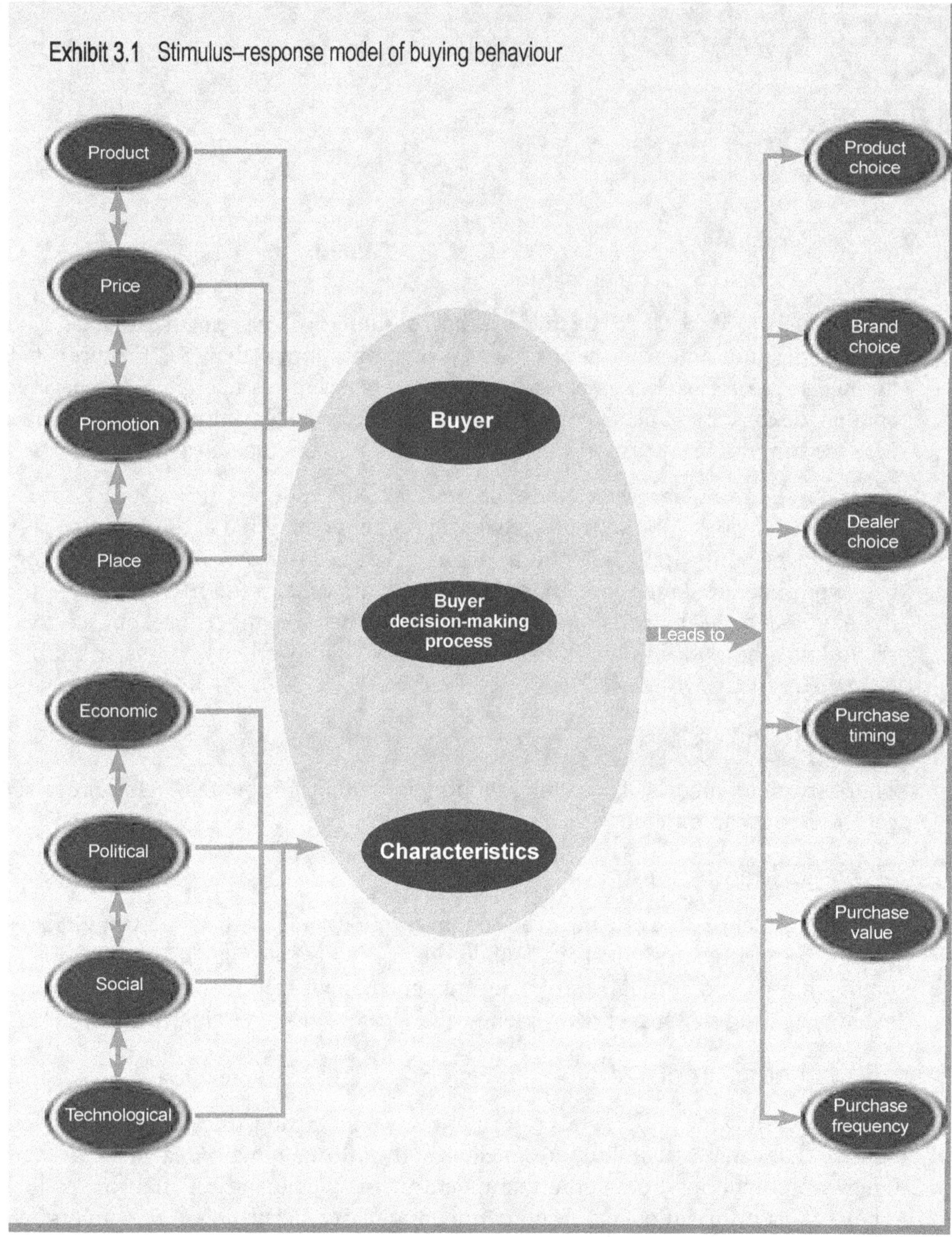

Exhibit 3.1 Stimulus–response model of buying behaviour

cost-conscious, they collect information on price particulars also. A few customers do not gather information; they straight away go for buying it as they are confident about the manufacturer. We cannot correctly judge the customer's intentions and behaviour. Sometimes we can; some other times we cannot. Predicting what the customer will buy and will not buy do not require squeezing your brain these days because today's average customers are conscious of all the important factors that require consideration. The recurring recessions across the globe have made them conscious of the value of their money. We shall discuss this aspect in more detail at another place in this chapter.

The amount of effort a consumer puts into searching depends on a number of factors such as the *market* (how many competitors are there, and how great are differences between brands expected to be?), *product characteristics* (how important is this product? How complex is the product? How obvious are indications of quality?), *consumer characteristics* (how interested is a consumer, generally, in analysing product characteristics and making the best possible deal?), and *situational* characteristics.

A customer can obtain information from personal sources like family, friends, neighbours and the like, commercial sources like advertising, salespeople, retailers, dealers, packaging, and point-of-sale displays, and experiential sources like handling, examining, using the product. However, these are conventional methods. The preferred method of search these days is the Internet, with mobile coming second when consumers are out and about:

1. Web
    i. Major search engines (Google, Yahoo, MSN)
    ii. Local search engines (Google Maps, Yahoo Local, MSN Live)
    iii. Internet Yellow Pages (YellowPages, Citysearch, Superpages)
2. Website
    i. Corporate website
    ii. Mobile website
    iii. Local websites
3. Mobile devices
    i. Cell phones
    ii. Smart phones
    iii. GPS
    iv. In-car navigation
    v. Portable navigation

Step III Studying Products

After gathering necessary information, the consumer studies different products available in the market. Remember well that only a few customers do intensive search and study the plus points and the minus points of buying the product.

Step IV Making the Purchase Decision

Sometimes the buyer makes the decision after a discussion with the family members; but not with all the buyers. Buyers make individual decisions frequently. Family decision-making is considered when huge expenditure is made because the funds involved may be the collective earnings of the family. Buying luxury items will involve the whole family deciding the brand and its advantages. When a proposal for a house purchase or a large shopping complex comes before the family, the entire family members might get involved in the decision-making process. When it comes to small purchases like buying a DVD player or an LCD television, the family may not necessarily be the final authority. But some families do collective shopping even for tiny items. Therefore the behaviour of the buyer is very difficult to assess.

Step V Using the Product

Expensive purchases can lead to what is known as cognitive dissonance—a fear that the customer has not made the right decision. Your job is to reassure the customer by offering good customer care, simple instruction manuals and loyalty schemes. They should still be exposed to testimonial advertising to reassure them that they have made the right decision.

BUSINESS CUSTOMER'S BUYING PROCESS

A big share of the market for goods and services is attributable to *organisational or business*, as opposed to individual, buyers. In general, organisational buyers, who make buying decisions for their companies for a living, tend to be somewhat more sophisticated than ordinary consumers.

Organisational buyers follow more or less similar procedure for making their purchase which is followed by a rational customer. Firms follow any one of these procedures to procure their supplies: i) centralised buying, ii) decentralised buying, and iii) a hybrid system. These buying systems have their merits as well as demerits.

There are several types of business buyers.

* Resellers involve either wholesalers or retailers who buy from one organisation and resell to some other entity. For example, large distributors or wholesalers buy goods in large quantities and resell them to retailers or end users who buy in bulk.

* Sometimes producers also buy products from smaller manufacturers to create a finished product. For example, rather than manufacturing the parts themselves, computer manufacturers often buy accessories like hard drives, motherboards, cases, monitors, keyboards, and other components from manufacturers and assemble them together to create a finished product.

* Governments buy a great deal of things. For example, the military needs an incredible amount of supplies to feed and equip troops.

* Finally, large institutions buy products in huge quantities. For example, universities buy thousands of reams of paper every month.

Hutt and Speh[5] (1998) suggest that each business-to-business buying situation can be categorised into one of the below categories:

New task   In the new-task buying situation, the problem or need is perceived by organisational decision makers as totally different from previous experiences; therefore a significant amount of information is required for decision makers to explore alternative ways of solving the problem and to search for alternative suppliers.

Straight re-buy   Where there is a continuing or recurring requirement, buyers have substantial experience in dealing with the need, and they require little or no new information. Evaluation of new alternative solutions is unnecessary and unlikely to yield appreciable improvements.

Modified re-buy   In the modified re-buy situation, organisational decision-makers feel that significant benefits may be derived from a revaluation of alternatives. The buyers have experience in satisfying the continuing or recurring requirement, but they believe it worthwhile to seek additional information, and perhaps to consider alternative solutions.

There are some differences between consumer and business buying behaviour.

Nature of the relationship   In business markets, a lean towards supply-chain management leads to more enduring relationships, meaning firms are more likely to pay more attention to the roles of suppliers, products, distributors and end users.

Frequency of purchase   In business markets, purchases are usually higher in frequency as their requirements ought to be high and regular.

Size of order   The average business order is larger than in the customer market.

Length of the negotiation period   The period of negotiation in business sales are normally much longer than in customers' buying situations.

Higher service expectations   Greater service expectations are the norm in business markets. The main reasons include a fear of obsolescence and the need to be able to quickly integrate the product into the buying company's own system as quickly as possible.

Professional buyers. Organisations tend to use full-time professionals to source inputs for the organisation, making inputs highly scrutinised.

Company rules, procedures, and policies   The firm's rules, procedures, and policies are the deciding factors in organisational buying. Organisational goals also influence purchase decisions.

FACTORS INFLUENCING BUYER BEHAVIOUR

Consumer behaviour is affected by many uncontrollable factors. Let us discuss a few important ones among them.

Personal Factors

Personal factors include:

   i.   age and life cycle stage,
   ii. occupation,
   iii. economic conditions, and
   iv. lifestyle.

Age and life cycle stage   People change the goods and services they buy over their lifetimes. Tastes in food, clothes, furniture, and recreation are often age-related. Buying is also shaped by the stage of the family life cycle.

Occupation   A person's occupation affects the goods and services bought. Blue-collar workers tend to buy low-cost work clothes, whereas white-collar workers buy branded wear and business suits. A company can even specialise in making products needed by a given occupational segment. Thus, computer software companies will design different products for brand managers, accountants, engineers, lawyers, and doctors.

Economic situation   A person's economic status will affect the product choice. The economic status of a person is reflected in how much money he/she has at his/her disposal, and how much money he/she is ready to spend for purchasing things.

Lifestyle   Lifestyle is a person's pattern of living, understanding these forces involves measuring consumer's major *AIO* dimensions, i.e., activities (work, hobbies, shopping, support, etc.) interest (food, fashion, family recreation) and opinions (about themselves, business, products).

Social Factors

Consumer wants, learning, motives and the like are influenced by social factors like culture, person's family background, reference groups, social class, and opinion leaders.

Family   Family is the most basic group a person belongs to. Marketers must understand that many family decisions are made by the family unit and consumer behaviour starts in the family unit. Family roles and preferences are the model for children's future family. Family buying decisions are a mixture of family interactions and individual decision making. Family acts as an interpreter of social and cultural values for the individual.

The stage in which the family is placed presently, plays an important role in determining the buyer behaviour. Families go through stages; each stage creates different consumer demands:

* bachelor stage
* newly married, young, no children
* full nest I, youngest child under 6
* full nest II, youngest child 6 or over
* full nest III, older married couples with dependant children
* empty nest I, older married couples with no children living with them, head in labour force
* empty nest II, older married couples, no children living at home, head retired
* solitary survivor, in labour force
* solitary survivor, retired
* modernised life cycle includes divorced and no children

Individual identifies with the group to the extent that he/she takes on many of the values, attitudes or behaviours of the group members.

Culture   It is one factor that influences buyer behaviour. Simply culture is defined as our attitudes and beliefs. It is also the set of values, ideas, and attitudes that are accepted by a homogenous group of people and transmitted to the next generation. It is important to study briefly how these attitudes and beliefs are developed. As a child is growing up, it is influenced by the behaviour, love and affection of their parents, brothers, sisters and other family members. When in school, the teachers, classmates, and the school culture makes a good amount of impact on the students. They also learn about their religion and culture, which helps them develop these opinions, attitudes and beliefs.

Culture also determines what is acceptable with product advertising. Culture determines what people wear, eat, reside and travel. Cultural values in the

US are good health, education, individualism and freedom. In American culture, time scarcity is a growing problem. But in India, it is rare to find time-conscious people.

Hofstede's dimensions[6] Gert Hofstede, a Dutch researcher, was able to interview a large number of IBM executives in various countries, and found that cultural differences tended to centre around four key dimensions:

Individualism vs. collectivism To what extent do people believe in individual responsibility and reward rather than having these measures aimed at the larger group? Contrary to the stereotype, Japan actually ranks in the middle of this dimension, while Indonesia and West Africa rank toward the collectivistic side. The U.S., Britain, and the Netherlands rate toward individualism.

Power distance To what extent is there a strong separation of individuals based on rank? Power distance tends to be particularly high in Arab countries and some Latin American ones, while it is more modest in Northern Europe and the U.S.

Masculinity vs. femininity It involves a somewhat more nebulous concept. "Masculine" values involve competition and "conquering" nature by means such as large construction projects, while "feminine" values involve harmony and environmental protection.   Japan is one of the more masculine countries, while the Netherlands rank relatively low. The U.S. is close to the middle, slightly towards the masculine side.

Uncertainty avoidance It involves the extent to which a "structured" situation with clear rules is preferred to a more ambiguous one; in general, countries with lower uncertainty avoidance tend to be more tolerant of risk. Japan ranks very high. Few countries are very low in any absolute sense, but relatively speaking, Britain and Hong Kong are lower, and the U.S. is in the lower range of the distribution.

Although Hofstede's original work did not address this, a fifth dimension of *long-term vs. short-term orientation* has been proposed. In the US, managers like to see quick results, while Japanese managers are known for taking a long-term view, often accepting long periods before profitability is obtained.

Reference groups These are groups of people who enjoy respect and esteem from the buyers. Some people may consider the opinions of the members of reference group.

Opinion leaders They are those people whom you look up to because you respect their views and judgments and these views may influence consumer decisions. So it may be a friend who may influence your decision on what computer brand to buy. Above all, marketing and advertising of the firms obviously influence consumers in trying to evoke them to purchase a particular brand of product or service.

The last few years have witnessed tremendous change in the consumer profile in India, thanks to globalisation and growth in the IT industry. The beneficiary, no doubt, is the retail sector. Consumers in India have started revising their posotions in regard to spending and style of living. Their behaviour has changed drastically due to thier enhanced earnings and awareness in regard to hygeine and health. Most of the corporates in India have noticed this trend and devised new strategies to suit the new wave. Improved quality of the core product, improved packaging, better advertisements, more product information, better after-sales-service, etc. have become necessity for today's Indian consumer.

Psychological Factors

Psychological factors include *motives* for purchase of an item. A motive is an internal energising force that orients a person's activities towards satisfying a need or achieving a goal. Actions are effected by a set of motives, not just one. If marketers can identify motives then they can better develop a marketing mix.

Perception   It is another psychological factor that has its impact on the buying behaviour of the people. Perception is the process of selecting, organising and interpreting information inputs to produce meaning. We choose what information we pay attention to, organise it and interpret it. Information inputs are the sensations received through sight, taste, hearing, smell and touch. Advertisers that use comparative advertisements (pitching one product against another), have to be very careful that consumers do not distort the facts and perceive that the advertisement was for the competitor. These advertisements might confuse the customers sometimes; but shrewd customers catch the point.

Attitude   It is another psychological factor influencing the buyers' decision to buy. The individual develops attitudes through experience and interaction with other people. Consumer attitudes towards a firm and its products greatly influence the success or failure of the firm's marketing strategy. Attitudes are developed by varied experiences of the buyer during the course of his/her life.

Attitudes and attitude change are influenced by consumer's personality and lifestyle. Consumers screen information that conflicts with their attitudes. They tend to distort information to make it consistent and selectively retain information that reinforces our attitudes. You must note the difference between attitude and intention to buy.

Personality   It is the sum of all the internal traits and behaviours that make a person unique; uniqueness derives from a person's heredity and personal experience. Examples include:

* Workaholism
* Compulsiveness
* Self-confidence

* Friendliness
* Adaptability
* Ambitiousness
* Dogmatism
* Authoritarianism
* Introversion
* Extroversion
* Aggressiveness
* Competitiveness

Traits affect the way people behave. Marketers try to match the store image to the perceived image of their customers. However the strength of association between personality and buying behaviour needs to be established. However, it is certain that there is a good amount of correlation between these two variables.

WHAT DO FIRMS LEARN FROM RESEARCH ON BUYER BEHAVIOUR

Buyer behaviour involves both simple and complex mental processes. Marketers cannot capture human nature in its entirety but we can learn a lot about customers through research, observation and thinking. Here's Professor Theodore Levitt: *"I think it is a process of trying to think your way through why people behave in certain ways. Or if not why, then what that behaviour is likely to be given certain kinds of products, certain kinds of... just stop to think."*

According to Malhotra,[7] the purposes of gathering market research information are to

    i.   identify and define marketing opportunities and problems
    ii.   generate, refine and evaluate marketing actions
    iii.   monitor marketing performance
    iv.   improve the understanding of marketing as a process.

Research on consumer behaviour is an ongoing process. It is consumer research that revealed the effect of factors like personal, social, and psychological on consumer behaviour. But the big question is how many sellers undertake research to bring out the inner thoughts of their customers? There are a number of consumer research firms the world over especially in the U.S. These consulting firms carry out research on behalf of their client firms. Or they supply stored information to them on request. All the information found in the literature on consumer behaviour are the result of consumer research carried out by experts in the field.

Research helps find the real reasons why people buy what they buy. This requires time, money and expertise. Surprisingly several organisations don't really know exactly why their customers buy or don't buy their products. Yet understanding customers is at the heart of marketing. The research may be a simple process in case you choose to observe what is happening at the store while the buyer is about to buy your product. You may also decide to interview the buyer inside or outside the store. In some firms, the senior marketing managers personally make visits to observe the buyer behaviour. This kind of information search will be without any biases and the information so gathered will be of greater value than the information collected through hired sources.

It would be relevant here to mention what was given by Michael Treacy and Fred Wiersema in their book *The Discipline of Market Leaders.*[8] They suggested that most successful firms fall into one of the three categories:

Operationally excellent firms, which maintain a strong competitive advantage by maintaining exceptional efficiency, thus enabling the firm to provide reliable service to the customer at a significantly lower cost than those of less well-organised and well-run competitors. The emphasis here is mostly on low cost, subject to reliable performance, and less value is put on customising the offering for the specific customer. Wall Mart is an example of this discipline. Elaborate logistical designs allow goods to be moved at the lowest cost, with extensive systems predicting when specific quantities of supplies will be needed.

Customer intimate firms, which excel in serving the specific needs of the individual customer well. There is less emphasis on efficiency, which is sacrificed for providing more precisely what is wanted by the customer. Reliability is also stressed. Nordstrom's and IBM are examples of this discipline.

Technologically excellent firms, which produce the most advanced products currently available with the latest technology, constantly maintaining leadership in innovation. These firms, because they work with costly technology that needs constant refinement, cannot be as efficient as the operationally excellent firms and often cannot adapt their products as well to the needs of the individual customer. Intel is an example of this discipline.

The firms need to know the following through consumer research:

* the reasons why their products are accepted by the consumers,
* the reasons why their products are rejected by the consumers, and
* the measures to be taken to improve consumer acceptance of their products.

The businessmen of today have come to know of the secrets of success of a product in the market thanks to the quality movement led by Dr. W. Edwards Deming, Dr. Joseph Juran, Philip Crosby, and Armand V. Feigenbaum. Quality is the foremost priority of the consumer. There can be no second opinion. Of course the next important factor is price. These are the things which every seller knows. But how many sellers follow these prescriptions? Firms fail to take the advices of the experts, and this leads to problem situations at times of economic slowdowns and other difficult situations.

At the same time, we should not fail to recognise the truth that lies behind the success of the business barons in the international business scenario. Their success is the result of careful strategic planning and implementation of these plans with due precision through highly talented and dedicated people who are at their service. Anyone who is aware of these facts is bound to succeed in his endeavour. The firms, therefore, have to listen to the findings of the researchers with due concern.

The basic tenets of successful strategic marketing are:

* Underline the benefits your buyers would enjoy while buying your goods,
* Stress on the unique services you offer them,
* Keep doing something new, useful, and interesting for your customers,
* Anticipate changes in the market,
* Do not manufacture or sell variety of goods unless required by your customers, and
* Enlist their support by assuring them quality after-sales-service.

SUMMARY

* Buyer behaviour may be defined as *a series of response patterns of an individual or organisation that occur in search for products or services that are capable of satisfying the buyer's conscious and subconscious needs.* Blackwell, Miniard, and Engel define consumer behaviour as "activities people undertake when obtaining, consuming, and disposing products and services."

* A well-developed and tested model of buyer behaviour is known as the *stimulus– response* model. Marketing stimuli consists of the marketing mix, viz., product, price, place and promotion and other stimuli include other forces in the buyer's environment: economic, technological, political and cultural. All these inputs enter the buyer's brain, where they are turned into a set of observable buyer responses, i.e., product choice, brand choice, dealer choice, purchase timing and purchase amount.

* The steps involved in the buying process of the customer are:
  i. Need identification
  ii. Gathering information,

   iii. Studying products,

   iv. Making the purchase decision, and

   v. Using the product.

* Organisational buyers follow more or less similar procedure for making their purchase which is followed by a rational customer. Firms follow any one of these procedures to procure their supplies:

   i. centralised buying,

   ii. decentralised buying, and

   iii. a hybrid system.

   These buying systems have their merits as well as demerits.

* Several factors influence the buying behaviour of the individual. They are:

   i. personal factors which include age and life cycle stage, occupation, economic situation, and life style,

   ii. social factors which include family, culture, and reference groups, and

   iii. psychological factors which include perception, attitude, and personality.

* Research helps find the real reasons why people buy what they buy. This requires time, money and expertise. Surprisingly many other organisations don't really know exactly why their customers buy or don't buy from them. Yet understanding customers is at the heart of marketing.

REVIEW QUESTIONS

1. What is buyer behaviour?

2. "Assessing buying behaviour is never simple, yet understanding it is the essential task of marketing management." Why assessing buyer behaviour is not simple? As a marketer, what would you do to assess the buyer behaviour?

3. "Consumers are goal-oriented, and their purchase decisions are often (but not always certain) carefully calculated to provide the greatest amount of benefits received for the money spent." Do you agree with this statement? Give logical reasons for your answer.

4. Explain the stimulus–response model of buyer behaviour.

5. Explain the black-box model.

6. Explain the consumer-buying process.

7. "The buyer identifies the product that he/she is to buy through some method." Explain the methods the consumer uses to identify the product he/she proposes to buy.

8. Explain a business customer's-buying process.

9. What is cognitive resonance? Why is the customer forced to have cognitive resonance? What are the ways it can be avoided?

10. What are the factors that influence the buyer behaviour?

11. What do firms learn from research on buyer behaviour?

REFERENCES

1. Blackwell, R.D., Miniard, P.W. and Engel, J.F. (2001). *Consumer Behavior,* 9th edn. Hartcourt College Publishers, Fort Woth.

2. Solomon, M. (1998). *Consumer Behavior. Buying, Having and Being.* Prentice Hall, New York, p. 15.

3. Xavier Sala Bringué. "Introduction to the study of consumer behaviour." Please look at the website for more particulars of his article http://www.unav.es/empinf/psicologia/introduction.doc

4. Thorndike, E. (1932). *The Fundamentals of Learning.* Teachers College Press, New York.

5. Hutt, M.D. and Speh, T.W. (1998). *"Business Marketing Management— A Strategic View of Industrial and organisational Markets"*, Dryden Press.

6. http://loveforlife.com.au/content/08/03/15/welcome-geert-hofstedes-homepage

7. Malhotra, K. Naresha (2002). *Basic Marketing Research: A Decision-Making Approach.* Prentice Hall, Upper Saddle River, NJ.

8. Treacy, Michael and Wiersema, Fred. (1993). *The Discipline of Market Leaders: Choose Your Customers, Narrow Your Focus, Dominate Your Market*, Perseus Books, New York.

4

STRATEGIC MARKETING FACTORS FOR GROWTH[1]

After reading this chapter, you will be able to learn about the following strategic marketing factors:

- *Strategic Marketing Planning*
- *Marketing Communications*
- *Market Positioning*
- *Product Pricing*
- *Brand Management*
- *Winning Competitors*
- *Marketing Research*
- *Managing Product Life Cycle*
- *Salesforce Management*

KEY TERMS

- Strategic marketing plan
- Executive summary
- Vision statement
- Mission statement
- Corporate objectives
- Marketing objectives
- *MARCOMs*
- Public relations
- Personal selling
- Sales promotion
- Advertising
- Direct marketing
- Market positioning
- Cost plus pricing
- Target return pricing
- Psychological pricing
- Value-based pricing
- Brand management
- Self-appraisal
- Strategic marketing research
- Salesforce management

INTRODUCTION

Marketing today is a delicate function irrespective of the size of the organisation. This has become so in view of the dynamic environment surrounding it. An organisation's success is determined by the efficacy of marketing even though many other factors play in the game of business. An effective marketing manager can sell defective products quickly; but he cannot hold it long as the deficiencies of other functions will start playing the game and the organisation will soon find its decline. Therefore, what we can say is business is a team game. It is a system. Any damage done to any part of the system will reflect in other parts as well. Therefore, the success of the organisation depends on the teamwork of its people. At the base of it is *'the human resource'*—humans of calibre, humans of talents, and humans of foresight. What is required to win the game of business is people of foresight for your organisation. Nothing on this earth can equal the talents of human beings. It is possible that even a good research can fail before an effective manager's foresight. As marketing is a key function along with other functional areas, it is our task here to make it perfect. And in search of this perfection, we have to pinpoint the key marketing factors which require most of the attention of the top marketing executives.

STRATEGIC MARKETING FACTORS

The objective of this book is to stress the need for strategic approach to resolve the problems confronted by a marketing manager. In this quest, a few important factors are identified as keys for all marketing problems holding value not only today but also in the future. The strategic marketing factors are:

* Strategic Marketing Planning
* Marketing Communications
* Market Positioning
* Product Pricing
* Brand Management
* Winning Competitors
* Marketing Research
* Managing Product Life Cycle
* Salesforce Management

Let us now begin to explore the important aspects of these factors briefly. The detailed discussion will form the remaining part of this book.

Strategic Marketing Planning

First let us see what Theodore Levitt[2] says about a strategic plan's relevance to marketing: "*Strategic planning involves defining what's to be done. It is inescapably rooted in marketing matters, in the need to respond to realities, the actualities of the market's unyielding requisites.*"

Therefore, a strategic plan has a lot to do with strategic marketing planning. A well-constructed strategic marketing plan is all that is needed to begin the work. Earlier discussion defines marketing strategy planning as *the process of determining appropriate courses of action for achieving the marketing organisation's objectives.* A strategic marketing plan consists of a broad outline of specifications of what should be done to accomplish specific marketing objectives during a specified future period which is normally ten years. It is in tune with the organisation's stated vision and mission statements and the stated corporate objectives in the overall long-term strategy of the organisation. *The strategic marketing plan is a part of the overall strategic plan of the organisation.*

There is no specific format for a strategic marketing plan. Firms can design their own strategic marketing plans according to their requirements. A general framework for a strategic marketing plan of a manufacturing organisation is as follows:

- Executive Summary
- Corporate Vision and Mission
- Statement of Corporate Objectives
- Statement of Marketing Objectives
- Situation Analysis—Internal and External
- *SWOT* Analysis
- Portfolio Analysis
- Formulation of Marketing Strategies
- Marketing Action Plan
- Marketing Budget
- Project Performance Review

Executive summary   Executive summary consists of synopsis of a situation, and key aspects of the marketing plan. It has to be given briefly not exceeding one page. The summary should briefly describe your business and the major points of your plan. It must describe briefly the status of the economy and industry. A brief forecast of the future business trend may also be given. The information given must be from authentic sources.

Corporate vision and mission statements   These statements form basic to the firm's strategic plan and in turn the strategic marketing plan. Jeffrey Abrahams[3], *TRINOVA* Corporation defines a *mission statement* in the following way:" A mission statement is an enduring statement of purpose for an organisation that identifies the scope of its operations in product and market terms, and reflects its values and priorities." *Corporate vision* is a short, succinct, and inspiring statement of what the organisation intends to become and to achieve at some point in the future, often stated in competitive terms. Vision refers to the category of intentions that are broad, all-inclusive and broad thinking. It is the image that a business must have of its goals before it sets out to reach them. It describes aspirations for the future, without specifying the means that will be used to achieve those broad desired ends.

Statement of corporate objectives   *Corporate objectives* are the milestones that organisations must achieve to reach short-term or long-term goals. Objectives should be measurable, quantitative, challenging, realistic, consistent, and prioritised. It is these objectives from which the objectives of the different departments including the marketing department of the firm are derived.

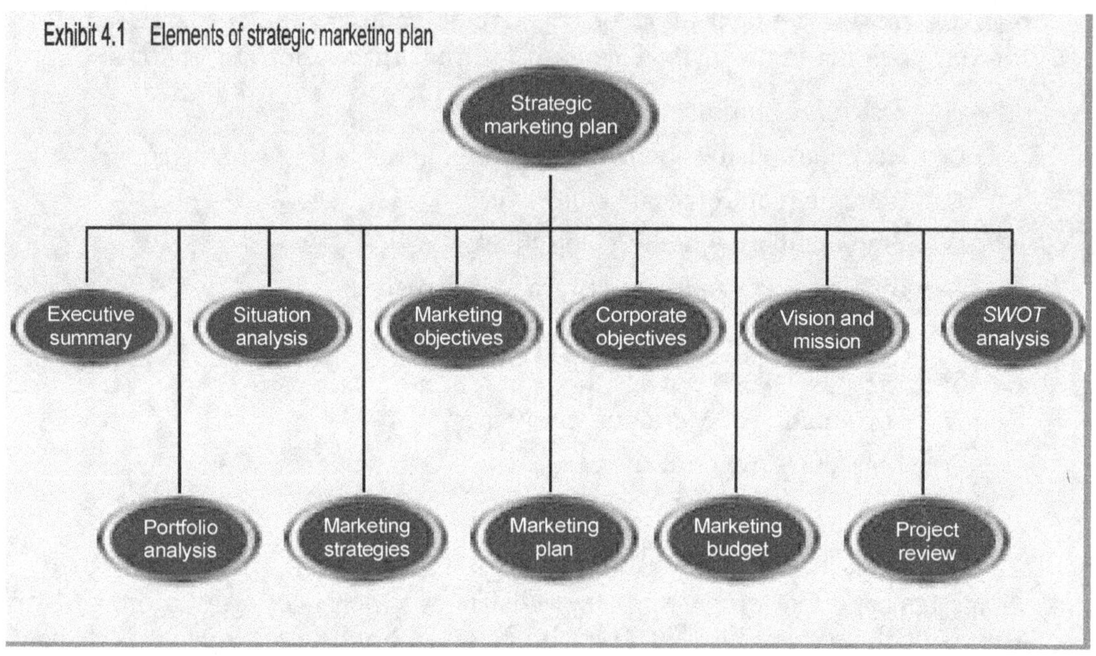

Statement of marketing objectives   Marketing objectives are the targets which must be achieved by the marketing personnel and these objectives are developed jointly by the senior marketing executives and the top management.

Situation analysis: internal and external   Situation analysis is an honest assessment of the internal and external environment of the marketing organisation. The situation analysis looks at the current business environment and can be elaborate or very simple. The components examined are competition, the size of the market, types of customers, channels of distribution, the present and proposed government policies, the aspects of physical environment which have bearing on the firm's marketing programmes, and economic conditions. By taking an overview of the whole picture and stating your strengths and weaknesses, you'll have a clearer understanding of how well your company will compete. Sometimes situation analysis includes the *SWOT* analysis also.

SWOT analysis   *SWOT* is the abbreviation used in management to mean strengths, weaknesses, opportunities and threats. This model is the basic commandment for any organisation. If this model is applied in perfect condition, the firm will be able to confront any challenge that might appear on the scene.

Marketing portfolio analysis   In order to optimise the overall performance of its portfolio of products, the organisation must monitor and analyse the performance of each of its strategic business units (products). This analysis has to be conducted by the firm in order to decide which strategic business units to build, maintain, harvest, and divest. One of the best known and widely used models for this purpose is the Boston Consulting Group Product Portfolio Analysis model.

Formulation of marketing strategies   A *strategy* is the direction of the company's programmes in the long-run in order to achieve its objectives. The firm may have a single marketing strategy or multiple strategies depending on its needs. Some products may be in a dominant position relative to competitors, while others may be in a weaker position. Each product will have its own strategy, and may face several competitive products having their own marketing strategies. Some products may be profitable while others may need cash to finance growth or to fight competition. Faced with this complex situation, the organisation must allocate its limited resources among these products in order to optimise its overall performance.

Marketing action plan   The statement of marketing action plan contains details of smaller plans or tactics to be followed by the marketing department in order to achieve the targets or marketing objectives.

Marketing budget   A marketing budget contains the projected costs and timeline related to the execution of the firm's marketing tactics.

Project performance review   The final part of the strategic marketing is the review of the projects while they are in operation. This review is important because any deviation from the scheduled path can be detected on time and remedial steps can be taken immediately. The strategic marketing plan suggests the methodology to be followed in carrying out the project performance review.

A detailed discussion of these factors will be taken up in the next chapter.

Marketing Communications (MARCOMs)

Marketing Communications (or MarComs or Integrated Marketing Communications) are information and related media used to communicate with a market. Those who practice advertising, branding, direct marketing, graphic design, marketing, packaging, promotion, publicity, sponsorship, public relations, sales, sales promotion and online marketing are termed marketing communicators, marketing communication managers, or more briefly as marcom managers. We can say that everything the firm does forms part of marketing communication. Every act of the firm conveys some message to the stakeholders.

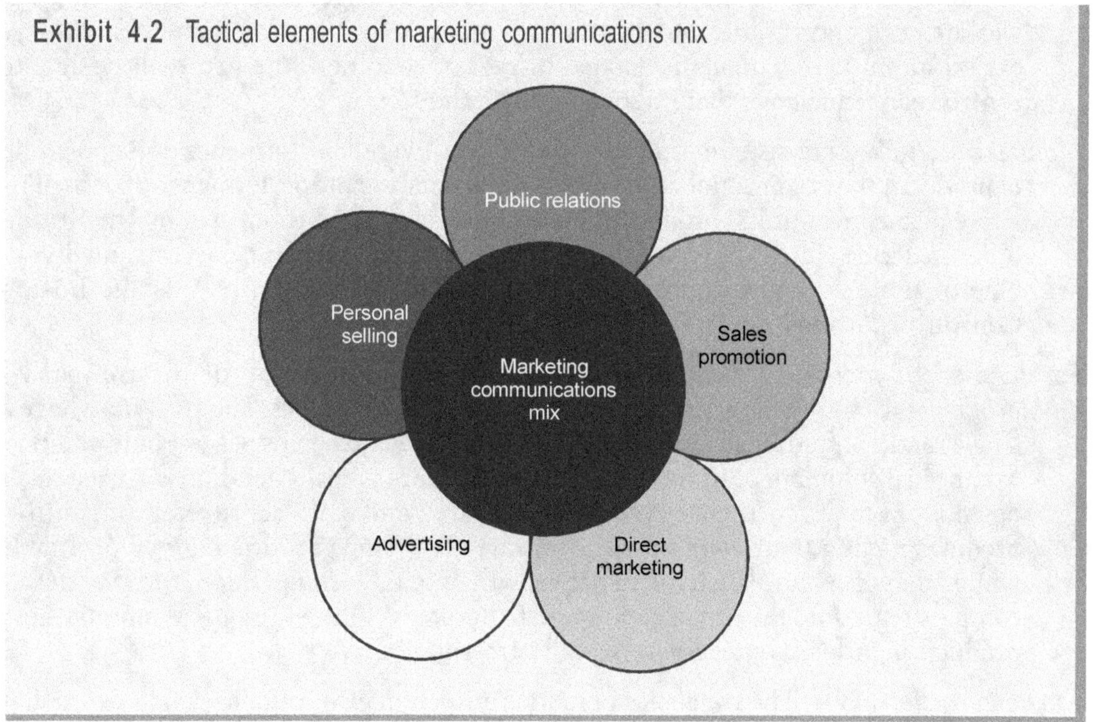

Exhibit 4.2 Tactical elements of marketing communications mix

Most important elements of *MARCOMs* are:

1. *Advertising*   It is any paid form of non-personal communication link, initiated by an identified marketer, to establish or continue exchange relationships with customers and at times, with other stakeholders (Exhibit 4.3).

2. *Sales promotion* It is a direct inducement that offers an extra value or incentive for a product, to the trade or consumer, with the objective of creating an immediate sale .Thus, there can be two types, consumer-oriented or trade-oriented.

3. *Direct marketing*   It is any communication to a consumer that is designed to generate a *behavioural* response, and usually it is used to sell, e.g., Dell, Amazon. It is also the

case with personal selling. Communication may be direct, viz., direct mail, or through mass media like TV, e.g., direct-response advertising and telemarketing.

4. *Personal selling*   It is the personal presentation by the firm's salesforce for the purpose of making sales and building customer relationships.

5. *Public relations*   It is an activity that fosters goodwill between an organisation, and its stakeholders. When the function of public relations is managed effectively, it can be useful. Otherwise, it can be damaging, e.g., Microsoft funding to cut funds for the Justice Dept! Thus, public relations can be a double-edged sword.

Market Positioning

Market positioning is a bundle of efforts to influence consumer perception of a brand or product relative to the perception of competing brands or products. Its objective is to occupy a clear, unique, and advantageous "position" in the consumer's mind such as "the best driving car," "the most economical car," or "the safest car."

Positioning is a perceptual location. It's where the firm's product or service fits into the marketplace. Effective positioning puts the firm first in line in the minds of potential customers. Positioning is a powerful tool that creates an image. This image may be positive or negative. The firm should not put itself in the bad books of the customers.

Image is the outward representation of being what the firm wants to be, doing what it wants to do, and having what it wants to have. If the firm does not define its product or service, a competitor will do it for the firm.

The firm's position in the marketplace evolves from the defining characteristics of its product. The primary elements of positioning are:

Pricing   You must decide the right type of pricing taking into account the kind of segment you are going to serve. Is your product a luxury item, somewhere in the middle, or cheap? Evaluate the expectations of the customers in your segment. And give them what they want.

Right quality   Total quality is a much used and abused phrase. What is needed for the customer is the right quality. The ordinary customer does not want a car that gives 100 miles per gallon at a cost of $200,000. What the consumers look for is the right quality and should not take their car often to the garage. The firm must recognise what the customer *actually* wants. Is your product well produced? What controls are in place to assure consistency? Do you back your quality claim with customer-friendly guarantees, warranties, and return policies?

Service   The consumer of today is very specific about the kind of after sales services offered by the firm. Do you offer the added value of customer service and support? Is your product customised and personalised?

Distribution   How do customers obtain your product? The channel or distribution is part of positioning. The customer should not find it a cumbersome process to search for your product.

Packaging   Packaging makes a strong statement. Make sure it's delivering the message you intend.

Exhibit 4.3   An advertisement communicating a message

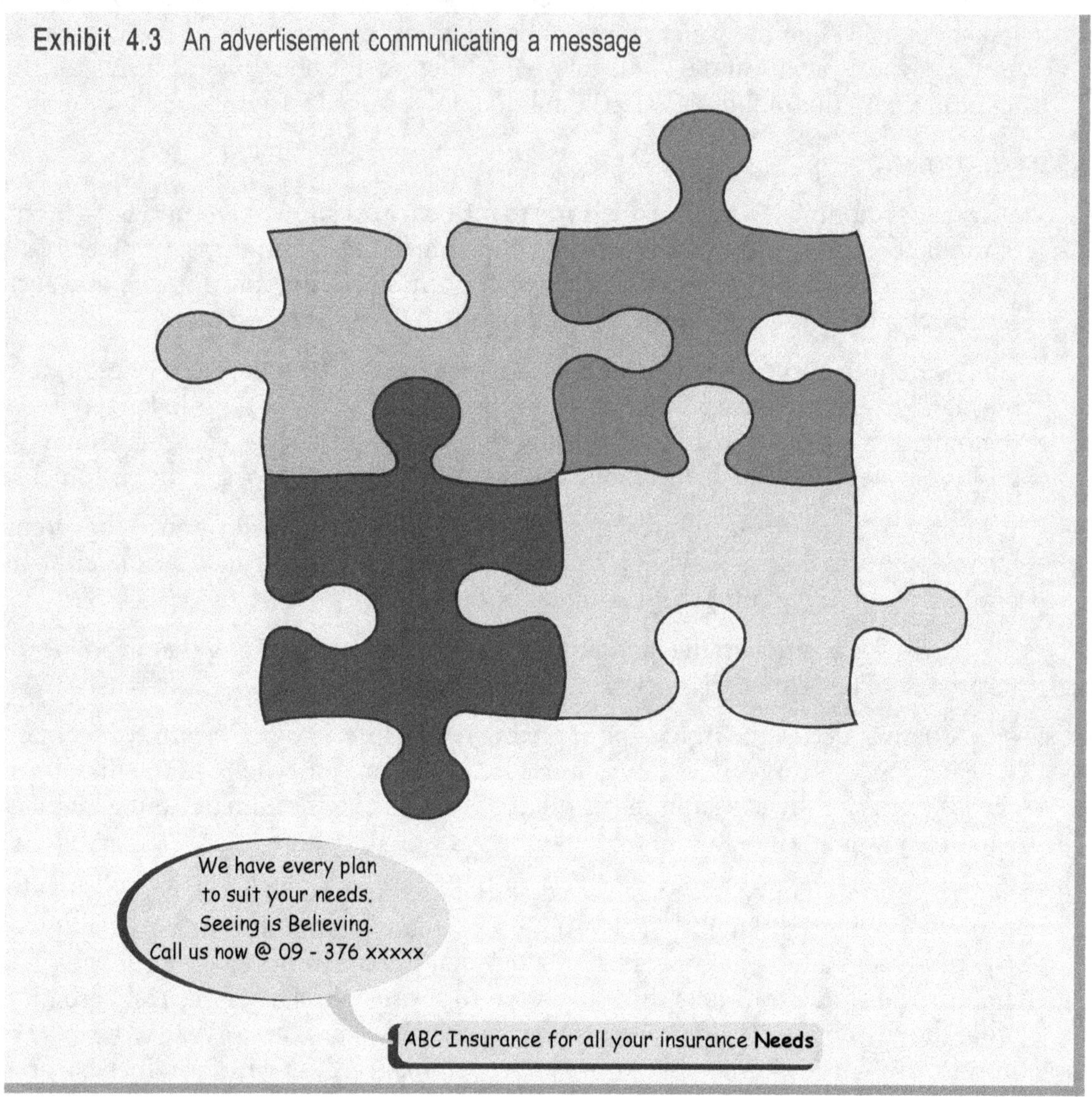

Product Pricing

Product pricing is a strategic factor that determines the positioning of the firm in the industry. Before deciding an appropriate pricing strategy, you have to consider various factors such as manufacturing cost, promotion cost, research and development cost, market situation, our position in the market, and the firm's policy.

There are two kinds of strategies available for the marketer: i) market skimming, and ii) market penetration. Market skimming attempts to skim the cream off the upmarket by setting a high price and selling to those customers who are less price-sensitive and who follow the habit of buying the top end product in the market. Penetration pricing method attempts to satisfy the objective of quantity maximisation by offering the product for a low price. This method aims to capture the consumers who are highly price-sensitive and at the same time financially less comfortable.

The major types of pricing methods are i) cost-plus pricing, ii) target return pricing, iii) value-based pricing, and iv) psychological pricing. There are other innovative pricing methods which are extensively used by the firms. Sometimes the marketer asks the customers what they think the service is worth. This is called as *outside-in pricing*. Value-based pricing methods are widely adopted nowadays.

Different types of price discounts are also offered to the customers. They are i) quantity discount, ii) cumulative quantity discount, iii) seasonal discount, iv) cash discount, v) promotional discount, and vi) trade discount.

Brand Management

The American Marketing Association (AMA) defines a brand as a "name, term, sign, symbol or design, or a combination of them intended to identify the goods and services of one seller or group of sellers and to differentiate them from those of other sellers". It is the sum total of their experiences and perceptions, some of which you can influence, and some that you cannot. A good brand

- confirms your credibility
- delivers the message clearly
- connects your target prospects emotionally
- motivates the buyer
- reinforces user loyalty

Remember, your brand is living in the hearts and minds of customers, clients, and prospects. Therefore, brand is silently working for the success of the organisation. But the making of a brand is not that easy. Several years of dedicated work of both employees and the management has made it. Brand is the powerful ambassador as well as the spokesperson of the organisation.

Brand management is the application of marketing techniques to a specific product, product line, or brand. It seeks to increase the product's perceived value to the customer and thereby increase brand franchise and brand equity. Brand management is an art and a total approach to managing companies, and as such includes much about changing minds. CEOs have long realised that the real strength of a company can be traced to the value of its brands. Brand marketing managers seek to create and develop brand value by converting consumer insights into consumer loyalty. Other things being same, the key to the success of a marketing organisation is to integrate brand management activities across your organisation so your marketers can be creators.

Winning Competitors

Business is an unending game with the stakeholders and competitors. The difference between these two types of games, viz., game with the stakeholders and game with the competitors lies in their goals. The aim of the game with the stakeholders including the customers is a win–win situation. This game aims at mutual benefit whereas the game with the competitors is fierce and heart-breaking. The later game may lead to a fatal outcome. Businessmen must understand this fact and learn not to tax the customers too much. Customers are the people who support business and vice versa. Too much of exploitation of the customers will take the business to its end. But take the competitors seriously and show no sympathy for them. Understand their moves and take counter moves on time. Try to take the initiative and use your creativity in finding solutions to problems related to the competitors.

Most firms know that they should do competitive analysis, but often they do not know exactly what to do, when to do it, and how to do it with the most value and least cost. Technology and globalisation are making it increasingly difficult to compete. A business must satisfy its customers, earn their satisfaction and loyalty, gradually achieve the maximum share of its target market, and finally the day will come when its brand power is impeccable. This is what the firm has been striving for!

An important point you must keep in mind is that there is no ready-made recipe to win the competitor's moves. You have to understand the situation and act accordingly. Your brain power alone can triumph. You cannot easily forecast what your competitor is going to do next. Remain prepared for any eventuality. There are plenty of marketing consultants who promise to help you tide over the situation. Some of them may do good; but most of them do not have the solution readily.

Let us now study what you should do to see that the competitors are not able to come nearer to your firm.

Do an honest self-appraisal   The first and foremost thing you must do is an honest self-appraisal. Without knowing who you are, what your strengths are, what your weaknesses are, what your position is, and where you stand, it would be difficult to make an attempt to thwart the moves of your competitors. You must know

* the efficacy of your system,
* your market positioning,
* your financial strength,
* your manpower quality,
* your brand power,
* your innovation power,
* your marketing communication skills, and
* your distribution system

Streamline your system   After recognising your strengths and weaknesses, the next task before you is to *quickly* and *perfectly* revamp the system. This will take you to your destination smoothly and show the light that you have been searching for.

One of the quickest ways to streamline your business is firstly, to look at the paper flows in your business. Eliminate unnecessary points. Secondly, empower your employees. The best employees have been with the company a long time and know the processes and decisions inside-out. Thirdly, install a system that would find permanent solutions for problems. Fourthly, have a look whether your organisation needs regrouping the departments. Next, revisit your marketing communications system. Plug the holes if you find any. Develop a communications system that would keep your customers by your side. Think over newer areas that may require improvement. But see that you do all this *quickly* and *perfectly*. If necessary, seek the assistance of outside expert.

Know your customers   To be successful in business and attain excellence, you must centre on what actually matters to your customers. Great market leaders bring to the customer something that redefines what customers can do or accomplish today. Beating the competition simply allows firms to be more efficient in what customers can already do today. It is the customer who decides your destiny. Whatever the size of your firm may be, it is the customer that matters. Whether you are in a very high side of the business or not does not matter. Do not underestimate the power of your customers. Give them due respect. See that they are satisfied and make repeat purchase.

One of the very important points about your customers is that do not make your customer become skeptical of your moves. When you say some thing, you must mean it. See that you do not lose your credibility with your customers. When you make offers or price cuts, do them with all seriousness. Do not make fake offers. Do not try to fool your customer. This will not do any good to your business. Instead, it will do enough harm to your image. Consider the long-term impact of your act.

You have to be doubly cautious when you are dealing with B2B customers. You have to follow all the prescriptions given in the previous paragraph with enough care. In their case, you have to know about the customers of your customers as well.

Know your competitors   Make a *SWOT* analysis as if you were the competitor. Assess the strengths and weaknesses. Make an assessment of the customers. Find out who their customers are and also find out what they actually get from their seller. Do they get anything extra? Are they educated? What are their expectations? Your salespersons' role is vital to study about the competitor and their customers. Train your salespersons how they must work for drawing them to your side. But see that you do not overact. This will create suspicion in the minds of the competitor's customers.

Develop your strategy   Now that you have come to the final step, you must formulate the suitable strategy to use in the market against your competitor. By now you must have come to a conclusion about the strategy you must adopt to tackle your competitor. Any strategy you would follow will finally reach the customer. So the target is the customer and not the competitor. Remember it.

Strategic Marketing Research

Strategic marketing research is a process of gathering information in order to probe into the future of the market on specific issues taking into account the environment of the organisation and its influence on the variables of research. Marketing research is primarily concerned with finding out the *feelings* or opinion of the customers. It fails to take into account the environmental aspects and its impact on the market. Therefore strategic marketing research is vital for the organisation for making right decisions. A research conducted in its right spirit will unearth so much of valuable information for the organisation from the market.

Strategic marketing research is the process of researching everything connected to marketing in an organisation. Information is the key to decision-making for all the organisations. Despite the difficulties organisations face in gathering relevant information, organisations continue to collect information and make decisions. It must be remembered that not all organisations conduct systematic and scientific research for their marketing needs because doing research is a costly affair. Even big companies make decisions out of foresight sometimes. Nevertheless research is an essential part of especially a marketing organisation. Conducting research needs special expertise and sincere work.

You have to be careful about the research findings. You should not go with it without considering the logics behind the results. Of course the evaluation of results is very difficult because they are about future. Not all marketing research findings prove to be good at all times even for big multinationals like *Toyota*. Japan's *Toyota* entered the Chinese auto industry late, but in the end, the potential of the domestic market, softening of Chinese policies towards foreign companies and low-cost manufacturing advantages made the decision inevitable. However, *Toyota* lags behind many of its rivals in the market, a legacy of its decision in the 1980s to focus on the United States rather than heeding Beijing's request for greater investment in China. *Toyota's* market intelligence system failed to predict the turn of events in China. It doesn't mean that marketing research is a futile exercise. May be that *Toyota* would not have liked to enter the Chinese market in the beginning. Only *Toyota* people know what happened inside it.

Product Life Cycle Management

Do you know why some firms never bother spending millions of dollars on new projects? Do you know that out of 3000 raw ideas only one emerges successful? Do you know that most of the success stories are from large firms? Do you know the reasons why only large firms succeed in their new product development? Do you know why these firms work so hard to keep a product in the market?

If you follow these questions closely, you will be able to find out the answers too! Big companies are financially well-off and since they know the path to success, they daringly get themselves involved in new ventures. After all, business is all about risk taking. When the going gets tough, the tough get going! Large firms employ right people in their organisations paying huge sums of money as compensation which smaller firms do not do. These highly paid people are under pressure to find new things. It is a fact that they are willingly doing it. They happily do it as they get the due recognition from the management. Same is the case when a firm uses new strategies to extend the life of its product in its every stage in the market.

Let us consider here the findings of a key market study.[4] Linton, Matysiak and Wilkes, Inc.'s market study has made the following findings on new product introductions in the retail grocery industry:

* The failure rate for new product introduction in the retail grocery industry is 70–80 per cent.
* The US Top 20 enjoys a 76 per cent success rate for new product introductions.
* The bottom 20,000 US food companies have an 11.6 per cent success rate for new product introductions.
* A major difference between top 20 new product introductions and bottom 20,000 introductions is the apparent lack of research and strategic marketing done by the bottom 20,000.

Managing the product life cycle is an art. It is an interesting as well as challenging task and there are people who crave after such tasks. These executives find the task interesting and they constantly apply their minds with the determination to win the game. Here the highest level of need suggested by Abraham Maslow works. It is true that there are people who want to prove their skills to the world or the community around them.

Organisations must explore new strategies to prolong the life of a product on which the firms have spent lot of money on their research; finding out a similar product in the future is not that easy. This is the reason for organisations striving hard to maintain their products in the market.

Exhibit 4.4 Look at the reality!

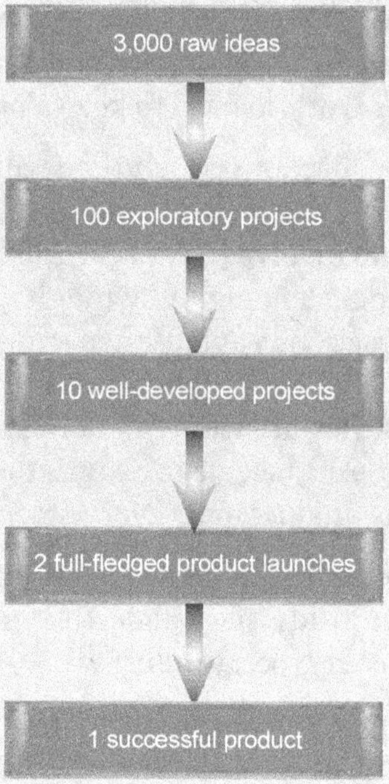

Source: Stevens, G.A. and Burley, J. "3,000 Raw Ideas = 1 Commercial Success!", (May/June 1997) Research Technology Management, Vol. 40

Salesforce Management

An effective salesforce strategy is critical to achieving sales targets and aligning the salesforce with the strategic direction of the firm. Salesforce management is all about organisation, planning, and recognising the strengths and weaknesses of the individual members of your salesforce. They are frequently combined with a marketing communications (*MARCOMs*) system, in which case they are often called customer relationship management (CRM) systems.

Effective salesforce management is very much about selection of right people for the job, imparting them relevant training, paying them satisfactorily, and effective motivation. All manufacturing and selling organisations which do well in other functions pay special attention to this aspect of management because they want to see that their efforts on the other fronts must bear fruits. And this is possible only when the salespersons are managed effectively.

SUMMARY

The chapter made a brief study of the important strategic marketing factors. These factors deserve special attention of management in order to see that the organisation excels in the marketplace. The strategic marketing factors are:

- Strategic Marketing Planning
- Marketing Communications
- Market Positioning
- Product Pricing
- Brand Management
- Winning Competitors
- Marketing Research
- Managing Product Life Cycle
- Salesforce Management

REVIEW QUESTIONS

1. "Too much of exploitation of the customers will take the business to its end." Do you agree? Give your arguments in concrete terms.
2. What are the contents of a strategic marketing plan? Explain them.
3. "Technology and globalisation are making it increasingly difficult to compete." State why it is so by explaining the impact of technology and globalisation on business.

4. Explain marketing positioning. What are the primary elements of positioning?
5. Discuss the strategies of winning the competitors.
6. Explain the need for strategic marketing research.
7. Discuss the importance of product life cycle management.

REFERENCES

1. Soundaian, S. (2011). *New Dimensions in Management.* MJP Publishers, Chennai.
2. Levitt, Theodore. *The Marketing Imagination.* The Free Press. New York/London.
3. Linton, D.B. (1997). "Market study results released: new product introduction success, failure rates analyzed." *Frozen Food Digest.* 12(5): 76.
4. Abrahams, Jeffrey. (1995). *The Mission Statement Book.* Ten Speed Press. Berkeley, California.

5

STRATEGIC MARKETING PLANNING[1]

After reading this chapter, you will be able to

- *understand the concept of strategic marketing planning, and the steps involved in formulating the plan,*

- *learn the art of formulating marketing objectives,*

- *know about the method of analysing external and internal situation,*

- *learn about marketing portfolio analysis,*

- *identify the areas for which marketing strategies must be formulated, and*

- *learn the process of marketing strategy performance, evaluation, and review.*

KEY TERMS

Strategic management	Corporate mission	Stakeholders
Strategic planning	Corporate objectives	*SMART*
Strategic marketing planning	Environmental scan	Situation analysis
Dynamic strategy model	*SWOT* analysis	Marketing portfolio
Five forces analysis	Corporate strategy	Strategic business unit
Corporate vision	Executive summary	Marketing action plan
MARCOMs	Marketing budget	

INTRODUCTION

Management is a term that attracts all people. Only a handful of people do not like to be part of management. Most people like it because in their view, it includes a sophisticated lifestyle, commanding position, attractive remuneration, dressing in style, travelling in luxurious cars, and living in posh localities. People see all these things in their every day life. These things make management people the high class. But a big majority of these people fail to understand the nature of the function of management which involves brain-breaking work day and night. Managers spend sleepless nights and their thoughts remain around the organisation ever. They have to find newer strategies to tackle problems and threats coming from all around all the times. This requires great business acumen, education, and training which ordinary people can never think of.

During those days, management's responsibility was to *get things done.* Once the target was achieved, the job would be over. The efficiency of the organisation was measured on the basis of the accomplishment of the goals. But how they get things done was considered immaterial and the means used to accomplish tasks were not questioned.

In today's large organisations, these strategies won't work. As organisations grow in size, the gap between ownership and management becomes wider and wider, and this feature of today's organisations shapes the way the organisation must be managed. You need to have the full support of the key people and these key people have to be very effective as well as confident lieutenants of the CEO so that the CEO can manage organisations of any size. The first task of management is to do planning.

WHAT IS PLANNING

Planning, in real sense, involves deciding the organisation's goals for the next period which must be in commensurate with the resources, charting out the programme of action, listing out of activities to be performed to achieve these goals, determining who is to do what and when, and empowering people. The concept of planning is to identify what the organisation wants to do by using the four questions which are "where are we today in terms of our business or strategy planning? Where are we going? Where do we want to go? How are we going to get there?..."[2]

To execute the plan, the CEO has to perform many functions like organising, staffing, and motivating, and finally, the management has to compare its performance with the results and decide the steps to be taken to rectify deviations, if any, from the fixed path.

In the course of its work, the traditional management did not consider the marketing of goods as a major task because the market of those days was full of consumers who were not aware of several factors which affected their interests. The management was also ignorant of several things until people like Ralph Nader appeared on the scene and created awareness not only among the consumers but also among the CEOs of organisations.

Planning was considered a ritual and the execution part was left to situational management. It goes without saying that the management was fully engrossed in situational management before the concept of strategic management came to the rescue of the CEOs. More than three-fourths of the management's time had to be spent for managing unforeseen and unplanned work in the organisation. This happened so because the management ignored the importance of the internal environment and paid only a formal look at external environment. The analysis of environment from strategic point was not performed. This is the prime weakness of planning as was done by the CEOs of those days. You must remember that even today there are some CEOs who very much undermine the need for strategic management. The sooner they correct their ways, the better will be their organisations.

WHAT IS STRATEGIC MANAGEMENT

Strategic management content and process emerged in the 1970's with the works of Rumelt, Mintzberg, and Ansoff. They suggested methods to evaluate and implement critical aspects of formulated strategy. In 1979, Michael Porter introduced his concept of Five Forces Analysis[3] of industry attractiveness to develop competitive advantage through generic strategies. In the 1990's, Bartlett, Hamel, Prahalad,[4] and others developed a resource-based view of strategy. In 2000, a new paradigm for strategic management was given by Hamel, Sutton, and others. This new paradigm resulted in a shift of focus of organisations to learning, knowledge, and innovation. Their Dynamic Strategy Model stressed the need of the firms to obtain valuable information, create knowledge, and accumulate intangible capabilities through the process of learning. The new integrated information technology systems are playing a vital role in today's concept of strategic management.

Strategic management tries to solve problems of management by attempting to study the environment, internal and external, which is the springboard of all threats, and opportunities that are the concerns of the CEOs worldwide, and by creating a focal point to the organisation, viz., corporate strategy through the statement of the firm's vision and mission. The major advantage of strategic management is its stress on the firm's vision and mission, and its stress on developing competitive advantages in order to excel in the industry. Strategic management is also very much concerned about the development of talents in the organisation and it urges the CEOs to find people of talents from wherever they are available.

Through its ability to forecast the future events by the study of environment, strategic management is able to reduce the burden of today's management, and management today is very much relieved from the stress they underwent before the concept of strategic management was in place. Today, the CEOs are able to predict the future turn of events with greater accuracy than ever before. Look at large companies that practice strategic management! and, see how far they were affected by the greatest recession after the Great Depression the world faced during the 1930's. Large multinational corporations were not affected much by the impact of the great recession which swept across the developed world in 2008 and the first half of 2009.

The need for situational management has come down very much, as the concept of strategic management takes care of it. By more or less accurately assessing the future environment, management is able to play the game safely.

WHAT IS STRATEGIC PLANNING

As we saw earlier, planning is an old concept; but during those days planning was certainly a big improvement in managing the organisations. Time has changed the history, and today, planning has become a course of formal management education. Strategic planning has replaced it as the new concept is many times better than the old one.

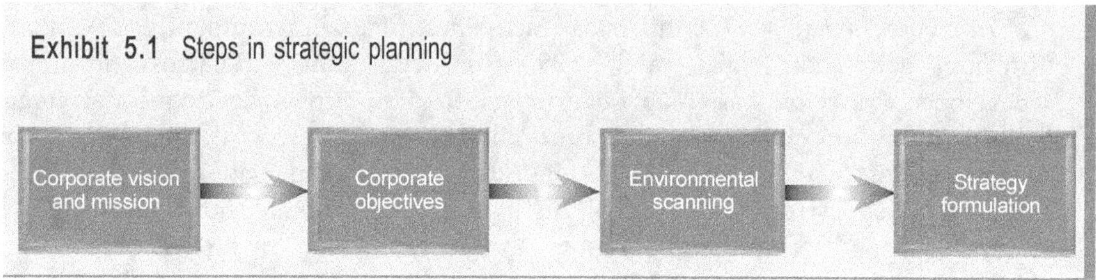

Exhibit 5.1 Steps in strategic planning

Strategic planning determines where an organisation should reach at a future period (vision), say, 10 years, outlines the broad policy of the firm to be followed in the process (mission), determines the firm's objectives, scans the internal and external environment during the period under consideration, and drafts a suitable road map (strategy) to reach the spot or achieve the corporate objectives. Exhibit 5.1 gives the process of making a strategic plan.

WHAT IS STRATEGIC MARKETING PLANNING

Strategic marketing planning is the process of determining appropriate courses of action for achieving the marketing organisation's objectives. The marketing organisation's objectives are derived from the overall objectives of the firm.

For instance, the firm's overall objective is to achieve a 300% growth in terms of the firm's cash reserves, say, in the next 5 years. The firm must make a complete analysis as to what must be done to reach this objective. This plan is known as strategic plan. The strategic plan would spell out the strategy of the firm briefly. The functional heads of the firm must analyse as to what must be done in their respective departments to achieve this target. Chief Marketing Officers may have to increase their sales levels by 40% each year. This will be the objective of the marketing department.

A strategic marketing plan consists of a broad outline of specifications of what should be done to accomplish specific marketing objectives during a specified future period which is normally ten years. It is in tune with the organisation's stated vision and mission statements and the stated corporate objectives in the overall long-term strategy of the organisation. *The strategic marketing plan is a part of the overall strategic plan of the organisation.* A well-constructed strategic marketing plan is all what we need to begin the work.

There is no specific format for a strategic marketing plan. Firms can design their own strategic marketing plans according to their requirements. Here we will see a general framework for a strategic marketing plan of a manufacturing organisation.

* Executive Summary
* Corporate Vision and Mission
* Statement of Corporate Objectives
* Statement of Marketing Objectives
* Situation Analysis—Internal and External
* Portfolio Analysis
* Formulation of Marketing Strategies
* Marketing Action Plan
* Marketing Budget
* Marketing Strategy Performance Evaluation and Review

Executive Summary

As said earlier, executive summary consists of synopsis of a situation, and key aspects of the marketing plan. It has to be given briefly not exceeding one page. The summary should briefly describe your business and the major points of your plan. It must describe briefly the status of the economy and industry. A brief forecast of the future business trend may also be given. See that whatever you give must be from authentic sources.

Exhibit 5.2 Executive summary of the firm's strategic marketing plan

i. Corporate vision	"To become market leader in providing best products and services to consumers worldwide in the consumer electronics industry."
ii. Corporate mission	"To use knowledge power, and innovation in providing quality goods at affordable costs and services to the stakeholders without disturbing the ecosystems of the globe."
iii. Corporate objectives	"Our objective is to strive for profit, growth, customer focus, and commitment to stakeholders and to become the global leader ultimately."
iv. Environmental scan and SWOT analysis	i. *Internal* Employee loyalty is high; we will continue to enjoy their support in achieving what we intend to achieve; and the finances will be excellent.
	ii. *External* Competitors are expected to operate with aggressive postures; the industry will be buoyant; the global inflation rate will rise abnormally; and consumers will find it difficult to make their purchases.
v. Corporate strategy (functionwise)	i. *Operations strategy* The firm will aim at shorter production cycle, standardised variety, and low-cost for right-quality.
	ii. *Marketing strategy* The firm will continue to pursue same strategies in relation to market segments, new products, market positioning, and pricing. Aggressive responses will be on the cards to the competitors' provocations.
	iii. *Human resources strategy* The firm will continue to have cordial relations with employees and try to provide them maximum benefits for their services.
	iv. *Financial strategies* The firm proposes to alter its capital structure in a way that will provide full benefits to its shareholders.
	v. *Legal strategies* The firm will make sincere attempts to solve all the pending disputes out of the court of law.
	vi. *Information technology management strategies* The firm is determined to go for outsourcing if it gives substantial saving in the firm's expenditure.

Exhibit 5.2 is a sample executive summary of a large firm. The executive summary gives important aspects of the strategic marketing plan in a compressed form.

Corporate Vision and Mission Statements

These statements form basic to the firm's strategic plan and in turn the strategic marketing plan. Jeffrey Abrahams[5], *TRINOVA* Corporation defines a *mission statement* in the following way: "A mission statement is an enduring statement of purpose for an organisation that identifies the scope of its operations in product and market terms, and reflects its values and priorities." *Corporate vision* is a short, succinct, and inspiring statement of what the organisation intends to become and to achieve at some point in the future, often stated in competitive terms. Vision refers to the category of intentions that are broad, all-inclusive and broad thinking. It is the image that a business must have of its goals before it sets out to reach them. It describes aspirations for the future, without specifying the means that will be used to achieve those broad desired ends.

The mission statement should be a concise statement of business strategy and is developed from the customer's perspective and it should fit with the vision for the business. The mission should answer three questions:

1. What do we do?
2. How do we do it?
3. For whom do we do it?

What do we do?   This question has to be considered not in terms of what is physically delivered to customers, but by the real and/or psychological needs of the customers. Customers buy goods to satisfy a variety of needs. Some of the needs are fulfilled and some go unfulfilled or even unnoticed by customers themselves. It is our duty to make them not to forget their needs. We have to formulate strategies in this direction. Good advertisements with factual information can make the customers become aware of their forgotten needs. Therefore your task is a multi-faceted and multi-purpose packed one. Therefore, we have to be conscious of what we do for the customers. We have to make an in-depth study of whether we can offer better services to the customers at reduced costs. The benefit of reduced cost should not be enjoyed by us alone; the customers must also be given a slice of the benefit.

How do we do it?   The physical product has to be taken here. The technical aspects of the service must be in commensurate with the real needs of the customers. Needs may be real or created. New products which are offered to the customers create new needs. If the product is an existing one, we must do justice to the customers by making the product worth the price. The customer should, in no way feel cheated. Many businesses of today are not serious on this point. For survival in the long run, the business should act selflessly. We should fix the price reasonably except when we have to recover the investment in research to find out the product. The product must contain features that facilitate for easy and harmless use of it. The customers are ignorant and this ignorance should not be misused by the organisation.

For whom do we do it?   The answer to this question is important; as it will help you focus your marketing efforts. Though many small business owners would like to believe otherwise, not everyone is a potential customer, as customers will almost always have both demographic and geographic limitations. When starting out, it is generally a good idea to define the demographic characteristics (age, income, and the like) of customers who are likely to buy and then define a geographic area in which your business can gain a presence. As you grow, you can add new customer groups and expand your geographic focus.

An additional consideration with mission statements is that most businesses will have multiple customer groups that purchase for different reasons. In these cases, one mission statement can be written to answer each of the three questions for each customer group or multiple mission statements can be developed. Also, as a final thought, remember that your vision and mission statements are meant to help guide the business, and not to lock you into a particular direction. As your company grows and as the competitive environment changes, your mission may require change to include additional or different needs that are to be fulfilled, delivery systems, or customer groups. With this in mind, your vision and mission should be revisited periodically to determine where modifications are desirable.

Today's large firms make statements about their intentions in the form of different titles which they consider the focal point of their activities. Most companies do not declare their visions and missions these days. They declare their position on sustainability and corporate citizenship in their websites.

Exhibit 5.3   Vision and mission statements

AT & T's mission statement   "Delivering a valuable customer experience is crucial to the success of any business. At AT&T, it is at the centre of everything we do, everyday.

Our goal is to treat all of our customers as if they are our only customer. We do this by providing thoughtful, caring and prompt attention. Our focus is on:

- Connecting people with their world, everywhere they live and work.
- Driving innovation in wireless, entertainment and other communications services.

❈ Consistently demonstrating a passionate commitment to customer care.

❈ Listening to our customers and responding to their needs."

General electric's policy statement "Responsible leadership and operational excellence are hallmarks of GE. Our citizenship framework—make money, make it ethically and make a difference—enables us to make contributions and create value for society in ways that are aligned to the business strategy of the company.

Our approach involves setting accountabilities just as we do in other parts of our business. We highlight our citizenship performance with data points, metrics, actions and progress made on issues material to GE's business and in relation to global trends in these key categories:

❈ Compliance and governance

❈ Environment, health and safety

❈ Public policy

❈ Suppliers

❈ Customers

❈ Employers

❈ Products and services

❈ Human rights

❈ Communities and philanthropy

WalMart stores' business approach "At WalMart, we see sustainability as one of the most important opportunities for both the future of our business and the future of our world.

Our opportunity is to become a better company by looking at every facet of our business—from the products we offer to the energy we use—through the lens of sustainability."

Bharti Airtel's vision statement "By 2010 Airtel will be the most admired brand in India i) loved by more customers, ii) targeted by top talent, and iii) benchmarked by more businesses."

Oil and Natural Gas Corporation's vision and mission statement "To be a world-class Oil and Gas Company integrated in energy business with dominant Indian leadership and global presence.

❈ Dedicated to excellence by leveraging competitive advantages in R&D and technology with involved people.

- Imbibe high standards of business ethics and organisational values.
- Abiding commitment to safety, health and environment to enrich quality of community life.
- Foster a culture of trust, openness and mutual concern to make working a stimulating and challenging experience for our people.
- Strive for customer delight through quality products and services.
- Integrated in energy business
- Focus on domestic and international oil and gas exploration and production of business opportunities.
- Provide value linkages in other sectors of energy business.
- Create growth opportunities and maximise shareholder value.
- Dominant Indian leadership
- Retain dominant position in Indian petroleum sector and enhance India's energy availability.

Statement of Corporate Objectives

Corporate objectives are the milestones that organisations must achieve to reach goals of short-term or long-term. Objectives should be measurable, quantitative, challenging, realistic, consistent, and prioritised. It is these objectives from which the objectives of the different departments including the marketing department of the firm are derived.

The following is a sample statement of corporate objectives of a global electronics goods manufacturer:

Growth   We recognise the need for sustainable growth and exploit every opportunity available in the environment for growth that builds upon our strengths and competencies.

Customer focus   We recognise the value of our customers in our endeavour and our every decision shall be customer-focused, and customer-oriented.

Commitment to stakeholders   We will make sincere attempts to satisfy the expectations of our stakeholders including the society who are the backbone of our organisation. We are keen that our focus on social responsibility is no less than that of leading organisations in the world and we will strive to find new avenues of becoming a true global citizen.

The SPIRIT of Performance

Exhibit 5.4 The *SPIRIT* values of ConocoPhillips

ConocoPhillips is committed to setting the standard of excellence in everything we do. Our "Purpose and Values" are essential building blocks in the continued success of the company. Together, these ideas represent "**The SPIRIT of Performance**" and are an integral part of our search for greatness.

Purpose   Use our pioneering spirit to responsibly deliver energy to the world.

Values

Safety

We operate safely.

People

We respect one another, recognising that our success depends upon the commitment, capabilities and diversity of our employees.

Integrity

We are ethical and trustworthy in our relationships with all stakeholders.

Responsibility

We are accountable for our actions. We are a good neighbour and citizen in the communities where we operate.

Innovation

We anticipate change and respond with creative solutions. We are agile and responsive to the changing needs of stakeholders and embrace learning opportunities from our experiences around the world.

Teamwork

Our "can do" spirit delivers top performance. We encourage collaboration, celebrate success and build and nurture long-standing, mutually beneficial relationships.

Profit   Profit is the driving force for any organisation. Therefore we will strive rigorously to increase profits by reducing costs rather than raising prices.

Global leader   We will strive to become corporate leader within the shortest possible time."

HP's corporate objectives have guided the company in the conduct of its business since 1957, when first written by co-founders Bill Hewlett and Dave Packard.

Statement of Marketing Objectives

Marketing objectives are the targets which must be achieved by the marketing personnel and these objectives are developed jointly by the senior marketing executives and the top management. They are derived from the corporate objectives which have been formulated by the top management. Corporate objectives are formulated by a committee consisting of the functional heads because coordination is very important in formulating them as all the functional heads must give their consent for the corporate objectives. The functional heads consider their capabilities in relation to the organisation's resource mobilisation capability.

Marketing objectives should:

* be clear
* be measurable, and
* have a timeframe for accomplishment.

A simple acronym used to set objectives is called *SMART*. SMART stands for:

1. *Specific*   Objectives should specify what they want to achieve.
2. *Measurable*   You should be able to measure whether you are meeting the objectives or not.
3. *Achievable*   Are the objectives you set, achievable and attainable?
4. *Realistic*   Can you realistically achieve the objectives with the resources you have?
5. *Time*   When do you want to achieve the set objectives?

The following is an example of the marketing objectives for an organisation:

* *Profitability objectives*   To achieve a 50% return on capital employed by the FY 2014–15.
* *Market share objectives*   To gain 15% market share in the cosmetics industry of the country by the year 2014.
* *Survival objectives*   To survive the present wave of depression with minimum depletion of profit.

* *Promotional objectives* To increase awareness of the need for using quality electrical materials for buildings among the general public.

* *Growth objectives* To grow in sales size from the present $2.75 billion to $5.5 billion within the next 4 years.

* *Brand objectives* To promote brand loyalty among the buyers by creating awareness among them about the quality and durability of our products.

* *New product objectives* To become a leader in introducing useful new products in the next three years in our market.

* *Market withdrawal objectives* To withdraw unsuccessful products from the market on time.

Exhibit 5.5 HP's corporate objectives

Our Corporate Objectives

Customer loyalty

We earn customer respect and loyalty by consistently providing the highest quality and value.

Profit

We achieve sufficient profit to finance growth, create value for our shareholders and achieve our corporate objectives.

Growth

We recognise and seize opportunities for growth that builds upon our strengths and competencies.

Market leadership

We lead in the marketplace by developing and delivering useful and innovative products, services and solutions.

Commitment to employees

We demonstrate our commitment to employees by promoting and rewarding based on the performance and by creating a work environment that reflects our values.

Leadership capability

We develop leaders at all levels who achieve business results, exemplify our values and lead us to grow and win.

Global citizenship

We fulfil our responsibility to society by being an economic, intellectual and social asset to each country and community where we do business.

Situation Analysis—Internal and External

Situation analysis is elaborately discussed in Chapter 6 and therefore, let us make a brief discussion on it here. Situation analysis is an honest assessment of the internal and external environment of the marketing organisation. The situation analysis looks at the current business environment and can be elaborate or very simple. The components examined are competition, the size of the market, the target group of customers, channels of distribution, the present and proposed government policies, the aspects of physical environment which have a bearing on the firm's marketing programmes, and economic conditions. By taking an overview of the whole picture and stating your strengths and weaknesses, you will have a clearer understanding of how well your company will compete. A situation analysis describes an organisation's competitive position, operating and financial condition and general state of internal and external affairs. Situation analysis includes the SWOT analysis also. Of course the main objective of situation analysis is to find out strengths, weaknesses, opportunities, and threats expected to be present in the future environment of business.

SWOT is the abbreviation used in management to mean strengths, weaknesses, opportunities and threats. This mode is the basic commandment for any organisation. If this model is applied in perfect condition, the firm will be able to confront any challenge that might appear on the scene. A SWOT analysis is often conducted as a major part of a situation analysis.

Internal situation   Internal situation consists of the internal factors that have a bearing on the marketing capability of the organisation. These factors include the following:

1. ***The quality of marketing manpower***   This is one of the key success factors for the organisation. The entire marketing team is responsible for the performance of its department. The quality of manpower must be assessed and their ability to live up to the expectations of the marketing organisation need to be ascertained. Even though the process of performance appraisal is continuous in the organisation, the training imparted to the salesforce and the personal factors might have prompted them to improve their skills. The organisation must have on its roll effective and dedicated people only. This factor may even be a competitive advantage for the marketing organisation of the firm. The salesforce needs to be continuously motivated by management in order to make good of the hidden talents of people.

2. ***Employee morale***   The level of the employee morale is another key success factor. High employee morale is an important requirement for a good organisation. The ability of the organisation to motivate the employees decides where the organisation stands in relation to the morale levels of the organisation.

3. *Management–employee relations*   The situation in the organisation with regard to the relationship between the employees and management must be studied. There may be grievances which may remain hidden in the employees. The outward behaviour of employees cannot be a decisive factor.

4. *Management commitment*   Sometimes the management may not be willing to stress on organisational development. They exploit the employees too much and still they may not be satisfied. Such managements must change their *attitude* and they too must work towards the growth of the organisation. This situation may be found common in smaller organisations.

5. *Resourcefulness of the organisation*   This problem is common in most of the progressive business organisations. Organisations find it difficult to allocate funds internally and procure especially at times of tight monetary policies pursued by the funding agencies. This situation must be managed effectively by prioritising the expenditures so that the firm can proceed with its programmes with confidence.

External situation   The external situation mostly consists of forces beyond the control of the organisation. The major concerns of the marketer are to find out the changes that take place in the external environment as and when they occur, and to find out whether these changes can be turned to the benefit of the organisation by converting them as opportunities. The marketer needs skills to look at the situation strategically and make them contribute to the organisation's cash reserves. The following are the major external factors which have strong bearing on the firm's performance:

1. *The macroeconomic conditions*   Macroeconomics studies aggregated indicators such as GDP, unemployment rates, and price indices to understand how the whole economy functions. Macroeconomists develop models that explain the relationship between such factors as national income, output, consumption, unemployment, inflation, savings, investment, international trade and international finance. These factors very much influence the market conditions not only domestically but also internationally. The global economy may also show its impact on the firm's market, as international economy plays truant. These aspects are a matter of grave concern for multinational corporations and the investors who have put in billions of dollars in foreign markets by way of investments. The firm, in such cases, has no other way than adjusting its strategy to the new economic environment.

2. *The microeconomic conditions*   Microeconomics is primarily focused on the actions of individual agents, such as firms and consumers, and how their behaviour determines prices and quantities in specific markets. It examines how these decisions and behaviours affect the supply and demand for goods and services, which determines the prices; and how prices, in turn, determine the supply and demand of goods and services. The marketing CEO must in this case also take steps to alter the marketing

strategies of the firm if necessary. You must note that not all the firms are affected by the turbulent changes in microeconomic conditions. There are also firms which remain unaffected. If your firm belongs to this category, you must analyse how well you can utilise the opportunity arisen out of the new situation.

3. *Changes in government policies*   It is hard to say that the same policy will be in place in future. Even stable governments make drastic policy changes. In such a situation, you must analyse how well you can capitalise the new situation. It is a notable point that in November 2009, the American Medical Association has urged the federal government to reconsider its classification of marijuana as a dangerous drug with no accepted medical use, a significant shift that puts the prestigious group behind calls for more research. If the federal government does not accept the demand of the medical association, it will have a sea change in the world trading policies and practices in the pharma world. It will open up the doors to many firms and at the same time it will be a big blow to several firms.

4. *Technological changes*   Technology poses a threat to many firms. Fast changing technologies are matters of grave concern for industries across the globe. Perhaps the most volatile aspect of American society these days is the rate of technological growth, and the U.S. government has responded to new technological issues as well. In many cases, whole new sectors of government have been created to deal with technological change, such as the Federal Communications Commission (founded in 1934), the Federal Aviation Administration (FAA) and NASA (both in 1958), and the Federal Department of Transportation (1966). One recent government response to technological change (and a direct result of American society's passion for wireless technology) is the FCC's ruling that television stations must transmit all-digital signals by June 12, 2009.

5. *Global climatic changes*   It is a fact that the unwanted aspects of the global climatic change have put the world population in grave danger. The Union of Concerned Scientists has warned that global warming is one of the most serious challenges we face today. To protect the health and economic wellbeing of present and future generations, we must reduce the emission of heat-trapping gases by using the technology know-how, and practical solutions already at our disposal. There is a danger of islands going under the sea in the next 100 years or so, if steps are not taken to reduce global warming. These steps, if taken steadily by world governments, will bring in untold hardships to industries across the globe. This is the reason why many governments are not initiating concrete steps in this direction. They are afraid that there will be another Great Depression and ultimately, it will lead to loss of millions of jobs and, in turn, to closure of several industries in the developed world as well as the emerging economies like China and India.

6. *Drastic changes in climatic conditions*   Droughts, floods, etc., have their impact on business. These changes lead to reduced agricultural output and the agro-based industries suffer for want of raw materials. It is difficult to forecast precisely the future changes in the climatic conditions especially in countries like India which depend on monsoons for their irrigation requirements.

7. *Vagaries of nature*   Earthquakes, tsunamis, and the like have their impact on business. These are conditions which are difficult to predict early, but there has been a global effort working towards developing a technology to predict and forewarn the business sector.

Predictable external situation   There is another category of external factors, viz., the factors which can be predicted with reasonable accuracy. They are consumer preferences, tastes, and behaviour. These factors are forecasted by experts in the field. Experts may be employed by the firm or hired as marketing consultants. The findings of consumer research are valuable to the decision makers and medium-sized and big firms to carry out systematic marketing research.

Marketing Portfolio Analysis

A company manufactures an array of products to satisfy different categories of consumers. It has to find out the right quantum of each product to be manufactured so that the company will be in a position to supply the products to the satisfaction of its consumers. This has to be analysed and the right mix of products must be ascertained by the marketer. Marketing portfolio analysis tries to fix the right mix of the products the company should manufacture. Many models are available for the purpose. The most important one among them is the Boston Consulting Group Product Portfolio Analysis Model.

The *product portfolio* is the collection of products that make up the company's product mix. The best product portfolio is one that fits the company's strengths and helps exploit the most attractive opportunities. The company must:

1.   analyse its current business portfolio and decide which businesses should receive more or less investment, and

2.   develop growth strategies for adding new products and businesses to the portfolio, whilst at the same time deciding when products and businesses should no longer be retained.

Methods of portfolio planning   The two best-known portfolio planning methods are from the Boston Consulting Group and by General Electric/Shell. In both the methods, the first step is to identify the various strategic business units ("SBUs") in a company portfolio. An SBU is a unit of the company that has a separate mission and objectives and that can be planned independently from the other businesses. An SBU can be a company division, a product line or even individual brands—it all depends on how the company is organised.

Exhibit 5.6   The Boston consulting group box ("BCG Box")

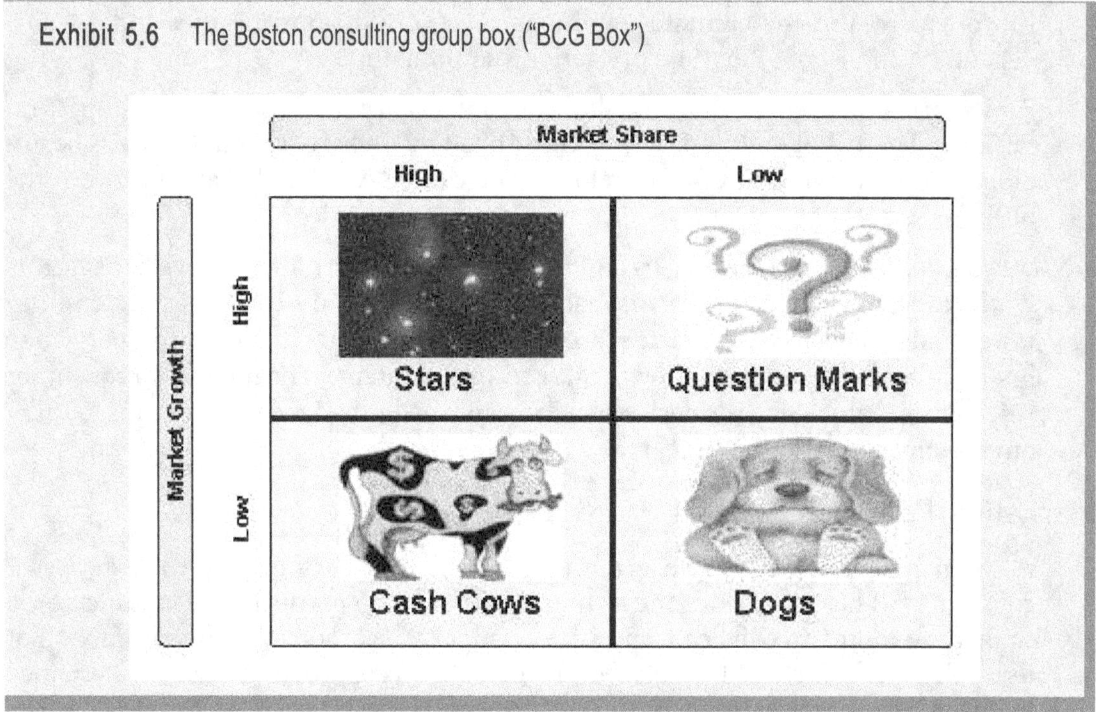

Using the BCG Box a company classifies all its SBUs according to two dimensions:

On the horizontal axis: relative market share—this serves as a measure of SBU strength in the market

On the vertical axis: market growth rate—this provides a measure of market attractiveness

By dividing the matrix into four areas, four types of SBU can be distinguished:

Stars   Stars are high growth businesses or products competing in markets where they are relatively strong compared with the competition. Often they need heavy investment to sustain their growth. Eventually their growth will slow and, assuming they maintain their relative market share, will become cash cows.

Cash cows   Cash cows are low-growth businesses or products with a relatively high market share. These are mature, successful businesses with relatively little need for investment. They need to be managed for continued profit—so that they continue to generate the strong cash flows that the company needs for its Stars.

Question marks   Question marks are businesses or products with low market share but which operate in higher growth markets. This suggests that they have potential, but may require substantial investment in order to grow market share at the expense of more powerful competitors. Management has to think hard about "question marks"—which ones should they invest in? Which ones should they allow to fail or shrink?

Dogs   Unsurprisingly, the term 'dogs' refers to businesses or products that have low relative share in unattractive, low-growth markets. Dogs may generate enough cash to break-even, but they are rarely, if ever, worth investing in.

Using the BCG box to determine strategy   Once a company has classified its SBUs, it must decide what to do with them. In the diagram above, the company has one large cash cow (the size of the circle is proportional to the SBU's sales), a large dog and two, smaller stars and question marks.

Conventional strategic thinking suggests there are four possible strategies for each SBU:

1. *Build share*   Here the company can invest to increase market share (for example turning a "question mark" into a star).

2. *Hold*   Here the company invests just enough to keep the SBU in its present position.

3. *Harvest*   Here the company reduces the amount of investment in order to maximise the short-term cash flows and profits from the SBU. This may have the effect of turning Stars into Cash Cows.

4. *Divest*   The company can divest the SBU by phasing it out or selling it—in order to use the resources elsewhere (e.g., investing in the more promising "question marks").

The Boston box model depends on the following premises:

1. The profits and cash generated from a product are a function of its market share. Profits and market share correlate directly.
2. Revenue growth requires investments. In the context of the Boston Box, investments are mainly expenses for marketing, distribution and product development. The extent of these expenses depends on the general market growth for that product.
3. High market shares require additional investments.
4. No business or market can grow infinitely.

Formulation of Marketing Strategies

A *strategy* is the direction of the company's programmes in the long-run in order to achieve its objectives. The *marketing strategy* is the means by which a marketing objective is achieved. The marketing strategies are related to the components of marketing mix, viz., product, price, place (distribution) and promotion. In addition, the firm must plan for improving its marketing capabilities. It must plan strategies for imparting training to the salesforce.

The firm may have a single marketing strategy or multiple strategies depending on its needs. Some products may be in a dominant position relative to competitors, while others may be in a weaker position. Each product will have its own strategy, and may face several competitive products having their own marketing strategies. Some products may be profitable while others may need cash to finance growth or to fight competition. Faced with this complex situation, the organisation must allocate its limited resources among these products in order to optimise its overall performance.

Marketing strategy includes the decision about the launch of a product in a specific market, the pricing strategy, location, features of the product for a specific target group and ways of promotion. Let us dwell at some length into the important marketing strategies which include the components of marketing mix.

The marketing strategist must formulate marketing strategies for the following areas:

1. new products planning,
2. managing product life cycles of the existing products,
3. customer relationship management,
4. retention of current customers,
5. adding new customers,
6. pricing for individual products,
7. components of promotional mix, and
8. managing channel members.

Marketing Action Plan

The statement of marketing action plan contains details of smaller plans or tactics to be followed by the marketing department in order to achieve the targets or marketing objectives. A marketing action plan sets out how you are going to put your marketing strategy into practice. Besides marketing communications, your marketing plan should span the full mix of marketing activities. Developing new products and building your distribution network might be important parts of your strategy. You might also want to strengthen your marketing capabilities.

Constructing the marketing action plan   Preparing the marketing action plan (MAP) requires careful consideration of all the relevant factors. Each marketing strategy requires separate marketing plans. However, there are important guidelines for the construction of the MAPs. These guidelines are to be framed taking into account the firm's marketing policies. Any contravention will lead to misunderstanding between key people; therefore, the guidelines must be set out in simple language.

Exhibit 5.7   The war strategy of a winning emperor

Sun Tzu and the Essential Components of Victory

Sun Tzu is one of the most renowned Chinese strategists in history. Although his strategy was about warfare, the principles are still used today in Asia. Sun Tzu said these are the considerations to obtain victory:

1. Know when to fight and when not to fight.

There is a time for everything. Act with forethought and dispassion instead of succumbing to emotion. Superiority of numbers or position is not always necessary for victory. The one who understands the rhythm of the battle and is able to freely utilise other natural advantages can realise victory with a smaller force or inferior position.

2. Obtain the whole-hearted support of your troops.

The one who understands how to obtain the unconditional support of his troops by creating a common objective will have a great advantage over his opponent.

3. Be well-prepared to seize favourable opportunities.

One must sharpen his intuition in order to recognise favourable opportunities and be prepared to seize them.

4. Free yourself from interference.

If a superior is constantly giving orders to his general (manager), the general cannot fight an effective battle. Freedom from such interference is essential. If a general has been chosen well, he will insist on being given the freedom to win the battle.

5. When the time is right, act swiftly and decisively.

Do not act precipitously, but do not hesitate when the conditions for victory are present.

6. The highest form of victory is to conquer by strategy.

To win a battle by actually fighting is not the most desirable way. To conquer the enemy without resorting to war, conquering the enemy by strategy is the highest, most desirable form of generalship. The next best form of generalship is to conquer the enemy by alliance. The next is to conquer the enemy by battle on open ground. The worst form of generalship is to conquer the enemy by besieging walled cities ... those most skilled in warfare are those who conquer the enemy without fighting battles, who capture cities without laying siege to them, and who annex states without prolonged warfare. They can preserve their forces whole and intact while struggling for the mastery of their opponent. They can win a complete victory without as much as wearying their men. All this is due to the use of strategy.

7. The Opportunity for victory is provided by the enemy

Sun Tzu says that an army can only make itself secure against defeat; the opportunity for victory must be provided by the enemy. The wise commander cannot achieve victory unless his enemy presents him with an opportunity.

Source: The Art of War by Sun Tzu

The action plan may be salespersonwise or productawise. It depends on the nature of the product or market. The marketing action plan must contain the following aspects:

1. details of specific assignment for the salesperson,
2. specific product objectives for individual products or product lines,
3. clear but brief reasoning for non-routine activities,
4. the agenda of the member of the salesforce to achieve the assigned target,
5. time frame for carrying out activities put out in the agenda, and
6. the mode of end-of-the-day reporting by the member of the salesforce.

Marketing Budget

A marketing budget contains the projected costs and timeline related to the execution of the firm's marketing tactics. Expenses involved in marketing are actually investments and the return from these investments is received during future periods. The firm cannot accurately find out the point of time when the marketing expenses stop their return to the firm.

The firm incurs expenses on the following counts:

1. Marketing office expenses
2. Salaries for marketing staff including managers and assistants
3. Fixtures and fittings
4. Travel costs

5. Advertising agency commissions

6. Sales promotion expenses like free gifts, vouchers, discounted prices, joint promotions, free samples, and competitions and prize draws

7. Marketing communications *(MARCOMs)* costs:

    i. Personal selling expenses

    ii. Public relations expenses like printing, mailing, website development and hosting, and brochure design

    iii. Advertising expenses like TV, radio advertising and magazine advertising

    iv. Direct marketing expenses like sms, e-mail, telemarketing, couponing, and special campaigns

The funds allocated to marketing expenses may be fixed through using one of these methods:

1. *Percentage-of-sales*   Allocating a specified percentage of sales revenue is one of the most popular methods for developing a marketing budget. The actual amount of allocation depends on the marketing needs of individual organisations.

2. *The dollar method*   Many businesses simply set a flat dollar amount for their marketing budget. This method is particularly useful for small businesses. They can base marketing budgets on what they think the company can afford instead of the company's sales.

3. *Matching competitors*   Analysing and estimating what the competitor is spending and copying them is another method for fixing amount for marketing expenses. This is another simple way to set a budget, since maintaining costs comparable with competitors keeps the business in line with others in the field.

Marketing Strategy Performance Evaluation and Review

The final part of the strategic marketing is the review of the projects and strategies while they are in operation. This review is important because any deviation from the scheduled path can be detected on time and remedial steps can be taken immediately. The strategic marketing plan suggests the methodology to be followed in carrying out the project performance review.

The objectives of the strategy performance evaluation are to:

* establish whether the strategy has met its objectives;

* establish whether the execution of strategy has been value for money;

❋ determine whether participants have found the strategy worthwhile; and

❋ identify ways the strategy could have been improved.

Steps in strategy performance evaluation and review The following procedure may be followed to evaluate the performance of strategies and make appropriate adjustments so that the future strategy will be sans previous defects.

1. Revisit strategy's objectives,
2. Collect performance data,
3. Discuss with key participants,
4. Compare performance with objectives, and
5. Identify areas of improvement, and
6. Prepare the improved version of the strategy for future application

SUMMARY

❋ Strategic marketing planning is *the process of determining appropriate courses of action for achieving the marketing organisation's objectives.* The marketing organisation's objectives are derived from the overall objectives of the firm.

❋ There is no specific format for a strategic marketing plan. Firms can design their own strategic marketing plans according to their requirements.

❋ The following are the important components of the strategic marketing plan:

 ❋ Executive Summary
 ❋ Corporate Vision and Mission
 ❋ Statement of Corporate Objectives
 ❋ Statement of Marketing Objectives
 ❋ Situation Analysis—Internal and External
 ❋ *SWOT* Analysis
 ❋ Portfolio Analysis
 ❋ Formulation of Marketing Strategies
 ❋ Marketing Action Plan
 ❋ Marketing Budget
 ❋ Marketing Strategy Performance Evaluation and Review

REVIEW QUESTIONS

1. Explain strategic marketing planning.

2. Discuss the need for and importance of corporate vision and mission statements.

3. "Most companies do not declare their visions and missions these days." What do you think to be as the reasons for not declaring their vision and mission statements? What are the disadvantages of such an act?

4. What are marketing objectives? Give examples of them.

5. Draft a simple strategic marketing plan for a company of your choice.

6. Explain the four types of strategic business units according to the Boston Box Model.

7. Explain the process of formulation of a marketing action plan.

REFERENCES

1. Soundaian, S. (2011). *New Dimensions of Management*. MJP Publishers, Chennai.

2. Dalziel, Murray, and Stephen, C. Schoonover. (1988). "Changing ways: A practical tool for implementing change within organisations." Amacom/American Management Association, New York.

3. Porter, M.E. (1979). *How Competitive Forces Shape Strategy, Harvard Business Review*.

4. Hamel, Gary and Prahlad, C.K. (1996). Competing for the Future, Harvard Business School Publishing.

5. Abrahams, Jeffrey. (1995). *The Mission Statement Book*. Ten Speed Press. Berkeley, California.

6

SITUATION ANALYSIS

After reading this chapter, you will be able to

- ❂ *learn about SWOT analysis and its importance in strategic marketing management,*

- ❂ *know the process of internal situation analysis, and*

- ❂ *know about the relationship between external situation analysis and strategic marketing management.*

KEY TERMS

- ❂ Internal situation analysis
- ❂ Hawthorne effect
- ❂ Consumer policy statement
- ❂ Marketing information system
- ❂ Prospects
- ❂ Physical environment
- ❂ Socio-cultural environment
- ❂ Legal environment
- ❂ Economic environment
- ❂ Technological environment
- ❂ Political environment
- ❂ Total situation analysis
- ❂ Customer relationship management

INTRODUCTION

Situation analysis is an essential aspect of any organisation. Let us take the example of our own family. The head of the family must know the *in*-and-*outs* of his family members. In a traditional family, the head shoulders the responsibility of running the house. He has to find the resources and give them to his family's executive, namely, wife. The executive manages the resources and allocates them with care to different heads of accounts. The head of the family must also be knowledgeable about the characteristics of each family member, his/her strengths and weak points, the potentials of each member so that he can arrange for suitable placement in the family assignments. The family assignments may be business or work in the family farm. If there is no family business or farm, the head has to arrange for higher studies for his children in order to make them lead an independent life. In any case, a good family head must recognise the talents of his sons, daughters, father, mother, and others and try to make use of them in order to augment the family's finance. This is known as *internal situation analysis* or *micro-environmental analysis* when applied to a business organisation. The *family* head in a business is none other than the CEO.

When the family head looks for opportunities for himself and for his children outside his control area, it is called as external situation analysis. The outside world consists of good things as well as unwanted things. The family head analyses all the conditions using his talents to find the favourable aspects in the external environment so as to place his dependents in good position. When he searches for good educational institutions or when he searches for quality products for the consumption of his family, he is considered probing his external environment. This is called as *external situation analysis*. External situational analyses are performed by the business organisations to find out new opportunities or threats which may hamper their growth. It is also called as *macro-environmental analysis* by business organisations.

SITUATION ANALYSIS AND STRATEGIC MARKETING MANAGEMENT

It is an obvious fact that the concepts of strategic management can be applied to marketing management. The important concepts of strategic management are:

* identification of the firm's objectives in the long run,
* formulation of suitable strategies to accomplish these objectives,
* identification of core competencies in the firm,
* identification of sustainable competitive advantages,
* making an assessment of the firm's strengths and weaknesses,
* creation of core competencies and competitive advantages if they are not available within,

❋ implementation of strategies, and

❋ making an evaluation and review of the process of strategy execution.

In fact, situation analysis is nothing but *SWOT analysis*. Internal situation analysis is the process of making an assessment of the firm's *strengths* and *weaknesses*. It is the study of the internal environment as to what capabilities are present in the organisation, and what deficiencies are found in it. The internal situation analysis is the process of making an honest self-appraisal, the purpose of which is to identify i) the plus points which can be utilised fully for the welfare of the firm, and ii) the minus points of the organisation. The firm will be able to eliminate the minus points in the organisation by taking constructive steps to convert them into plus points.

The external situation analysis is concerned with the identification of *opportunities* and *threats* present in the external environment. The firm has to study the environment and find out the opportunities and try to make the best use of them. At the same time, the firm must explore the possibilities of converting the possible threats into opportunities or at least the firm must take steps to see that these threats do not come in the way of the firm's growth.

When the concepts of strategic management are applied to the marketing function of the firm, it is called strategic marketing management. As in strategic management, an internal and external situation analyses must be performed to identify the strengths, and weaknesses of the marketing organisation and also the opportunities and threats present in the external environment of the firm.

PROCESS OF INTERNAL SITUATION ANALYSIS

The internal situation analysis may also be called as micro-environmental analysis. The process of internal situation analysis in the marketing department is concerned with identification of the strengths and weaknesses of the marketing department's functioning in relation to its members, customers, prospects, channel members, and media people. In addition the management's relationship with the marketing department must also be studied because it is necessary to ascertain the extent of support extended by the management to the marketing department which is important in deciding the direction of the department's activities. The internal situation analysis of the marketing department may be performed under the following headings:

1. Employee-oriented situation analysis
2. Customer-oriented situation analysis
3. Prospects-oriented situation analysis
4. Distribution-oriented situation analysis
5. Media-oriented situation analysis
6. Management-oriented situation analysis.

It is necessary to prepare a report on internal situation analysis which will be later used for preparing a consolidated report of total situation analysis. The consolidated report of situation analysis can be used for formulating marketing strategies of the firm.

Let us probe into the activities of the marketing department which will be the focus of the remainder of this chapter.

Employee-oriented Situation Analysis

Human resource is a very important part of any organisation. Employees are the partners in the progress of the organisation. They make it or sink it. *Employee Engagement Report* by Blessing White (April 2008) has revealed that only 29% of employees are actively engaged in their jobs. These employees work with passion and feel a profound connection to their company. People who are actively engaged, help move the organisation forward. 84% of highly engaged employees believe they can positively impact the quality of their organisation's products, compared with only 31% of the disengaged. 72% of highly engaged employees believe they can positively affect customer service, versus 27% of the disengaged. Seijts, Gerard H. and Dan Crim (2006) have found in their "*The Ten C's of Employee Engagement*", (*Ivey Business Journal*), that engaged employees care about the future of the company and are willing to invest in the discretionary effort. 68% of highly engaged employees believe they can positively impact costs in their job or unit, compared with just 19% of the disengaged.

The following factors are very important for making the employee-oriented situation analysis:

1. employee skills in relation to their education and training levels,
2. their job performance,
3. their relationship with peers, subordinates, and superiors,
4. their attitude towards organisational policies, and
5. their state of motivation.

Employee skills and job performance The capabilities of the members of the marketing organisation are the significant factors in determining their performance levels. These capabilities are the result of the combined impact of their education levels, and the quality of training imparted to them. However, there are people who refuse to learn even when sufficient motives are there to learn.

Whatever their level of education and training be, what matters for the organisation is whether the employees have done it or not. The actual performance is the yardstick used to measure the on-the-job performance of the members of the marketing organisation. For example, marketing officers may be indifferent towards their job; but their subordinates may take things seriously and they would have produced marvellous results in their territories. Who is accountable for this extraordinary performance? The marketing officer? Or, the subordinates? It is necessary to find out the members' skill levels in handling the sales. Therefore, the firm must keep confidential files which record the efficiency levels of the members of the organisation. If the particular person is not improving in performance despite opportunities like training, the management may initiate disciplinary action against the person.

Continuous appraisal of the employee performance at regular intervals is a must for any organisation. It is a kind of Hawthorne Effect. When employees feel that someone is assessing their performance, their performance levels are bound to increase. The Hawthorne effect is a form of reactivity whereby subjects improve an aspect of their behaviour being experimentally measured simply in response to the fact that they are being studied, not in response to any particular experimental manipulation.

The quality of manpower employed is one of the key success factors for the organisation. The entire marketing team is responsible for the performance of its department. The quality of manpower must be assessed and their ability to live up to the expectations of the marketing organisation need to be ascertained. Employee performance must be recorded at regular intervals and this record may be used when sanctioning *pay rises* to the employees. Here the important point is to take stock of performance levels of the employees so that this aspect may be considered while making important management decisions.

Nature of human relations in the workplace The organisation's mission in the workplace is to create a working environment that promotes the satisfaction and well-being of every employee, enabling them to flourish and fulfil their potential as far as possible for their greatest possible benefit, as well as that of their team and consequently their organisation. Everything begins with the individual, regardless of his or her place in the organisation. It is the sum of attitudes of all individuals that determines the level of relations between human beings within an organisation.

Our objective here is to assess the kind of human relations prevailing among the members of the marketing organisation. An employee survey can do the job. Cordial human relation is a prerequisite for executing a programme of strategic marketing in the marketing department.

The prerequisites of a good climate in the workplace are:

* transparency of objectives, risks and results,
* allocation of clearly defined tasks according to each individual's abilities and aspirations

- enriching content of work: learning, acquisition of new skills, and employability,
- providing the means to carry out work and attain objectives,
- high-quality environment and working conditions,
- encouragement of independence and initiative,
- cooperation and value placed on participation and team work,
- the search for a consensus in decision making,
- active watch over dissatisfaction, unhappiness and well-being in the organisation,
- acceptance, sharing and management of the difficulties and risks connected with each individual's tasks, and
- shared responsibility and support.

Employee attitude   Studies show that attitudes of employees correlate closely with customer satisfaction, which correlates with business profitability. Customers prefer to do business with employees who have positive attitudes and this preference brings customers back time and again. Since it costs less to support a sale to a returning customer than attracting new customers, a high percentage of retained customers correlate with higher business profitability.

Attitude is defined as any strong belief or feeling towards people and situations. Attitudes are not quick judgments that one makes casually and can easily change. One possesses acquired attitudes throughout his work-life in the organisation. Employee attitudes represent a powerful force in any organisation. An attitude of *trust* can pave the way for better communication between an employee and supervisor. Firms do not want to hire job seekers who are expected to demonstrate negative attitudes. One can have the best education, experience, resume, and skills in the world, but if the person's attitude is wrong, it will be difficult to get hired.

Attitude surveys must be conducted to ascertain the employee attitude toward the organisation. It is not that easy to bring out information from the employees about their organisation. The researcher has to use techniques that can gather information from people having contacts with the marketing organisation. But a talented researcher can find out what the employees think about their superior, department, and the organisation.

Motivational levels   Performance is considered to be a function of ability and motivation. Ability depends on education, training, and experience of the employee. It is a slow as well as time-consuming process. But motivation is different altogether. Motivation can be improved quickly. Very powerful words are enough. The managers have to find out these words and use them at the right situations. Timing is important.

Words used at the wrong time will lead to negative motivation. In this way, we can say that motivation is a delicate process. An effective executive can do it just like that. It is as simple as wearing a shirt.

The marketing organisation must conduct employee motivation surveys. A standard employee motivation survey covers nearly every facet of employee motivation, including:

* Overall satisfaction
* Corporate culture
* Supervisor relations
* Training
* Pay and benefits
* Work environment
* Communications

To motivate employees, it is important for managers to realise that it is difficult to motivate employees unless the manager is adequately self-motivated. Managers and supervisors who are constantly looking stressed out and who show no enthusiasm for their work easily pass on these negative traits to their employees. Therefore no amount of friendly suggestions or monetary considerations will make such employees motivated. By conducting motivation surveys, the firm can find out where it stands with respect to its motivation of employees.

Customer-oriented Situation Analysis

Customer-oriented situation analysis is concerned with the search for the nature of relationship between the customers and the marketing people in a firm. Customers are the focal point of the firm. It is needless to say much about the customer vis-à-vis the firm because not only literature but also experiences of business people are aplenty to prove the point.

In large and medium-sized organisations, customers are contacted through the channel members. Even though the channel members are selling directly to the customers, the firm is dependent on the customers indirectly. The channel members are acting as the firm's agents.

The firm has to find its efficacy regarding the following aspects for finding the customer-oriented situation:

1. the marketing organisation's customer/consumer policy statement
2. the marketing information system
3. the working of the consumer grievance handling mechanism

Let us make a brief analysis of the above variables and their position in the firm.

Exhibit 6.1   Consumer Return Policy Statement

H.H. Brown Shoe Company, Inc. produces quality footwear that serves many different purposes. We stand behind the products that we produce. At times, despite our best efforts to assure the best quality, a product purchased from a retailer may have a defect in materials and or workmanship as there are many components and processes that go into footwear manufacturing.

If a consumer believes that a manufacturer's defect has caused unusual wear or otherwise affects the use of the footwear, we require the consumer to return the footwear to the retailer where the footwear was originally purchased. The original selling retailer has its own policies and processes in place to satisfy the consumer including an initial inspection for normal wear. In the event that the selling retailer cannot reasonably satisfy the consumer, that consumer may then contact the brand manufacturer. If someone other than the original purchaser contacts or attempts to contact H.H. Brown Shoe Company, Inc. or any of its divisions or affiliated companies, it will be necessary for us to receive the appropriate written authorisation from the original purchaser authorising H.H. Brown Shoe Company, Inc. to discuss the matter with the representative and to deal with the representative in resolving the matter.

H.H. Brown Shoe Company, Inc. requires that a consumer have the original sales receipt within one year of purchase and can identify the retailer that the footwear was purchased from. We may use reasonable efforts to contact that retailer on the consumer's behalf to ensure full satisfaction. In the event that this is not possible the consumer may choose to return the footwear to us for inspection. If a determination is made that there is in fact a defect H.H. Brown Shoe Company, Inc. has, at its option, the right to either repair, credit in full against the purchase of inventory currently in stock at MSRP, prorate the value of the original purchase, as appropriate or replace the footwear with the same or comparably valued footwear. If no defect is apparent the inspected footwear will be returned to the consumer.

The firm's consumer policy statement   It is quite common for large firms to declare their consumer policies along with their vision and mission statements. It is a good corporate practice which conveys messages to the existing and prospective customers the intention of the firm. But the question is how far these firms conform to these policies. It is well and good if the firm is sincere in its motives. In this connection, the company must make a self-appraisal to see the extent to which the company is translating its words into deeds. It is an important component of the situation analysis.

The marketing information system (MIS)   The MIS is a computerised system that is designed to provide an organised flow of information to enable and support the marketing activities of an organisation. In a knowledge-intensive economy, the ability to collect, analyse and act upon marketing information more rapidly than the competition is the core competency from which competitive advantage flows. Marketing information systems provide the information technology backbone for the marketing organisation's strategic operations.

Through the use of market research and marketing intelligence activities the MIS can aid the identification of emerging market segments, and the monitoring of the market environment for changes in consumer behaviour, competitor activities, new technologies, economic conditions and governmental policies. Market research is situational in nature and focuses on specific strategic or tactical marketing initiatives. Marketing intelligence is continuous in nature and involves monitoring and analysing a broad range of market-based activities and information sources.

The MIS provides the information necessary to develop marketing strategy. It supports strategy development for new products, product positioning, marketing communications (advertising, public relations, and sales promotion), pricing, personal selling, distribution, customer service and partnerships and alliances. The MIS provides support for product launches, enables the coordination of marketing strategies, and is an integral part of salesforce automation (SFA), customer relationship management (CRM), and customer service systems.

Consumer grievance handling mechanism   A good consumer grievance handling mechanism is the gateway to earn loyal customers. Look at the oft-heard statements:

- It costs about five times as much to attract a new customer as it costs to keep an old one.

- For every customer who bothers to complain to the average business, there are twenty-six who remain silent.

- Over 91% of unhappy customers will never purchase goods or services from you again.

- The average 'wronged' customer will tell eight to sixteen people. More than 10% will tell more than twenty people.

When a customer purchases a product or pays for a service, there is an expectation of some benefit that will be derived from the product or the service. If the customer's expectation is met, the result is bound to be customer satisfaction. While customer satisfaction does not automatically lead to loyalty, satisfied customers are more likely to become loyal customers, and the increase in satisfaction also increases loyalty.

The present status of the consumer grievance handling mechanism needs to be studied in order to take stock of the situation. An effective grievance handling procedure brings to the organisation a good number of loyal customers.

Prospects-oriented Situation Analysis

Potential customers are the future of the organisation. Therefore it is necessary to make an audit of what the firm has been doing to attract new customers. Websites are wonderful magnets that attract new visitors who, in turn, become customers of the firm. Website can be treated as your online representative who directly interacts with your visitors 24 × 7. Make a list of your activities for attracting new customers. Evaluate them. Find out how many website visitors have turned into your customers.

Next, find out what your marketing people are doing to contact potential customers. The firm must ascertain the following to unearth the facts regarding the employees' relations with the potential customers.

1. What methods are they following to identify the potential customers?
2. What is the nature of their contact with them?
3. Do they look at them with friendliness?

All these things will help assess the efficacy of the marketing organisation in taking concrete steps for wooing potential customers.

Distribution-oriented Situation Analysis

A channel of distribution or trade channel is the path or route along which goods move from producers to ultimate consumers. It is a distribution network through which producers put their products in the hands of actual users. A trade or marketing channel consists of the producer, consumers or users and the various middlemen who intervene between the two. The channel serves as a connecting link between the producer and consumers. By bridging the gap between the point of production and the point of consumption, a channel creates time, place and possession utilities.

Channel members are the people who support the organisation with their expertise in customer relationship and their network of operations. At the same time they need the support of the firm as well. It is a kind of partnership. As long as both the firm and the channel members act in good faith, the relationship continues forever. It is necessary to study the strategy followed by them to find customers for the products. When the channel members follow world class and flawless strategies, it is well and good; but if they do not adhere to the directions of the firm on the issue of customer relations, it may do enough harm to the sales level of the firm in near as well as distant future. The dreams of the firm in executing marketing strategies will be like building castles in the air.

The firm must make an assessment of the channel members' activities vis-à-vis to our organisation. This is an essential part of the internal situation analysis that the firm is pursuing vigorously. The assessment may be done on the following lines.

* whether the channel member is adhering to the instructions of the firm
* whether the channel member is fulfilling their part of the agreement correctly
* whether the channel member is managing the cash received from the customers as per agreed norms
* whether the channel member communicates with the firm about the grievances of the customers in time
* whether the strategies followed by the channel members to find customers are satisfactory

After making an assessment of the above factors, the firm must prepare a report of channel members' performance and this report must be kept ready along with the other reports on situation analysis for consolidation purposes.

Media-oriented Situation Analysis

As corporate competition is increasing, so is the need for returns on massive expenditures on advertising. Firms spend millions, even billions of dollars to win the hearts and minds of people, to convert them as their customers, and to influence the people's choices towards their products and services. Even a reputed company like Coca Cola continually spends money on media advertising to support recognition of their products. Every year Coca Cola is spending more than $100 million to keep its name in the forefront of the public's eyes. When the firm proposes to advertise, it needs to choose the right media that will effectively deliver the message to the target market.

A good firm looks at two things:

* the amount of money to be spent on advertising, and
* the effectiveness of advertising.

The effectiveness of advertising, in turn, depends on two factors;

* the quality of the advertisement copy, and
* the reputation of the actual media.

The firm has to consider these factors before it parts with its money.

A survey to assess the effectiveness of the advertisement must be undertaken. The media-oriented situation analysis aims at:

- the effectiveness of the media used to advertise, and
- the effectiveness of the content of the commercial.

The firm must see that it makes a perfect job on these two fronts. An analysis of the media is necessary to evolve a suitable marketing strategy which will complement the firm's efforts to excel in the market. In the task of accomplishing the firm's objectives, no function is less important in business. Success comes as a result of coordinated efforts of so many people in the organisation. There is no function as more important and less important. All the functions are important and even small activities, sometimes, do wonders. Organisation is teamwork.

Management-oriented Situation Analysis

The management must shoulder the responsibility for the results of an organisation. It is the management that decides the policies; it is the management that activates business; it is the management that makes things happen; it is management that commands people and resources; and it is the management that harvests. Therefore, it is necessary for the management to see that there are no let-ups on its side. Management's responsibility is to provide resources on the basis of consultation and concurrence with the executives concerned. In today's organisations, management cannot force things upon executives. After all the workers too have their own say in today's work environment. When such is the situation of today, management cannot have total command over the executives and it is management's responsibility to provide what is required by the marketing people.

A management-oriented situation analysis tries to find out the following:

1. whether the management has good rapport with the marketing department
2. whether the management provides necessary finance for the marketing projects
3. whether the management provides funds with skepticism or reservations
4. whether the management and marketing executives see things eye-to-eye

EXTERNAL SITUATION ANALYSIS AND STRATEGIC MARKETING MANAGEMENT[1]

The marketing executive must make a study of the external environment and the way it affects the marketing function on a continuous basis. The important external factors are discussed in this section of the chapter. The broad social and other forces that influence every business or non-business organisation constitute the external situation or the macro-environment of the marketing organisation. A firm operating in the US, India and China has to devise a strategy that will satisfy all the consumers of these countries or individual strategies to suit the consumers of respective countries.

In the course of making the external situation analysis, the marketing executives/ the experts must identify the opportunities and threats in the external environment. They must make an analysis whether these opportunities can be cashed in on by the marketing organisation of the firm. The main objective of making the external analysis is to identify these factors. When doing so, the executive will be able to find out ways and means of thwarting the threats at its budding point.

The external factors that can affect the marketing organisation of the firm are:

* *Physical*—how the country's physical factors like territorial size, geographical location, natural resources, climate, rivers, lakes and forests impact business.

* *Socio-cultural*—how consumers, households and communities behave and their beliefs. For instance, changes in attitude towards health, or a greater number of pensioners in a population.

* *Legal*—the way in which legislation in society affects the business, for example, changes in employment laws on working hours.

* *Economic*—how the economy affects a business in terms of taxation, government spending, general demand, interest rates, exchange rates and European and global economic factors.

* *Technological*—how the rapid pace of change in production processes and product innovation affect a business.

* *Political*—how changes in government policy might affect the business, e.g., a decision to subsidise building new houses in an area could be good for a local brick works.

* *Ethical*—what is regarded as morally right or wrong for a business to do. For instance should it trade with countries which have a poor record on human rights.

* *Competitive*—what our competitors are doing to outperform our marketing efforts.

Physical Environment

Even though the physical environment does not have direct impact on a firm's functioning, still it can impact upon your success in business and consequently needs to be considered. A country's territorial size, geographical location, natural resources, climate, rivers, lakes and forests constitute its physical environment. The physical environment influences political and economic activities, shapes cultural characteristics such as language and religion, and determines land usage, transportation, and commercial flows. When planning domestic and international marketing activities, the possible impact of the physical environment should be taken into account. For example:

* Population distribution will be affected by topography (that is, a country's rivers, mountains, deserts, and so on) and climate—people tend to settle where the climate is moderate, and there is an adequate supply of water.

* Certain climatic conditions may dictate adaptations to the product—some glues and oils, for example, will not function in very cold climates.

* Climate also influences the logistics of packaging, protective packing and safeguarding the product while it is in transit or in storage. Products which are particularly vulnerable to climatic conditions are those that are adversely affected by extremes in temperature or excessive humidity changes (fruits being transported to hot climates or across the equator, for example).

* Abnormal weather conditions (for example, typhoon season in Asia) can disrupt the transportation of export products while unforeseen changes in the weather can threaten companies which produce seasonal goods.

* Topography will influence the routing of goods and the choice of transport mode, which in turn will affect cost and thus will have an impact on the price offered to the buyer.

Socio-cultural Environment

Language is central to the expression of culture. Within each cultural group, the use of words reflects the lifestyle, attitudes and many of the customs of that group. Language is not only a key to understanding the group, but also it is the principal way of communicating within it. A language usually defines the parameters of a particular culture. Thus if several languages are spoken within the borders of a country, that country is seen to have diverse cultures.

Material culture relates to the way in which a society organises and views its economic activities. It includes the techniques and know-how used in the creation of goods and services, the manner in which the people of the society use their capabilities, and the resulting benefits. When one refers to an "industrialised" or a "developing" nation, one is really referring to a material culture.

The material culture of a particular market will affect the nature and extent of demand for a product. Whereas a luxury item, such as a sophisticated piece of computer hardware, may have a ready market in a country such as France, demand for it may be non-existent in a developing country which is hampered by inadequate facilities and/or foreign exchange shortages. The material culture of a country may also necessitate modifications to the product.

Exhibit 6.2 The Meaning of Colour to Different People

Colour and Culture

The significance of colours may vary considerably from one culture to another. For example, in many societies, colours are often associated with emotions: "to see red", "to be green with envy" or "to be feeling blue".

Green, a popular colour in many Moslem countries, is often associated with disease in countries with dense, green jungles. It is associated with cosmetics by the French, Dutch and Swedes and increasingly with an environment-conscious world.

Various colours represent death. Black signifies death to Americans and many Europeans, but in Japan and many other Asian countries, white represents death. (Obviously, white wedding gowns are not popular in parts of Asia.) Latin Americans generally associate purple with death, but dark red is the appropriate mourning colour along the Ivory Coast. And even though white is the colour representing death to some, it expresses joy to those living in Ghana.

In many countries, bright colours such as yellow and orange, express joy. To most of the world, blue is thought to be a masculine colour but it is not as manly as red in the United Kingdom or France. In Iran, blue represents a bad colour. Although pink is believed to be the foremost feminine colour by Americans, most of the rest of the world considers yellow to be the most feminine colour. Red is felt to be blasphemous in some African countries but is generally considered to be a colour reflecting wealth or luxury elsewhere. A red circle has been successfully used on many packages sold in Latin America; but it is unpopular in some parts of Asia. To them, it conjures up images of the Japanese flag.

(*Source:* D. A. Ricks, *Big Business Blunders*)

A culture's aesthetics refer to its ideas concerning good taste and beauty as expressed in the fine arts—music, art, drama and dance—and in the appreciation of colour and form. Insensitivity to aesthetic values can not only lead to ineffective advertising and package design for products, it can also offend prospective customers. Aesthetics also embrace people's dress and appearance, i.e., their outward garments and adornments or accessories. Distinctive national attire, for instance, includes the Japanese kimono, Dutch clogs, and the Englishman's bowler hat and brollie.

Social organisation refers to the ways in which people relate to one another, form groups and organise their activities, teach acceptable behaviour and govern themselves. It thus comprises the social, educational and political systems of a society.

In a culture where great importance is attached to the family unit, promotional efforts should be directed at the family as a whole rather than the individual. The size of the family unit differs from one culture to another. It can range from the nuclear family, that is, mother, father, and children, to the extended family which includes many relatives and whose role is to provide protection, support and economic security to its members. In the extended family, characteristic of developing countries, consumption and decision-making takes place in a larger unit and purchasing power patterns may be different from those evident in western cultures.

In any society, certain occupations carry more prestige, social status and monetary reward than others. In India, for example, there is a strong reluctance amongst people with university education to perform 'menial' tasks using their hands, even answering the telephone. In many countries, including France, Italy and Singapore, financial independence is considered essential for occupation-related prestige. In Japan, however, the majority of university-educated professionals tend to prefer working for large multinational firms to self-employment.

A religious system refers to the spiritual side of a culture or its approach to the supernatural. Western culture is accepted as having been largely influenced by the Judeo-Christian traditions, while Eastern or Oriental cultures have been strongly influenced by Buddhism, Confucianism, Taoism and Hinduism. Although very few religions influence business activities directly, the impact of religion on human value systems and decision-making is significant. Thus, religion exerts a considerable influence on people's actions and outlook on life, as well as on the products they buy. In certain parts of the world, such as Latin America, the influence of religion extends even beyond the individual or family and is manifested in a whole community's deep involvement in, and devotion to, the church.

Legal Environment

Domestic laws govern marketing within a country, for example, the physical attributes of a product will be influenced by laws (designed to protect consumers) relating to the purity, safety or performance of the product. Domestic laws might also constrain marketers in the areas of product packaging, marking and labelling, and contracts with agents. Most countries also have certain laws regulating advertising, for example, Britain does not permit any cigarette or liquor advertisment on TV and India also has similar regulations.

The legal systems of most of the non-socialist countries can be grouped into common law and code law. Common law is generally based on precedents or past practices, while a code, which is a comprehensive set of volumes having statutory force and covering virtually the whole spectrum of the country's law, is established by arbitrary methods, for example, a speed limit of 80 kmph or, a three-day period for cancelling a contract.

Economic Environment

The primary concern in analysing the economic environment is to assess the opportunities for marketing the company's products abroad or possibly for locating some of the company's production and distribution facilities outside the country. Indeed, when striving to identify potential countries to focus on, one of the major differentiating factors will be the differences in the economic environments that exist between potential target countries.

Decisions about how much of a product people buy and which products they choose to buy are largely influenced by their purchasing power. If a large portion of a country's population is poor, the market potential for many products may be lower than it would be if they were reasonably prosperous. If a country is expected to enjoy rapid economic growth and large sectors of the population are expected to share in the increased wealth, the sales prospects for many products would clearly be more promising than if the economy were stagnating.

The important aspects of economic environment that have impact on business are: i) gross domestic product, ii) disposable income levels, iii) demographic factors, iv) competitive and complementary factors, and v) degree of government intervention.

Technological Environment

Technology can be defined as the method or technique for converting inputs to outputs in accomplishing a specific task. Thus, the terms 'method' and 'technique' refer not only to the knowledge but also to the skills and the means for accomplishing a task. Technological innovation, then, refers to the increase in knowledge, the improvement in skills, or the discovery of a new or improved means that extends people's ability to achieve a given task.

Technology can be classified in several ways. For example, blueprints, machinery, equipment and other capital goods are sometimes referred to as hard technology while soft technology includes management know-how, finance, marketing and administrative techniques. When a relatively primitive technology is used in the production process, the technology is usually referred to as labour-intensive. A highly advanced technology, on the other hand, is generally termed capital-intensive.

Changes in the technological environment have had some of the most dramatic effects on business. A company may be thoroughly committed to a particular type of technology, and may have made major investments in equipment and training only to see a new, more innovative and cost-effective technology emerging. Indeed, the managing director of a multinational organisation manufacturing heavy machinery once said that the hardest part of his/her job had nothing to do with unions, pay or products, but with whether or not to spend money on the latest technologically improved equipment.

Computer technology has had an enormous impact on education and health care. The advancements in medical technology, for example, have contributed to longevity of human life in many societies. In addition, the introduction of robots in many factories has reduced the need for labour and occupational hazards that labour faced, and the use of VCR's and microcomputers have become commonplace in many homes and businesses.

Unfortunately, there is a negative side to technological progress. The introduction of nuclear weapons, for example, has made the destruction of the human race a frightening possibility. In addition, factories using modern technologies have polluted both air and water and contributed to various environmental and health-related problems.

Political Environment

When America's founders wrote the US Constitution in 1787, they did not envision political parties playing a role in the government. Rather, they expected that constitutional provisions such as separation of powers, checks and balances, federalism and indirect election of the president by an electoral college would deter the formation of parties.

Despite these provisions, the United States in 1800 became the first nation to develop political parties organised on a national level and to transfer executive power from one party to another via an election. By the 1830s, political parties were an established part of the US political environment.

Today, the Republican and Democratic parties are the two main political parties in the United States. Most elected officials serving as president, congressional representative, state governor or state legislator are members of one of these parties. The Republicans and Democrats have dominated American politics since the 1860s, and every president since 1852 has been either a Republican or Democrat.

TOTAL SITUATION ANALYSIS

Situation analysis helps us to identify our strengths and weaknesses, and also to discover the opportunities and threats, the external environment has in store for our firm. This process will be of great use to the decision makers of the organisation. The organisation will be able to decide the extent in doing the situation analysis and the firm must be able to identify the *dividing point* beyond which the organisation should not venture into.

A total situation analysis report must be prepared to see the whole picture. This will help to identify the opportunities available in the market and also the threats the environment has in stock for us. A list of opportunities along with their timings and a list of threats can guide the management in making right decision on time. Ignoring the opportunities as well as threats would cost the organisation dearly. Therefore it is essential to look into them and select suitable opportunities and make profit out of them. Threats are no less important and they need timely attention and action so that the organisation can sail smoothly. Threats from small competitors also must be looked into with due care. Those threats that might require lot of time and money and which do not justify the benefits the organisation would get may be ignored.

SUMMARY

* The firm's marketing executive must make a situation analysis which contains i) internal situation analysis, and ii) external situation analysis.

* Internal situation analysis is nothing but the making of an assessment of the firm's strengths and weaknesses. It is the study of the internal environment as to what capabilities are present in the organisation, and what deficiencies are found in it. The internal situation analysis is the process of making an honest self-appraisal, the purpose of which is to identify i) the plus points which can be utilized fully for the welfare of the firm, and ii) the minus points of the organisation. The firm will be able to eliminate the minus points in the organisation by taking constructive steps in converting them into plus points to the firm.

* The internal situation analysis of the marketing department may be performed under the following headings:
  1. Employee-oriented situation analysis
  2. Customer-oriented situation analysis
  3. Prospects-oriented situation analysis
  4. Distribution-oriented situation analysis

5.   Media-oriented situation analysis

6.   Management-oriented situation analysis.

- The marketing executives must make a study of the external environment and the way it affects their marketing function as a continuous basis. The factors that can affect the marketing organisation of a firm are:

  - *Physical*—how the country's physical factors like territorial size, geographical location, natural resources, climate, rivers, lakes and forests impact business.

  - *Socio-cultural*—how consumers, households and communities behave and their beliefs. For instance, changes in attitude towards health, or a greater number of pensioners in a population.

  - *Legal*—the way in which legislation in society affects the business. (for example, changes in employment laws on working hours).

  - *Economic*—how the economy affects a business in terms of taxation, government spending, general demand, interest rates, exchange rates and European and global economic factors.

  - *Technological*—how the rapid pace of change in production processes and product innovation affect a business.

  - *Political*—how changes in government policy might affect the business for example, a decision to subsidize building new houses in an area could be good for a local brick works.

  - *Ethical*—what is regarded as morally right or wrong for doing a business. For instance should it trade with countries which have a poor record on human rights.

  - *Competitive*—what our competitors are doing to outperform our marketing efforts.

- Finally the marketing executive must prepare a total situation analysis report which is a consolidated form of internal and external situation reports.

REVIEW QUESTIONS

1. Explain the process of internal situation analysis.

2. "In fact, situation analysis is nothing but *SWOT Analysis*." Elaborate the statement by giving examples from the real world.

3. Explain how to undertake an employee-oriented situation analysis.

4. *"Employee Engagement Report* by Blessing White (April 2008) has revealed that only 29% of employees are actively engaged in their jobs." Discuss the implications of the findings of the report for organisations.

5. "Whatever their level of education and training be, what matters for the organisation is whether the employees have done it or not." Do you agree? Substantiate your stand with some valid points.

6. What are the prerequisites of good climate in the organisation?

7. Explain how to undertake a customer-oriented situation analysis.

8. "Studies show that attitudes of employees correlate closely with customer satisfaction." What are the implications of this finding for a marketing organisation?

9. "To motivate employees, it is important for managers to realise that it is difficult to motivate employees unless the manager is well-motivated." Explain how far this statement is valid. Give your points succinctly.

10. Are consumer policy statements necessary to an organisation? Explain your answer with a vivid analysis.

11. "Potential customers are the future of the organisation." Do you agree? Bring out your strategies to rope in the prospects into the fold of the organisation.

12. Explain how to undertake a distribution-oriented situation analysis.

13. "It is the customers alone to be satisfied; but the channel members also need to be satisfied." Do you agree? Explain your position with strong points.

14. Explain how to undertake a media-oriented situation analysis.

15. "An analysis of the media is necessary to evolve a suitable marketing strategy which will complement the firm's efforts to excel in the market." Explain how far the statement is true.

16. Explain how to undertake an external situation analysis.

17. "Even today, religion exerts a considerable influence on people's actions and outlook on their life." Substantiate the statement with valid points.

REFERENCE

1. Soundaian, S. (2011). *New Dimensions of Management.* MJP Publishers, Chennai.

7

MARKET SEGMENTATION AND PRODUCT POSITIONING

After reading this chapter, you will be able to

- *recognise the need for market segmentation*

- *know about the approaches and common bases to segmentation,*

- *learn the process of segmentation,*

- *understand the process of product positioning, and*

- *learn about ten commandments for perfect positioning of the firm.*

INTRODUCTION

People are not entirely identical. Nor they are entirely different. In some ways, they are identical; and, in some other ways they are different. This is why several companies survive in the same industry. This is why some firms excel and some other firms fail. Shrewd people make it to their advantage; people with mediocre capabilities just survive; and people with relatively less skills are doomed to fail.

Firms cannot manufacture goods to suit individual needs; this is quite impossible. They offer certain varieties and consumers are forced to buy from what is available in the market. In the case of many products, consumers do not know what to buy and how to buy until they are educated by the manufacturers. Manufacturers suggest to them to buy this or that. They offer limited choices and tell the customers that their products contain features that will suit their requirements. Some customers study them and decide; some others buy them because they *liked* it for reasons unknown to them. May be that they loved it at first sight! Customers get themselves grouped knowingly or unknowingly and these groups are identified by the firms; these groups became to be called as *segments* by the firms.

NEED FOR SEGMENTATION

Marketing segmentation is a logical outgrowth of marketing concept.[1] According to Barwell, the customer-focused philosophy is known as the "marketing concept." The marketing concept is a philosophy, not a system of marketing or an organisational structure. It is founded on the belief that profitable sales and satisfactory returns on investment can only be achieved by identifying, anticipating and satisfying customer needs and desires. As marketing tries to unearth even hidden needs of the consumers, it has become as not only a philosophy but also an art. This function can be effectively performed when the marketer is able to find out which section of people wants what. Here comes the relevance of market segmentation.

Segmentation of the market is not mandatory for the marketing organisation. The firm may choose mass marketing strategy if the product is of such nature that it is consumed by a vast majority of people in the province or country and that the product has an appeal to the common man. Mass marketing refers to consideration of the market as a homogeneous group and offering the same marketing mix to all consumers. It allows economies of scale to be realised through mass production, mass distribution, and mass communication. The fast moving consumer goods (FMCGs) belong to this group. The drawback in this strategy is that the same product is offered to all consumers despite variations in their tastes and preferences.

In most of the cases, segmenting the market becomes necessary for the manufacturer in view of the following reasons:

1. Marketers can effectively serve the consumers if they know who their customers are. The marketers will find it difficult to plan their work if they do not know whom to contact for marketing their goods. They are able to know the expectations of the customers as they are in touch with them through personal contacts or customer surveys.

2. The marketer can make effective use of the resources if the prospective customers are identified. Wasteful expenditure can be avoided and the time and funds at disposal can be properly used.

3. Segmentation helps to decide the best strategy to create and retain the customers since the customers and their expectations are identified.

4. Focused task is better than diffused task. Segments help the marketer to focus the attention on a specific group of customers.

5. The firm is able to satisfy the customers and thus, the customers are happy with the service. The firm stands to gain from repeated purchases which then lead to customer loyalty which is the biggest asset to the organisation.

WHAT IS MARKET SEGMENTATION

Segmenting the market is a strategy that involves dividing a market into subsets of consumers who have common needs and applications for the goods and services offered in the market. These subsets of consumers have something in common They may belong to the same income group or, they may belong to the same age group. If they do not belong to the same income/age group, they may have similar wavelength of thoughts.

Consumers are not alike. A rich man goes to buy a car. He has already collected all the information via the Internet. He has certain expectations in his mind. The class of car he proposes to buy should give him maximum mileage with maximum features. Two brands of cars satisfied most of his expectations. He is not worried about the styling of the car. He is not worried about the price range or colour. He visits a particular reputed dealer's showroom and places the order for the car. Another man, also rich, visits the showroom and places the order instantaneously. When the dealer requested him to get all the particulars about the car, he simply replied that he had already driven the car a few times and that he liked the performance and the stylish looks. Both the customers are rich; but their expectations are different. You may be surprised to learn that even lower middle class consumers buy cars of high class. Why? The answer is that no two persons are identical in all respects. He wanted to buy the car because he liked it and wanted to live with it. That's all. He attributed no special reason for his decision.

Market segmentation is the process of dividing the whole market into several submarkets on the basis of customer characteristics or behaviours in order to find out a suitable category of customers who may be targeted by the firm to market its goods. This definition contains four points:

1. Dividing the whole market into submarkets,
2. Doing it on the basis of customer characteristics or behaviours,
3. Searching for a suitable group of customers, and
4. Targeting the group for marketing the goods.

The whole market, i.e., city, provincial, national, or international may be divided as per the nature of the market of the firm. The bases for dividing the market are many in number and the business must select the appropriate base for its product. Customers' characteristics are the most suitable base for all organisations. The customers with the specific set of characteristics and behavioural patterns must be identified and the marketing strategy of the organisation must be formulated accordingly.

APPROACHES TO SEGMENTATION

The first approach to market segmentation is the *top-down approach*. The firm decides which segment of the market is most suitable for its operations. Then the firm formulates its strategies to attract the customers in this segment. Since the marketer initiates the segmentation process, it is known as the *top-down* approach.

Even if the marketer does not formulate a method to identify specific segment, the market gets segmented by itself. The marketer conveys the message about the product through a popular medium. The key to segmentation is to let the marketplace segment itself. It is prudent for the marketers to identify in which segment the product has already fit in the market by observing what category of people buy their products. This approach to segmentation is *bottom-up approach*. This will help them to formulate strategies to reinforce the segment of the market. When a group of customers buy a product, they form the segment.

Let us now look at the characteristics of market segment.

1. The segments have needs and behaviours which exist despite any company's products or services.
2. These segments will not change their behaviour to accommodate you or your products unless you offer extraordinary value.
3. The buying patterns, usage patterns and attitudes causing segmentation are rational and provide insight into increasing market share within a segment.

4. Segmenting customers into groups of loyal buyers, price shoppers and customers who are loyal to competitors is logical and is based on the knowledge and experience base of the customer.

Therefore, the task of the marketer is to identify the segment in order to understand the needs of the customers who make the segment.

COMMON BASES FOR SEGMENTATION

Literature on marketing suggests several bases for segmenting the market. The following segments are popular even though many other bases are available. It is always good to limit our choices and select the best segment for our need. Let us now discuss briefly the popular segments used for segmenting consumer markets.

Geographic Segmentation

Geographic segmentation is an important process particularly for multinational and global businesses and brands. Many such companies have regional and national marketing programmes which alter their products, advertising, and promotion to meet the individual needs of geographic units. Marketers will tailor marketing programmes to fit the needs of individual geographic areas, localising the products, advertising, and sales effort to geographic differences in needs and wants. Marketers will also study the population density or regional climate as factors of geographic segmentation. The following are some of the geographic variables often used in segmentation:

- Region—by continent, country, state, or sometimes even neighbourhood
- Size of metropolitan area—population within ranges or above a certain level
- Population density—often classified as urban, suburban, or rural
- Climate—according to weather patterns which are common to certain geographic regions.

Demographic Segmentation

Gathering customer data such as a person's age, his or her lifestyle, employment, the average size of a family, marital status, religion and life cycle are all part of the factors involved in a demographic segment. A detailed study of the population will show how individual preferences change as they mature or gain better living conditions as their income grows. The following are some of the demographic segmentation variables:

- age
- gender
- family size

* family life cycle
* income
* education
* ethnicity
* nationality
* religion
* social class

Psychographic Segmentation

Psychographic segmentation categorises customers on the basis of their lifestyles. Activities, interests, and opinion surveys are some of the tools for measuring lifestyle. Psychographic segmentation has demonstrated its use as a practical marketing tool in consumer markets. Psychographic variables have been a popular segmentation variable, particularly in consumer marketing of fast moving goods. They are any attributes relating to personality, values, attitudes, interests, or lifestyles. They are also called IAO variables (for Interests, Activities, and Opinions). Psychographics can also be seen as an equivalent of the concept of "culture" as used most commonly in national segmentation. Some of the psychographic variables include the following:

* Activities
* Interests
* Opinions
* Attitudes
* Values

Behavioural Segmentation

Behavioural segmentation is also called as attitudinal segmentation. This type of segmentation is based on actual customer behaviour towards the product. Behavioural segmentation encourages the marketer to truly understand the customers. The marketer attempts to categorise and eventually target. When one begins to deal with behavioural segmentation, measuring often becomes more of an art than a science. These variables include the following:

* benefits sought
* usage rate
* brand loyalty
* user status—potential, first time, regular, and so on
* occasions, holidays and events that stimulate purchases

FEATURES OF SEGMENTS

You cannot assume things and go for segmentation. The segments must satisfy some of the conditions of the marketer. Let us now see what conditions these *segments* must fulfil.

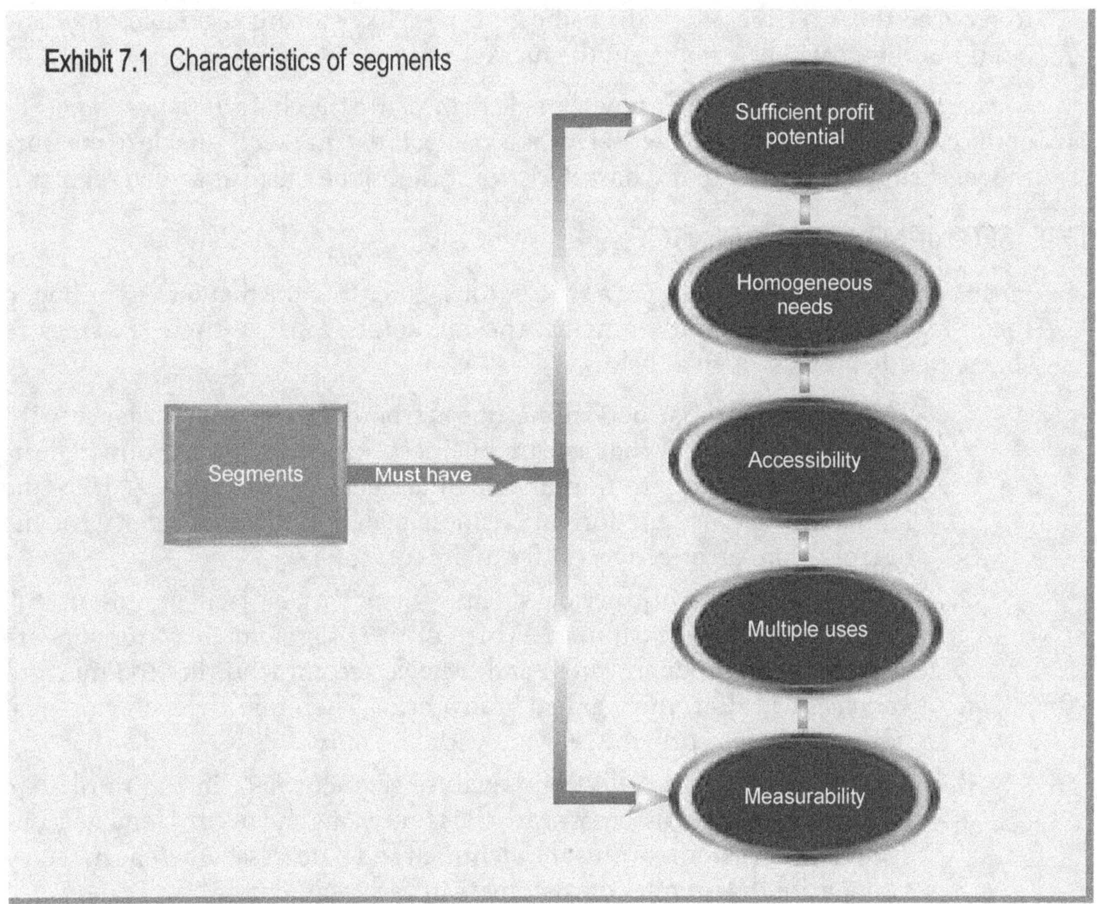

Exhibit 7.1 Characteristics of segments

Sufficient profit potential   Segments must have enough profit potential to justify developing and maintaining a strategy. The size of the segment and the nature of the customers who make the segment must justify to be called itself as a segment. A segment without profit potential is of no use for the marketer. The marketer must be able to differentiate between a profitable segment and a segment with poor profit potential.

Homogeneous needs   The consumers in the segment must have more or less similar, if not identical, needs. This requirement is important in the sense that serving a segment of customers with heterogeneous needs will be an exercise in futile.

Accessiblity   The segment must be reachable to the marketer. A product that is unable to reach the customer cannot have a segment for that customer. The marketer cannot have a strategy for reaching customers who are located in Siberia.

Multiple uses   The marketer will be prudent if he is able to find customers who have multiple applications for his product. Such a segment will encourage the marketer to serve better. A refrigerator with a single purpose like storing vegetables only and not other things will be a failure in the market.

Measurability   The marketer must be able to measure the characteristics and needs of the customers to establish themselves as a group. If the market is unable to measure the segment with respect to its characteristics, it cannot be called as a good segment.

THE SEGMENTATION PROCESS

Hiem and Schewe[2] have suggested a process for segmenting the market. According to them, after establishing the segments, the marketers can use their six steps to segmentation process given as below.

1. The marketer must determine market boundaries in accordance with business strategy. What is our business focus? Who are our generic competitors? What are the fundamental needs of this market? Here the marketer must use the formal business plan and then consider what the organisation can effectively offer to the customers.

2. The marketer must also decide which segment variables will be most useful. Who is our typical customer? Which of their segment characteristics are related to our product? Hiem and Schewe recommend that too much of variables will affect the segmentation process. Therefore, the marketer must be careful in selecting the relevant variables only.

3. The marketer must collect and analyse segment data in the third step, identifying specific customers with the same wants and needs. Homogeneous segments of customers must be identified and if necessary, he/she must try to quantify the number of customers in each segment.

4. The marketer has to now draw a profile of each segment that with variable information to form a picture of buying behaviour. This involves selecting those variables which are most closely related to customer's buying behaviour.

5. Then the marketer must target the segments by looking for the best opportunities that come from matching the company's resources with those opportunities. In targeting a particular segment, the marketer should look for opportunities that perfectly match the resources of the organisation.

6. Finally, the marketer must formulate a suitable marketing plan that best highlights the product features and creates the image that will appeal to the

targeted segment. Determine the best method for reaching that group. Product attributes as expected by the customers must be identified by the marketer. This process will enable the marketer to offer the best possible service or product to the customer.

The segmentation process explained below will be more pragmatic than that of Hiem and Schewe. It is generally regarded as consisting of four steps: segmentation, targeting, positioning, and strategy planning.

Step 1 Segmentation

The first stage of the segmentation process involves the selection of suitable variables for grouping customers. These are also referred to as base variables or the segmentation basis. There is rarely one best way of segmenting a market and more than one variable can be used. There are a number of segmentation variables that can be used for consumer and business-to-business markets. Segmentation analysis requires a range of data from a wide variety of sources on markets, customers' attitudes, motives and behaviour as well as competitor information.

As discussed earlier in this chapter, the marketer may use any one of the two approaches, namely, *top-down* approach, and *bottom-up* approach.

Top-down approach   The marketer selects the appropriate segment or segments which is most suitable for the organisation. In doing so, the following factors must be considered.

1. nature of the product which includes the price, durable or non-durable, nature of consumption, viz., mass or not, branded or not, and convenient or not,
2. probable category of consumers who would use the product, viz., age group, income groups, education level, and so on,
3. the most suitable marketing outlets,
4. the comparative market trends, and
5. the results of consumer surveys conducted for the purpose, if any

Let us take the example of toilet soap. Our purpose is to identify the suitable segment of the market. We have to follow the following factors:

i. *Price*   Averagely priced; semi-durable; mass consumption; convenience; brand-oriented sale; stresses quality ingredients of the product.
ii. *Probable category of consumers*   Adults; middle income group; education not a criterion.
iii. *Suitable marketing outlets*   Chain stores, departmental stores, any convenience outlet.

iv. *Comparable market trend*   Middle-income group and lower high-income group and upper low-income group.

Suggestion   Since the product may belong to mass consumption category and is averagely priced, the suitable segment is people of average and upper-middle income class category, above the age of eighteen, and educated people. Variables selected: i) income, ii) age, and iii) education.

Bottom-up approach   The marketer advertises through mass medium so as to convey the message about the product for sometime. The marketer then collects the information about the purchasers from the retail outlets as a consequence of prior arrangement with selected outlets. He analyses the data collected from the retail outlets and decides the variables on the basis of which segmentation is to be done.

Step 2 Targeting

Targeting is the next step in the sequential process and involves a business making choices about segment(s) on which resources are to be focused. There are five major targeting strategies: single segment or concentrated, selective specialisation, product specialisation, market specialisation, and full market coverage.

During this process the business must balance its resources and capabilities against the attractiveness of different segments.

i. *Single segment strategy*   It is a target market strategy in which only one segment of the market is chosen and a suitable marketing strategy is designed for that market. Normally this single-market strategy is used by small firms with limited resources. The firm concentrates on this segment and tries to make the best use of the segment.

Exhibit 7.2 Single segment strategy

ii. *Selective segmentation strategy*   This is a multiple-segment strategy, also known as a differentiated marketing strategy. Two or more than two segments are chosen by the firm depending on its resources and capabilities and the firm applies different strategies depending on the nature of the segments and its requirements.

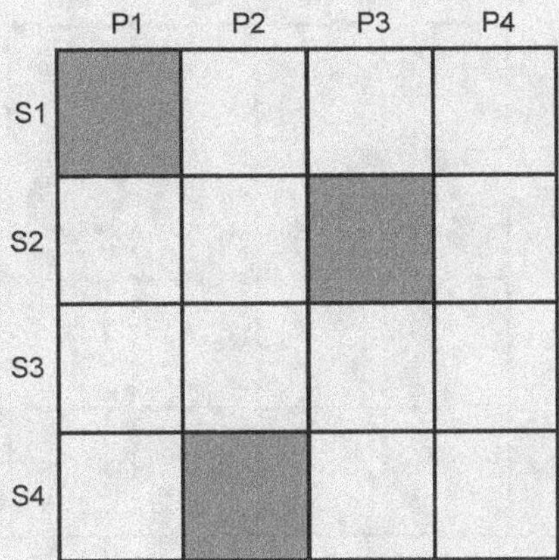

Exhibit 7.3   Selective segmentation strategy

iii. *Product specialisation strategy*   As the firm has limited number of products, usually single or two, it concentrates on those segments which are in need of these specific products. The firm specialises in specific strategies as well and employs these strategies to make use of in the market.

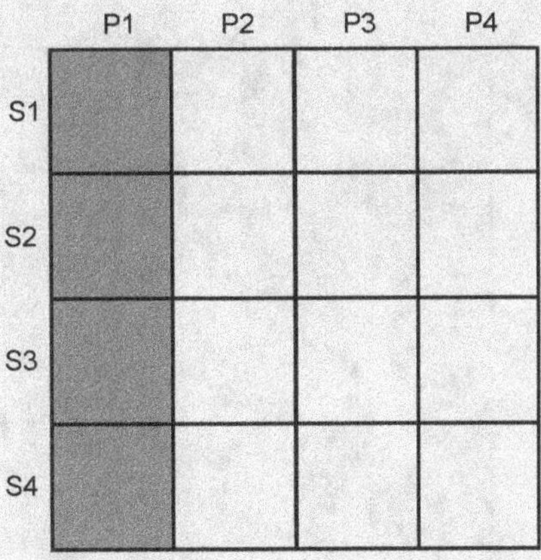

Exhibit 7.4   Product specialisation strategy

iv. *Market specialisation strategy*   The firm specialises in serving a particular market segment by understanding the characteristics of that market segment fully. Thus the firm becomes confident of handling the consumers belonging to that market and uses a strategy that would fully attract the consumers of that segment to the firm's fold.

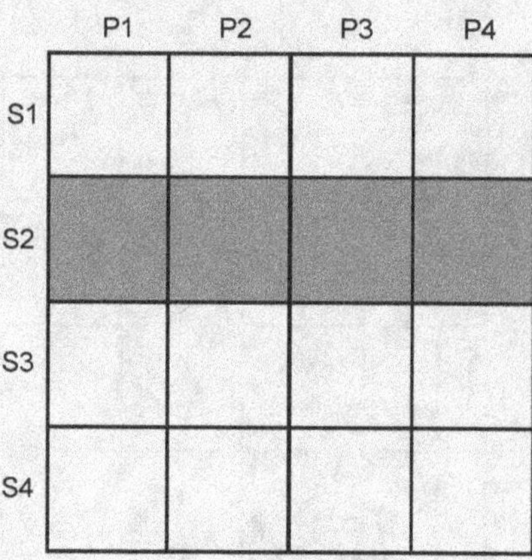

Exhibit 7.5   Market specialisation strategy

v. *Full market coverage strategy*   The firm attempts to serve the entire market. This coverage can be achieved by means of either a mass marketing strategy in which a single undifferentiated marketing mix is offered to the entire market, or by a differentiated strategy in which a separate marketing strategy is offered to each segment.

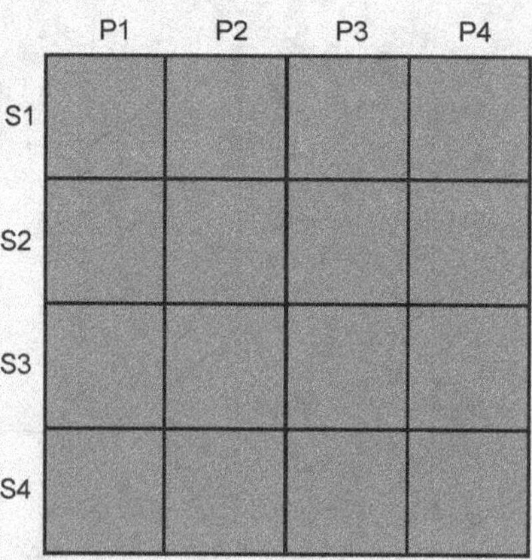

Exhibit 7.6   Full market coverage strategy

Step 3 Positioning

Positioning is the art of matching the firm's marketing message, with the desires, feelings, and beliefs of the particular type of customer that the firm knows it can service better than anybody else. Positioning follows on logically from the segmentation and targeting stages. Customer perceptions are central to the product position especially in relation to the competition's offering. The product or service has to satisfy key customer requirements and this has to be clearly communicated to customers.

When you speak about a product, one special attribute must come to the mind of the customer about the product instantaneously. That attribute must be a *good, special, and unforgettable* thing about the product. For many products, some negative aspects come instantaneously to the minds of the customers. The first step is to identify one specific attribute that sets the company, product, service or brand apart from competitors. When you say *Toyota*, you mean durability. When you say *BMW* or *VolksWagon*, you mean richness and quality. When you say *WalMart*, you mean quality, and low price. When you say *Volvo,* that one thing is *safety*. When it is *McDonalds*, it is a *fun place for kids.*

Let us study now what makes the process of fixing a position for a product, service, or a firm. But remember one thing! You must do this process very honestly.

Step 1   Prepare a list of attributes of the firm's product. Define your present position in the market as it is in the minds of the customers. Also state the place you want to reach.

Step 2   Make a list of all significant competitors and list out the features of their products. State their present position in the market.

Step 3   Now identify a specific attribute about your product that can differentiate it from the competition in a way that some consumers will find desirable. Kindly don't say your product does not have any special attribute. Yours has one.

Step 4   If you don't really have one special character for your product, you must create it. Do some research, and you will come out with it. Probe the possibility of creating awareness in the minds of your customers. Find out the strategy of creating a good place for you in the customers' mind.

Step 5   Chart out a step-by-step procedure in order that you will find a permanent place in the hearts of your customers.

Step 4   The Action Plan

The action plan contains the firm's strategy regarding the four P's of marketing. You must take these P's one by one and determine the activities you must perform to take a place in the market. Having identified the segmentation variables, the firm is in an advantageous position to chart out its course of action. Let us see what the action plan should contain.

1. The specifics regarding the changes you propose in your product, viz., the design, packaging, introducing more features, and so on.

2. The proposed pricing pattern and the factors the firm is to consider, if there is any change. The factors may include i) the income group of the segment(s) chosen for positioning, ii) the media selected for promotion, and iii) the preferences of the target consumers.

3. The proposed channel for the new positioning, the contract details with the new partners, viz., channel members, and the decisions regarding the launch of the product via the new channel.

4. The proposed changes in the promotional mix, viz., the content of the advertisement commercial, the media selection, proposal for any personal selling decision, the details of promotional package, and details of public relations proposals like demonstration and product campaigning.

A simple action plan   A simple action plan may contain the following activities:

* arranging with the artists to design the packaging cover
* determining the packaging material
* determining about minor changes in product design after consultation with a team of production and quality experts
* consulting with the management regarding the proposed changes in the price, whether it is an upward or a downward revision.
* preparing the details of agreement with the channel members in consultation with the firm's attorney.
* meeting the channel members in their places or in own premises and determining specific provisions of the contract.
* determining the specific details about the new promotional package like discounts, coupons, etc.
* determining the details of demonstration or product campaign in selected retail outlets.

One-to-one marketing   One-to-one marketing (sometimes expressed as *1:1 marketing*) is a customer relationship management (CRM) strategy emphasising personalised interactions with customers. The personalisation of interactions is thought to foster greater customer loyalty and better return on marketing investment. The concept of one-to-one marketing as a CRM approach is believed to be advanced by Don Peppers and Martha Rogers.[3] However, it may be said that only the term is new; the approach is almost as old as commerce itself. In the past, for example, proprietors of a general store would naturally take a one-to-one approach, remembering details about each customer's preferences and characteristics and using that knowledge to provide better service. One-to-one marketing seeks to reinvest marketing with the personal touch absent from many modern business interactions.

COMPETITIVE FORCES AND SEGMENTATION

An important factor that will affect segmentation in the future is the role of competitive forces. Michael Porter's 5-forces model[4] is relevant here. Porter's model of competitive forces assumes that there are five competitive forces that identify the competitive power in a business situation. These five competitive forces identified by the Michael Porter are:

1. Threat of substitute products
2. Threat of new entrants
3. Intense rivalry among existing players
4. Bargaining power of suppliers
5. Bargaining power of buyers

Threat of substitute products means how easily your customers can switch to your competitor's product. Threat of substitute is high when

* there are many substitute products available.
* customer can easily find the product or service that you are offering at the same or less price.
* quality of the competitors' product is better.
* substitute product is from a company earning high profits and can reduce prices to the lowest level.

A new entry of a competitor into your market also weakens your power. Threat of new entry depends upon entry and exit barriers. Threat of new entry is high when

* capital requirements to start the business are less.
* few economies of scale are in place.
* customers can easily switch (low switching cost).
* your key technology is not hard to acquire or is not protected well.
* your product is not differentiated.

Industry rivalry means the intensity of competition among the existing competitors in the market. Intensity of rivalry depends on the number of competitors and their capabilities. Industry rivalry is high when

- there are number of small or equal competitors and less when there is a clear market leader.
- customers have low switching costs.
- industry is growing.
- exit barriers are high and rivals stay and compete.
- fixed costs are high, resulting in huge production and reduction in prices.

Bargaining power of supplier means how strong is the position of a seller. How much your supplier has control over increasing the price of supplies. Suppliers are more powerful when

- suppliers are concentrated and well-organised.
- only a few substitutes are available to suppliers.
- their products are most effective or unique.
- switching cost, from one supplier to another, is high.
- you are not an important customer to the supplier.

Buyer's bargaining power may be lowered down by offering differentiated product. If you are serving a few but huge quantity of ordering buyers, then they have the power to dictate you.

PROCESS OF PRODUCT/FIRM POSITIONING FOR MASS MARKETING FIRMS

The process of finding a sure place for the product in the minds of the customers is called as positioning. It is concerned with the finding of a special place in their *minds*. When positioning is perfect, the firm can serve its customers better, and this will lead to successful marketing and will help in achieving corporate objectives. Therefore positioning plays a very important role in strategic marketing management.

Some products are of such nature that they need undifferentiated marketing. They are mainly fast moving consumer goods (FMCGs), and consumer electronic items. The products may be manufactured by small, medium or large companies. These companies market their products at local, provincial, or national levels. Undifferentiated marketing is also called as *mass marketing*. Mass marketing is concerned about advertising on a large-scale through mass media like television and radios. The entire market is treated as single segment and the marketing efforts of the firm are directed towards the whole market. The marketing strategies are designed in such a way that they attract all categories of customers.

Let us now study briefly the steps involved in the process of product positioning for mass marketing firms.

Step 1 *Design the product and its packaging suitably*   The first step in the process of product positioning is to design the product in such a way that its extrinsic and intrinsic features attract all the categories of consumers. This applies to packaging as well.

Step 2 *Price it reasonably*   Pricing must not be too low and at the same time, it should not be too high. The reason is obvious. If the price is too low it may not be preferred by rich people; if it is too high, the middle and lower class people may not afford to buy.

Step 3 *Build a strong brand for the product*   Products of mass marketing need a strong brand support. The brand will attract people from all classes. Brand building efforts must be made to create a strong brand base.

Step 4 *Make the product available at all outlets*   This step is very important in the sense that the nature of outlet is important for the consumer because not all the people would like to visit a departmental store for buying your product. Take the example of Proctor & Gamble's *Vicks Vaporub*. This product is available invariably in all kinds of stores ranging from a grocery store to a big departmental store.

PROCESS OF PRODUCT/FIRM POSITIONING FOR DIFFERENTIATED MARKETING FIRMS

First of all, one must decide whether the product is suitable for this kind of marketing because in this type of marketing the number of the consumers ought to be less. In differentiated marketing, the firm aims at specific set of customers who may possess more or less similar characteristics with regard to buying behaviour. The firm has to take all the steps to earn name and fame among the customers. Even though product/ firm positioning is important for a firm doing differentiated marketing, the same is necessary for firms doing undifferentiated marketing. Firms doing mass marketing spend millions of dollars to find place in the minds of customers, whereas in the other case, the sellers chart out strategies that will aim at specific group of consumers. This type of marketing is also known as niche marketing.

The success of niche marketing depends on how well one identifies his/her group of consumers and how well he/she designs the strategies to capture the niche market. The key is finding the market that most needs this product as well as can afford this product. You must collect necessary information from the market and then decide on the strategy to follow. For example, if you are a small manufacturer, your market may be near your place. If your product is a speciality product, you may have to advertise in the suitable media so that the message will reach the customers. Here, advertising plays a vital role in capturing the market. The ten commandments which you will find in the following section of the chapter can guide you rightly in approaching and formulating strategies for a niche market.

THE TEN COMMANDMENTS FOR PERFECT POSITIONING

Here we have ten useful ideas to place your product/service/firm in the hearts of the customers. Follow them and you will see light at the end. These strategies are valuable for consumer marketing as well as B2B marketing.

1. *Have satisfying quality in your product*   Quality is what matters for most of the customers. Customers won't be reluctant to buy your product if the quality of the product is able to satisfy them. We know the theory of consumer's surplus in economics. What does it say? Customers must have the feeling that they have paid for their product less than what it deserves and that they have enjoyed more out of the product. Follow the concept of consumer's surplus.

2. *Aim high. small profit is enough for the present*   You must aim high. You must aim at the larger market. Price your product/service with a small profit for the time being. You will get that time soon when whatever you do will work for you in the market. See that when you hike your price, there must be a genuine reason. The customer must not feel the pinch of your action. It is like inserting a sharp needle in a banana.

3. *Show reasonable concern for the customer*   Your concern for the customers must be well-measured. Too much of concern will create suspicion in the customers' mind. Guide them correctly. Have a pleasing face. Don't laugh loudly oftentimes during interaction with the customers. Enjoy the good points presented by the customer.

4. *Going too near the customer will have a negative impact*   The customers will go too far if you go too near to them. See that you keep the right distance. Your innocent act at the wrong time will drive away your customer. Don't be too much concerned about the customer.

5. *Present the facts and let him decide*   Recognise the fact that your duty is to present the facts. You cannot make a horse to eat the grass to your desire. The horse must have the need. So is a customer. You can never force a customer buy. Deciding to buy or not is their prerogative. Don't interfere in their freedom. Let them decide.

6. *Don't over-react to the customer's observations. Politely explain your position*   Customers are not identical. They have varied mental statures and it is your to respond carefully to any kind of situation. Don't get dragged into unnecessary arguments with a bad-tempered customer. When you see your customers, first read them through their face. Your assessment of the customers will be mostly perfect. You should not get angry with the customers when they raise irrelevant issues. Explain calmly and show the customers the door. Not all customers are seller-friendly.

7. *Ensure that no other seller has a better deal*   If customers say that another seller offers a better package, you may politely advise them to buy it. This shows your

confidence in your product/service. You can assure the customer about the quality and price of your product.

8 *Have strong points on your side* You must have very good reasons for the buyer to buy your product. You must have strong points on your side. Not all the customers are same in their preferences. Individuals differ in their tastes and preferences. When you say *safety* is your prime concern, there is a set of customers who prefer safety alone. They never look at other things. When you say your machine is *maintenance-free*, there is a set of customers who prefer to buy products which are *maintenance-free*. They do not bother about the life of the product or its price.

9 *Have the best promotional mix* You must formulate the best promotional mix for your product. If you do not have enough knowledge about it, seek the help of a good consultant. He/she will do it for you.

10 *You need to be an Arjuna to win the game* In Mahabharata, a great epic of India, the guru of the princes, Drona, asks his boys to aim at a bird sitting on a tree. One by one came for shooting the bird down and when the boys were about to shoot their arrows at the bird, Drona asked them to stop. He asked them what they saw when they aimed for shooting the bird. All the boys except Arjuna said they saw the tree, they saw the leaves and fruits with the bird, and they saw patches of cloud also along with the bird. Do you know what Arjuna said? Arjuna said that he saw the eye of the bird only and he saw nothing else. The lesson of this story is that you must pay your fullest attention to the task at hand, and that any deviation will fail you and you will be losing a lot.

SUMMARY

* Segmentation is necessary for most of the manufacturers in view of the benefits it bestows upon them. Mass marketing may be chosen if the product deserves it.

* Segmenting the market is a strategy that involves dividing a market into subsets of consumers who have common needs and applications for the goods and services offered in the market. Market segmentation is *the process of dividing the whole market into several submarkets on the basis of customer characteristics or behaviours in order to find out a suitable category of customers who may be targeted by the firm to market its goods.*

* There are two kinds of approaches for segmentation. The first approach is *top-down* approach. The second is *bottom-up* approach. In the former, the firm decides which segment of the market is most suitable for its operations. It is prudent for the marketer to identify in which segment his/her product has already

fit in the market by observing what category of people buys his/her products. This approach to segmentation is *bottom-up* approach.

* Literature on marketing suggests several bases for segmenting the market: geographic, demographic, psychographic, and behavioural.

* The features of segments are i) sufficient profit potential, ii) homogeneous needs, iii) accessible, iv) multiple uses, and v) measurability.

* The segmentation process is generally regarded as consisting of four stages: segmentation, targeting, positioning, and strategy planning.

* Porter's model of competitive forces assumes that there are five competitive forces that identify the competitive power in a business situation. These five competitive forces identified by Michael Porter are i) threat of substitute products, ii) threat of new entrants, iii) intense rivalry among existing players, iv) bargaining power of suppliers, and v) bargaining power of buyers.

* Ten strategies in the form of commandments have been given to place the product/service/firm in the hearts of the customers. They must be followed by them and light will be found at the end. These strategies are valuable for consumer marketing as well as B2B marketing.

REVIEW QUESTIONS

1. "Firms cannot manufacture goods to suit individual needs; this is quite impossible." Do you agree? Substantiate your answer.
2. Define market segmentation.
3. "Marketing segmentation is a logical outgrowth of marketing concept." Explain the statement with suitable arguments.
4. Explain the need for market segmentation.
5. "Segmentation of the market is not mandatory for the marketing organisation." Do you agree?
6. Explain the approaches to segmentation.
7. "Even if the marketer does not formulate a method to identify his/her segment, the market gets segmented by itself." Explain the logic behind this statement.
8. Explain the common bases used in segmentation.
9. "It is always good to limit our choices and select the best segment for our need." Is this statement agreeable to you? Explain your stand with suitable arguments.
10. Explain the features of market segments.

11. Explain the segmentation process suggested by Hiem and Schewe. State the defects present in their process.

12. Explain the four stages in the process of market segmentation.

13. Explain the target market strategies.

14. What are the steps in the process of positioning of a product?

15. What is one-to-one marketing?

16. "When you speak about a product, one special attribute must come to the mind of the customer about the product instantaneously." Do you agree? Substantiate your answer with valid points.

17. Explain the process of segmenting the market in the case of air conditioners.

18. Explain the 5-forces model of Michael Porter.

19. Explain briefly the steps involved in the process of product positioning for mass marketing firms.

20. How will you position a product of a differentiated marketing firm?

21. What are the ten commandments to be followed for perfect positioning of a product?

REFERENCES

1. Barwell, C. (1965). "The marketing concept." In: Wilson, A. (Ed.). *The Marketing of Industrial Products.* Hutchison, London.

2. Hiem, A. and Schewe, C.D. (1992). *The Portable MBA in Marketing.* Wiley.

3. Peppers, Don and Rogers, Martha. (1994). *The One to One Future.* Piakus, London.

4. Porter, M.E. (1979). *How Competitive Forces Shape Strategy.* Harvard Business Review, New Jersey.

8

STRATEGIC PRODUCT PRICING

After reading this chapter, you will be able to

- *understand the concept of strategic pricing,*

- *recognise the need for and importance of strategic pricing, and*

- *learn the process of strategic pricing.*

KEY TERMS

- Rational decision
- Pricing mechanism
- Strategic pricing
- Customer relationship management
- Strategic management process
- Consumer surplus
- Consumer panel

INTRODUCTION

Pricing is one of the key elements of marketing. Although it is only a part of the marketing mix, it is critical in achieving desired outcomes and specific marketing objectives. It is a tricky issue for an organisation which likes to do it with care and customers in mind because it is the pricing style that determines the firm's profit and sales levels. Of course, pricing is not a lone factor that decides the sales/profit of an organisation. Many other factors play in the game. For example, quality of the product is another key factor. Whatever price you fix, you cannot sell a product if it lacks the requisite quality. At the same time, the package has to be attractive; the firm must supply the product through the right channel; it must have the right kind of advertisement that would draw people to the product. There are many other factors that play their role in bringing the sales to the firm. These factors individually and collectively do their work and make the customer buy the product. This way the method of pricing and the strategy adopted to fix the price are very much a part of strategic product pricing. "Pricing is a bit like the weather. People complain about it, they worry about it, and in the end, they feel there is not much they can do about it."[1]

If the price is high, the customer may not buy the product. Similarly if the quality is poor, the product will have similar fate. If the price is low, it would not give the firm the required amount of margin. It is true that in some cases, even if the price is high, the customers buy it because it may be a matter of prestige for the buyer to be in possession of it. Some people may not buy a product because its price is very low. They may be under a perception that all the highly priced products are of high quality and that all the low-priced products are of poor quality. Studying the buyers' behaviour is truly a complicated task and many times the seller is unable to ascertain what customers have in their mind regarding the product. Of course, there are a number of surveys and studies that are used to find it out. But many of these surveys do not present the right picture because of their weaknesses.

Experts say that it is the emotional factor that helps make the buying decision. But we have to analyse what leads to this emotional decision. Emotional decision is not based on any hunch. When buyers decide to buy a car, they make a study of the features available in a particular car. Car buyers never sacrifice the safety aspects in a car which they propose to buy. Even in the case of buyers who are very much attracted towards a car because it looks so nice that they fall in love with the car, are not prepared to sacrifice the safety aspect in that car. They consider it the primary factor before buying the car. They may be even prepared to buy a car which may give poor mileage. Every car buyers have a secondary consideration before them when they buy the car. Of course safety becomes their first consideration. After safety what? Here comes their second requirement. It may be anything like the look, comfort, features, mileage, price, and maintenance. Sometimes, the buyers may like to have all these requirements in their car. If they want to have all these features in their car, then they may be called as a rational buyer. The truth is: buyers become emotional when they are satisfied that the particular car offers all that they require. They want to buy it as soon as possible. This is where emotion plays its role. Depending on the nature of the product, the emotional factor will work in the minds of the buyers.

The pricing process is a task to be performed by highly responsible people in a business organisation. Most of the companies in India do not consider it as a serious job because of the ignorance of a vast majority of Indian consumers. But the businesses cannot rule out the fact that the Indian consumers are becoming more and more sophisticated and knowledgeable and that they are going to play a big role in deciding the fate of many big business houses. These business houses do not have the requisite foresight and the ability to see the ground reality. They forget every rule when they enjoy bumper profits each year. They forget the fact that east or west, honesty is the best policy. They forget the fact the consumers must get value for their money in the *real* sense. In an era of globalisation, it is important that businesses must give the consumers what they *really* want. The consumers will repay the company for its gesture in the form of loyalty to the product.

There are many conventional methods of pricing like cost plus pricing, psychological pricing, target return pricing, marginal cost pricing, market-oriented pricing, premium pricing, penetration pricing, and so on. Whatever the method followed by the firm, it should not overlook the strategic aspect of the pricing policy.

WHAT IS STRATEGIC PRICING

A basic definition of strategic pricing is "… to price more profitably by capturing more value, not necessarily by making more sales." It is used to avoid the circumstance where "… vendors find themselves perpetually locked into a passive stance in which they are reacting to the tactics of customers and competitors, rather than proactively managing them."[2] We define strategic pricing this way: it is the process of identifying key factors which play a prominent role in the buying decision of the customer, ascertaining the real value, the product is expected to offer the customers, determining the price strategically giving due consideration to these factors, and capturing the market by employing proactive measures.

Strategic pricing is the coordination of interrelated marketing, competitive, and financial decisions to set prices profitably. For most companies, strategic pricing requires more than a change in attitude; it requires a change in when, how, and who makes pricing decisions. Perhaps, most important strategic pricing requires a new relationship between marketing and finance. Strategic pricing is actually the interface between marketing and finance. It involves finding a balance between the customer's desire to obtain good value and the firm's need to cover costs and earn profits.[3]

Strategic pricing involves recognising that not all pricing problems involve changing price as the best solution. The reason why pricing is ineffective is frequently not that the pricers have done a poor job. It is that decisions were made about costs, customers, and competitive strategy without correctly thinking through their broader financial implications.[4] As one marketing expert[5] aptly stated, "For marketing strategists, pricing is the moment of truth—all of marketing comes to focus in the pricing decision." Strategic pricing requires the management of the company to take responsibility for establishing a coherent set of pricing policies and procedures, consistent with its strategic goals for the company.[6]

The difference between price setting and strategic pricing is the difference between reacting to market conditions and proactively managing them. It is the reason why companies with similar market shares and technologies earn such different rewards for their efforts. An approach to pricing from a reactive point of view means that pricing decisions are made in reaction to a pricing problem, whereas proactive pricing is planned to exploit an opportunity.

WHEN DOES THE PRICING MATTER

Pricing is a signal to the whole market: customers and competitors. Customers are not identical in their thoughts and perceptions. We find wide variations in their opinions and behaviours. There are different types of customers. The brand-conscious customers are ready to pay any price for a product with which they have developed a liking and a permanent *connection*. Such customers are not price sensitive. Because of the bond they have developed over the years, they refuse to *change* their brand. This is known as brand loyalty.

A particular product may be appreciated by a customer as very good; but the same product may be branded by a different customer belonging to the same income and age group as useless and awkward. It is all the individual differences that make the difference. Researchers find it difficult to find reasons for difference in their behaviours. To understand consumer behaviour is to understand how the person interacts with the marketing mix. As described by Cohen, the marketing mix inputs (or the four P's of price, place, promotion, and product) are adapted and focused upon the consumer.

The customers do not always choose goods and services solely on price, performance and availability. The truth is that many purchases are influenced by a whole host of emotional reasons like esteem and image. Many of these non-rational reasons are hidden deep in their subconscious minds. Buyer behaviour involves both simple and complex mental processes. Marketers cannot capture human nature in its entirety but we can learn a lot about customers through research, observation and thinking. Here's Professor Theodore Levitt: "I think it is a process of trying to think your way through why people behave in certain ways. Or if not why, then what that behaviour is likely to be given certain kinds of products, certain kinds of... just stop to think." This is why customers are offered a variety of products in the same category. They are given sufficient choice by the producer and an opportunity to satisfy their expectations while buying a product.

We suggest here some reasons for why and when price matters for a customer.

1. *When the customer makes a rational decision*   Many consultants argue that most of the buying decisions are born out of emotions. This may be true in some cases but not always. A buying decision based on rational buying motives is generally the result of an objective review of available information. Some examples include: (i) profit potential or enhancement, (ii) quality of service, and (iii) availability of technical assistance. Rational buyers look for maximum benefit from the product. They do not get tempted by the outer look or package of the product. These customers make an evaluation regarding the money they pay and the value they receive. They make a study of these factors and finally decide whether to buy it or not.

2. *When the customer has limited resources at disposal*   The customers attach more importance to price when they are in financial crunch. When the customers are in such a condition that their financial position will not get corrected in the near future, they go for a product which offers the maximum for a lower price. It is quite natural that people go after a low-priced product, when they have many other commitments during the month or the next. They select their buys very carefully and try to save as much money as possible.

3. *When there are wide price variations among popular brands*   Certainly people start thinking when they find that the branded products are priced with wide variations. Their subconscious minds develop suspicion about their favourable product which is priced much higher. This customer rethinks on the next purchase "why my brand is sold at a much higher price?" and "why not try the other product this time?"

4. *When companions suggest a cheaper product with similar value*   Customers change their mind when a friend/companion makes a suggestion or criticises their way of buying. If they do not follow the suggestion of the companions they may become isolated in the society.

5. *When the customer had a bitter experience with a high-priced product*   It is true that some of the products which are high-priced lead to customer dissatisfaction because the product has consistently given poor performance to the customer. The customers become irked and change their policy altogether. They decide to buy products which are priced lower but give true value.

NEED FOR STRATEGIC PRICING

Michael Schneider, head of ABeam's CRM practice in Europe and co-author of the study on Strategic Pricing in Europe, explains: "When a company raises its prices, the expected consequence is a drop in demand. But how do some providers manage to improve their profit margins substantially while still keeping their sales volumes more or less steady? The answer is strategic pricing—a systematic approach to establishing and developing pricing strategies and systems."[7]

Pricing, at a particular stage, becomes one of the important competitive advantages for a company that manages its pricing process intelligently. It even becomes unbeatable and stands as a strong pillar for the organisation. It is true that such a pricing strategy, once found, becomes as a profit driver for the firm. An intelligent CEO looks for ways of not only cost cutting but also other intelligent ways in order to increase the profit levels of the organisation. Efforts must be made to maximise the profit without having the need to raise the price of the product. It is the best policy for all times, normal or abnormal. Strategic pricing is the way of pricing the product with the objective of turning the price into a competitive advantage of the firm. The slogans of strategic pricing are, "right value for right price" and "value for money".

We find companies selling their products for a much lower price and at the same time reducing the size of the product. These companies fail to recognise the fact that customers are not the same as they were earlier. They have become smarter and more sophisticated in their purchases. In India, we find this type of strategies very common among the manufacturers. The customers are very well aware that the company is offering the same product for a lower price but for a disproportionately smaller bottle/can. The irony is that even companies with high reputation do it. The real thing the company must do is, it must work hard to find ways and means to reduce the cost of manufacturing. You cannot argue that there is no way to do it.

Britannia Industries, a reputed biscuits company based at Kolkata, has been following the practice of maintaining the price but reducing the thickness of the product at the same time as in the case of its MarieGold. This is not a good practice. One has to be honest towards the customers. The biscuits manufacturer's act amounts to cheating the consumer. The company might argue that they have disclosed all the information on the package and that they are not doing anything unlawful. If they argue that the customers would not have a dissent for this act, they could have very well raised the price without reducing the weight of the pack instead of cutting the size of its product.

At times of recessionary situation, the following primary drivers of pricing decisions are affected. Therefore, in such a situation, strategic pricing must be practiced to bail out the organisation.

1. *Willingness to spend*   Consumers across all income segments will be looking for ways not to spend in order to keep their liquidity to meet most essential expenditures.

2. *Competitors' prices*   In a condition of recession, competitors will be tempted to reduce prices and sell their products in the market to maintain minimum liquidity in their companies. Of course, this would lead to price wars, and even advertisement wars.

3. *Company cash flows*   Fluctuation in commodity costs and uncertainty about volume will continue to disrupt supply chain costs.

4. *Pressing needs of customers*   Customers will be forced to spend on essential items which will be sold at higher prices even at times of recessionary trends.

In this environment, the company has to act intelligently and one important remedy that can help the company is strategic pricing. It can combat extreme price sensitivity with lower perceived prices, and manage the risk of price wars. For most companies, strategic pricing requires more than a change in attitude, it requires a change in when a pricing decision is made, how a pricing decision is made and who makes pricing decisions. For instance strategic pricing requires anticipating price levels before beginning product development.[8]

Whereas, price setting is one tactical decision in sales effort, the day-to-day management of pricing strategy is the coordination of multiple activities to achieve a common objective. While strategic pricing decisions can lead to long-term competitive advantage, tactical pricing often yields bigger and an immediate pay-off, it is the guerilla maneuvering to achieve the day's victory.[9]

Tactical pricing can be very helpful for a company in daily decision making process, it will help to

1. shift the mix of orders towards more profitable products.
2. reduce the amount of money left on the table in winning situations.
3. gain share by selectively cutting price with specific customers.
4. avoid the risk of price war.
5. exert upward pressure on industry prices in order to misdirect and confuse competitors.[10]

J. D. Richards, John Reynolds and Matt Hammerstein[11] have defined the organisational conditions for developing an integrated strategic pricing capability which will yield dramatic improvements in financial as well as organisational performance. First of all companies have to gain *talent* through training programmes to broaden and deepen technical pricing expertise and knowledge of company overall strategy. The next step should be the so-called strategic management process to be formed by a new pricing management team who would report to the executive committee, and take the responsibility for debating alternative pricing strategies, ensuring the decisions are consistent with the company's strategy. Last but not least, companies need a change in their *mindset and culture.*

A core group of managers with the expertise needed to develop pricing decisions that would be grounded in not only the company's own economics, but also competitor and market realities. The adoption of this model will generate new behaviours in the company life:

1. pricing will be based on strategic intent, not on profit targets
2. prices will be set proactively, not reactively
3. pricing changes will be agreed quickly and based on an evolving fact base
4. pricing decisions will be consequential and transparent, inducing a virtuous circle of performance.

THE STRATEGIC PRICING PROCESS

Pricing becomes strategic when management attaches due importance to the key factors involved in the buying decision of the customers. Fixing the right price for a product is an art and an art deserves appreciation and praise when it is performed with the necessary skills. Therefore, it goes without saying that the process of pricing requires the right skill to do it. The management must do it in style.

According to Bernhard Ebel, Markus Hofer, and Onno Oldeman of Simon, Kucher and Partners, a reputed international pricing consultant firm, management should concentrate more on "intelligent" price increases than on other measures like cost- cutting. They further state in their article *Strategic Pricing for Value* that managers and decision makers should acknowledge the price as the primary profit driver. Relative to cost-cutting, price optimisation offers three opportunities—it gains time, avoids additional upfront expenses, and has a stronger impact on profit. They add, many companies today do not follow systematic pricing process. Such a process is comprised of a system of organisational rules, guidelines, and measures intended to determine, manage and implement prices. Companies should apply innovative price strategies that focus on the customers' needs—so called value pricing—and implement such strategies by using an effective pricing process.

Bernhard Ebel, Markus Hofer, and Onno Oldeman suggest a strategic pricing process which is depicted in the Exhibit 8.1. The five phases of the strategic pricing process are—strategic guidelines, status quo check, price decision, implementation, and controlling/monitoring.

Exhibit 8.1 Five phases of strategic pricing process. Reproduced with permission of Onno Oldeman, Simon-Kucher and Partners, Amsterdam from their article Strategic Pricing for Value

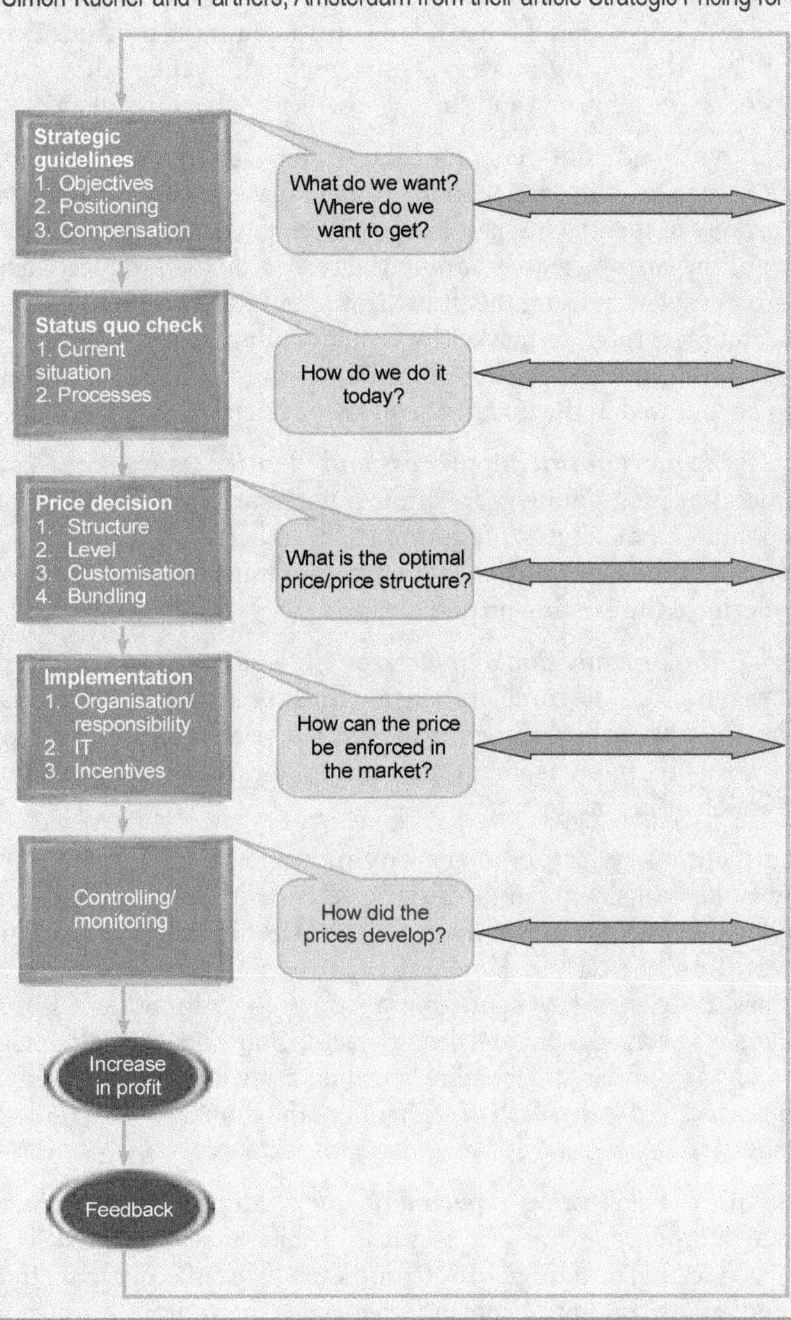

In the first phase, guidelines are framed. Questions like what do we want? and where do we want to get? are answered. In the second phase, the current situation, the existing pricing policies and processes are recorded. In the third phase, an appropriate price decision is made taking into account the previous two phases. In the fourth phase, the pricing process is implemented. In the fifth and final phase, the entire process is monitored and suitable corrective steps are taken.

Let us now study our version of the strategic pricing process. Our definition of strategic pricing gives the direction in this regard. We have defined the strategic pricing as the process of identifying key factors which play a prominent role in the buying decision of the customer, ascertaining the real value the product is expected to offer the customers, determining the price strategically giving due consideration to these factors, and capturing the market by employing proactive measures. We can derive the steps in the strategic pricing process from our definition. The following are the steps to be followed in the making of strategic pricing:

1. *Study the present pricing process and identify its weaknesses*   Whenever a new process or programme is drawn, it is necessary to identify the plus points and minus points of that process/programme. This is because the same defects should not get repeated in the new process. Therefore care must be taken to find out the merits and demerits of the existing process.

2. *Revisit the organisation's objectives*   It is necessary to take note of the goals of the organisation. The company's vision must be kept in mind because the vision of the company tells us how the company should be after a certain period of time. It is necessary that harmony is important on this point. Any deviation may not do good for the vision of the organisation.

3. **Identify the key factors in the buying decision**   The third step is to identify the key factors considered in the buying decision of the customer. In the case of the car buying decision, the most important key factor invariably for all customers is the safety feature of the vehicle. Almost all the customers look for it. After satisfying that the car has sufficient safety features, a customer looks for other features. Some of the customers may consider price as the key factor. Some others may consider mileage as the key factor. Similarly, depending on their taste and other aspects, the customer may look for several other features. Therefore the company must find out the primary and secondary key factors.

4. *Find out the real value expected of the product*   The most important step in the strategic product pricing process is to ascertain the real value expected to be offered by the product. Let us now go back to our knowledge of economics. In economics, we have studied the concept of consumer surplus. The concept of consumer surplus is

very relevant in the strategic pricing process. It is the measure of the welfare that people gain from the consumption of goods and services, or a measure of the benefits they derive from the exchange of goods. It is the difference between the total amount that the consumers are willing and able to pay for a good or service and the total amount that they actually do pay (that is, the market price of the product). Suppose that a consumer has purchased a product for ₹ 750. While consuming/using the product, the consumer feels that the product is worth more than ₹ 750, say, ₹ 1450. The difference between the actual price and the price the customer is ready to pay is ₹ 700. This amount is known as the consumer surplus.

The organisation, therefore, must find out the consumer surplus offered by its product. Sometimes there may be a consumer deficit. These consumer deficit products not only bring loss to the company but also damage the goodwill of the company. Such products must be withdrawn from the market. The company must employ the right method to ascertain the consumer surplus of a product. Many organisations have consumer panels. These consumer panels consist of the consumers who do their judgment without any bias. They speak out the truth regarding the quality of the product. They offer their comments about the pricing of the products when called for. The only important requirement is that these councils must consist of the *right* members.

Once the price the consumer is ready to pay is ascertained, the company must make a comparison of its prices with those of its close substitutes in the market. The company when fixing the price based on the consumer surplus must not ignore the prices prevalent in the market. The truth is that no customer will buy the product if the company fixes the price taking into account the data collected from the study of consumer surplus, unless it is market-based. Therefore the company must exercise utmost care while fixing the price based on value while there are close substitutes in the market. In the case of a new product this question does not arise.

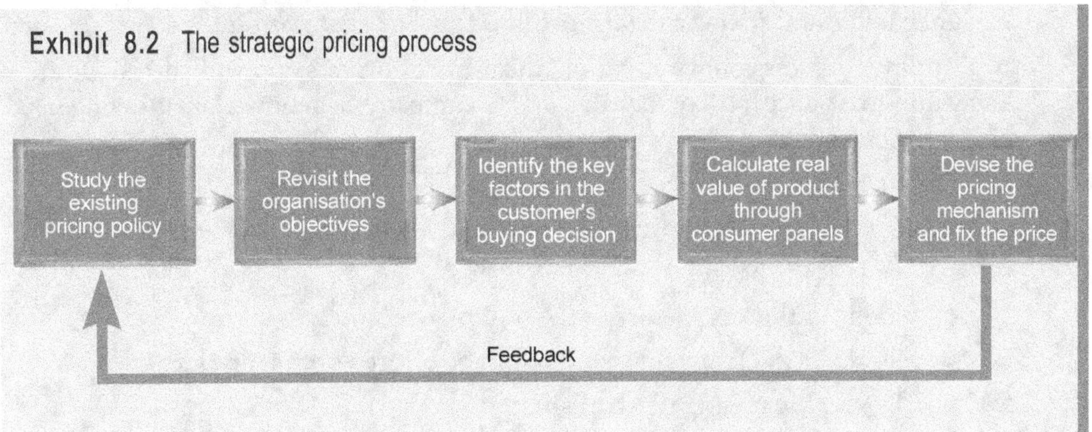

Exhibit 8.2 The strategic pricing process

5. *Devise the pricing mechanism*   In the final step, the organisation must devise a suitable pricing mechanism that would provide perfect pricing to the product. Here the management must decide how much of the consumer surplus must be charged and how much may be left to the advantage of the customer. The organisation should not be very optimistic in the sense that the customer would tolerate a nil-surplus. This may take the company to a point of no return. As a general rule and as a safety net, a fifty percentage of consumer surplus may be permitted to the benefit of the customer and the remaining may be added to the company's price.

SUMMARY

- Pricing is one of the key elements of marketing. Although it is only a part of the marketing mix, it is critical in achieving desired outcomes and specific marketing objectives. It is a tricky issue for an organisation which likes to do it with care and customers in mind because it is the pricing style that determines the firm's profit and sales levels.

- Strategic pricing is the process of identifying key factors which play a prominent role in the buying decision of the customer, ascertaining the real value the product is expected to offer the customers, determining the price strategically giving due consideration to these factors, and capturing the market by employing proactive measures.

- Buyer behaviour involves both simple and complex mental processes. Marketers cannot capture human nature in its entirety but we can learn a lot about customers through research, observation and thinking.

- Pricing, at a particular stage, becomes one of the important competitive advantages for a company that manages its pricing process intelligently. It even becomes unbeatable and stands as a strong pillar for the organisation.

- At times of recessionary situation, the primary drivers of pricing decisions are— willingness to spend, competitive prices, company cash flows, and pressing needs of the customers.

- The strategic pricing process involves the following steps:
    - Study the present pricing process and identify its weaknesses
    - Revisit the organisation's objectives
    - Identify the key factors in the buying decision
    - Find out the real value expected to be offered by the product
    - Devise the pricing mechanism

REVIEW QUESTIONS

1. "Pricing is a bit like the weather. People complain about it, they worry about it, and in the end, they feel there is not much they can do about it." Substantiate the statement with suitable arguments.

2. "Experts say that it is the emotional factor that helps make the buying decision." Explain the statement giving suitable arguments for your position.

3. Explain the concept of strategic pricing.

4. When does pricing matter? Explain your answer with suitable examples from reality.

5. "Pricing, at a particular stage, becomes one of the important competitive advantages for a company." Do you agree? Explain your points in detail.

6. "We find companies selling their products for much lower price and at the same time reducing the size of the product." Explore the truth in the statement.

7. How do you tackle the problem of pricing during recessionary trend?

8. What do you do in tactical pricing?

9. Explain in detail the process of strategic pricing.

10. "Once the price the consumer is ready to pay is ascertained, the company must make a comparison of its prices with those of its close substitutes in the market." How would you proceed with this comparison? What steps would you follow in the process?

REFERENCES

1. Robert, A. Garda. (1992). "Tactical pricing." *The McKinsey Quarterly.* No. 3, p. 1

2. Thomas Nagle and John Hogan. (2006). *The Strategy and Tactics of Pricing.* Pearson Prentice Hall, New Jersey.

3. Micu Adrian and Coita Dorin-Cristian. (2009). *"Strategic pricing role in settling the firm position on the market." Journal of Marketing.* 4: 725.

4. *Ibid* p. 727.

5. Corey, R. (1983). *Industrial Marketing: Cases and Concepts,* 3rd edn. Prentice-Hall Inc., Englewood Cliffs, NJ. p. 311.

6. Nagle, T. Thomas and Hogan, E. John (2006). *The Strategy and Tactics of Pricing: A Guide to Growing More Profitably,* 4th edn. Pearson/Prentice Hall. Upper Saddle River, NJ. p. 2.

7.   A report titled 'ABeam Consulting Releases Results of European Strategic Pricing Survey'; URL: http://www.abeam.com/global/article/2008/11/03/abeam-consulting-releases-results-of-european-strategic-pricing-survey.html

8.   Andrea Erika Nyárádi. (2007). *Strategic Pricing–A Part of Company's Strategy.* 5th International Conference on Management, Enterprise and Benchmarking, June 1-2, Budapest, Hungary. p. 135.

9.   *Ibid* p. 136.

10.   Robert A. Garda. (1992). "Tactical pricing." *The McKinsey Quarterly.* No. 3, p. 3.

11.   Richards, J. D. , John Reynolds, Matt Hammerstein. (2005). "The Neglected Art of Strategic Pricing." *Financial Executive.* p. 4.

THE DISTRIBUTION STRATEGY

9

After reading this chapter, you will be able to

- *recognise the need for middlemen,*

- *understand the factors determining the right channel of distribution for a product,*

- *learn the concept of multi-channel marketing,*

- *understand about the strategic channel alliances, and*

- *learn about vertical marketing systems.*

KEY TERMS

- Multiple channel
- Multi-channel marketing
- Strategic channel alliances
- Horizontal marketing system
- Competitive advantage
- Vertical marketing systems
- Media-mix strategy
- Conventional marketing system
- Corporate VMS
- Administered VMS
- Contractual VMS
- Channel management

INTRODUCTION

Management is a peculiar function. In a business organisation, the executives cannot show any kind of slackness to even a remote or relatively small factor like distribution. They cannot say that this is more important and that is less important in an organisation. The businessperson/executive must take utmost care in managing the affairs of a business. In their task of accomplishing the stated objective, the executive, like a director of a movie, has to pay attention to all the aspects of the organisation. They are very lucky when they have with them people of talents, sincerity, and honesty. Only such people can remain relaxed in their seat/home. The same is the case for a superior in a department. When the superiors are surrounded by talented people, they can hope for successful accomplishment of the assigned job. Therefore, it is clear now that everything depends on the calibre of the employees. In this regard, the management cannot ignore the importance of distribution. At crucial times, a perfect distribution strategy can give the organisation a good amount of profit. This may happen if the products offered by the close rivals are identical in all respects like quality, price, and so on and the difference exists only in the distribution strategy. In this case, the distribution strategy can help produce a reasonable amount of profits by cutting the cost of distribution. Therefore, distribution is an important function in an organisation; but the most important point is that it must be monitored by the management continually once a perfect strategy gets implemented.

WHAT IS A CHANNEL OF DISTRIBUTION

Stern and El-Ansary[1] define: "Marketing channels are sets of interdependent organisations involved in the process of making a product or service available for use or consumption." The product must reach the consumer from the producer and it is the producer's responsibility to see to it that it reaches the consumer on time. If the product does not reach the consumer at the right time, the organisation is bound to lose money and goodwill. Therefore, the producer decides to take the product to the consumer through a specific route. This route/path along which goods move in the process is called the channel of distribution. Between the producer and the consumer, there may be any number of middlemen depending upon various factors. There may be a single middleman; or two, or three, or more. The exact number depends on several factors. It depends mostly on the distance between the producer and the consumer, and the nature of the product. If the producer is located in India and the customer is in Africa, the route taken by the product to reach the consumer is bound to be lengthy and it is no surprise that in this case, many people will be involved in the process. At the same time, if the consumer is located next door, reaching the product to the consumer is no problem. In this case, the price of the product will also be much less leading to mutual benefit to the manufacturer and the buyer. Exhibit 9.1 tells us a few of the options the producer may use to take the goods to the consumer.

The number of middlemen will vary depending upon the nature of the market, product, and so on. A direct marketing channel consists of just two members—a producer and a consumer. By contrast, a channel that includes one or more intermediaries (wholesaler, distributor, or broker or agent) is an indirect channel. Companies often utilise multiple channels to reach more customers and increase their effectiveness. The channels vary for an industrial goods producer. In most cases, it involves direct marketing through company salespersons. Sometimes, the company may entrust the task to an industrial distributor or agent/broker who makes all the arrangements to market the goods of the industrial producer.

Exhibit 9.1   A few channels of distribution

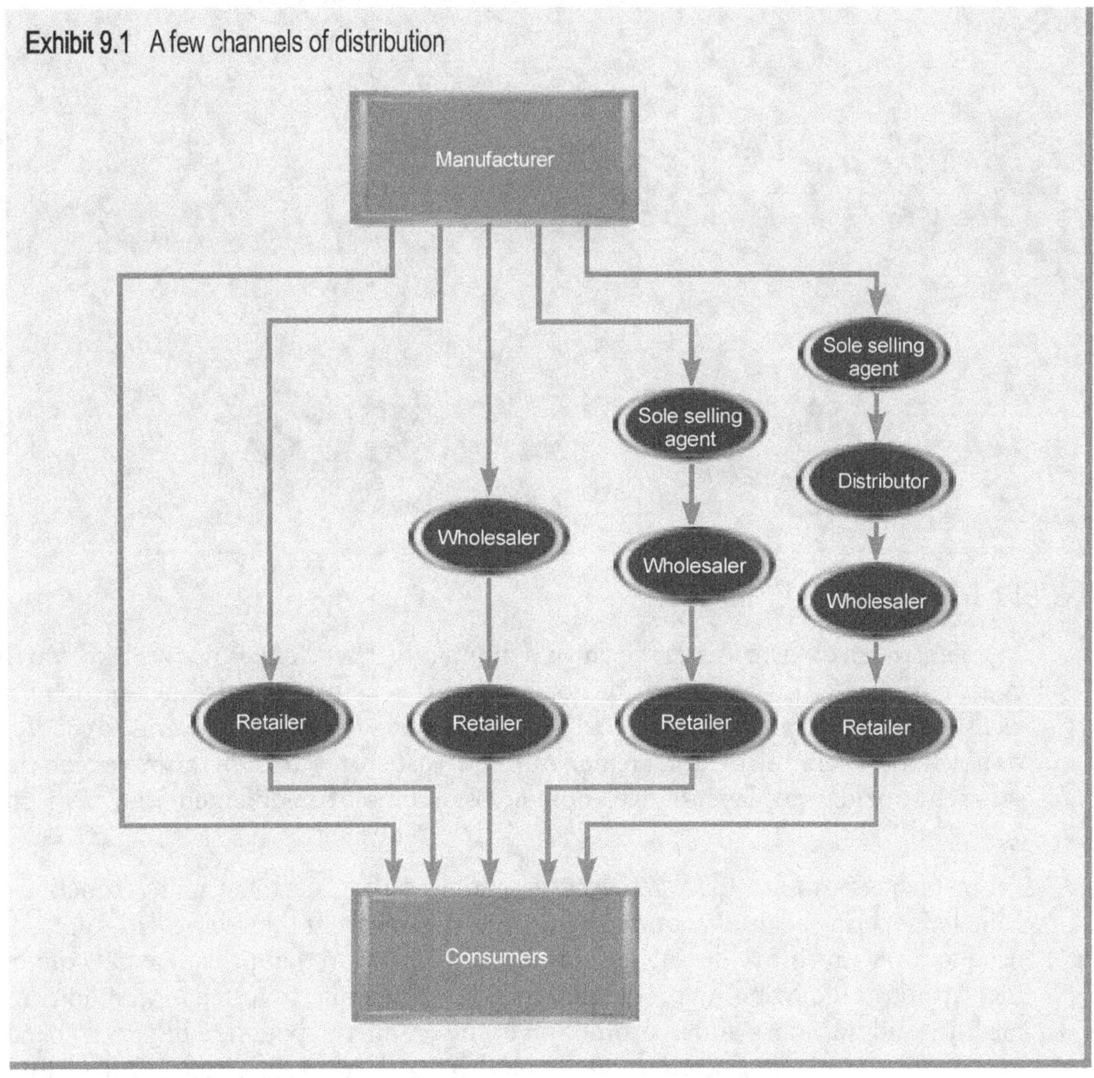

A marketing channel is critical to large and small businesses because they use these distribution channels to meet their marketing objectives by providing or delivering products and services that generate profit and customer base. Therefore, the decision to choose a particular channel becomes very important.

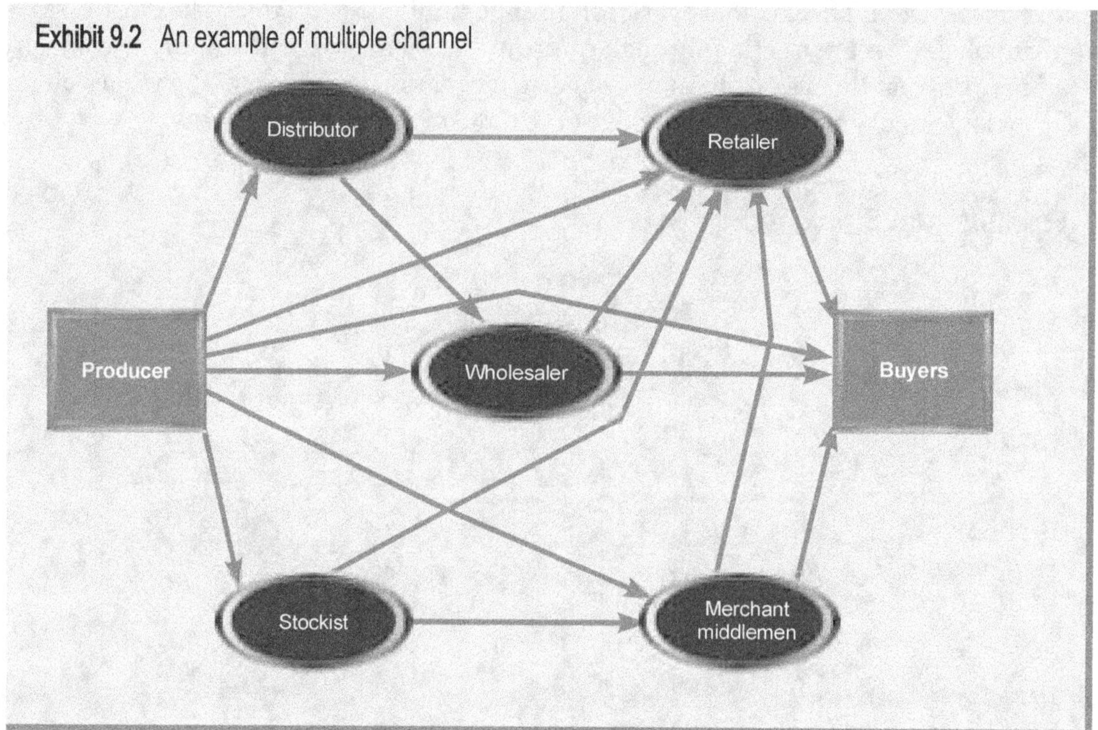

Exhibit 9.2 An example of multiple channel

NEED FOR MIDDLEMEN

Middlemen have existed since the dawn of humanity. Every one is not well-known to every other one. In this situation, one needs the help of a third person who is well-known to him and at the same time to the person with whom he wants to conduct transactions. Therefore the middleman must be trustworthy to both the buyer and the seller. In our day to day life, we come across scores of middlemen who help life go smooth.

In business, middlemen are very essential as they perform many functions. Middlemen bring additional capital to the industry segment they serve. This capital is used to carry inventory during periods of low demand so that peak demands can be met without wide swings in production rates. Capital is also invested in warehousing facilities and transport, and in promotion of the product to potential buyers. When a supplier operates in one location and their buyers are located at a distance, middlemen who are located near the buyers add value in the form of market knowledge, personal relationships, and intimate knowledge of the prevailing culture and laws.

Middlemen as Suppliers

A middleman finds out the source of the goods and brings them to the doorsteps of the consumer. He possesses lot of knowledge about the whereabouts of the goods and reaches out to the producer and makes judgment on the quality and other aspects of the goods. He decides whether the goods are the same ones required by the consumers in his place. He buys them in required quantities and keeps a good stock of them so that he supplies them to his customers without any interruption.

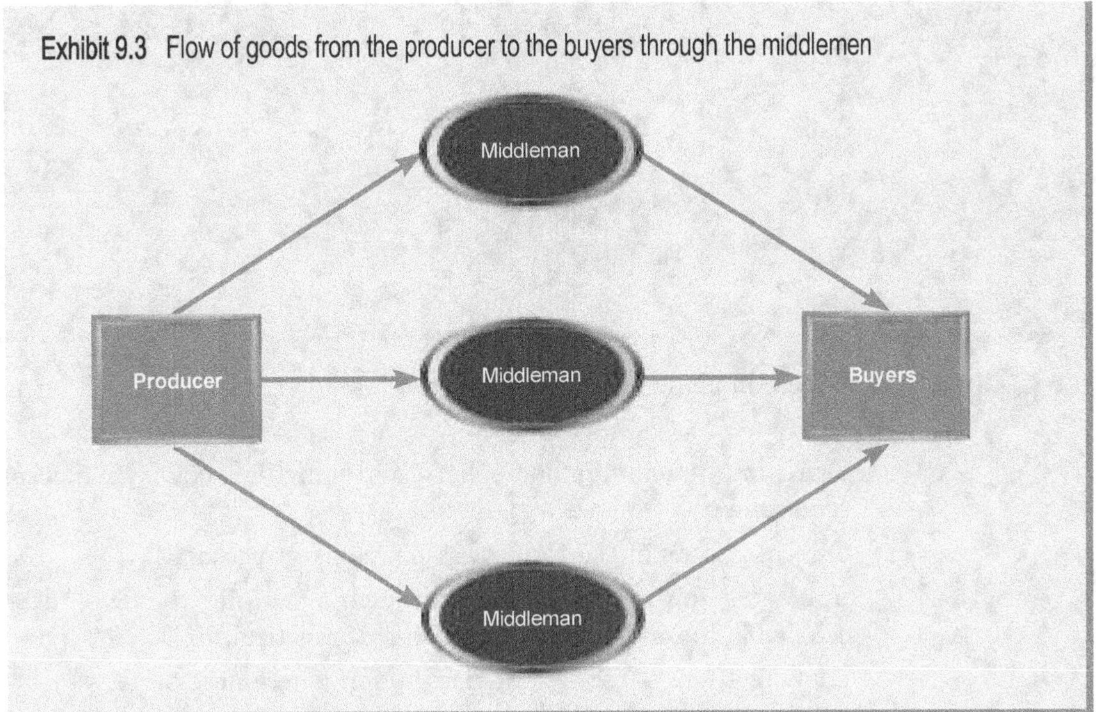

Exhibit 9.3   Flow of goods from the producer to the buyers through the middlemen

Middlemen as Providers

The channel members collect important information about the customers, their behaviour and change in their tastes and attitudes to the manufacturer. This information helps the organisation in many ways. The company is able to formulate its marketing strategy based on the information provided by sincere middlemen. Sometimes the wholesaler buys goods on cash basis from manufacturers and sells them on credit to retailers. In this way he provides financial help both to the producers and retailers. If necessary, the wholesaler also provides financial help by way of advance payment to producers.

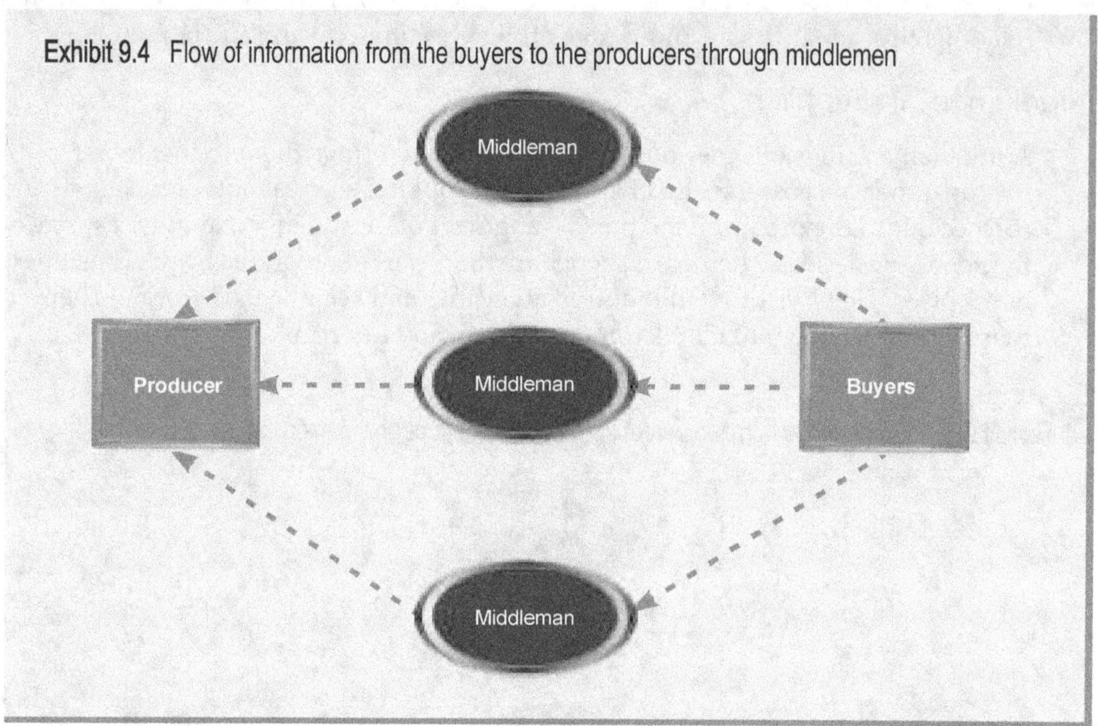

In addition, the middlemen are helpful to the manufacturer in the following ways:

1. Searching out buyers and sellers, and matching goods to market requirements.

2. Offering goods in the form of assortments or packages.

3. Implementing pricing policies in such a manner that would be acceptable to buyers and ensure effective distribution.

4. Looking after the process of distribution where necessary.

5. Participating actively in the creation and establishment of a market for a new product.

6. Offering after-sale services to consumers.

7. Offering credit to retailers and consumers.

8. Risk bearing with reference to stock hoarding/transport.

Middlemen in business help the seller and buyer in accomplishing their objectives. Since they are knowledgeable people in their field, they are very much required for a business to succeed.

FACTORS DETERMINING THE RIGHT CHANNEL

Effective distribution channels are essential for a successful organisation. The first important point is the company must be able to deliver the goods on time to the customer. The second important thing is the quality of the product. The quality must be the *right* one, not *very superior*, and certainly not below the quality of goods available in the market at the time. High quality may involve lot of money to produce. Therefore, logically the third point is the price. The price must be affordable to the customer. As far as the channel members are concerned, the mantra for the organisation is this: the less "middle men" that are in the delivery chain the better, as every link has a potential cost. The organisation must not fail to note the point that these channel members put in their experience, their money, and talents to the successful marketing of the products.

Choosing the right channel to move the products to the end user is a long-term strategic decision. Decisions like this cannot be changed according to the whims and fancies of the organisation. Since channels involve outsiders to the organisation, the executive in charge of the channel-decision must approach the issue carefully. A well-chosen channel is necessary because it constitutes significant competitive advantage to the organisation. The prospective channel must save on cost, improve and increase efficiency, and reduce channel-related conflicts. Poorly chosen channels can have long- term consequences and can, in turn, lead to product failures in the market. Therefore, enough care must be taken in determining the right channel for the organisation. Let us now dwell at the factors that must be considered at the time of channel selection.

Market Factors

Market factors include the family lifestyles of the consumers, market size, competition, segmentation, and so on. These market factors need to be considered by the management while determining the channel for its organisation. The consumers' lifestyle in India, today, has greatly changed. They have started using internet for making purchases which was a trend that was visible in the US. Internet marketing, which is not playing a major role today, is expected to pick up in the country very soon. Electronic commerce which is an important component of internet marketing helps to trace the manufacturers with ease and comfort and this reduces the need for middlemen for many products. The latest statistics reveal that 400 million people access internet regularly in India and that is a jump of 700% in the last six years. If the market size is sufficiently large and highly dispersed, the company has to have many middlemen in order to reach out for the customer. When the customers are located in high density, the company need not possess a large number of middlemen. The nature of the market, including segmentation, and its size are important factors in determining the nature of the channel.

Consumer Factors

Questions like who are your customers? from where do they buy? and how do they buy? can help to understand the connection between the channel and the consumers. Answers to these and other similar questions can guide one to the right solution.

If the customers belong to high income group, it would be wise to choose the channel which would help them to reach out to the particular outlet quickly. These customers cannot be reached by selling through ordinary retail outlets. The goods need to be sold in sophisticated outlets like departmental stores with facility for car parking.

Product Factors

Product factors include product sophistication, cost of the product, product standardisation, stage in the life cycle, and so on. Sophisticated products require channels manned by suitable people and the company has to search for specific channels which can sell these goods.

Organisational Factors

Organisational factors include the financial resources, available human resources, technological capabilities, managerial talents, marketing talents, and the organisation's desire for control over the channel members.

All the factors listed above collectively lead to the channel-decision. The management has to find out a balance giving priority to critical factors because it is these critical factors that determine the success of the channel-policy of the organisation. All the other factors must be considered from their relevance point of view to the organisation's need.

MULTI-CHANNEL MARKETING

Multi-channel marketing uses more than one purchasing mode to give customers access to products and services. These different channels could include websites, retail stores, mail order catalogues, direct mail and e-mail. Multi-channel marketing involves using two or more of these channels to provide increased benefits to both the company and its customers. One should not get confused with multiple channel. Multi-channel is totally different from multiple channel. Multiple channel marketing offers customers more than one channel to buy from or interact with a company, and can incorporate both traditional and newer media like sending catalogues through mail and sending e-mails. The company may use conservative channels like wholesalers and retailers. With a multi-channel approach, the marketing executive would use the same list of prospects to promote an event through two or more integrated disciplines, such as an e-mail with an embedded link to a website, or an SMS (short message service) message reminding recipients to call to register. Delivering multiple impressions and giving prospects a variety of ways to respond can dramatically improve results.

Although multi-channel marketing is not a new concept, it is becoming popular nowadays the world over. It has its roots in the erstwhile media-mix strategy which was followed by a large number of organisations. But this media-mix strategy did not become popular due to reasons unknown and it is reborn in the form of multi-channel marketing strategy. The following are the reasons why this strategy is becoming popular today.

1. Competition in the market is increasing day-by-day. The manufacturers are after the consumers using all the possible means to get their support.

2. The cost for acquiring a customer is increasing causing changes in the strategy of the manufacturers.

3. Satisfied customers have become a good source for new business. They bring in new customers thus considerably reducing the efforts of the organisation to find new customers.

4. The number of new channels available has increased. In the pre-information technology era, the middlemen available were limited in number and the channels were conventional. But today, we find a score of new kinds of channels even though they have a few disadvantages. Consumers are directly communicated by the manufacturers reducing the effort, time, and cost considerably. The evident fact is that consumers prefer personalised communication by the manufacturers.

Manufacturers opting for new and personalised channels create wonderful campaigns for attracting the customers. Once these customers are satisfied with the services of the manufacturers/suppliers, they remain rock solid with them for ever. This is the biggest advantage of these new personalised channels like e-mail marketing. Good campaigns reach the customers in a systematic manner. Personalised greetings to the consumers make them happy. In this way, firms are increasingly taking advantage of this innovative method of carrying out multi-channel campaigns for their customers.

The channels that may be used under a multi-channel marketing programme may be as follows:

* **RSS feeds** The marketing executive leverages RSS (Really Simple Syndication) technology to deliver fresh, relevant content directly to prospects, through campaign e-mails and hosted web pages.

- ✻ **SMS** The marketing executive builds higher levels of engagement with his/her prospects by communicating to them in a format they desire, via personalised short text messages to a mobile phone.

- ✻ **Call on demand** The marketing executive leverages the low cost and speed of delivery that integrated call services offer, communicating to prospects via personalised text-to-speech messages or recorded voice messages.

- ✻ **Fax** He/she taps into the simple, cost-effective means of reaching contacts through personalised fax communications.

- ✻ **Print mail** The marketing executive has to create automatically customised, digital direct mail documents and offers that outperform static mailers and conventional communications.

- ✻ **Hypersites** Creates customised URLs that engage the prospects in a personalised, relevant dialogue.

STRATEGIC CHANNEL ALLIANCES

Strategic alliances are a significant part of every business, from marketing to finance to manufacturing and service. According to Steve Steinhilber[2], Cisco Vice President of Strategic Alliances, "a strategic alliance is a relationship between one or more organisations that through the combination of resources can create significant and sustainable value for everyone involved." The strategic alliance can be worked out for marketing channels of organisations participating in the alliance.

Competitive advantage is gained by an organisation's ability to assemble collaborative teams from across the alliances in real time to harness the knowledge of the collective as fast as possible.[3] This new work paradigm has given rise to many technology trends that enable better communications and collaboration between the various constituents of the extended enterprise. A strategic alliance may encompass an entire array of organisational functions or a specific function. The competitive advantage may be gained by strategic channel alliances too. Channel sales alliances help extend the reach of one's brand and solutions into markets where localised sales, service and support is required to assist the customers.

A strategic channel alliance is an agreement whereby the products of one organisation are distributed through the marketing channels of another. This kind of distribution is also known as horizontal marketing system. In this strategy, two or more corporations on the same level join together for the purposes of pursuing a new marketing opportunity. Usually a horizontal marketing system is established so that the individual members can combine resources to make the most out of the marketing situation. This enables a company to use another company's well-established channel.

This is done because creation and nurturing of new channels will not only consume lot of time but also the performance of such newly created channels is not assured.

Ramco Systems Enterprise Networking Solutions[4], one of the leading networking integrators in the country, entered into a strategic channel alliance with 3Com India Ltd., the Indian arm of the $5.6 billion global networking major, to distribute their entire range of hubs and switches in India. The tie-up covers the entire Indian Corporate and Small and Medium Enterprise markets.

The range of 3Com networking products now available through Ramco Systems' eight sales and support offices and its 150 channel partners across the country, includes the entire family of Superstack II switches; NetBuilder and PathBuilder switches; and stackable and unstackable hubs. 3Com e-Networks support the next generation of mission critical voice, video and data applications which speed up and extend enterprise activities and open up a whole world of e-business opportunities.

It is also interesting to note that Ramco Systems has an exclusive channel programme called Ramco Systems Partner Programme which is designed to provide the partner the right expertise, train and educate the partner in providing end-to-end networking solutions and help the partner in achieving his/her business objective by adopting a collaborative approach.

Let us see a few latest strategic marketing channel alliances present in India and abroad.

1. The alliance[5] between Max New York Life Insurance, one of India's leading Life Insurance Companies, and Etawah Urban Cooperative Bank is worth noting. Max New York Life Insurance will utilise the branch network of the Bank to sell its life insurance products. The tie-up with Etawaha Urban Cooperative Bank will provide Max New York Life Insurance a channel to reach out to the Bank's customers, and in turn provide solutions to all financial needs of the customers under one roof.

2. AGC Networks[6] has entered into a strategic agreement with NEC India to distribute, install and support products from its Private Network Solutions (PNS) division. With this strategic arrangement, AGC Networks will offer NEC's Key Telephone Systems, PBX and IP PBX systems through its channel partners and system integrators in the country.

3. To facilitate the shift toward collaboration as a business-process enabler, Cisco has partnered with several leading IT solution providers and vendors, including Accenture, Apple, AT&T, British Telecom, Fujitsu, IBM, Italtel, Johnson Controls, Microsoft, Nokia, Tata Consultancy, and Wipro. Cisco's vision is to enable boundary-less collaboration for customers and their partners, suppliers, and customers. They are deeply committed to working

with other market experts to deliver solutions around collaboration. This commitment to partnering offers customers a choice of "best-of-class" solutions. The Cisco partner community is very broad, enabling them to serve the diverse needs of their customers.

4. Harley-Davidson has a strategic channel alliance with Best Western.

5. Reliance Communications (RCOM)[7], India's largest and only telecom operator offering nationwide CDMA and GSM mobile services, and GetJar, the world's second largest Apps Store announced in April 2010, a strategic alliance between the two companies. According to this alliance, GetJar will offer Reliance Communications its extensive catalog of over 65,000 free mobile applications. Reliance Communication's over 100 million subscribers will gain immediate access to GetJar's massive library of applications via a GetJar Apps Store through RCOM's VAS platform R-World. GetJar will also enable RCOM to offer its Apps Store to a large bandwidth of mobile handsets across multiple brands and not remain restricted to a few high-end smartphones. Reliance Communications will offer the GetJar Apps Store across GSM and CDMA networks.

VERTICAL MARKETING SYSTEMS

A vertical marketing system (VMS) is a strategy of creating a new kind of channel activity in which a single channel member coordinates the activities of all the major channel members in order to maximise the marketing efficiency of all the channel members by cooperating with each other without any confrontation among the members of the organisation's channels. The coordinating channel member manages channel activities to achieve efficient, low cost distribution aimed at satisfying the target market customers. Vertical marketing strategy is akin to vertical integration. The difference between them is the presence of the spirit of cooperation under the vertical marketing system.

In conventional marketing systems, producers, wholesalers, and retailers are separate businesses that are all trying to maximise their profits. When the effort of one channel member to maximise profits comes at the expense of other members, conflicts can arise that reduce profits for the entire channel. To address this problem, more and more companies are forming vertical marketing systems.

There are three types[8] of vertical marketing systems: corporate, administered, and contractual. Under a corporate vertical marketing system, all the links/members in the vertical supply chain are owned and/or controlled by a single corporate entity. Contractual vertical marketing systems come about when multiple members in the supply chain agree to operate cooperatively to develop their business with terms and conditions agreeable to all of them. An administered vertical marketing system happens when some businesses in the supply chain are dependent on a dominant channel member in the supply chain. Therefore, the dominant business usually dictates the decisions of the other businesses in the chain. The dominant member takes care of the business health of the other members and does not try to eliminate or eat away the profit of other members.

A very important advantage of the vertical marketing strategy is that the manufacturer and the channel members stand to gain from the new arrangement. Cooperation is the mantra of this strategy. The manufacturer and the channel members create a network and thus a strategy is framed to effectively function in the market. This strategy of vertical marketing system also helps the channel members to exchange their experiences and evolve new methods to provide satisfaction to the customers.

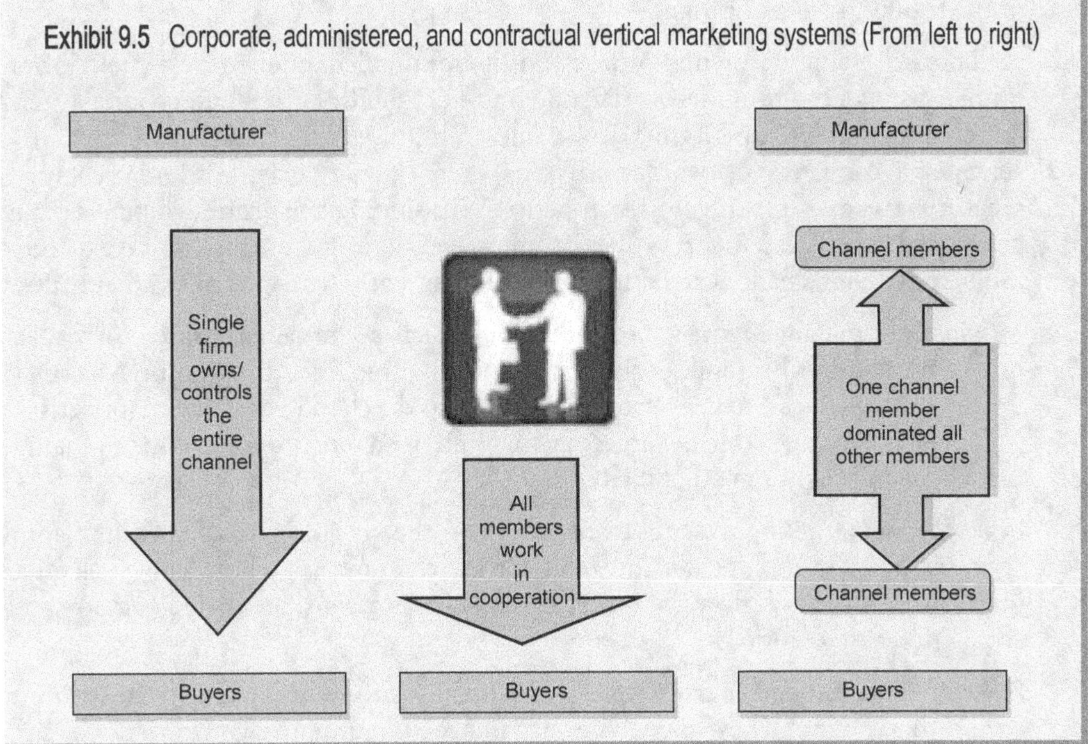

Exhibit 9.5 Corporate, administered, and contractual vertical marketing systems (From left to right)

Another important advantage of the vertical marketing system is that it helps to wipe out altogether conflicts between channel members. In an ordinary channel of distribution, conflicts among the channel members are very common. Avoidance of conflicts leads to a competitive advantage to the manufacturer. Conferences are convened often by the manufacturer to create an understanding between the channel members. These conferences provide a platform to the channel members to share their experiences in the marketplace.

CHANNEL MANAGEMENT

Channel management serves as one of the most critical ways that a company can better serve its customers and establish competitive advantage. Customer satisfaction is not solely achieved through a superior product. Establishing and leveraging a targeted channel strategy enables companies to align their supply chains with customers' requirements—and to do so profitably. But today's complex distribution systems make this a challenging task. But any task, however challenging it may look, can be accomplished through the effective application of mind and devising an effective action plan and executing it. This action plan is called by us as strategy. Strategies are born out of systematic application of mind. Therefore what is needed is systematic application of the thinking power of man.

Like all elements of marketing and operations, channel management offers numerous chances to improve revenue and profitability. Effective channels serve targeted customer segments, maximise sales, minimise cost and provide companies a sustainable competitive advantage. By analysing how important different channels are to a company's total revenue, competitive positioning and profits, channels can be prioritised for enhancement. With customer needs in mind, the marketing executive can help redesign channel structure and management to enhance sales and profits.

Channel management, as a process by which a company creates formalised programmes for selling and servicing customers within a specific channel, can really impact one's business. To get started, first segment the channels by like characteristics (their needs, buying patterns, success factors, and so on) and then customise a channel management programme that includes:

1. *Goals*   The marketing executives must define the specific goals for each channel segment. They must consider the goals for the channel as a whole as well as on an individual basis. And, they should also remember to consider their goals for both acquisition and retention.

2. *Policies*   They must construct well-defined policies for administering the accounts within this channel. They have to be sure to keep the unique characteristics of each segment in mind when defining policies for account set-up, order management, product fulfilment, and so on.

3. *Products*   The marketing executives must identify which product in their offering is most suited for each segment and create appropriate messaging. Also, they must determine where their upsell opportunities lie.

4.　*Sales/marketing programmes*　The marketing executives must design support programmes for their channel that meet the organisation's needs, not what their idea of its needs are. To do this, they should start by asking their customers within this segment, "how can we best support you in the selling and marketing of our products?" That being said, the standard considerations are product training, cooperative advertising, seasonal promotions, and merchandising. Again, this is not a one-size-fits-all, so be diligent about addressing this segment's specific needs in these areas.

SUMMARY

* Marketing channels are sets of interdependent organisations involved in the process of making a product or service available for use or consumption.

* Middlemen in business help the seller and buyer in accomplishing their objectives. Since they are knowledgeable people in their field, they are very much required for a business to succeed.

* The factors that are to be considered by the marketing executive while choosing a marketing channel can be grouped as market factors, consumer factors, product factors, and organisational factors.

* Multi-channel marketing uses more than one purchasing mode to give customers access to products and services. These different channels could include websites, retail stores, mail order catalogues, direct mail and e-mail.

* A strategic channel alliance is an agreement whereby the products of one organisation are distributed through the marketing channels of another. This kind of distribution is also known as horizontal marketing system. In this strategy, two or more corporations on the same level join together for the purposes of pursuing a new marketing opportunity.

* A vertical marketing system is a strategy of creating a new kind of channel activity in which a single channel member coordinates the activities of all the major channel members in order to maximise the marketing efficiency of all the channel members by cooperating with each other without any confrontation among the members of the organisation's channels.

* Channel management serves as one of the most critical ways that a company can better serve its customers and establish competitive advantage. It is a process by which a company creates formalised programmes for selling and servicing customers within a specific channel.

REVIEW QUESTIONS

1. What is a channel of distribution?

2. In what ways the decision on marketing channels are important for an organisation?

3. "The middleman must be trustworthy to both the buyer and the seller." Do you agree? Substantiate your position with valid arguments.

4. "The company must be able to deliver the goods on time to the customer." Give appropriate reasons for this emphasis on time.

5. Explain the need for and role of middlemen in marketing.

6. "Electronic commerce which is an important component of internet marketing helps to trace the manufacturers with ease and comfort." Is it true? Give your arguments in support of your point.

7. "Sophisticated products require channels manned by suitable people and the company has to search for specific channels which can sell these goods." Give an example of such a product and explain the qualities of "suitable people".

8. What are the determinants of a right channel of distribution?

9. Explain multi-channel marketing.

10. "Delivering multiple impressions and giving prospects a variety of ways to respond can dramatically improve results." What do you mean by this statement? What is the need for such a strategy?

11. "Satisfied customers have become a good source for new business." Explain how they make it to the success of the business.

12. "Manufacturers opting for new and personalised channels create wonderful campaigns for attracting the customers." Give any one of these wonderful campaigns and explain its benefits to the organisation.

13. What are the channels that may be used under a multi-channel marketing programme?

14. "Multi-channel is totally different from multiple channel." Explain the difference between the two.

15. Discuss the connection between multi-channel strategy and media-mix strategy.

16. Explain in detail the strategic channel alliances with examples.

17. "The competitive advantage may be gained by strategic channel alliances too." What do you mean by strategic channel alliances? Give at least any three of such an alliance.

18. What are vertical marketing systems? Explain the types of these systems.

19. "This strategy of vertical marketing system also helps the channel members to exchange their experiences and evolve new methods to provide satisfaction to the customers." State how a vertical marketing system can provide satisfaction to the customers.

20. Explain the need for and importance of channel management.

21. "Like all elements of marketing and operations, channel management offers numerous chances to improve revenue and profitability." What are these numerous chances? Explain them.

REFERENCES

1. Stern, L.W. and El-Ansary, A.I. (1992). *Marketing Channels.* Prentice-Hall, Englewood Cliffs, NJ. p. 1

2. Steve Steinhilber. (2008). *Strategic Alliances. Three Ways to Make Them Work.* Harvard Business Press.

3. Kerravala, Zeus, *Strategic Alliances: The Value of Partners,* see the web site http://www.cisco.com/en/US/prod/collateral/voicesw/c22-558396 00_value_partners_so.pdf.

4. A Report titled "3Com and Ramco Systems strike strategic alliance for Indian Market" See the web site http://business.webindia.com/pr13129901.htm

5. A Report titled "Max New York Life Insurance Forges Strategic Business Alliance With Indian Mercantile Co-operative Bank" *Travel Business Review* March 6 2009.

6. A Report titled "AGC Networks Enters into Strategic Agreement with NEC" Posted June 24, 2010 by ITVARNews Network .

7. A Report by *GetJar* titled "Reliance Communications signs strategic alliance with GetJar to create India's largest and free mobile Apps Store" April 27, 2010.

8. Kotler, P. and Armstrong, G. (2001). *Principles of Marketing.* Prentice Hall, USA.

10

PRODUCT LIFE CYCLE MANAGEMENT STRATEGIES

After reading this chapter, you will be able to

- *recollect the various strategies that a marketer would follow during the different stages of the product life cycle,*

- *recognise how the idea of strategic management can help an organisation in excelling in the process of product cycle management, and*

- *learn in detail the steps to be followed in the process of strategic product life cycle management.*

KEY TERMS

- Competitive environment
- New-to-the-world product
- New-to-the-company product
- Idea generation
- Product development
- New product market probing
- Test marketing
- Promotional expenditure
- Exit strategies
- Milking strategy
- Sunset strategy

INTRODUCTION

Product life cycles are a matter of concern not only to most of the marketing executives but also to the business organisations and its CEOs worldwide. They are anxious as well as concerned about the stage in which their products are passing through. As everyone is aware, these cycles may end in a few months for some products, and may extend for an infinitely long period for some other products. Products succeed wonderfully or fail miserably in the market due the reasons known and unknown. The TVS 50 moped which was launched in 1980 is still going very strong. Perfetti Van Melle's Alpenliebe, Center Fresh and Big Babool have been a big success in the Indian market. These products gave the company a very good name after Italy, its home country. There are many other successful products like Tata Indica, Pepsodent, Surf Excel Supreme, Hero Honda Splendor, Lizol floor cleaning liquid and Nokia handsets.

Let us also look at the other side. IPhone's launch in India has been dubbed the biggest failure of a top-notch brand from a well-regarded company in recent times. It had a short life in India. The reasons are many. Its price has been considered to be very high. The consumer confidence level was low. The company failed to understand the Indian handsets market. Tata's Tanishq introduced their 18 carat jewellery and the product was positioned at elite segment and it too failed miserably in a very short span of time. TVS Spectra which was launched in 1998 was a failure. Kellogg's Corn Flakes was a failure in India because of its failure to understand Indian consumers. The company thought that like Americans, Indians would use Corn Flakes for their breakfast. But it failed to understand the fact that Indians start or end their meal with hot food. Corn Flakes and cold milk could never be a match for Indians. If hot milk is poured on the corn, it would lose its taste. Many new products fail because they don't create sufficient value for customers, or because their pricing strategy is not consistent with the value the product delivers, or the producers do not understand the customer behaviour.

PRODUCT LIFE CYCLE STAGES REVISITED

The product life-cycle is a series of different stages a product goes through, beginning from its introduction into the market and ending at its discontinuation. A product's life cycle consists of four stages, namely, introduction, growth, maturity, decline and the subsequent withdrawal from the market. During the earlier parts of the product life cycle, the cost of promoting the product may be larger than the revenue it brings in. However, for successful products that are marketed effectively, the product will become increasingly profitable during the growth and maturity phases. A typical life cycle for a well-managed product is shown in Exhibit 10.1. There are many products that do not follow the usual shape of the product life cycle graph. [1]

The duration of each life cycle phase can be controlled, to a certain extent. This is particularly true of the maturity stage. This is the most important one to extend from a financial point of view because this is the period when the product is at its most profitable position.

Introduction Stage

Since the customers are yet to become aware of the product, the sales volume is very low and therefore the business also suffers from loss. This is due to huge expenditure on the promotion of the new product. The company has to formulate powerful promotional strategies ignoring quantum of investment involved for promoting the product. The marketing executive must plan aggressive measures to capture the market. This is the case for both industrial and consumer products. However the marketing strategies adopted to capture the market will vary for these two products.

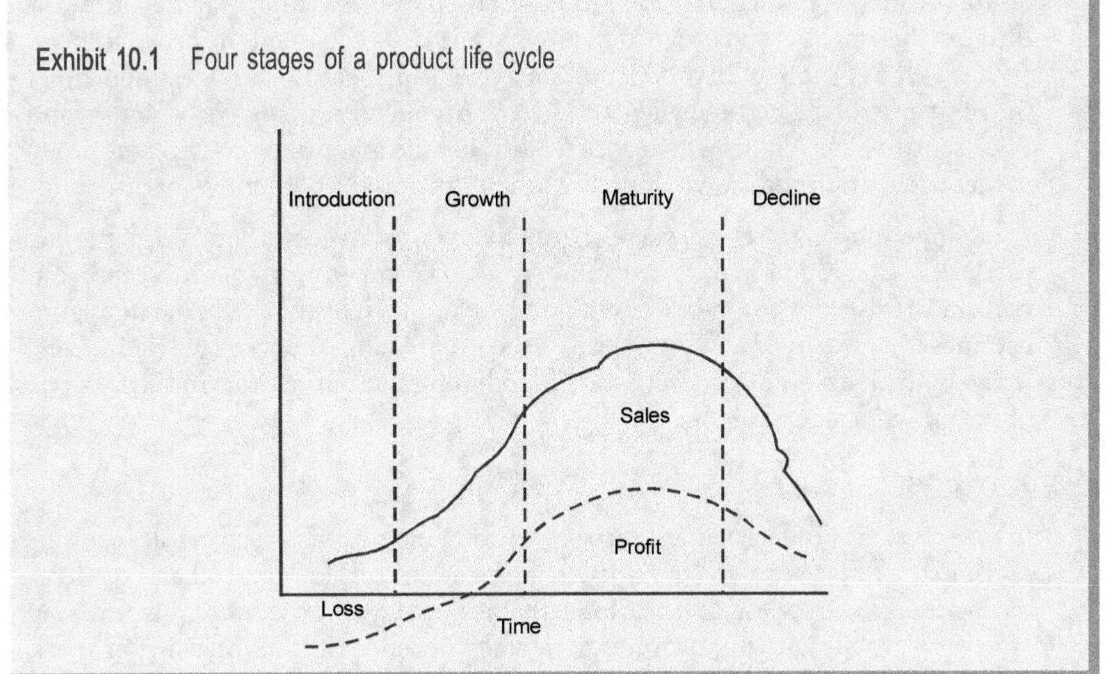

Exhibit 10.1   Four stages of a product life cycle

In this stage, it is difficult to find competitors in the market as the product is new to the market. But once the competitors sense that the new product is going to succeed in the market, the market will soon find competitors. The competitors will be keenly observing the progress made by the product. If they find any positive signals from the market, they will begin to introduce their versions of the product. However, it will take some more time. But we can expect that once the competitors decide to compete in the market, they will do it aggressively.

Growth Stage

Once the product has entered the growth stage, surely it is a positive signal for the product as well as to the organisation. The marketing executive now must try to capitalise upon the reputation of the product and its market position. Consumers become knowledgeable about the product. Sales increases rapidly because consumers spread word-of-mouth messages to their near and dear. There is no better advertisement than this. The organisation must take steps to cope with the galloping customer expectations. It is pointless to increase customer expectations and product demand without having arranged for relative production capacity. A company must not make the mistake of over-committing. This will result into losing customers not finding the product "on the shelf".[2]

If the consumers accept the product, they start making repeated purchases in the case of consumer products. If it is a consumer-durable product, they convey the message through their friends and other companions. The cost of making the product shows a decline as the economies of production start operating because of huge production by the company forced by rising demand for the product. Profit also rises significantly. Price-sensitive consumers who form a majority of the market start buying the product in the latter part of the growth stage. This helps the product enter the maturity stage.

Competition in the initial stage of growth will not be severe; however in the latter part of the stage, the market will find scores of competitors vying to capture the market. At this point of time, differentiating the product from those of the competitors becomes the priority for the marketing executive. Claims and counter claims can be found in the market. Advertising wars rage among the competitors in the latter part of the growth stage.

Maturity Stage

In this stage, the product demand increases further up to a certain stage. Sales continues to rise in the early part of the maturity stage but at a much slower rate than experienced during the growth phase. In this stage, the company will experience the peak stage. How long it will take to reach the peak stage depends on the intensity of market activity of the organisation and its competitors. Again how long the company will enjoy the peak position also depends on the kind of strategies followed by the competitors in the market. If the competitors are strong in the market, and if they offer better quality products at more competitive rates, then the organisation may have to give up its peak and the market shows slackness for the company as the competitors become more vigorous in their strategies. The battle of distribution continues using multi-distribution channels.[3]

However, it all depends on how well the marketing executives design their strategies to counter the strategies of the competitors.

Costs begin to rise during maturity because of market saturation and continually intensifying competition. When this slowing of sales is combined with the increasing costs associated with this stage, the result is that profits will have reached their highest level and must, from this point on, decline. The only remaining customers to enter the market will be the *laggards*. These customer groups are by far the most risk averse and most hesitant to adopt new products. These customers are quite price sensitive and they have been waiting for the situation where the market will offer the products for low prices. These consumers are the people who are prepared to sacrifice their comforts until they find a favourable market. And, as a result, they will not buy products until prices have seen significant declines.

Decline Stage

Sales continues to decline unless the marketing executive and the top management join together to make key decisions to revise the strategy and increase the sales and compete in the market. In this stage, profit also looks down and sometimes, it may start to show a negative trend. Even though competitors are still found in the market, smaller ones will leave the market. This stage is a bonanza for the laggards who have been waiting for this stage to make the purchase.

STRATEGIC PRODUCT LIFE CYCLE MANAGEMENT

The idea of strategic management can be applied to management of product life cycle and the business can benefit from it to a great extent. It can help the organisation to extend its thinking beyond conventional management of the product life cycle. Strategic product life cycle management makes only a marginal difference from the conventional techniques of product life cycle management. The strategic management of product life cycle stresses the importance of the marketing function in contributing to the strategic marketing goals of the organisation. The strategic marketing goals are tied to the overall business strategy of the organisation. Therefore, the strategic marketing executive must fully exploit the new product market for the sake of the organisation. At the same time, care is to be taken to see that the organisational overall strategy does not get hurt by the overambitious actions of the strategic marketing manager. One has to apply all the talents available at disposal to reap the best harvest from out of the new product.

In this section of the chapter, we will study how strategic ways of thinking can help in each process including the development stage. The basic idea is that there is one best way of doing things. But it is difficult to reach that point. It is a big question whether all the organisations are working towards that point. It is the unbelievable truth that only a few organisations have this concept in their minds and these organisations work tirelessly for reaching that point. However, this point will elude them from reaching it because one does not know whether the best solution has reached or not. Until that point is reached, the goal of the organisation is to find better ways of handling things. The pity is that many executives don't believe in the concept of one best way of doing things.

An important characteristic of strategic management is its emphasis on competitive environments. Organisations collect data from the environments, interpret them and then arrive at conclusions. This process is unique to strategic management. Before the idea of strategic management was conceived, the organisations collected data with regard to competition and consumer tastes and preferences alone. Detailed analysis of the entire environment was not emphasised during those days. But today's business has to necessarily take a full look on what is happening around the organisation extending from the neighbourhood to the most distant place on the earth for the organisation. This is due to the recent upsurge in business and trade world over, maybe because of the establishment of the WTO which made trade and business a disciplined system. This forced all the organisations which are concerned in their welfare, or in their destiny too, to have a new look on their strategies and methods in approaching the business. The result is strategic management.

Let us now go ahead with how the idea of strategic management can help an organisation in excelling in the process of product cycle management. Here we include the decision to develop, idea generation, and the development stages in our analysis as they are essential ingredients of product life cycle analysis from strategic management point of view.

Decision to Develop a New Product

Daft and Weick[4] suggested that organisations differed in their modes of scanning, depending on management's beliefs about the analysability of the external environment, and the extent to which the organisation intruded into the environment to understand it. An organisation that believes the environment to be analysable, in which events and processes are determinable and measurable, might seek to discover the 'correct' interpretation through systematic information gathering and analysis. Therefore, basically it is the decision of the organisation to develop a new product or not. This decision, of course, is very much related to its vision and its intensity of determination to pursue the organisational goals.

A new product may be new to the world or new to the company. The former requires detailed study on whether the product would be accepted by the market or not. It has to satisfy several parameters as given below:

1. The customers' expectations must be satisfied by the new product.
2. The company must have the confidence to create the market for the product.
3. The product must possess the characteristics which will make the competitors difficult to enter the market soon.

The decision to develop such a product will bear fruit for the company. If a product does not satisfy even one of the above three parameters, the company making the decision to make a new-to-the-world product may not be successful in the market.

The second choice of the company is a new-to-the-company product. The company may follow the market leader swiftly and make the product with better features and offer them to the customers.

The decision to get into the field of new products has to be made necessarily in order to survive the turmoil of the market. Gone are the days when whatever produced was sold out in the market. The number of producers was small. The demand was heavy. But things changed as many enterprising people started their production facilities in order to satisfy the growing needs of the population and vied each other to capture the market. Also people have their own preferences in choosing products of their choice. The quality conscious consumers started looking for better features in the product they wanted to buy. The result was the quality movement that grabbed the manufacturers to win the race. Japanese were the first to realise the need for quality to succeed in the market and their subsequent entry and success in the American as well as Western automobile markets proved it beyond doubt. The automobile success of the Japanese manufacturers made the consumer durable goods manufacturers of Japan to think in similar lines and they too manufactured electronic and other consumer durable goods at prices which their American counterparts could not afford to offer. It took a few decades for the Americans to find the way out. But by then the Japanese had created loyal consumers by their impeccable designs, price, and performance. These factors had a salutary effect among the American consumers who did not heed the appeals from government heads and other prominent Americans to buy American goods. All these appeals went in vain. But the Americans also started developing quality products and they too recovered some of their lost markets.

The decision to find out new products which could change the fortune of a company is very basic for a business. This decision is very much related to the organisational objectives. The firm's objectives must permit an organisation to go ahead with a new product development programme. A dynamic organisation would always like to carry out projects to find out new products in order to survive in the market. The vision of the organisation must also permit the firm to go ahead with the new project. An organisation which is wedded to a strategic management programme alone can systematically engage itself in the new product development process.

Idea Generation

The idea of a new product must come from the creative people in the organisation and it must be endorsed by the management. It can come from any person in the organisation or even outside it. In the case the ideas are available outside the organisation like research institutions and universities, the organisation must take steps to use them. The company can also source the ideas from the suggestion schemes meant for the employees. The responsibility to generate new ideas rests mainly with the research and development department of the organisation.

A good new product idea will possess the following characteristics:

* The new product idea must be able to satisfy the needs of the organisation.

* The idea must correspond to the requirements of the market.

* The product idea must be able to satisfy the consumer in a way to encourage the customer to purchase the product repeatedly.

* The idea must create a new product sooner in order that it will not become obsolete.

* It must require minimum cost to convert itself into a product.

* It must be able to create confidence in the minds of those involved in the development of the new product.

Product Development

The strategic marketing executive, in consultation with the top management, must chart out the long-run new product objectives of the organisation. Obviously these objectives must be in conformity with the organisational objectives. The organisation must look deeper into the future and predict the future developments in the new product scenario that may appear in the market. This may be called as *new product market probing*. This will be studied in detail in Chapter 11.

Product development is the task to be performed by the research and development department of the organisation. When they do it, the research and development executive will be in constant touch with the marketing executive because it is the marketing executive who will be able to suggest improvements in the product being developed. A preliminary meeting of research and development executive, production executive, and the marketing executive must be held before any work on the development of the product begins. The meeting must reach a consensus on the approach to the new product. It must define the basic product qualities in order that the new product will find its market and patronage among consumers quickly.

The expectations of the customers which will be satisfied must be listed out and a detailed discussion must be made on each aspect of the customer expectations.

If the product is an entirely new one which the market has not seen so far, it requires more detailed probing on whether the idea will be a hit in the market. Since the demand is to be created for such a product afresh, the nature of the product and its concept, and the prospective consumers must be analysed in detail. The organisation's ability to spend on new product promotion and the kind of marketing strategy to be adopted must be considered by the top executives of the organisation.

Once the product is completed, it must be given to the consumer panel which is already functioning in the organisation. The panel's opinion must be given due consideration by the top management and steps necessary to carry out the alterations, if any, must be taken. Thereafter the company must proceed with test marketing and the findings of the test marketing must be carefully analysed.

Product introduction   Introducing the product in the market must be done at the right time and at the right place. New products often fail because of unanticipated market shifts that result in missed opportunities and misused channels of distribution. Competitive pressures, cost issues, and customer expectations decide the timing of product introduction. A strategic marketing executive considers the long-term implications of introducing the product in the market. The organisation must not be in a hurry to put the product in the market. At the same time any undue delay in introducing the product might also lead to customer disinterest. Once announcement is made in the press or any other media, the company should launch the product as promised; otherwise, it will damage the reputation of the organisation and there are chances that an oscillating customer may switch loyalty to the substitutes. Therefore, delays in introducing the product must be avoided.

A strategic marketing manager must look at new product introduction as part of the overall corporate strategy. The objectives of new product introduction must be in conformity with the company's vision statement. The process must contribute substantially to the goals of the company. From the strategic marketing management point of view, the following are the important aspects to be considered.

1.   The first aspect that might impact the organisation is the pricing of the new product. Pricing decision must be made in such a way that it would not affect the organisation's reputation. Pricing depends upon various factors. The important factors are customer expectations, market trend, consumer surplus, cost, and so on. Pricing the product at high level might hamper the marketing prospects. At the same time, if pricing is low, the company may not be able to earn reasonable profit. All these factors must be balanced and the right decision must be taken.

2. The second aspect is about promotional measures for the new product. In the product introduction stage, the company is under an urgency to spend heavily on promotions. The marketing executive must take into account the nature of the customers, channels available, the organisation's practices, and the like.

3. The competitors' activities must be closely monitored in order to see whether they are planning for a chase. But if our company is a market leader, it is certain that the competitors in the market would follow our product and they would try to make their versions of the product as quick as possible. Therefore, it is necessary that the company must create an unforgettable image about our product by providing hard facts to them. The marketing executive must remember that consumers today are very intelligent and well-educated. The company should not hide any fact from the customers. Passing on false information to them will harm the product's future. Sometimes it may even lead to product failure.

4. Selection of the city for test marketing is very important because it will spread the message about the success or the failure of the product. There are cities which are considered as test cities. In India, good test cities are Chennai, and Bangalore.

Product growth Growth is a stage which must be fully exploited by the company. If the company finds success in the market, obviously competitors start their operations to make money by offering their versions of the product. However, it will take some more time for them to develop their versions. This gap is the right time for the company to take strong roots in the market. When the competitors enter the market and try hard to make money which might lead to a slow-down in the company's sales at the end of the growth stage, the company must introduce new features or variants that are ready in the company's sales plan. This would make the company maintain or even improve its sales level eventually leading to the next stage.

It would be a shock to the competitors when they find new features or variants in the market. Some of the competitors, sensing this type of strategy from the company, would also do the same thing. Sometimes, they might try to overtake the company by introducing new features. The introduction of handsets with double sim cards by the Chinese manufacturers is a good example. Even with competition beginning to offer their products in the new category, the original company still dominates the market because many consumers believe that the original manufacturer is the pioneer as well as an expert in the field. In this stage, the company should be seeing where its demand is coming from, and which of its efforts are worth spending time and energy on.

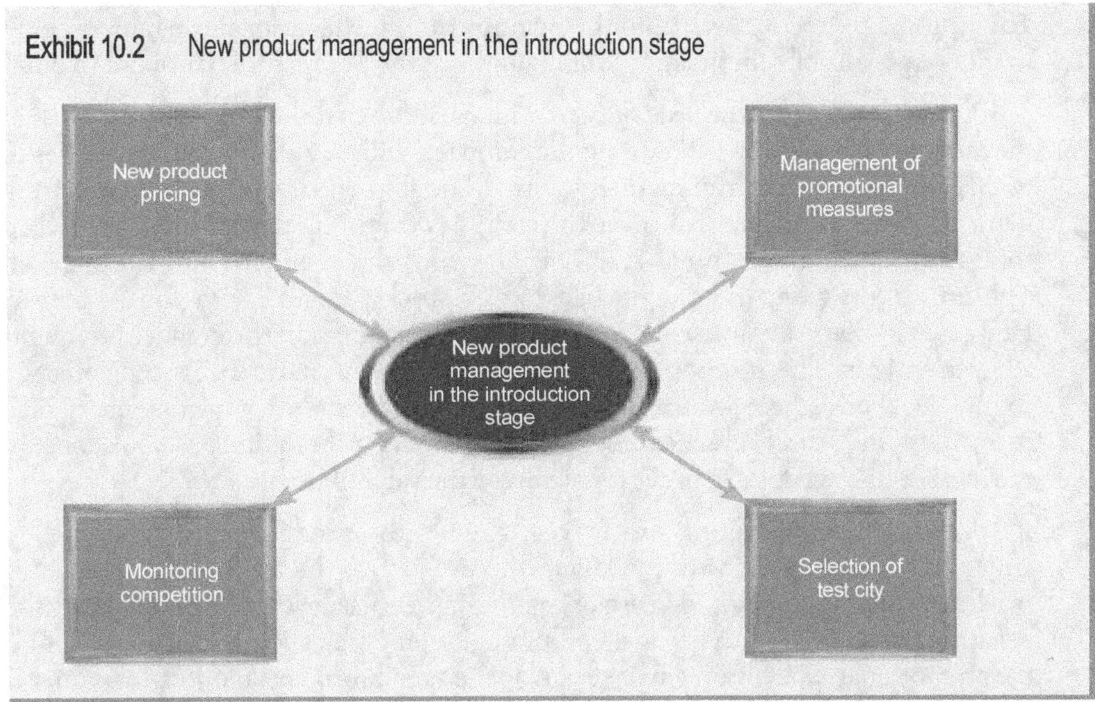

Exhibit 10.2   New product management in the introduction stage

Marketing is a game. It must be played with every care. An alert marketing executive can tackle any kind of situation in the market. As the competition enters the market, they will probably be offering products at prices lower than the price of the original product. This is a penetration pricing policy designed to take sales away from the market leader. If the original company used a skimming pricing policy, its continued use would surely lead to rapid loss of sales to the competition unless it is altered. Prices should be lowered so that sales can continue to grow, and the competition kept at bay. It is important that too much of lowering of the price by the pioneer might lead to erosion of profit and also loss of reputation of the company. However, price reduction becomes inevitable for the company as competitors started offering at very low prices. As long as the company is able to gain a comfortable margin, price may continue to be reduced. As the consumers are today well aware of the efforts of the company to find out a new product and cost involved in it, they will not find fault with the company's decision to price the product at a higher level in the early stages of the product.

Product maturity   The presence of a large number of competitors characterise the market. By now the consumers become well aware of the utility of the product and the number of consumers also increases. A wide variety of the product is available in the market because of the entry of a large number of competitors. The original company that introduced the product must recognise the ground reality and take steps accordingly. Many of the customers think in terms of quality, styling, features, and pricing.

The customers expect offers from the manufacturers. The rational consumers begin to think in terms of benefits they would get from the product they propose to buy.

Product maturity is the peak or maximum position that the company can reach in the market. The question is how long the company will stay there. The answer lies in the fact that extending the maturity period largely depends on the talents of the marketing executive. However, once the company finds that the product has reached the saturation point, it must start withdrawing the product from the market. The important thing is that no backlog of stock remains with the company. However the company must show its presence in the market through less frequent advertisements. The promotional schemes during the maturity period must be continued. Novel schemes can attract customers; therefore, the company must engage itself in finding out novel schemes of promotion. A lot of thinking has to be done by the marketing executive in order to maximise the sales of the product.

Product decline The marketing executives extends the product maturity stage by employing novel methods of managing the product in the market. But a point is reached when they cannot increase or maintain the sales level any more. This is the beginning point of product decline. The strategic marketing executive must minimise the promotional expenditure; may even stop the spending on promotional activities if it is evident that any further spending will not add any benefit to the organisation. The company can maintain production at low levels up to a certain period to satisfy the loyal customers. It can decide to withdraw the product at an appropriate time.

Sales may decline because the product has lost its sheen, or the product has become obsolete, or the market trend reverses due to change in customer preferences. In this situation, the most preferred strategy regarding pricing is not to reduce the prices and keep very small stock of the product. The marketing executive has to look at the sales figures everyday and make decisions accordingly. The company will have to concentrate more on producing spares in the case of durable goods. This is important because the customers must be supplied with good quality spares for the products they purchased from the company, or else the company will have to face the fury of the customers. This position will very much damage the future sales of the company and it will be blocking the company's aspirations for a bigger role in future.

EXIT STRATEGIES

Exit strategies are implemented when a company decides that it is no longer beneficial to remain active in a given market or industry. The company must plan for the suitable exit strategy once the product has reached the decline stage. The most preferred strategy is "the milking strategy". But while using this strategy, the marketing executive must follow certain rules. They must not try to sell the product at the cost of the reputation of the company. Too much of price-cutting will harm the reputation of the company. Therefore, it is better to withdraw the product from the market. The marketing executives can continue to supply the product to the market if a sizable number of loyal customers are still after the product. In the case of these customers, there is no need to cut the price. Disciplined and responsible withdrawal will do more good than an abrupt withdrawal. The latter is the case of AIWA in India. The company suddenly closed its operations in India leaving its customers in the dark. The disciplined exit strategy is known as "sunset strategy". The company doing a sunset strategy announces sufficiently in advance about the withdrawal of its product from the market.

Some companies resort to cannibalisation. In the normal case of cannibalisation, an improved version of a product replaces an existing product as the existing product reaches its sales peak in the market. The new product is sold at a high price to sustain the sales, as the old product approaches the end of its life cycle. IBM made some severe mistakes in the past by avoiding cannibalising because it was the market leader, letting competitors succeed. Cannibalisation should be approached cautiously when there are hints that it may have an unfavourable economic effect to the company, such as lower sales and profits, higher technical skills and great retooling.

Conrad Berenson[5] posited an exit model in 1963 that identified five categories of criteria used to evaluate a product abandonment decision:

1. Financial security, which entails determining if the minimum return on investment is being met for the firm;

2. Financial opportunity, or calculating the return on alternative uses of the firm's resources;

3. Marketing strategy, which determines the value of the product above pure financial profit, such as brand name worth and the value of established distribution channels;

4. Social responsibility, or criteria that encompass the firm's responsibilities to customers, employees, suppliers, and so forth; and

5. Organised intervention, which takes into account actions by government, society, or labour groups as a result of the decision to exit.

In addition to Berenson's criteria for determining the value of an exit decision, R.S. Alexander's model[6] identified six signs that suggest that a firm may have to consider exiting a market: (1) falling sales; (2) deteriorating prices; (3) declining profitability; (4) an increase in the popularity of substitute products, such as margarine instead of butter; (5) obsolescence of a product or idea; and (6) increasing consumption of management resources to keep the product viable. These symptoms must be closely followed and steps to rectify the errors where they are found must be taken immediately.

It is interesting to note that some companies decide to withdraw its product when its product is at the peak. Their purpose is to accommodate new technologies in their products. They look at the pulse of their customers and if their customers expect a better product, they withdraw the present one ignoring its position in the product life cycle. Intel Corporation is one of the companies that usually withdraw products during their peak to replace them with other ones of better and newer technology.

SUMMARY

* Product life cycles are a matter of concern not only to most of the marketing executives but also to the business organisations and its CEOs worldwide. They are anxious as well as concerned about the stage in which their products are passing through.

* A product's life cycle consists of four stages, namely, introduction, growth, maturity, and decline and the subsequent withdrawal from the market.

* Strategic product life cycle management makes only a marginal difference from the conventional techniques of product life cycle management. The strategic management of product life cycle stresses the importance of the marketing function in contributing to the strategic marketing goals of the organisation.

* The decision to get into the field of new products has to be made necessarily in order to survive the turmoil of the market. Gone are the days when whatever produced was sold out in the market. The number of producers was small in number. The demand was heavy.

* The idea of a new product must come from the creative people in the organisation and it must be endorsed by the management. It can come from any person in the organisation or even outside it.

* The strategic marketing executive, in consultation with the top management, must chart out the long-run new product objectives of the organisation. Obviously these objectives must be in conformity with the organisational objectives.

* Introducing the product in the market must be done at the right time and at the right place. New products often fail because of unanticipated market shifts that result in missed opportunities and misused channels of distribution.

* Product maturity is the peak or maximum position that the company can reach in the market. The question is how long the company will stay there. The answer lies in the fact that extending the maturity period largely depends on the talents of the marketing executive.

✹ The marketing executives extends the product maturity stage by employing novel methods of managing the product in the market. But a point is reached when they cannot increase or maintain the sales level any more.

✹ Exit strategies are implemented when a company decides that it is no longer beneficial to remain active in a given market or industry. The company must plan for the suitable exit strategy once the product has reached the decline stage.

REVIEW QUESTIONS

1. Explain the stages which a product comes across in its life.
2. Discuss the role of competitors during the life of a product.
3. Explain the parameters that a product must satisfy in order to succeed in the market.
4. "The decision to find out new products which could change the fortune of a company is very basic for a business. This decision is very much related to the organisational objectives." Explain how this decision is related to organisation's objectives by giving practical examples.
5. "An organisation which is wedded to a strategic management programme alone can systematically engage itself in the new product development process." Do you agree? Give your arguments in a succinct manner.
6. "New products often fail because of unanticipated market shifts that result in missed opportunities and misused channels of distribution." Probe the reasons for new product failure in the market.
7. How would you manage a product when it is in the growth phase of its life cycle?
8. "The decision to find out new products which could change the fortune of a company is very basic for a business." Explain the need for such a decision.
9. Explain how creativity can help generate ideas for finding new products for an organisation.
10. "If the product is an entirely new one which the market has not seen so far, it requires more detailed probing on whether the idea will be a hit in the market." What kind of probing will you do under the context?
11. "Once announcement is made in the press or any other media, the company should launch the product as promised." If not what will be the consequences? Explain.

12. "The objectives of new product introduction must be in conformity with the company's vision statement." Explain the statement with a good example.

13. Explain how you would manage a new product in the introduction stage.

14. Explain in detail Conrad Berenson's exit strategies to be adopted for a product.

15. Explain R.S. Alexander's model that suggest that a firm may have to consider exiting a market.

REFERENCES

1. Professor Cox was able to identify six different shapes of the product life cycle graph in his research of 256 pharmaceutical products.

2. Komninos, Ioannis Faculty of Engineering, Aristotle University of Thessaloniki Urban and Regional Innovation Research Unit, *Product Life Cycle Management,* p. 7.

3. Multi-distribution channel is one that offers back up distribution ways. A good example is the use of retail stores and the use of Internet. The former requires a completely different distribution channel than the latter and a product usually is distributed through the former first.

4. Daft, R.L. and Weick, K.E. (1984). "Toward a model of organizations as interpretation systems." *Academy of Management Review.* 9(2): 284–295.

5. Berenson, Conrad. (1963). "Pruning the product line." *Business Horizons,* Summer. 63–70.

6. Alexander, R.S. (1964)."Death and burial of 'sick' products." *Journal of Marketing.* pp. 1–7.

11

NEW PRODUCT STRATEGIES

After reading this chapter, you will become knowledgeable about the following new product strategies:

- *Creating value for the customer*
- *Delivering the right quality*
- *Offering lovable design*
- *Superior after-sales service*
- *Right pricing*
- *Meaningful promotional measures*
- *Right timing of new product launch*

INTRODUCTION

It is the successful new products which help organisations survive in the industry. If the organisations stick to their conventional products, they would be eliminated from the industry sooner or later. Successful new products become money spinners of the organisation and all the key executives have to work for its success. Not only products but also the strategies ought to be new in order to meet growing competition in the market. Had Xerox Corporation continued its original methods without resorting to benchmarking, it would have disappeared from the industrial map of the world. Coca Cola's New Coke, Pepsi's Crystal Pepsi, Apple's Lisa, Levi's Type 1 Jeans and Ford's Edsel were a few great failures. Toyota had to recall lakhs of its cars for its steering system defect in the US. Nokia too had to recall its handsets for overheating and bursting its BL-5C batteries (manufactured in China) while charging the handsets. In 1994 Maruti Udyog recalled Maruti 800 cars due to some problem in front axle components which endangered customer safety on road. These are a few examples of poor quality systems in their products. These companies have failed in their new product strategies owing to poor quality management of their new products.

New product strategies have to be formulated keeping in mind their strategic importance and the organisation's vision for the future. Strategic management is the process that the companies use to formulate their vision, mission and objectives in the long run, analyse their external and internal environment, and select one or more strategies to use to create value for customers and other stakeholders, especially shareholders. This concept of strategic management pervades all the activities of an organisation and new product management is no exception. New product strategies must be formulated in order to see that they do not fail in the market for any reason. There has to be a zero failure of new products and a strategic approach helps a lot in this process.

THE WHOLE PRODUCT

We have to first understand what a product is and what its components are. A product is the physical object, or service from which the customer gets direct utility plus a number of other factors that help to satisfy him. A product needs to be a whole product. When it is a whole product, customers go after it. The customer is not aware of several things that are contained in a product. It is the duty of the organisation to educate the customer about the whole product. Guy Smith, Silicon Strategies Marketing, defines a whole product as a product that encompasses everything the manufacturer delivers, including features, price, support and the shade of red on the packaging. Exhibit 11.1 tells us what a whole product contains.

The generic product is the product which is the rudimentary or core thing without which the manufacturer cannot enter the market. It is the product for which the manufacturer actually contracts with the buyer. It contains the minimum specifications of the buyer.

The expected product includes the customer's minimal expectations like delivery conditions, installation services, and after-sales services.

The augmented product is the non-physical part of the product. It usually consists of lots of added value, for which one may or may not pay a premium. So when one buys a car, part of the augmented product would be the warranty, the customer service support offered by the car's manufacturer, and any after-sales service.

The potential product is all what can be done as physical enhancements to the core product. These improvements on the product will better satisfy the consumer; he may not be aware of these improvements until he is educated.

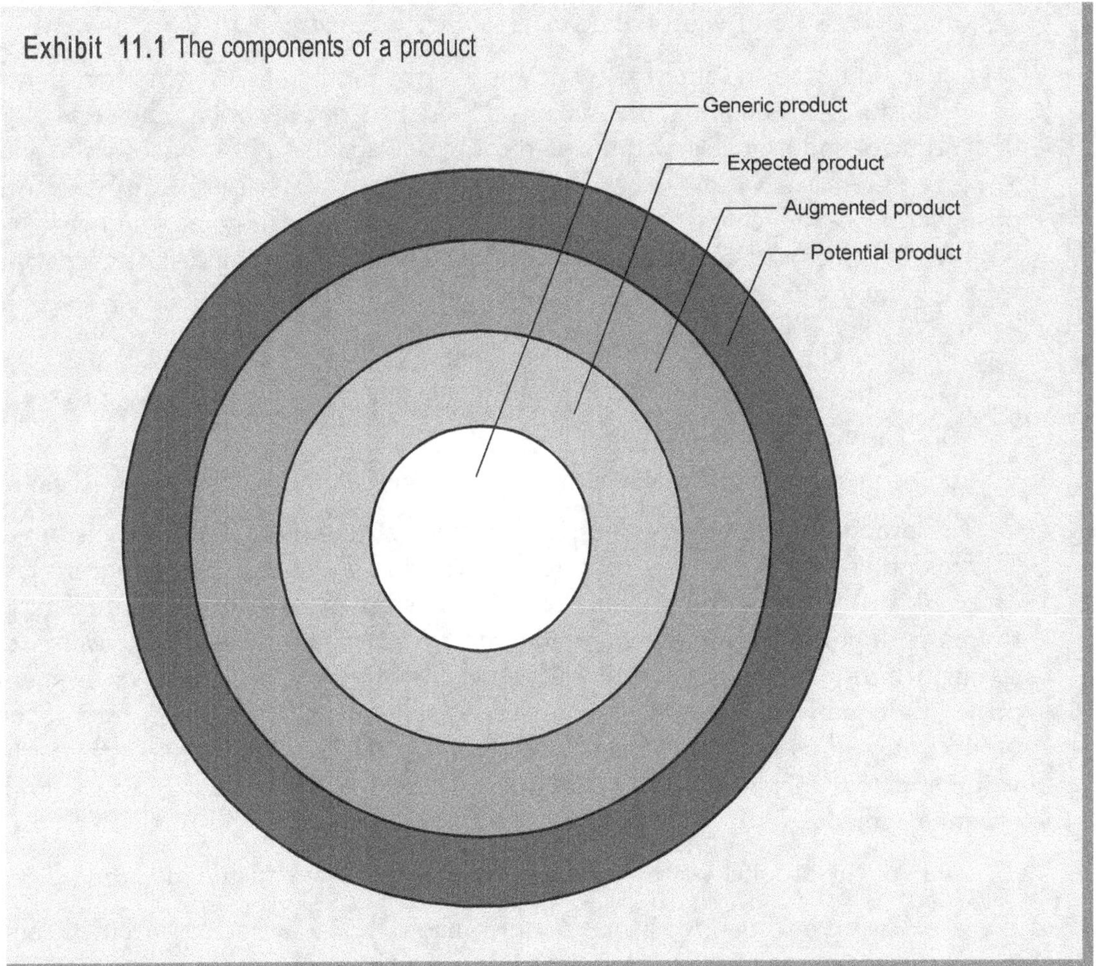

Exhibit 11.1 The components of a product

NEW PRODUCT STRATEGIES

The strategies to be adopted from the stage of finding out a new product through research up to the stage of making it successful in the market have to be flawless so that the overall objectives of the organisation can be achieved which would lead to the realisation of the company's strategic goals.

1. Creating Value for the Customer

Value for money (VFM) is one of the definitions given for quality. It has developed itself into a concept. The manufacturers and the consumers as well attach so much of importance to this concept. The emphasis of value for money has changed through the years from a focus on competition to encompassing issues of quality and service improvement through best value, to achieving efficiencies and, most recently, to ensuring that issues of equity and sustainability are addressed.

Erlendsson[1] states: Value for money is a term used to assess whether or not an organisation has obtained the maximum benefit from the goods and services it both acquires and provides, within the resources available to it. He goes on to add: Some elements may be subjective, difficult to measure, intangible and misunderstood. Judgement is therefore required when considering whether VFM has been satisfactorily achieved or not. It not only measures the cost of goods and services, but also takes account of

- the mix of quality, cost, resource use,
- fitness for purpose,
- timeliness, and
- convenience to judge whether or not, together, they constitute good value.

The product must possess the right value for money paid by the customer. The customer should not feel that he/she has paid more than what the product deserved. Instead, the product must offer the customer consumer surplus. This is the most important strategy to be adopted by an organisation which wants to accomplish its strategic goals. A disenchanted customer is like a bad advertisement made in a popular newspaper. Such an advertisement will spoil the future of the product as well as of the company. The product offered must possess the right value and this fact must be brought to the notice of the customer through prominent media.

Value of the product can be enhanced in different ways including:

- reducing costs (for example, labour costs, better procurement and commissioning) for the same outputs

* reducing inputs (for example, people, assets, energy, materials) for the same outputs

* getting greater outputs with improved quality (for example, extra service or productivity) for the same inputs

* getting proportionally more outputs or improved quality in return for an increase in resources.

These ways help to reduce the cost and subsequent reduction in price which would enhance the value for the customer.

2. Delivering the Right Quality

The term "quality" has been defined in many ways by different experts on quality. Let us see some of these definitions.

Joseph Juran and Frank Gryna   "Quality is fitness for use."

Armand Feigenbaum   "...the totality of characteristics of an entity that bear on its ability to satisfy stated or implied needs."

American Society for Quality (ASQ)   "Quality is a customer determination based upon a customer's actual experience with a product or service, measured against his or her requirements—stated or unstated, conscious or merely sensed, technically operational or entirely subjective and always representing a moving target in a competitive market."

Peter Senge et al., The Fifth Discipline   "Quality denotes an excellence in goods and services, especially to the degree they conform to requirements and satisfy customers."

Anonymous   "Quality is the ongoing process of building and sustaining relationships by assessing, anticipating, and fulfilling stated and implied needs."

All these definitions are right and we cannot say a particular definition is wrong. But many manufacturers fail to understand the importance and need for the right quality. They must recognise the fact that quality of the product is one of the most important factors that the consumer expects from the manufacturer. But the manufacturer cannot provide all that demanded by the consumer. The consumer may demand error-free functioning of the mixer-grinder for twenty five years or a suiting cloth that does not fade away for at least ten years. No manufacturer can afford to give a quality of this magnitude to the consumer. The manufacturer has limitations. The manufacturer may incur high costs to produce a product of such a quality. Or the technology may not be available to keep the suiting as new as the original one up to ten years. There may be many other limitations for the manufacturer. Therefore, what the manufacturer may do is to provide the *right* quality to the consumer.

Then what is the meaning of right quality? How can it be defined? We may say that a product possesses the right quality if it gives satisfaction for a reasonable period of time. Therefore, the right quality is that quality which gives satisfactory performance to the consumer for a reasonable period of time.

This is the mantra for the marketing success of an organisation: Give the right product to the right customer at the right time for the right price at the right place. If these three conditions are satisfied then the marketing executive's task will become very simple. The customer must be given the right product, not very superior or very inferior. An average customer likes such products and never hesitates to buy them.

3. Offering Lovable Design

Product design is a critical factor in organisational success because it sets the characteristics, features, and performance of the service or good that consumers demand. The objective of product design is to create a product with excellent functional utility and sales appeal at an acceptable cost and within a reasonable time. The product needs to be manufactured using high-quality, low-cost materials and methods. It should be produced on equipment that is available when production begins. The resulting product should be competitive with or better than similar products on the market in terms of quality, appearance, performance, service life, and price.

Hayes and Wheelwrights give five impeccable design strategies that a manufacturer may adopt. These strategies will ultimately result in a design on which the consumer will fall in love. They are given as follows.

1. *Cost advantage*   Minimise the component, assembly and production costs.

2. *Design prominence*   Focus on aesthetics, ergonomics, packaging, presentation, and innovative materials and concepts to deliver consumer value. This will come in the form of enhancements to product usability and sensory perception that will stir up emotional reactions in shoppers related to their needs and desires.

3. *Feature leadership*   Deliver cutting-edge and highly innovative solutions, then highlight how the features of your product deliver these benefits.

4. *Concentrated application*   Design the product to be tailored to the needs and wants of a particular type of customer. Make it the most appropriate option available to them in terms of fit and performance.

5. *Desirable alternative*   Design the product's features and benefits within the scope of an existing product category or an established leader therein. This strategy will often work well within sales channels with room for category growth, but will need accompanying strategies to differentiate the product when competition heats up.

Hayes and Wheelwright state that focus of the manufacturer must be on aesthetics, ergonomics, packaging, presentation, and innovative materials and concepts to deliver consumer value. These characteristics of the product undoubtedly catch the attention as well as the loyalty of the customer. More importantly, it is true that people fall in love on first sight of the product. Once people are satisfied with the image of the company, this finding of falling in love on first look is true. The design of the product, the kind of look, and the unparalleled packaging style are very important factors that give an edge for a company among the companies of its class.

The principles of design to be used will, of course, depend on the project at hand which may be of architectural, automotive, machinery, and/or computer development. All of these are scientific in nature, and therefore, also hope to achieve different results as opposed to communicative design which includes designs applied to magazines, advertisements, books, and websites, amongst others. Good product designs are born out of creativity. Creative people are able to invent good designs appropriate to the time and the market. Only those designs which match the customers' preferences will succeed in the market.

Product design is more important today than ever because customers are demanding greater variety and are switching more quickly to products with state-of-the-art technology. The impacts of greater product variety and shorter product life cycles have a multiplicative effect on the number of new products and derivative products that need to be designed.

4. Superior After-sales Service

The last few decades have seen a growing trend toward aggressive global competition, increased marketplace demands and accelerated technological changes. These changes have forced the organisations to take a close look at their marketing strategies which include after-sales services offered by them. Many value-conscious customers are demanding that not only a company's products offer more value than its competitor's not only in its design and manufacturing, but also in its product delivery and support. Today, more companies recognise the importance of after-sales service as a means of enhancing brand value, strengthening customer relationships, and boosting revenue streams. Moreover, feedback from service activities is necessary in tracking maintenance and product configurations in the field.

Increasingly, distribution and service support options available for a product are the key factors in determining consumers' product purchase decision. After-sales service is being recognised today as one of the competitive differentiators for most companies. Paul[2] believes that an essential part of marketing strength is service support.

When customers buy a product, they expect certain levels of post-purchase support to go along with it. Identifying those expectations of customers is essential for marketing success of the organisation and will be even more important when markets mature. Parasuraman[3] says if any company focuses on customer service effectively and defiantly, it is able to make customer retention and this will really help company to be more compatible in the market and enable them to implement their marketing plan.

According to Eppientte, customer service has been emerging as a competitive weapon for business firms. He says: "It is becoming harder and harder to compete on manufacturing excellence alone. Manufacturers who thrive… will compete by bundling services with products." The importance of customer service can be more recognised, when Michael Porter[4] considers it as a parameter for his value-chain analysis model that makes the margin for the company. According to him, to create value costs are incurred; the difference between costs and revenue is margin. To increase margin, the enterprise can increase value for the customer (primary activities). Generically primary activities are inbound logistics, operations, outbound logistics, marketing and sales, and continuing service.

In India, the status of after-sales service is in a pathetic condition excepting a few organisations. Customers do not find the same warmth received at the time of placing an order, when he/she visits the showroom or service station for even a small complaint about the product. The situation is still worse as companies become smaller and smaller. The customers, as they find similar treatment everywhere they go, have started ignoring or forgetting the disrespect shown by the seller or the staff. People have become accustomed to this type of treatment meted out to them by most of the sellers. Therefore, they prefer those sellers who show *some* respect or recognition to them.

5. Right Pricing

Pricing is the method adopted by a company to set the selling price of its product. It usually depends on the company's average costs, and on the customer's perceived value of the product in comparison to his or her perceived value of the competing products. Pricing is one of the four P's of the marketing mix. Pricing decisions made hastily without sufficient research, analysis, and strategic evaluation can lead to the marketing organisation losing revenue. Prices set too high can also impact revenue as it prevents interested customers from purchasing the product. Setting the right price level often takes considerable market knowledge and testing of different pricing options, especially with new products. Often customers' perception of a product is formed as soon as they learn the price, such as when a product is first seen when walking down the aisle of a store.

Exhibit 11.2 After-sales services in Siemens

Success factors in after-sales service

As a maker of capital goods, you provide your customers with outstanding products and after-sales services to match. Your service spectrum is tailored to your service strategy and the market situation. Some services are standard, are expected by your customers, and are considered "must-have" services. These include:

* Maintenance and inspection
* Repair
* Spare parts supply
* Update and upgrade services
* Customer support

The potential for after-sales service goes far beyond this list. Services are an important differentiating feature of your core business and can even become a significant profit centre for your company. What is needed is reliable and efficient service processes. For innovative companies, the provision and management of a service base on the customer's premises over the entire life cycle of products is a central strategic objective. With complex products, this life cycle can mean 20 to 30 years of potentially lucrative service.

Two factors contribute to success in this business:

* Familiarity with the installed product base and secondary mechanisms. Studies show that successful manufacturers today are familiar with just 50% of their installed base and only half know where their products are being used around the world.

* The contact with and the geographical proximity to your customers through qualified staff onsite, who know the language and understand the mentality of your customer. At the same time, your customers expect individualised, yet international service concepts. That calls for new business models, which go beyond mere spare parts supply or product oriented services.

Many companies have responded to this need and provide their customers, for example, with operator and financing models. Such companies are well ahead of the competition if they also provide efficient and reliable basic service processes on a global scale.

The price is an integral part of the whole product mix and sets up consumer expectations about quality. Therefore, more expensive products are likely to be considered as better quality than cheaper products. Underpricing hurts the product as much as overpricing does. If the price is too low, potential customers will think it can't be that good. This is particularly true for high-end, prestige brands. Therefore, the most important element of an effective market strategy is the ability to maximise and protect the price of the product. Price is the final measure of customer value and competitive advantage.

The company first has to decide what it wants to accomplish with the particular product. If the company has selected its target market and market positioning carefully, then its marketing-mix strategy, including price, will be fairly straightforward. The following conditions favour setting a low price:

- The market is highly price-sensitive, and a low price stimulates more market growth;

- Production and distribution costs fall with accumulated production experience;

- A low price discourages actual and potential competition.

Many companies favour setting high prices to "skim" the market. The company sets a price that makes it just worthwhile for some segments of the market to adopt the new material. Each time sales slows down, the company lowers the price to draw in the next price-sensitive layer of customers. In this way, company skims a maximum amount of revenue from the various segments of the market. Market skimming makes sense under the following conditions:

- A sufficient number of buyers have current demand;

- The unit costs of producing a small volume are not so much higher that they cancel the advantage of charging what the traffic will bear;

- The high initial price will not attract more competitors;

- The high price supports the image of a superior product.

A company might aim to be the product-quality leader in the market. It will charge a high price to cover the high product quality and high R&D cost. Caterpillar is a prime example of a firm pursuing product-quality leadership. It builds high-quality construction equipment and offers excellent service, with the result that it is able to price its equipment at a premium.

6. Meaningful Promotional Measures

Promotion is an attempt to influence. Promotional activities are designed to inform, persuade, or remind the market of the firm and its products and ultimately to influence consumers' feelings, beliefs, and behaviour. A successful promotion programme should include all the communication tools that can deliver a message to a target audience. A promotion programme can include five components: advertising, sales promotion, public relations, sales force, and direct marketing. The promotional measures taken must be meaningful which accommodates all the needs of the organisation and of the customers as well.

Advertising is a paid form of non-personal communication by an identified sponsor. The mass media used include TV, radio, magazine, billboards, newspapers, and direct mailing. Advertising is the most effective tool for building awareness of a company, product or service. It is also relatively inexpensive based on the cost per thousand people reached.

Sales promotion changes the behaviour of the buyers. Customers will act upon a sale, an offer, or a chance to win something. Sales promotion activities include coupons, discounts, in-store displays, trade shows, samples, in-store demonstrations, and contests. A company can also sponsor trade promotion, in which supermarkets or other retailers are given discounts to promote a specific product. The big minus point of excessive sales promotion is that it will spoil the image of the company among the more loyal customers. They may feel that *their* company has gone to rock-bottom to sell its products.

A programme of public relations is designed to create a positive image of the company to a target market. It uses non-paid communication by presenting commercially significant news in a published medium or obtaining favourable presentation of the business or product on radio or television. Tools to create publicity include publications (reports and brochures); events (sponsoring activities and trade shows); news (favourable stories about the company, its people, and products); community involvement (time or money invested in local interests); identity media (business cards, stationary, and signs); lobbying activity; and social responsibility to the environment and society.

The more complex the product or service, the more necessary to use salespeople who can answer questions and help customers. However, a company's salesforce is one of the most expensive marketing communication tools. More money is spent on personal selling than on any other form of promotion. In addition to hiring good people, a company should help its salespeople be more productive by providing them sales tools, i.e., computers, fax machine, and e-mail.

Direct marketing by mail, phone, or personal contact can be used to effectively communicate with a very narrowly targeted group. Lists for direct marketing purposes can be purchased from different sources. However, for direct marketing to be effective, it is important to maintain a comprehensive customer database in the company and manage the database in a way that it can be divided into subcategories for different promotional programmes.

7. Right Timing of New Product Launch

Apple's iPhone 3G[5] went on sale in twenty-one countries on July 11, 2008. Three days later, the company announced that one million units had been sold. Other news reports from the launch painted a familiar picture of high-profile product launches: long lines and some customers going away empty-handed. Some of the people empty-handed might have asked, "Why didn't they produce more?" The demand is highly unpredictable and may oscillate either way. One of the requisites of a product success is to keep the customers supplied with the product. The product's launch timing was so perfect that even though the company had enough stock of the product, it could not satisfy all the customers. Amazon introduced its Kindle e-book reader in 2007 with insufficient supply. Video game consoles have a bad track record on this front: Microsoft had shortages of the Xbox 360 in 2005 and Nintendo had shortages of the Wii in 2006. When Maruti Suzuki launched Swift Dzire, it faced shortage of cars. With these products, why is there urgency to launch? Competitive threats are an important reason.

Timing is everything and often timing a launch can mean all the difference in the world. The timing of the new product launch event may be predetermined by a key industry trade show or other major event. Whatever the case, as you go through your launch planning process, identify the times and locations that afford maximum leverage. Anthony Di Beneditto[6] found that the timing of the launch (i.e., when the launch is conducted from the point of view of the company, the competition, and the customer) is just as important as whether the activities are performed. More managerial attention should be devoted to launch timing with respect to all of these viewpoints in order to improve the chances of success.

According to Abell,[7] a new product must be launched when the *strategic windows* are open for the organisation in the market. The strategic window is open when the 'fit' between the key requirements of a market and the particular key competencies of a firm competing in that market is at an optimum. Introduction of a product must be timed to coincide with periods in which such a strategic window is open. According to him, a market is a temporary vehicle for growth, a vehicle which may be used or abandoned as circumstances dictate—the reason being that the firm is often slower to evolve and change than is the market in which it competes.

Timing of the launch may be incidental or critical, depending on what the competition is up to or how the market is shifting. Usually there's a sense of urgency because of the need to meet a perceived market demand, but the launch, the product, and your budget will all be better off if you have time on your side. The company must give its agency the right amount of time to plan and publicise the product. The period depends on the nature of the product and the market. One to two years is an ideal amount of time to plan the launch, he says. At a minimum, a company should meet with its advertising or public relations firm six months ahead of the launch date.

Robert E. Cannon[8] developed the following checklist to make certain that the timing of the product launch is perfect.

1. Target the audience
2. Train and focus the salesforce
3. Samples and demos are ready and in place
4. Pricing is set
5. Promotions are in place
6. Displays are ready
7. Distribution is ready
8. Inventory is in stock
9. Advertising is set
10. Press releases are timed

SUMMARY

* New product strategies have to be formulated keeping in mind their strategic importance and the organisation's vision for the future.

* A whole product consists of generic product, expected product, augmented product, and potential product. A product needs to be a whole product. When it is a whole product, customers go after it. The customer himself does not know several things that are contained in a product.

* The product must possess the right value for money paid by the customer. He should not feel that he has paid more than what the product deserved. Instead, the product must offer him consumer surplus. This is the most important strategy to be adopted by an organisation which wants to accomplish its strategic goals.

* The customer must be offered a product that possesses the right quality. The right quality is that quality which gives satisfactory performance to the consumer for a reasonable period of time.

❈ The product must possess a design that is liked by the consumers. The design of the product, the kind of look, and the unparalleled packaging style are very important factors that give an edge for a company among the companies of its class.

❈ After-sales service is being recognised today as one of the competitive differentiators for most companies. An essential part of marketing strength is service support. When customers buy a product, they expect certain levels of post-purchase support to go along with it.

❈ Pricing decisions made hastily without sufficient research, analysis, and strategic evaluation can lead to the marketing organisation losing revenue. The product must be rightly priced, not overpriced or underpriced.

❈ The promotional measures taken must be meaningful which accommodates all the needs of the organisation and of the customers as well.

❈ Timing is everything and often timing a launch can mean all the difference in the world. The timing of the new product launch event may be predetermined by a key industry trade show or other major event.

REVIEW QUESTIONS

1. Explain the concept of "whole product".
2. Analyse the "value for money" angle of quality. Give its merits and demerits.
3. Explain the ways in which the value of a product can be enhanced.
4. Explain the different new product strategies available for the marketer.
5. "The right quality is that quality which gives satisfactory performance to the consumer for a reasonable period of time." Do you agree with the statement? Substantiate your answer with suitable points.
6. Explain the five impeccable design strategies that a manufacturer may adopt as given by Hayes and Wheelwright.
7. Why is after-sales service recognised today as one of the competitive differentiators for most companies? Explain your points thoroughly.
8. "Underpricing hurts the product as much as overpricing does." Do you agree? Explain your position with suitable arguments.
9. Do you think excessive sales promotion will spoil the image of the company among the more loyal customers? Give reasons for your answer.
10. What are the reasons for stressing the suitable timing for the launch of a new product?

REFERENCES

1. Erlendsson, J. (2002). Value For Money Studies in Higher Education http://www.hi.is/~joner/eaps/wh_vfmhe.htm 04 January 2002.

2. Paul, A. Herbig and Frederick Palumbo. (1993). "Serving the aftermarket in Japan and the United States." *Industrial Marketing Management.* 22: 339–346.

3. Parasuraman, A.(1998). "Customer service in business-to-business markets: An agenda for research." *Journal of Business and Industrial Marketing.* 13 (4/5): 309–321.

4. Michael Porter in 1985 introduced in his book 'The Competitive Advantage' the concept of the Value Chain. He suggested that activities within the organisation add value to the service and products that the organisation produces, and all these activities should be run at optimum level if the organisation is to gain any real competitive advantage.

5. http://apple.iphonesreview.com/about.aspx?detail=a1303-16gb

6. Anthony Di Benedetto.(1999). "Identifying the key success factors in new product launch." *Journal of Product Innovation Management.* 16(5): 530–544.

7. Abell, F. Derek. (1978). "Strategic windows." *Journal of Marketing.* 42: 21–26.

8. Robert, E. Cannon. (2005). Management Consultant in his blog *The Cannon Advantage* titled 'Taking Aim.' 4 (6).

12

COMPETITION-WINNING STRATEGIES

After reading this chapter, you will be able to

- ❊ *recognise the need for effective management of competition in the marketplace,*
- ❊ *understand the need for key assumptions before proceeding further,*
- ❊ *become knowledgeable about the strategies to be used by a market leader, the market challengers, and the market follower during the different stages of the product cycle, and*
- ❊ *know about niche marketing.*

INTRODUCTION

Competition! Many marketers are very much weary of this term. Therefore they hate it. Even many smart people hate it. But really smart people take it as a joy to *play* with the competitors. They are there to make smart people think and use their brains. It is a pity that some marketers are afraid of even to make a brief summary of the developments taking place in the marketplace. Competition educates smart marketers and shows the way to deal with it.

A strategic marketing manager acts swiftly to the market changes, as is concerned with the long-term concerns of the organisation. Some people might ask why a strategic marketing manager must indulge in short-run or current activities like confronting competition. I would like to clarify to them that every "long-term" consists several "short-terms". When we consider, for example, the vision of the organisation, it can very well be for one year or two years or more. It need not necessarily be for a long period of ten years. But organisations formulate their vision statements for a minimum period of ten years. Why? It is because all the planning is carried out keeping in mind the vision of the organisation. Therefore, it is the duty of the strategic marketing manager to safeguard the "short-terms" also for the organisation's well-being in the long-run.

When competitors appear on the scene, they bring with them a bundle of information or clues to the organisation. The job of the smart marketing executive is to take the thread and read the message hidden therein. Suppose a competitor creates an advertisement and makes it in a reputed magazine. The message contained therein provides lot of messages to the company against which the advertisement is meant. The strategic marketing executive is able to understand the cues available in the advertisement and thereby this advertisement helps to determine the counter measures. The irony is that many of the competitor's advertisements need no counter measures. The competitor's ad will die down on its own. It is not only ads but other forms of promotion which vie to overthrow the market leader from its position.

This chapter tries to suggest important strategies to be followed by the market leader, and the market followers. However, it requires wisdom and well-calculated conclusions for the Chief Marketing Officer (CMO) concerned. Mere following of these strategies, sometimes, may not work. But these strategies can give the CMO the direction to proceed and the point where to begin the work in order to find a way to defeat the competitor. Therefore, the CMOs are advised not to take these strategies literally.

KEY ASSUMPTIONS

The strategies suggested hereby have with them some key assumptions and the CMOs have to make doubly sure that these assumptions are first satisfied by their products and their organisation. The following are the assumptions:

1. The price of the product is worth the quality of the product.
2. The buyer enjoys sufficient consumer surplus from the consumption of the product.
3. The quality of the product is better than the competitor's at least marginally.
4. The advertisement media used are same or better than those of the competitors.
5. The quality of the advertisement copy used is similar, if not identical.
6. The distribution channels are more or less similar.
7. The products are sufficiently available in the market.
8. The sales staff is loyal and talented.
9. The quality of packaging is more or less similar.

STRATEGIES FOR MARKET LEADERS

In this section of the chapter, we assume that it is the market leader who introduces a new product in the market. It is a fact that market challengers also equally try to perform better than the market leaders and innovate and introduce new products in the marketplace. Sometimes, a market challenger overtakes the market leader. Therefore, this section of the chapter is equally applicable to a market challenger also who introduces new products in the market. In this situation, the roles are reversed and the market leader becomes a close competitor to the market challenger.

Studying the market in its right perspective needs not only a thorough knowledge of it but also the ability to interpret the trends correctly. The Chief Marketing Officer must possess these skills invariably. It needs keen observation of people and events because, though being a market leader, one cannot sit relaxed and spend time enjoying a movie. Even while enjoying a movie, one must look for clues and information from the people around. But, at the same time, one cannot come to a conclusion because a few people had a particular opinion about the product. If it is a good opinion, then the task is to look for reasons for their opinion. If the reasons are genuine, the marketers may be happy with their product. If they had a negative opinion, it is important to consider the reasons cited by them. Again, if the reasons are perfect, accept them and find out the ways to rectify the mistakes cited by them as early as possible. One may even talk to them to elicit more ideas, as a stranger to the product and also as if he/she has never seen the product. Let us now study the strategies that may be followed by the market leader.

What is required is a relentless pursue of policies and strategies that would work unfailingly in the market. This requires a good amount of thinking in the right perspective and a clearly logical approach. The strategic marketer requires *good skill* to predict what will happen if a particular measure is taken in the market. The creativity level of the marketer or the team needs to be very high in order to succeed in the marketplace. Only a dedicated team of marketers can do this task more effectively.

Strategies in the Introduction Stage

The market leader is one who is consistently working on new products and the one who introduces them in the market as often as necessary. The research and development department of the market leader is brimming with activities and the people there are well-motivated and highly loyal to the organisation.

Competitors keep watching the performance of the new product from the market leader. However, they have the presumption that the new product will succeed in the market. Therefore, the competitors begin to produce an identical product. By the time they complete production of their version of the product, the original manufacturer would have earned sufficient reputation in the market for the new product. The competitors adopt the strategy of reduced prices and improved designs and other features in their products, when they enter the market with their products. By that time the original manufacturer would have completed the introduction stage of the product. Therefore, competition will be very marginal and competitors are not very active during the introduction stage.

Let us now study the strategies to be adopted by the market leader during the introduction stage.

Do not offer all the features at the introduction stage The market leader must not download in the product all the features of the new product during the introduction stage itself. Some of the key features of the product should be kept in reserve for future use to confront the competitors. Even a guru does not reveal everything to his students. Even the most obedient student cannot learn all the lessons from his guru. The guru reserves for himself one or two key secrets. This is how India lost a lot of valuable knowledge from ancient times. The CMO must see that the new product must contain one or two key features, and must keep in reserve three or more key features for future usage. Some of the marketers may raise the ethical issue in this regard. But there is no question of ethics here. It is a question of knowledge. After all every company is working for earning more and more money from the technology they found. Blow the iron while it is hot!

Study the strategies of the competitor as they introduce their product in the market The market leader should have an excellent market communication system which would supply market reports regularly regarding all the aspects of the market. One of the sub-systems must send reports about the role played by the competitors when they introduce their version of the market leader's product. Although patent rights are able to safeguard the original product and its design, only hi-tech products come under its jurisdiction. Most of the FMCGs may not be brought under the patent rights. Certain designs and formulae may be safeguarded through patent rights. However, the competitors may invent their own version of the product sooner or later. If the competitor takes a lot of time for it, it becomes as a boon to the original manufacturer and can reap bumper harvests in the market. But, when the competitor comes out with competitive product very soon, it is a situation of grave concern for the original manufacturer. In this case, they have to respond to the competitor's claims in a suitable way.

It is important to study the strategies adopted by the competitors at this point of time. The competitor may follow one or more of the following strategies for promoting the product in the market.

1. Offering better quality and design,
2. Offering the product at competitive prices, and
3. Intensive advertising campaigns.

Let us study these strategies and the suitable responses to be made by the market leader.

Challenge No. 1: Offering better quality and design   This is a powerful strategy because it touches the very root of the strategy adopted by the market leader. If the competitor is able to offer the product with a better design and quality, it would become a challenge to the leader. When the competitor's product is much better in quality and design, it would be a tough task to the leader to beat the competitor in the market. It is a matter of grave concern to the leader. But any situation can be tackled by the use of mind power and creativity. The leader must recognise the fact that there is always a better way of doing things. This applies to all players in the market including the leader.

The strategy to be followed in this situation is to swiftly react to the competitor by offering still better quality and design to the customer. As I said already, the leader would have reserved some of the key features of the product for future use. One of such features may be the design of the product. The leader must have deliberately designed the product that way in the beginning. Now is the time to respond to the competitor. The price of the product is reduced in such a way that the margin from the product is very low. The purpose is to clear the stocks of the product available with the dealers in order to pave way for the newer version of leader's better designed product.

Challenge No. 2: Offering the product at competitive prices   We must recognise the fact that after all every business person's ultimate goal is to earn more profit from their products. And the competitor is no exception. Therefore, what the leader must infer from this truth is that the competitor cannot afford to offer the product beyond a certain price level. This is a limitation to the competitor and an advantage to the leader. The leader must capitalise the situation by offering the product at a slightly higher price. The purpose of the leader is to remain in the good books of the loyal and other customers and to defeat the designs of the competitor. Note that at no point, the leader should fix a lower price for the product. The price must be one small step above the competitor's price.

Challenge No. 3: Intensive advertising and other promotional measures
The strategy of the competitors to undertake intensive advertising and other promotional measures is quite natural because it is their duty to see that they overtake or at least follow closely the sales levels of the leader. However, the aim of the leader is to keep the competitor at a greater distance. The strategy of the competitor to undertake rich advertising campaigns and other promotional measures will erode the profit levels of the competitor. However it becomes mandatory to offer an identical or better product to the loyal customers. Otherwise, the competitor will lose a good chunk of loyal customers. Therefore, the competitor is under a compulsion to offer the product and satisfy the customers.

The leader must respond using one or more of the following strategies:

1. Convey simple and concrete messages to the market through world class advertisements in the right media.

2. Make intelligent offers to the customers without affecting much the finance of the company.

3. Avoid aggressive measures to defeat the competitor because the leader must be sensitive to ethical issues involved. Let the competitor also survive. But if the competitor starts encroaching the leader's market, do not show any sympathy and take bold steps to remove the competitor from the market.

4. If the competitor makes untrue claims in their advertisements, make the fact public by challenging the claim of the competitor.

Strategies in the Growth Stage

In the beginning of the growth stage, the market does not witness very active roles by the competitors because the competitors have to chart out their strategies and make a superior product compared to that of the market leader. It takes some more time and the market witnesses hectic activities from the middle part of growth stage. It is between the later period of the introduction stage and the early period of the decline stage that the leader or any player in the market earns good profits from the market. The market leaders must capitalise the situation to their favour and this process must be continued relentlessly until the product is declared unviable during the decline stage. Once a product proves itself successful in the market, it would be a boon to the player who introduced the product in the market.

Let us now dwell briefly on the market conditions during the growth stage. As the product has been found to be successful, competitors will throng the market. Competition becomes intense with price wars, promotional strategies and the like. The market leader has to leverage on marketing skills for making the growth stage successful. The competitors follow the strategies similar to that are found during the introduction stage. The differences are the following.

1. The number of competitors soars.
2. Price wars become intense.
3. Technologywise also, competition increases.
4. Competitors employ strategies which focus on market penetration.
5. The market becomes more active searching for strategies to beat one another.
6. The competitors target the market leader in their strategies and the market leader has to find out new strategies to weed out competition in the market.

The market looks like a battlefield. The players have to work hard to win the market. The role of the market leader, who has twin tasks, becomes very important. One task is to find out strategies to beat the competitors and the other is to adopt strategies to retain the existing customers and create new ones. In this situation, the market leader can expect the competitors to adopt the following strategies to capture a good share of the market.

1. The competitors enter the market with a market penetration strategy. Pricing of the product is the focus of the competitors. It involves low prices. Competitors fix low prices for their products.
2. The competitors use very attractive promotional measures to woo the customers.
3. They bring in their products with more features.
4. They concentrate on several cost-cutting measures in order to offer the product for still lower prices.

Let us study these strategies and the suitable responses to be made by the market leader.

Challenge No. 1: Market penetration strategy   In the market penetration strategy, the competitor fixes the prices very low expecting the product to reach all sections of the customers. The product will reach even unexpected quarters of the market and it becomes affordable to purchase by a very large section of the customers.

The market leaders will not feel the pinch till the middle of the growth stage. Thereafter, they must begin to respond to the competitors' actions by following quick strategies that will reach the customers very quickly. The market leaders may adopt one or more of the following strategies to counter the measures taken by their competitors:

1. The market leaders must make a decent reduction in their prices. But, as the market leaders are under the compulsion to react to the competition they should reduce the prices such that it will not affect their reputation and will bring in cat-on-the-wall customers and others to their fold. By this we mean that the customers should understand that they have not been exploited too much by the market leader.

2. The market leaders must make use of their reputation as a leader by not making too much of price cutting. Too much of price reduction will truly affect the reputation of the market leaders.

3. The market leaders must educate the buyers on the more important aspects to be considered while making a purchase decision. They must stress on the need to consider the other aspects of the product like the invisible services being offered along with the product. For example, the quality of after-sales-services truly matters to all of the customers. For the market leaders, it must be a competitive advantage. They must have a pucca after-sales-service system at their disposal. The market leaders must make surprise visits and inspections on the facilities of their dealers. It will go a long way in roping in a number of new customers while retaining the existing ones. It is an unassailable weapon in the armoury of the market leaders.

Challenge No. 2: Attractive promotional measures At the outset, attractive promotional measures may seem to be effective and truly it is so *till* a certain stage. But it will not work for long. It will work like a boomerang and will hit back the shooter with a deadly blow. Today's customers are not that unwise to fall into the trap laid by the competitors in the name of promotional measures. It is a false notion that people are guided by the physical offerings. But, at the same time, we cannot deny the fact that there is a small section of customers who are after attractive offers and discounts without going into details of such offers and discounts. However, the market leader must also offer simple and less costly offers to satisfy this small section of the customers who say that their brands do not offer any offer of price cuts. It is difficult for a genuine manufacturer to offer big price cuts whatever cost-cutting measures they may adopt.

Challenge No. 3: Products in-built with more features It is a true challenge in front of the market leader. Some of the competitors employ great people with big brains in their marketing department or administrative department. These people offer highly standard ideas to the CEOs who execute their ideas invariably. This is a real challenge to the market leader.

We have discussed earlier that the market leader must keep in reserve some of the key features of the product for incorporating them in future in the product. Now is the time to release one or two key features in the market depending on the kind of features contained in the competitors' products. The trump card feature of the product must be released as a final weapon when the competitors are at their best regarding the features of their products.

Challenge No. 4: Cost-cutting measures   The competitors' most important strategy is that of manufacturing their products using substandard materials which will obviously cost less. Sure, these products will be to the satisfaction of the customers. But the product's durability becomes questionable. In the initial periods, the products offer flawless service to the consumer. But as time passes on it starts showing its colour. Either the product becomes a total waste, or it incurs heavy costs for maintaining the quality. But it is true that one cannot bring the original performance of the product for any cost. All these things do not mean that the market leader should not take steps to cost-saving strategies to reduce the price. The market leader must use all the expertise to bring down the cost of manufacture and other costs, at the same time never resorting to cost-cutting measures using substandard materials.

Strategies in the Maturity Stage

The maturity stage is the point where competition becomes cut-throat. The competitors employ all the strategies, ethical and unethical, to capture the market share. Some of the competitors are bold enough to unfold a series of lies in their advertisements under the notion that no one is going to check all these details.

The maturity stage offers the leaders maximum return to the organisation and the cow should be milked to the maximum. Knowing fully well that the product will reach the decline stage sooner or later, the market leaders have to look for opportunities and strategies to the best out of the market. They may adopt one or more of the following strategies to maximise their profits.

1. The market leader must introduce the most important feature of the product in the market which is the final weapon at disposal. The timing of this step is very important. When the leader feels that the end of the maturity period is nearer with no other strategy on hand, the final step is to incorporate the most important feature in the product.

2. Reasonable expenditure for promotional activities like advertising and sales promotional measures could be allowed. Heavy expenditure must be avoided during the later part of the maturity stage.

3. During the later part of the maturity stage, a marginal reduction in prices is advised because there are laggards in the market waiting for such an opportunity. These people wait for the market leader's move to make the reduction in the price. There are two kinds of laggards. The first kind of laggards lose patience and avail the opportunity offered by the market leader after the product has taken a very long journey in the market. The second kind of laggards wait for some more time and they act when many of the competitors withdraw from the market because these laggards think that no more reduction in price is possible and they will finally buy the product.

Strategies in the Decline Stage

During the decline stage, many small competitors disappear from the scene or offer their products at rock bottom prices with a very small margin. The second type of laggards as mentioned in the previous section is seized of the opportunity. These people make their purchase at last confirming that the manufacturers will not make any more price cuts. Only a few sellers remain in the market in the later part of the declining market. The market leader and only a few close competitors stay in the market making an all out effort to extend the life of the product. Some of them also succeed in their objective to stay in the market for an extended period.

The sales figures available clearly show the position of the product in its life cycle. Following this, the marketer decides the next steps. Once confirmed that the product has started its decline in the market, the marketer is all set to alter the strategies. The market leader follows one or more of the following strategies during the decline stage:

1. The marketer must study the prospects of the product by analysing the possibility to give the product another lease of life. If the chances are bright, the idea of extending the product's life could be considered. If the chances are bleak, the marketer may decide not to go for extension of life of the product.

2. The promotional expenditure must be kept at low level; but the market presence of the product must be communicated regularly to the market through advertisements until the top management decides to stop the production of the particular product.

3. The marketer must wait for the right time for withdrawing the product from the market. If the close competitors have already withdrawn from the market, the leader may wait and watch the progress or otherwise of the product in the market. In this case the marketer can slightly step up the promotional measures to find out the renewed response, if any, from the market. If the trend is favourable, the promotional expenditure might be stepped up in order to benefit from the second life cycle of the product.

STRATEGIES FOR MARKET CHALLENGERS

Market challengers are those manufacturers who are close competitors to the market leader. Their marketing objective is to overthrow the market leader from the position as market leader. They formulate their strategies independently; but sometimes situation forces them to follow the market leader. They also have vast research and development facilities in their organisations. Hyundai, and Tata are market challengers to Maruti Suzuki in the pleasure car segment. Market challengers follow strategies similar to the market leader, when they introduce new products in the market. They also innovate and introduce new products in the marketplace. They challenge the market leader by offering a variety of products and more or less identical quality products to the customers. They also have vast customer base and highly reputed brands.

A market challenger plays two roles in the marketplace. They are

1. as a marketer introducing new products in the market, and
2. as a close competitor to the market leader.

As a marketer introducing new products in the marketplace, they adopt strategies discussed in the previous section of the chapter. As a close competitor to the market leader, the market challenger's attack is from all sides; quality, design, after-sales-service, customer relationship, and the like. You can give any names that are fancy for the strategies followed by the challenger. Price and quality wars are very common between the leader and the challengers.

Since we have already studied the first role of the market challenger as one who introduces new products, let us now study the marketing strategies to be followed by a market challenger as the one who is confronting the new product as a close competitor. The market challenger adopts one or more of the following strategies to beat the market leader.

1. Establishes a team of experts to track down the moves of the market leader,
2. Keeps the research and development team in full alert,
3. Readies the prototype swiftly, and
4. Builds the product with an enviable perfection with better features at an unbelievable cost of manufacture.

Let us now study the different strategies followed by the market challenger during the various stages of the life cycle of a product introduced by the market leader.

Strategies in the Introduction Stage

The initial part of the introduction stage involves hectic activity on the part of the market challenger. Now, the new product introduced by the market leader is available in the market. The team which has been assigned the task of monitoring the new product must carefully as well as *swiftly* assess the market prospects of the product. If the conclusion reached is a *yes*, the team must report its findings to the top management through the chief marketing officer. The management considers all the aspects very carefully and makes a quick decision whether to engage itself in the new product. The decision is taken overnight. The next step is the process of making a prototype of the new product. The research and development facilities of the company carry out the work with razor precision, and the prototype is submitted to the top management. While developing the prototype, the research and development team of the company has certain objectives. They are

1. to make the prototype much better in performance, appearance, and general design.

2. to make the prototype at a lower cost using all the available cost reduction techniques so that the cost of manufacturing will be much less than that of the original product.

3. to consider all the aspects of ergonomics in order to see that the product offers better handling by the user.

4. not to violate the patent right laws.

The top management makes all the possible tests on the prototype including the usage of the product personally in the homes of senior executives for a few days or one or two weeks. If the result is positive, then the top management orders for commercial production of the product in its plant.

The time to be taken to introduce a better product in the market will vary depending on the following factors:

1. the nature of the product including the technology required,

2. the need for employment of manufacturing cost reduction techniques, and

3. the time required for testing the performance of the product,

These factors decide the amount of time required to complete the product. It is important to note here that the precision with which the prototype is made and the speed of manufacturing the product in the plant are the keys to the success of the product in the marketplace.

The next step is to decide the launching date. Once the product comes out with great success, the management is brimming with confidence and aims to beat the original product quickly. As far as launching is concerned, in today's marketplace, the following aspects play a key role.

1. The launching date
2. The launching place
3. The launching personality

The launching time must not coincide with any other major events in the country like cricket, and important festivals. If an important festival like Diwali is approaching, the launch date must be suitably advanced.

Incorporation of features   As far as the incorporation of features is concerned, the company must, in the beginning, incorporate the features which are one step above that of the original product. The very important or fanciful features must be reserved for future use when the competition is at its peak.

Need for effective promotional measures   The promotional measures too play a key role in deciding the success of the product. Therefore, the promotional measures adopted must be the best in the industry. This will go a long way in defeating the plans of the market leader. The promotional measures especially advertising must catch the attention of the customers quickly and they must prompt the customers to make the purchase decision in favour of the market challenger. This is the case not only during the introduction stage but also during the growth as well as the maturity stages.

Strategies in the Growth Stage

Growth stage strategies depend on the sales trend of the product during the introduction stage. If the sales figures are encouraging, the company and its executives become jubilant over the developments. It signals the beginning of success of the product. The marketer must act more forcefully in the marketplace. The company must undertake intensive promotional campaign highlighting the quality, price, and other features. The salespersons have to work a lot in this stage. Their role becomes the key in this stage.

Aggressive marketing   Aggressive marketing will help the company to bring in more sales revenue. The marketer must explore more avenues for expanding the market. All the potential customers must be converted into the company's customers. Simple offers during this stage can help the company to march ahead. But you must see that you are not spending too much on sales promotional activities. Keep advertising in important media so that the message will reach the target market. Keep a low profile of other forms of sales promotion.

Genuineness of advertisements   The strategic marketer must speak out the truth to the customers. Any false or untrue claims will damage the reputation of the organisation. This will stand in the way of the company reaching the first slot in the marketplace. Be genuine in your claims. The customers will like it. The potential customers will soon become your customers. Exaggerated advertisements are the first hurdles that stand in the way of the organisation's path to faster growth.

Significance of marketing information system   Daily market reports must be carefully analysed and suitable remedial action must be taken. Even a small sales decline in a particular territory must be taken note of and the concerned salespersons must be called to get their explanations. The marketer must be very responsive as well as sensitive to market changes.

Each and every move of the competitor must be tracked through the marketing information system of the organisation. The officers assigned for the purpose must be instructed to communicate even minor changes in the strategy of the competitor. Suppose that the competitors are making changes in their organisation to reduce your pace of growth in the marketplace, then in this case, you must also make a strategic move to counter this move. If the competitor is changing the marketing officer who is looking after the market strategies, you must analyse the pros and cons of this move of the competitor. The new officer may be shrewd enough to confront the competitor in the market and may possess great skills in the assigned task. This change must be analysed and the company must make suitable changes in its marketing organisation, if necessary.

The value of proactive measures   It is not that the marketer must be reactive only. Proactive measures will also go a long way in improving the sales figures of the company. Timely proactive measures alone will make the company march towards the goal of becoming as the market leader. When you take independent and proactive measures, the market leader will become frustrated and will make hasty decisions which will surely harm the market potential. Therefore, as a true challenger, you must attack the market leader from all sides forcing to revise the strategies again and again. This would be the greatest weakness of the market leader. The confused and frustrated market leader will not be able to make wise decisions. Mind that your staffs are no way inferior in talents and the ability to execute the plans.

Strategies in the Maturity Stage

Maturity stage offers the maximum return to the company. At the same time, it is a real battlefield in which you have to confront the competitors head on. Do not fail to note that the market leader is not your only competitor. Many other competitors will fight for their share of the market. Your objective must be to push them all back and lead the market with new strategies and features in the product. Maturity stage witnesses the deadliest competition in the marketplace. See that at no time you lose your blood and you must keep it cool. Only a cool mind will be able to create newer ideas. So make yourself and your people cool.

Introduce the best features of the product in the middle of the maturity stage Your strategy must be to introduce the best and hitherto unknown features of the product in the middle of the battle. Your new features must create storms in the market. You alone must be able to see through the storm. You have a special way to look into it. You must silently and confidently travel through the storm. Your competitors will be lost in the midst of the storm. You must recognise the fact that your competitors too may try to carry out similar exercises in the market. But you must prove that yours is the superior one and your features alone are user-friendly. The user-friendly features reach the market very quickly pushing your competitors way back. You must give them shock after shock. This is the only way available for you to become the market leader. See that you are not using unethical practices during your confrontation with your competitors. Using unethical practices will surely harm your reputation among the existing as well as potential customers.

Make genuine offers to your customers   These days, offers play an important role in roping in new customers. Not only the potential customers, but also your existing customers also expect something special from you. Do not forget to recognise their sentiments and expectations. Offers may be of many kinds. You may offer another product free along with your product. You may offer a small product or a big product to your customers. In this case, the product you are offering as an offer must be of good quality. The customers would very much appreciate your approach. Your buzzword must be quality, quality and finally quality only. Another way is to give an extra weight free to the customers for the same price for a limited period. Note that this must be a limited and one time offer. After the period has ended, you must roll back to your previous position.

Confront the competitors with confidence   As said already in the beginning of this section, the maturity period is a real battlefield for the strategic marketers. They must keep in mind the strategic objectives of their organisation and the role of their contribution in the accomplishment of the organisational objectives. The strategic marketers may take pride for their accomplishments; at the same time, they must recognise the fact that they are not the only persons to claim credit for the success. Organisation is teamwork. If anyone forgets their role in the organisation and starts foul playing, the efforts of all the others will go waste. At the same time the company will be pushed behind without any scope for recovery. It is the right of the strategic marketers to feel proud for their achievement; but they should not forget all the other people behind their feat. Therefore, they must share the credit with their co-workers in the organisation.

The battle must be taken to the doorsteps of the competitor, and the ball should be always in the other side only creating stress and tension to the players of the opponent team. You can do all this only if the strategic marketers possesses the requisite confidence in them. This confidence should not be like a castle in the air. It must be built on solid foundation. The marketer must have the ability to face the competitors with newer strategies. They must use their creative skills to discover new ways of working for the success of the organisation.

Strategies in the Decline Stage

The alarm will give the signal at the right time for packing-up. The sales level in the market of not only our company but also all the companies in the market will show the point where the slowdown begins. Once it has been found out that the product has started declining in the market, the strategic marketers must explore ways to begin the last journey as far as the new product is concerned. They must chalk out a plan to get maximum gain from the market by extending the life of the product. If it is found to be feasible after intensive deliberations with senior executives of the organisation, they can go ahead with the proposal. If the committee decides that any further moves in the market will to the detriment of the organisation, the company must decide for a slow but cautious withdrawal of the product.

Communicate your presence in the market   Any abrupt withdrawal from the market will do more harm to the organisation. The company will have to earn the resentment of the customers. Therefore, your withdrawal must be in a phased manner. However, until you remain in the market, you must keep telling your customers that you are still there to serve the customers. You must create confidence in the minds of the customers. Even though the market is declining, you are hand-in-hand with your customers. This will bring you the sympathy of the customers. Once you have earned the sympathy of the customers, then you can go ahead with your programme of phased withdrawal of the product.

Minimise your promotional expenditure   You must stop spending on sales promotions if you are sure that the product has entered the decline stage. You keep communicating the customers to convey your presence in the market through simple but effective advertisements.

Set the right time for the final withdrawal   Withdrawing from the market is, of course, a sad thing; but it is unavoidable. All the products must face it sometime in future. There is no product on this earth with an assured life for an infinite period of time. It is a matter of time. That's all. The timing of final withdrawal is important. The customers must be informed about it. It is not that a big announcement must be made in leading magazines. The withdrawal from the market must be silent and the message must be passed on to the customers through informal channels. In the case of long-time successful products, companies may announce the withdrawal through press meets.

THE CASE OF MARKET FOLLOWERS

Market followers are medium- or small-sized organisations which follow the actions and reactions of the market leader and the market challengers. There are two kinds of market followers. The first type belongs to the category of *silent players*. Silent players are the organisations which strictly follow the moves of the market leader or market challengers. They do not have any high ambitions for their future. They do not aspire for innovation; they simply follow the market leader in their strategies. The second category of market followers consists of companies which formulate long-term plans to become market challengers or market leaders. They are the *active players*. They are ambitious market followers who have their own research and development facilities to develop new products, and in a later stage they start employing creative people to develop new products to reach their goals.

NICHE MARKETING STRATEGY

The terms, target marketing, focused marketing, concentrated marketing and micromarketing are all used as synonyms for niche marketing. A niche market is a small segment of the market which has special requirements. It is a market which has a group of customers who possess similar characteristics. The special requirements of the niche market cannot be satisfied by mass marketing organisations like market leaders and market challengers. A market leader and the market challengers look for a big share of the market which the niche market cannot provide. Sometimes the market followers undertake niche marketing. However, sometimes large companies also do niche marketing. Take the example of Johnson & Johnson, a reputed healthcare company. It consists of 170 affiliates (business units), most of which pursue niche markets. In niche marketing you focus on the customer and you provide the customer with the products they need, now and in the future. The niche marketer is very close to the customer, who knows the specific needs of the individual customer and supplies with the right product that can satisfy the customer.

Highly luxurious cars, very special orders from special customers and the like belong to niche marketing. Niche marketers have few competitors as the customers contact the niche marketers and ask for a particular product. The niche marketer produces the particular product as per the specifications of the individual customers.

SUMMARY

* The key assumptions for studying the competitive-winning strategies are the following.
    * The price of the product is worth the quality of the product.
    * The buyer enjoys sufficient consumer surplus from the consumption of the product.
    * The quality of the product is better than the competitor's at least marginally.
    * The advertisement media used are same as those of the competitors.
    * The quality of the advertisement copy used is similar, if not identical.
    * The distribution channels are more or less similar.
    * The products are sufficiently available in the market.
    * The sales staff is loyal and talented.
* The competitive-winning strategies have been discussed from the view point of a new product introduced by the market leader.
* These strategies have been studied from the product life cycle point of view giving clearly the strategies to be followed in its each stage by a market leader, and market challengers.
* Market followers follow the actions and reactions of the market leader and the market challengers.
* The niche marketing strategy is followed by a manufacturer who wants to satisfy the needs of small groups of consumers who have identical characteristics.

REVIEW QUESTIONS

1. What are the strategies to be followed by the market leaders during the introduction stage?

2. What must the leader do in order to reduce the price of the product in such a way that the margin from the product is very low? In what situations, must such a strategy be followed by the market leader?

3. As a prudent marketer, how would you counter the moves of your competitor who offers a better quality product?

4. As a prudent marketer, how would you counter the moves of your competitor who offers their product at competitive prices?

5. As a prudent marketer, how would you counter the moves of your competitor who undertakes intensive advertisement campaigns to promote their product?

6. What are the strategies to be followed by the market leaders during the growth stage?

7. "It is not that the marketer must be reactive only. Proactive measures will also go a long way in improving the sales figures of the company." Do you agree? Substantiate your answer with valid points.

8. What are the challenges that the competitor will throw to you during the growth stage of your product? How will you confront them successfully?

9. How would you beat the market penetration strategy of your competitor?

10. "The battle must be taken to the doorsteps of the competitor, and the ball should be always in the other side only creating stress and tension to the players of the opponent team." Do you agree with the strategy? List out the merits and risks in following such a strategy.

11. What are the strategies that are to be followed by the market leaders at the time of the maturity stage of his product?

12. What are the strategies that are to be followed by the market leaders at the time of the decline stage of their product?

13. What strategies must be followed by the market challenger during the introduction stage of their product? Also explain how these strategies will work for them.

14. What are the strategies that must be followed by the market challenger in order to succeed in the market at the time of maturity stage of the product?

15. What are the strategies that must be followed by the market challenger at the time of decline of the product?

16. In what ways an abrupt withdrawal of the product from the market will harm the organisation?

13

ADVERTISING AND SALES PROMOTION STRATEGIES

After reading this chapter, you will be able to

- *take note of the assumptions on which the marketer needs to develop the advertising and sales promotion strategies,*
- *learn about the objectives of advertising,*
- *come to know about a number of advertising strategies that may be used to rope in new customers and to retain the existing ones,*
- *learn about various advertising strategies that use internet as the medium,*
- *learn about the sales promotional strategies that are used by the marketers, and*
- *recognise the significance of creativity in formulating advertising and sales promotional strategies for the benefit of the marketing organisation.*

KEY TERMS

Feature advertising	Patriotic advertising	Pay-per-click advertising
Testimonial advertising	Music-centred advertising	Affiliate marketing
Fact advertising	Mega advertising	Banner advertising
Appeal advertising	Up-to-the-point advertising	E-mail marketing
Challenge advertising	Tiger's assault advertising	Content advertising
Wit and humour advertising	Passive advertising	Viral advertising
Mixed strategy creativity	Cold advertising	Incentivised advertising
Task commitment	Internet advertising	Video advertising

INTRODUCTION

Advertisements when they are effective can turn things upside down. People are carried away by good advertisements and some of them even convert ordinary customers into special ones. Advertisements are that powerful. They very much help to create brand loyalty among the customers. Loyal customers are an asset to the organisation in the sense that the customers stand solidly behind the brand and they themselves are good advertisers as well as the torch bearers for the company. They speak for their brand in the crowd and when they are an influential person in the society, their role is still bigger in creating new customers for the organisation. A loyal customer is an unpaid ambassador of the organisation. One of the prominent men of American advertising, Bruce Fairchild Barton,[1] said this on advertisements: "Advertising is the very essence of democracy. An election goes on every minute of the business day across the counters of thousands of stores and shops where the customers state their preferences and determine which manufacturer and which product shall be the leader today, and which shall lead tomorrow."

In many companies, the advertising budget is the first to be cut when the economy begins to fizzle. Ironically, that means the publications and websites with which you have advertised in the past may now face a much more daunting challenge of hitting their sales targets. If your boss is considering cutting the advertising budget again, remind him of what Philip K. Wrigley, heir to the largest chewing gum company in the world, said when asked during a transcontinental flight why he still spent so much on advertising. He replied, "For the same reason the pilot of this airplane keeps the engines running when we're already 29,000 feet up."[2]

Sales promotion is not a less important activity when compared to the role of advertisements. Sales promotional measures create a suitable environment for the organisation. In such an environment, advertisements can become more effective. However, there are a few advertisements which create very good responses without the help of the sales promotional measures to roping in new customers. This way, we can say that advertisements are more powerful than the sales promotional measures. In fact sales promotional measures do well when advertisements inspire the customers to buy the product. Sales promotional measures serve as the reinforcing agent in the marketplace.

Experts say that the role of advertising has come down sharply in organisations when compared to promotions. But it cannot be so because the value of genuine and effective advertisement is very great. A good advertisement backed by a powerful product creates a want in the customers, inspires them to buy, and create brand loyalty. But most of the sales promotional measures create suspicion in the minds of customers and many customers become hostile to such measures. Therefore, we have to use the sales promotion strategies selectively only. In this chapter, clear tips are available on how to select the best promotional strategy among the available ones.

KEY ASSUMPTIONS

Whatever the role of an advertisement is and whatever the role of the sales promotional measures may be, the success of these efforts depend on the satisfaction of some key assumptions in the marketplace. These assumptions, if not satisfied, can make even the best advertisements ineffective and wasteful. Let us now list out these assumptions.

1. The quality of the product is more or less similar to those made available by leading manufacturers.
2. The packaging, pricing, and the like are also more or less similar to those of the leading brands.
3. The channels of distribution are also more or less similar.
4. The employee morale is also good.
5. The brand name is also equally good.
6. The company offers more or less similar after-sales-services to the customers.
7. The talents of the employees of the organisation are also more or less similar.

As a strategic marketer, you must see that you are no small in your methods, techniques, and strategies, while you are entering the market. This means that you have satisfied all the requirements stated above as key assumptions. Even if one of the requirements fails to be present, the organisation may not get the desired results.

NATURE OF ADVERTISING

Advertising has become an essential part of the business world. If you have a good product or an efficient service to offer, you need to master the art of advertising! While some of the advertising agencies might stick to the conventional advertising methods, others are resorting to modern advertising methods. There is a new cult of modern advertisers who are experimenting with ideas that are truly modern and innovative! Today we are able to find a variety of advertising techniques used by organisations. The important point in this connection is that the strategic marketer must choose the right kind of advertising that suits the requirements most.

Objectives of Advertising

The ultimate objective of any advertisement is to make more sales. However, there are some specific objectives the analysis of which can lead us to new ways of thinking and advertising. The following are the objectives:

1. To capture the attention of the prospects,
2. To keep alive their interest, and
3. To inspire them towards action.

Capturing the attention of the prospects   This is the prime objective of an advertisement. Capturing the attention of the prospects is no simple job. The prospects are the potential customers who would soon turn as our customers if they are accessed through proper media. But the irony is that many advertisers, in their anxiety to capture the attention of potential customers follow unethical practices for the purpose. We are able to see a lot of advertisements that make claims which are untrue or exaggerated on the face of it. Such advertisements, even though attract the attention of the people, do no good for the organisation. In fact, they produce negative results. We find some advertisements on the television screen claiming that if a housewife uses their detergent powder, even a shirt full of stains would turn as new one. A wise customer would never believe this claim. Today, we find a majority of consumers are rational as well as conscious of their needs. One cannot hope to falsely distract their attention through untrue statements. Another advertisement claims that their floor cleaning product would remove even toughest of the stains on the floor. What a pity! These advertisers, it seems, are not interested in their long term business. Even prudent customers get carried away by such advertisements and the next time, they won't turn to this product. But the irony is that since the market is full of such companies, they are able to survive in the market as the customers are left with no other alternative. If a good product arrives in the market, the other brands will sooner or later vanish like the morning dew. Until then they can do their business.

Keeping live the prospects' interest   The responses of the prospects vary depending on their needs and the kind of urgency to buy the product. Some of the prospects may be searching for a suitable product. These prospects follow some quick methods to make their purchase decision. If they need the product urgently, they rely on the reputation of the brand and make their purchase straight without taking any other course. Sometimes, they make enquiries with their friends and relatives who are already in possession of the particular product. But most of the prospects belong to the category which follows a "wait and watch" policy. In the case of this category, the objective of the advertisement must be to keep the message about the product alive until they come to a decisive conclusion. This can be possible only if the strategic marketer advertises the product frequently. However, too much of frequent advertisements might sometimes damage the reputation of the organisation. Look at the advertisements of Horlicks! They do not advertise heavily for promoting their product. They advertise only when they launch a new product in their series. Now they are planning to give a label of *complete food* for their brand in addition to what they have now as a *health drink*. Therefore, a carefully drafted strategy of advertising alone can make the prospects keep alive the message given through the advertisements.

Inspiring the prospects toward action The third objective of the advertisement is to make the prospects toward a concrete action. This depends on the kind of message passed on to the prospects through the advertisement. The advertisement copy plays the vital role in this connection. The most effective copy is one which makes the prospects buy immediately. This is the most successful advertisement. Whether the prospect is urgently in need of a product or not, the message given in the advertisement creates a need to buy the project urgently at once. Whether they have the resource or not is immaterial. In such cases, the prospects arrange the resource somehow and buy the product to satisfy their compelling mental pressure to buy the product. The prospects relax only after they complete the purchase of the product. Until then they never sleep.

There are some prospects who make the purchase very carefully without hurrying to the decision to buy the product. In such cases the objective of the advertisement must be to inspire them continuously so that they will make the purchase soon.

SPECIFIC ADVERTISING STRATEGIES

Let us now study the different advertising strategies available for the marketer.

Fact advertising This is a strategy which makes use of the facts about the product. The marketer chooses this method of advertising assuming that the market consists of many rational customers who evaluate a product on the basis of its merits. The alert consumer collects facts regarding different brands of the product available and compare them and makes the purchase decision. This method is an effective one for industrial products; however, this method is sometimes used for consumer products also, the belief being that a customer's mental faculty will retain all the plus points of a product and keep reminding of them whenever the customer has an opportunity to think about the need to buy the product.

Appeal advertising In advertising a product, some of the manufacturers use different appeals which, they believe, would do the job. Appeals may be prestige, richness, health, beauty, sex, youthfulness, safety, ease of use, and so on. Appeals are considered to be effective by the marketers. They believe that sometimes even quality becomes secondary and an appeal to one's basic instinct plays a major role in marketing the product. The marketer must have the knowledge of connection between appeals and nature of the products. They have to possess the talent to identify the right kind of appeal to the right product and make use of it in their advertising strategy.

Challenge advertising Today we find marketers throwing up challenges to the customers to disprove their claims on quality of their products, and in the case of any customer proving this claim against the product, would receive a lump sum as the prize money.

This type of challenges to the customers has become common in India today. Many marketers have started adopting the challenge strategy with a good rate of success.

Wit and humour advertising   Many customers like advertising based on humour and wits. *Vodofone* advertises their products this way. *Pass Pass* and *Alpanliebe* also use advertisements which are very attractive and humourous. Geuens and D. Pelsmacker[3] find that ads that are warm, erotic, or humourous all outperform ads that use non-emotional appeals.

Testimonial advertising   These are the advertisements in which popular personalities like Amitabh, Kiren Bedi, and Sharukh Khan appear and speak high of the products. However, this form of advertisements is expensive; therefore, only big companies can afford to appoint the brand ambassadors. The expectation of the marketer is that the followers or fans of the personalities would take the advice of the personalities and sales would hit a new mark.

Feature advertising   The unique or key feature of the product is given prominence in the advertisement. Thus the customer is taken to the concept of differentiation. The product is differentiated citing the unique or special feature/s available in the product. This is a kind of advertising used where the product enjoys superiority over others.

Patriotic advertising   Patriotic advertising is a kind of advertising made to evoke response from those customers who are highly patriotic when the competitor/s involved is/are foreigner/s. This kind of advertisement works well when people with patriotism are large in number in a country. Of late, even American companies have started giving advertisements using this kind of appeal among the Americans. Scholars have suggested that nationalism grows in intensity when a country is threatened or attacked.[4]

Music-centred advertising   You can see some of the advertisements on the television screen which present music without any spoken words. This way the advertiser is able to convey a message to the audience and in many cases such advertisements can be successful if produced in the right sense.

Mega advertising   This is a type of advertising which can be found in the junction points of the city. These advertisements look gigantic and attract the attention of the onlookers very easily. This is a powerful strategy to advertise the products of high value involving hi-tech products. Sometimes other companies like cement and communications also use this kind of advertising very effectively.

Up-to-the-point advertising   Some of the marketers are very careful not to use words that would give double meaning in the minds of viewers. Here the advertisers literally mean what they say. There is no room for misinterpretation. They give their points that would reach the customer instantly. The customers do not find it difficult to understand the message. This may also be called as point-to-point or plain advertising. This may be used for any kind of media.

"Tiger's assault" advertising   This is an advertising strategy in which the marketers wait for the right time to pounce into the market like a roaring tiger. The marketers release a series of messages to the market very frequently with strong points which will never fail them in the market. This strategy is adopted when the marketer introduces a highly worthy new product which may look like a close substitute but really is not. They leap forward by giving point after point so that the customer is fully convinced. This may also be called as an aggressive advertising strategy. This strategy involves heavy expenditure and can be adopted by large organisations only. When this strategy is used by the company, all the other companies take a back seat in their approach to advertising their products. Such is the force applied by this type of advertising.

Passive advertising   Passive advertising is made by organisations which convey messages regularly to their customers about the superiority of their products thereby assuring them of their best service to them.

Cold calling   Direct sale over the phone or in person is the oldest method of selling and it is cost effective; the marketers are usually only sacrificing their time. If they are going door to door, they have to make sure to have effective marketing material and talking points prepared, and keep good tracking records.

Bandwagon   Bandwagon is a form of propaganda that exploits the desire of most people to join the crowd or be on the winning side, and avoid winding up the losing side. Few of us would want to wear nerdy cloths, smell differently from everyone else, or be unpopular. The popularity of a product is important to many people. Even if most of us say we make our own choice when buying something, we often choose well-advertised items—the popular ones. Advertising copywriters must be careful with the bandwagon propaganda technique because most of us see ourselves as individuals who think for themselves. If bandwagon commercial is too obvious, viewers may reject the product outright.

Magic ingredients   The suggestion that some almost miraculous discovery makes the product exceptionally effective, e.g., a pharmaceutical manufacturer describes a special coating that makes their pain reliever less irritating to the stomach than a competitor's.

INTERNET ADVERTISING STRATEGIES

The role of the internet in getting exposure for the products is significant. Internet advertising is considered to be more expensive than print media but is cheaper than other mediums of advertising. Internet advertising is very flexible as the latest updates and other modifications can be done with minimum effort. The advertisers can make their choice by selecting those sites that relates best with the products and services offered by them. Televisions and internet play important role in advertising. For example, in the movie *E.T.*, the extraterrestrial eats Reese's Pieces candy. The candy was authentically integrated into the movie and sales of Reese's Pieces soared 80% after the movie, catapulting the new product to mainstream status.[5] However, inappropriate or excessive product placements may do more harm than good to the brand. It is also important to note that one exposure generates the highest proportion of sales and that additional exposures add very little to the effect of the first.[6]

Let us now study important methods of internet advertising.

Pay-per-click advertising   Pay-per-click (PPC) advertising is all about relevance, particularly with Google AdWords. For every click made by the visitor, the host charges a small sum as fees to the advertiser. If the marketer's advertisements don't get clicked on enough, they will be removed. The pay-per-click advertising programmes offered by Google and Yahoo have the greatest market reach. Google's programme called AdWords delivers targeted pay-per-click advertisements via its own search engine, websites and a host of partner sites. The interesting point of PPC advertising is the speed at which the marketers can reach their target market and the high quality of sales leads that can be generated. The downside is the price and the need for excellent conversion to sales.

Affiliate marketing   This is a more popular internet marketing/advertising technique. The technique is basically a scenario where a company agrees to pay commission or incentives to another web-based organisation or individual to advertise and market its product or service. For instance, an online company that sells forex software product could contract out an affiliate marketing programme (based on agreed commissions or incentives) to a web-based company that offers information on forex products. The affiliate programme is provided by the company needing the affiliate services, while the affiliate itself refers to the website that embarks on the promotion for the company who supplied them affiliate programme.

Banner advertising   Banner advertisements, simply put, are just HTML codes in a specific size and shape (differing from advertiser to advertiser) that present a small snippet of the product or service on a specific host site. Banner advertising has gained popularity at an increasing rate over the past few years due to the increasing popularity of internet as well as the fact that it has more audience and the ability to direct a prospective client to their website with just a click.

E-mail marketing   E-mail marketing is a low-cost internet marketing method for small business owners to improve their sales. Though it might be under threat from spammers abusing the medium, e-mail marketing is still a very effective strategy to market the product to the customers. Targeting the marketers' e-mails to the correct demographic segment establishes a strong foundation for their campaigns to be effective.

Content advertising   Content advertising, sometimes called contextual advertising, paired with a sound strategy has proved that it can help online advertisers obtain new sales, generate leads, and lower a company's online cost-per-acquisition. Content networks include premier publishers, blogs, forums, shopping portals, coupon sites, and so much more. Many of the websites in a content network are highly ranked organic websites. The expansive reach provides a business massive exposure to web users engaged in content relevant to the products and services.

Viral advertising   Viral advertising is spreading as a popular, efficient marketing tool, as consumers increasingly pick and choose what advertisements they watch and when. Viral is today's electronic equivalent of old-fashioned word of mouth. It's a marketing strategy that involves creating an online message that's novel or entertaining enough to prompt consumers to pass it on to others — spreading the message across the web like a virus at no cost to the advertiser. A word of caution here! When done well, it can significantly increase traffic to your site with its ability to 'travel' from computer to computer. When done poorly, it can alienate customers and even worse affect a brand's reputation.

Incentivised advertising   Under the incentivised advertising, the visitors are rewarded for visiting the marketer's website. Success in this type of advertising depends mainly on the marketer's offer and the way he presents it. Most advertisers who fail either do not have a good offer or they fail to deliver the benefit of their offer across to the target audience.

Video advertising   A promotional programme that has already been highly popular among the customers is video promotion. Videos have the capability to grab the attention of web visitors than any other form of advertising. They can also be effective enough to increase the visibility of your product ranges than conventional online promotional tools like banners. With almost every web surfer showing keen interest towards accessing videos in their daily browsing habits, website owners have been able to cash in on the platform thus bringing more value to their businesses. Videos are viewable on all browsers and they don't take much time in buffering. So, the marketers can easily take full advantage of the platform in marketing their products and services without any issues. Apart from product promotion, videos are also effective in letting the marketers tell their visitors about the company's achievements and progress of their corporate house.

SALES PROMOTIONAL STRATEGIES

The objectives of advertising and sales promotions are identical. They are 1) creation of wider customer base, and 2) increasing the sales level of the organisation.

However, advertising has another goal namely, conveying messages to the customers. Even though advertising is superior in some respects, sales promotion has its own advantages. It is true that many customers are after sales promotional measures announced by the organisations. In fact these customers are waiting for them. Until then they don't buy. They buy the product only when it becomes urgent. They postpone their purchases until the company announces an offer. It is evident that customers throng the dealers whenever companies announce offers or price cuts during particular seasons like Diwali, Pongal, Ugadi, Independence Day, and so on.

There are three categories of strategies namely push strategy, pull strategy and combination of both. Let us study these strategies available to the marketer.

Push Strategy

A push strategy engrosses the intermediary channel members to push the product through the distribution channels to end consumers through promotions. Companies promote the services or products though the resellers who in turn promote it to another buyer or to the end customer. These are the people who carry the brand throughout the channel to reach the end consumers. Buy-back guarantees, contests, discounts, premiums, and free trials are some of the tactics that are employed in push strategy. This kind of strategy is usually involved in products where there is fierce competition amongst producers and the intermediaries are given heavy margins by each producer to ensure his product is given the preference.

Pull Strategy

In pull strategy, the consumer requests for the products and pulls it through the distribution channel. The company concentrates on its marketing communications efforts on end consumers in the wish that it kindles interest and demand for the product at the end-user level. The tactics included in this strategy are coupons, cash refunds, loyalty programmes, and premiums and the like. By adopting this strategy the marketer works with the intermediaries, especially the retailers to better present the products not only in shelves but also improve its general outlook. The Bajaj Auto's scheme of *taking* home a scooter at ₹ 999 was a sales promotional offer communicated through effective advertising and was essentially a pull strategy.

Mixed Strategy

This kind of strategy is adopted when the company thinks that the products need a push from both sides. Neither the intermediaries are pushing the product of the company to the extent nor the customers have a knowledge of or are interested in the product. To make this thing really happen the company simultaneously launches a two prong battle. This strategy is obviously more cost bearing and takes more time to materialise. In this strategy the company not only gives heavy margins to the intermediaries like the wholesalers and distributors, but also tries to attract the customers by making its products more attractive in shelves and packaging. This is one of the most comprehensive sales promotion strategies. The company should properly plan for the expenses and the expected outcome. A misdirected campaign will not only result into great financial loss but may hurt the brand in the market.

DESIGNING THE SUITABLE PROMOTIONAL STRATEGY

When you are deciding upon the best promotional strategy for reaching your target market, you need to

- study the market by doing simple research
- keep your customer in mind
- be creative

Studying the market includes activities such as studying the target market and finding out what other businesses in the industry are doing. A relatively quick way to learn how the competitors communicate their marketing messages is to look in trade journals. This will give the marketer an idea of which features they believe are important and are emphasising.

Keeping your customer in mind will help prevent wasting money and time on ineffective promotional activities. For example, it obviously won't help to advertise in the newspaper if the target audience doesn't read it.

CREATIVITY IN ADVERTISING AND SALES PROMOTIONS[7]

Leo Tolstoy said: "The best stories don't come from "good vs. bad" but from "good vs. good." We can slightly modify the statement of Tolstoy this way—The best products don't come from "good vs. bad" but from "good vs. good." This is true. The marketer must offer the best product to the customer and at the same time, use the best advertising and sales promotion techniques. Creativity helps to find out new and worthy strategies which can bring in more customers into our fold. After all this is the sole objective of strategic marketing. The customer, so earned, must be retained with us forever. This is the ultimate goal of strategic marketing management.

What is Creativity

Creativity (or creativeness) is a mental process involving the generation of new ideas or concepts, or new associations between existing ideas or concepts. From a scientific point of view, the products of creative thought (sometimes referred to as divergent thought) are usually considered to have both originality and appropriateness. An alternative, more everyday conception of creativity, is that *it is simply the act of making something new.* Some of the authors attributed creativity variously to divine intervention, cognitive processes, the social environment, personality traits, and chance ("accident," "serendipity"). It has been associated with genius, mental illness and humour. Some say it is a trait we are born with; others say it can be taught with the application of simple techniques.

Organisational creativity is an inner urge or state of mind that drives a person knowingly or unknowingly toward finding a new or modified product/service/system/ process that contributes to the success of the organisation considerably. Look at what is said by Albert Rothenberg about creativity, "The problem of creativity is beset with mysticism, confused definitions, value judgments, psychoanalytic admonitions, and the crushing weight of philosophical speculation dating from ancient times."

Determinants of Creativity

In order to find out new strategies for advertising and sales promotion, it is essential to understand what determines creativity in a man. Creativity has been associated with a wide range of behavioural and mental characteristics, including associations between semantically remote ideas and contexts, application of multiple perspectives, curiosity, flexibility in thought and action, rapid generation of multiple, qualitatively different solutions and answers to problems and questions, tolerance for ambiguity and uncertainty, and unusual uses of familiar objects.

Creativity needs to be analysed in order to understand what it contains. It would help to comprehend its nature and to become creative. An understanding of creativity will encourage men and women to take up this sphere of life as a profession. They can develop the creative skill in them. Creators are not only born; they can be developed with appropriate training. Let us now discuss the determinants of creativity.

Mother Nature   Mother Nature is the biggest teacher. She teaches silently. Living beings are her students. Whoever wants to take lessons from her can do so at their will. Nature does not deny admission to its institution. She is a great source for creative ideas and thoughts.

Desire to learn   Man must possess the desire to learn. Desire to learn comes naturally to some people and for many people, their environment forces them to acquire the desire to learn. When it naturally occurs, it is well and good. At the same time, when man is forced by the environment to learn, it is also equally good. Sometimes, the latter works faster and better. In this case, there is a compulsion or motive, whereas in the former it is absent.

Task commitment   The researchers must set high standards for their work. These high standards will help them achieve the objective. It includes the ability to identify significant problems within an area of study. When the researchers are able to identify the specific areas, they are nearing the end of their research. A correct diagnosis will help the doctor cure the ailment quickly.

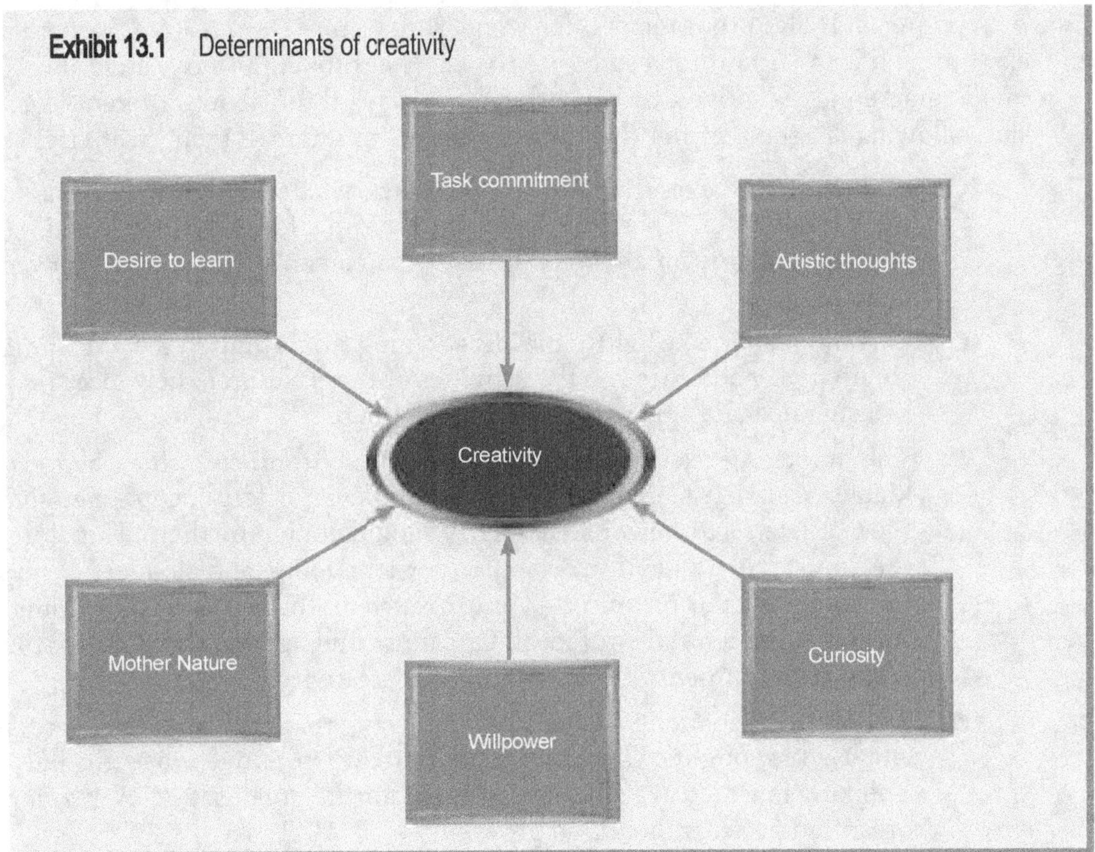

Exhibit 13.1   Determinants of creativity

Artistic thoughts   Art is a thing that is looked by the creator as a thing of beauty. Most of the artistic thoughts come naturally to the creator. However, today arts are taught in schools and colleges. These thoughts help the researcher to find new things by thinking in new directions. An artist thinks differently who approaches the problem from different angles.

Curiosity Curiosity is another important component of creativity. Only a curious person will have a liking for further probe into the matter. The creators have naturally in them the trait of curiosity. At the same time they are not in a hurry to see the results. They approach the problem logically and systematically.

Willpower The determination to finish a given task is the greatest asset of the creators. Willpower makes them patient, as well as determined. They plan their project in such a way that the probability of failure will be minimal.

How to Get the Marketer's Creativity Going

Advertising and sales promotions offer wonderful avenues for creative marketing executives. It is important to keep creativity, i.e., the thinking process, alive always by the marketing executives. Creative thinkers always think about different ideas. The following are some of the tips for the markets to improve their creativity.

* The marketing executive has to note down whatever that may come to mind at all times. Creativity can occur anytime. Ideas can flow anytime, anywhere, and from anybody. It may be a person's friend, wife, or even enemies.

* One should not take lightly the ideas coming from children too. Watching children play and through the activities of these children, new ideas may be generated and it is useful to elaborae them.

* The marketing executives must create an environment which helps to kindle creativity. Gathering of youths and even elderly people can give the marketers a number of ideas. They should not ignore them. Therefore, they must make a habit to be at places where young and old meet. While travelling in a bus or train they must watch all that is happening around them and get a number of ideas. One must find out ways of building the sort of environment that will encourage creativity.

* The strategic marketers must look for ways that will initiate different and useful thoughts. One must avoid thinking in terms of benefits only. Thinking must always stress on the gain for the organisation. A growing organisation helps them also grow.

* The marketers must try to find out how ideas are taking the roots and how they are developing into useful themes for the organisation.

* They must find out the reasons that while the first step is often the most difficult, it is also the most important.

Creativity is a process of reasonable imagination or thinking in the right direction that leads to splendid results. A person of good creativity skills keeps on analysing the possible newer methods or techniques that can be effectively used in the given circumstance. Creativity can occur any time. The advertising copy maker or the marketer in charge of devising sales promotional methods must possess a good sense of creativity.

SUMMARY

* Advertisements when they are effective can turn things upside down. People are carried away by good advertisements and some of them even convert ordinary customers into special. Advertisements are that powerful.

* Sales promotional measures do well when advertisements inspire the customers to buy the product. Sales promotional measures serve as the reinforcing agent in the marketplace.

* Whatever the role of an advertisement is and whatever the role of the sales promotional measures may be, the success of these efforts depend on the satisfaction of some key assumptions in the marketplace.

* The specific objectives of advertising and sales promotional strategies are 1) to capture the attention of the prospects, 2) to keep alive their interest, and 3) to inspire them toward action.

* A number of advertising strategies including internet advertising has been provided in order to make a thorough understanding of the subject.

* The role of creativity in finding out new advertising and sales promotional strategies for action by the strategic marketer is very important for a growing organisation.

REVIEW QUESTIONS

1. What are the key assumptions to be kept in mind while designing suitable advertising and sales promotion strategies for a manufacturing organisation?

2. Explain the nature of advertising strategies.

3. A loyal customer is an unpaid ambassador of the organisation. Is it true? Can you say that all the loyal customers are the ambassadors of the company? Put forth logical arguments to prove your stand.

4. Discuss any five specific advertising strategies.

5.   Explain the internet advertising strategies.

6.   "There are a few advertisements which create very good responses without the help of the sales promotional measures in roping in new customers." Give two or three examples of such advertisements and explain how they accomplish the job.

7.   What are the important sales promotional strategies?

8.   Discuss the role of creativity in advertising and sales promotions.

9.   What are the determinants of creativity?

REFERENCES

1.   Bruce Barton (1955). Chairman of BBDO, quoted in James B. Simpson, *Contemporary Quotations*, 1964, Vail-Ballou Press, Binghamton, NY. p. 82.

2.   http://www.scribd.com/doc/5877598/COMO-INCREMENTAR-LAS-VENTAS-DURANTE-UNA-RECESION

3.   Geuens and Pelsmacker, D. Feelings Evoked by Warm, Erotic, Humorous or Non-Emotional Print Advertisements for Alcoholic Beverages, *Academy of Marketing Science Review*, June 1998 No. 01.

4.   Sharma, S., Shimp, T.A. and Shin, J. (1995). "Consumer ethnocentrism: A test of antecedents and moderators." *Journal of the Academy of Marketing Science.* 23: 26–37.

5.   Susan Spillman. (1985). "Marketers race to leave their brand on films." *Advertising Age.* 56 (51): 3–4.

6.   John, P. Jones. (1995a). *When Ads Work: New Proof that Advertising Triggers Sales.* Lexington Books, New York.

7.   Soundaian, S. (2011). *New Dimensions of Management.* MJP Publishers, Chennai.

14

SALESFORCE MANAGEMENT STRATEGIES

After reading this chapter, you will be able to

- *Learn the objectives of salesforce management,*
- *Study how these objectives turn themselves into strategies of salesforce management,*
- *Recognise the need for creation of a loyal salesforce,*
- *Understand the importance of right kind of training to salespersons and the methodology to plan it,*
- *Recognise the importance of paying well for the services rendered by the salespersons, and*
- *Recognise the need for adopting positive motivational techniques to motivate the salesforce*

KEY TERMS

Teamwork	Training objectives	Instruction manual
Loyal salespeople	Communication skills	Feedback session
Personality tests	On-the-job training	Training programme evaluation
Halo effect	Off-the-job training	Sound remuneration plan
Transparency	Audio-visual methods	Commission

INTRODUCTION

Jack Welch, former CEO, General Electric said: Any company trying to compete must figure out a way to engage the mind of nearly every employee. It goes without saying that organisation is teamwork. All the people in the organisation must work in unison. If everyone in the organisation says that it is their contribution that made the organisation stand tall, one must answer them in the positive. It is a big *yes*. But if they say that it is because of their contribution alone that the company is doing well, they are certainly wrong and the answer would be a big *no*. The organisation is what is today because of the efforts put into it by people of all categories starting with the CEO ending with the worker in the factory. Everyone must make their contribution to the success of the organisation. The salespersons are no exception. They must work wholeheartedly recognising their role in the organisation. Still more important is that they must recognise the destiny of the organisation if they refuse to contribute their reasonable efforts to it. All the members of the organisation must learn to work as a team. Only such an organisation would excel in all spheres.

OBJECTIVES OF SALESFORCE MANAGEMENT

The salespeople represent the organisation in the market, and are looked upon as the company's ambassadors. What the salesperson speaks, does, and behaves tell upon the company and its future. One cannot rule out the significance of these key persons in the company. The CEO, the finance officers, the production engineers and supervisors, the personnel managers and their team, workers, and so on stay within the four walls of the company and prepare things required by the customers who are always in touch with the salespeople. Therefore, the salespeople need special attention, care and training.

The strategies of salesforce management are hidden in its objectives. They may be found out through an analysis of the objectives. The objectives of salesforce management are stated below.

1. To create loyal salespeople,
2. To impart the right kind of training to salespeople,
3. To see that they are rightly paid, and
4. To motivate them in the right direction.

These objectives are self-explanatory and need no further details. These objectives form the basis for the rest of the chapter.

Creation of Loyal Salespeople

Loyalty is a trait that is born with people. Therefore, finding people with the trait of loyalty is a tough job. The company may invite applications for loyal people and it might receive thousands of applications. Can we imply that all the applicants are loyal people? There may be a few loyal people in the crowd. But how will you identify them? You cannot so easily separate the loyal people from the rest in the crowd. Everyone would say they are loyal persons. What is the parameter to decide? One cannot determine the personality of a person on the first sight. However, there are a few experts who are able to find out the difference between loyal and disloyal people. But these experts themselves must be identified by the management. All these things are possible only through experience.

Role of tests   There are some methods which help to find out the traits of people. They are the so-called personality tests. Some experts make use of loyalty tests. There's quite a famous story for Christians, and that's the one about Abraham and Isaac. Basically the way the story goes is God's test to check Abraham's loyalty by commanding him to sacrifice his son. Abraham, being the dutiful lackey, goes about grabbing his son and tries to kill him with a sharp knife without giving the command a second thought. However, just as dutiful Abe was about to deliver the death cut, God sends an angel to say, "psyche!" and he didn't have to go through with it. You see, it was just a test, a loyalty test. God of course isn't supposed to be the coy type, so he didn't ask hypothetically, "what would be your response be if I asked you to remove some kids from your family?" or even rhetorically, "you wouldn't object to killing your son for me, would you?". No, God in the story commanded and like a loyal, faithful servant, Abe unquestionably set out to carry out the command. Such a loyalty test cannot be conducted in today's organisations.

Personality has a significant role to play in providing answers to some of the key questions concerned with selection of employees. In most working situations it's the personality of your co-workers and managers that affect the day-to-day success of the organisation. If the team doesn't work well together or a manager can't motivate their staff, then productivity and quality of service will suffer. If a test is able to reveal one's personality, well and good; the organisation would get sufficient number of loyal employees. But the problem is that the so-called personality tests lack reliability and validity. This is why most companies are reluctant to use these tests in selecting people for their organisations. In India, the need for loyal employees has been increasing steadily.

It is true that most of the companies that produce personality tests are very secretive about their methodologies and refuse to make public crucial information about how their tests were developed or how well they work, claiming that this information is "proprietary". The usefulness and accuracy of even the most well established tests, (for example, the Myers-Briggs[1] Type Indicator—first published in 1962 and the subject of thousands of research papers), remain highly controversial among psychologists. Despite all these revelations, there has been a dramatic increase in the use of personality tests over the past ten years or so.

Strategies for creating loyal salespeople   Let us now dwell at some length on the strategies that may be employed to create loyal salespeople. Since loyal salespeople are the backbone of the sales organisation, the management must make an all-out effort to create loyal salespeople. One of the successful executives said—Loyalty is not given by an employee; it is earned by the employer. What is the meaning of this statement? The employer must be loyal to his employees first; the employees will become spontaneously loyal. This is true in many cases.

Let us discuss a few strategies that may be used in creating loyal salespeople.

Select right persons for the job   The basic requirement for the success of the sales organisation lies in the fact that the right people are employed as salespersons. Every care must be taken to see that no wrong person enters the team. The best way to do this is to recruit people referred by the present loyal salespersons. There is no better way than this. Finding out the traits in a few hours or in a few days is a tough task. Halo effect may stand in the way. Therefore, every effort must be made to select the right candidates for the job. Recommendations from well known quarters can also do the job better. The organisation must have some kind of hold over the newly selected salespersons.

Reward the employee for his truthfulness   The beginning of loyalty lies in the fact that the trustworthiness of the employees must be recognised by proper means. Many employers think that it is the duty of the employees to remain truthful to the organisation as they receive due compensation for their services. But the fact is that most of the people like to be recognised when they have performed an act that extraordinarily depicts their truthfulness. They don't expect a big purse from the management. All they need is some kind of recognition from their employer or at least from the superior.

Make the company an attractive place to work   If you make your company into an attractive place to work, combining success, culture, training and excellent products, people will gravitate to you and will wait for an opening if the timing isn't quite right. More important, most of the top performers will not leave, even for more money, because they like where they are and what they are doing. Also they may be afraid that they may not be able to repeat the same performance in a new environment and therefore, they don't like to lose their position in the present organisational set-up. This makes loyalty one of the top jobs of the CEO because they create the company structure. Stay on top of your people's ambitions as well, so you can move them up the ladder if they have the talent, or enhance their role to fulfil their needs and still match their talents. Your best salespeople are not all cut out to be managers. Good sales professionals earn the respect of their peers by working hard. Work environments that foster mutual respect have high morale and are more productive.

Give salespeople freedom to take risks A salesperson does not work in a vacuum and must have the freedom to take risks to open new markets. They must also have the assurance that what has been promised can and will be delivered by others in the company. There are people who love risk-taking and also come out successful. Such salespersons must be encouraged and their achievements must be recognised by the management.

Transparency in dealings with salespeople Salespeople simply can't risk their personal reputations and livelihoods—and performers will inevitably gravitate to employers who value their opinions, anyway. Instead, as a good employer, share your reasoning. Understand how your decisions will impact customers—and don't be afraid to adjust in the light of unpleasant truths. Your sales team is closest to your clients; they must always know you're acting honourably. Tell them the consequences of a particular transaction. Discuss with them freely and frankly.

Impart Right Kind of Training

When we speak of training, most of us do not take it seriously. We think training people is the simplest of all jobs in the organisation. This notion is totally wrong. It leads to several unsolvable problems of the organisation in future. Training is the source where the salespersons or any other section of employees are groomed and they are prepared there for the future organisation. This fact must be recognised by the top management and due care must be taken by it to see that there is no leniency in the management of the training sessions.

Training the salesforce to our exact requirements is an important factor in its success on the field. Many organisations fail to do the job because they do not know what is exactly required of the trainees. Many government and a few private organisations fail because they do not know the intricacies of the training job. They think training is not serious matter. They consider it as a formality. This attitude of the people, both the trainers and the trainees, is a major cause for concern. Even many executives take it easy. Serious thought must be given to all the aspects of training as it is the breeding point for the future loyal salespersons of the organisation.

Steps required of an effective training programme Let us now study the steps and essential aspects of an effective training programme organised for salespersons. See that these steps are followed with great care and sense of belongingness by the concerned executives.

1. *Set training objectives* The objective of any training programme is same irrespective of its kind. The objective is to prepare the trainees for the task ahead. The specific objectives of a training programme for salespersons may be the following:

1. To teach the philosophy of training to the trainees, and emphasise their role in the organisation,

2. To make them recognise the significance of teamwork in the organisation,

3. To train them on the intricacies involved in managing the prospects as well as the existing customers,

4. To teach them the behaviour of the buyer, his/her reactions, and the role of the salespersons in all kinds of situations,

5. To educate them on the need for success in their career, and

6. To prepare them for the task of winning the customer.

2. *Select the right executive for the conduct of training programme*
The training programme must be conducted by an able executive. Do not entrust the job to the wrong person. If so, the purpose of the programme will be defeated without a point of return. Care must be taken to select a responsible officer to conduct and oversee the proceedings of the programme. The success or otherwise of the training depends on the attachment shown by the executive-in-charge of the training programme.

3. *Select people of talents for the position of instructors/trainers*
The instructors are the keys to the success of the training programme. They must be people who love teaching. They must possess the desire to teach the technique of salesmanship. In fact they must be trained in training skills, if necessary. The essential qualities of an effective salesperson are given below.

i. The trainer must possess good communication skills. Clear and simple language should be used to instruct, direct and coach. The trainer must have good listening skills to understand the points raised by the trainees and has to maintain eye contact to make the trainee listen and avoid distraction.

ii. The trainer must possess thorough understanding of the subject matter. Recalling examples from experience is good without overdoing it. Telling too much from the trainer's experience will have a negative impact. The trainer must possess up-to-date information on the subject of training.

iii. The trainer must have done the job already and must be able to explain in detail the complexities involved in the job.

iv. The trainer must be patient enough to clarify even very small points raised by the trainees and rather welcome even minute points. Since the trainees are raw hands, the trainer should not expect too much of knowledge from them. After all every one commits mistakes and the point is that the salesperson should not commit the same mistake repeatedly.

   v. The trainers must have a flair and desire for the teaching job. They must love the teaching assignment and must feel proud while seeing the students moving up in the ladder.

   vi. The trainer must have respect for people. The trainees view the trainer as being knowledgeable. The trainer must be a model to them.

   vii. The trainer must keenly observe the progress of the trainees and determine who requires more attention and must act accordingly.

   viii. The trainer must possess the right sense of humour. But too much of it may spoil the game. Don't give an overdose of it.

4. *Select the right training method*   There are several methods of training the salespersons. The executive-in-charge of the training must decide the right method of training. Usually two types of training methods are available for training purposes—on-the-job training and off-the-job training. The training executive must decide which method should be used to train the salespersons. The trainer must also decide what kind of audio-visual methods must be used during the training.

5. *Prepare a detailed manual for instruction*   The executive-in-charge of the training must prepare a training manual containing a step-by-step procedure for conducting the sessions. The manual must also contain the details regarding the lessons which are numbered and the executive-in-charge must make sure that no lesson is skipped by any instructor. It is imperative that the training sessions proceed as per the schedule and in the case any deviation is necessary, it must be accommodated at the right points. He must see that the course duration does not exceed except under extraordinary situations.

6. *Conduct a feedback session in the middle*   The executive-in-charge of the training programme must conduct a feedback session for the trainees and a free and frank discussion must be made in order to elicit necessary information from them. Information from everyone must be gathered in order to make sure that the programme is proceeding satisfactorily. Any shortcoming in the training programme must be set right.

7. *Consult with the trainers as and when necessary*   It is important that the trainers' or instructors' opinions must be documented by the training-in-charge executive so that worthy points given by them can be implemented immediately. This would help in making the programme relevant and meaningful. Many trainers have their suggestions to improve the programme. A meeting may be arranged with the trainers and their opinions may be ascertained to improve the training modules. The executive may also request them to speak out freely if they have any grievances to redress. All these steps would make the team cohesive and effective. The trainers must have mutual understanding with each other. Overlaps must be identified and avoided by special instructions so that when two trainees are involved both would not skip that part thinking that the other trainer would have covered the component. Many training programmes miss this aspect.

8. *Evaluate the training programme*   Training has no meaning if it does not serve the intended purpose. Therefore, it is essential to evaluate the trainees in respect of what they have learned from out of the training programme. Several methods of evaluation are available. Tests may be conducted and the scores may be the parameter to decide the effectiveness of the training programme. Interviews may be conducted and answers given by the trainees may be analysed to evaluate the training programme. Other creative methods like a simple conversation with the trainees, observing how they perform on the field immediately after their training may be used to study the effectiveness of the training programme.

Pay Them Well

Money is all. Money matters. People say after a given point of time earning money does not count. Is it true? No. It is not true. In exceptional cases, it may be so. An *average* human, with earnings high or low, is after money all the times. There are people at all levels of income who do not care for money. And the reverse is also true. Whether a person respects money or not, it is the duty of the employer to pay well. As an employer, one must be bound to make payments to the employees for their services to the organisation. The employer must not bother about the quantum of money the salesperson receives as salary, commission or incentive. In fact as an employer, one must encourage and appreciate the employees for their feat in their assignment. Look at the practices followed by the Life Insurance Corporation of India in this connection. They display the name/s of those who achieved extraordinarily every month on a prominent board in its office every month. It is a big credit to them. It is a message to the non-achievers to follow the achievers. Money is a great motivator.

A good remuneration plan for salespersons is a means of securing better control of their activities, greater incentive sales, more loyalty, higher morale and greater enthusiasm and interest. It should be planned in such a manner that both the employer and employee must stand to gain. The employer must get higher sales and the salespersons higher income. Such a compensation plan would serve the intended purpose of the organisation.

A sound remuneration plan has the following advantages.

1. It attracts best salespersons because improved performance needs a reward. Talented salesmen are attracted when the firm is prepared to pay well for hard work.

2. It increases the volume of profit and sales of the company.

3. Salespersons develop a sense of loyalty to the organisation. Thus the loyal employees become a permanent asset of the company assuring their best service to it.

4. It satisfies the salespersons because their hardworking efforts are paid well. A satisfied customer naturally puts heart and soul together to maximise work performance.

5. It establishes a healthy employer and employee relationship. Salespersons who are paid well and well-treated, have no scope for grudges or grumbling.

Motivate Them Well

Motivation is more of an art. It is a complex area. It differs from person to person. Where people find it difficult to align and associate with the organisational aims, then most motivational ideas and activities will have a reduced level of success. This alignment is very important as it determines the level of motivation.

A top performer needs no external push to get going on the next sale. They are a special breed of people who are highly self-motivated. They perform well because of the following reasons.

* They are responsible.
* They are full of confidence.
* They are eager to approach that next prospect.
* They love achievement.

Highly motivated salespeople are productive. Highly productive salespeople are highly self-motivated. If you can increase their production, you will automatically increase their motivation. Production and motivation go hand-in-hand. Increase one, and the other thing will get increased automatically. The top performers are generally a highly self-motivated individuals who devour their work because they really enjoy producing the results.

Even though today's salesforce is motivated by more than just a salary cheque, that doesn't mean compensation is unimportant. Commissions will always be the No.1 factor in getting salespeople to perform. Extra incentives like vacations and bonuses can go a long way in motivating the salesforce. The task of providing an environment that promotes enthusiasm for selling rests squarely on the sales executives. In addition to hard cash, today's salespeople also seek loyalty and recognition from their managers more intentionally than did their predecessors. They want to know that they are more than a cog in the company machine and that their contribution isn't being taken for granted.

Finding the right way to motivate each salesperson takes hard work and creativity. Motivational and inspirational quotes, poems, posters, motivational speakers and stories, team building games and activities develop salespersons' motivation. Motivational methods are wide-ranging, from inspirational quotes and poems, to team building games and activities, as ice-breakers, warm-ups and exercises for conferences, workshops, meetings and events, which in themselves can often be helpful for staff motivation too.

People often enjoy events which include new non-work activities, especially when superiors and subordinates take part in the same teams as their junior staff, which also helps cohesiveness and 'can-do' culture. Inspirational quotes, stories and poems all help motivation too. Powerful positive imagery stimulates visualisation in the conscious and sub-conscious brain, which encourages self-motivation, developmental behaviour, confidence and belief. Playing games enable people to experience winning and achieving in a way that their normal work might not.

There are three important things you can do to help the salespeople to increase their production.

* clarify the end-results of the job
* remove the barriers to performance
* provide support

When the above points are given due importance by the sales manager, the salespeople would do their best for the organisation.

SUMMARY

* It goes without saying that organisation is teamwork. All the people in the organisation must work in unison. The salespersons are no exception. They must work wholeheartedly recognising their role in the organisation.

* The strategies of salesforce management are hidden in its objectives. They are, 1) to create loyal salespeople, 2) to impart the right kind of training to salespeople, 3) to see that they are rightly paid, and 4) to motivate them in the right direction.

* Since loyal salespeople are the backbone of the sales organisation, the management must make an all-out effort to create loyal salespeople.

* Training is the source where the salespersons or any other section of employees are groomed and they are prepared there for the future organisation. This fact must be recognised by the top management and due care must be taken by it to see that there is no leniency in the management of the training sessions.

* Money is a great motivator. A good remuneration plan for salespersons is a means of securing better control of their activities, greater incentive sales, more loyalty, higher morale and greater enthusiasm and interest. It should be planned in such a manner that both the employer and employee must stand to gain.

* Motivation is more of an art. It is a complex area. It differs from person to person. Where people find it difficult to align and associate with the organisational aims, then most motivational ideas and activities will have a reduced level of success. This alignment is very important as it determines the level of motivation.

REVIEW QUESTIONS

1. What are the objectives of salesforce management strategies?

2. "The salespeople represent the organisation in the market." In the light of this statement, make an inquiry into the role of the salespeople. In what ways the salespeople can improve the performance of their organisation?

3. What are the strategies to be adopted for creating loyal salespeople?

4. "Loyalty is a trait that is born with people." Do you agree? Give relevant points for your stand on the statement.

5. "The best way to employ the right people is to recruit people suggested by the present loyal salespersons." Do you agree with this suggestion? What are the merits and demerits of this method of selecting salespeople for the selling job?

6. Explain the role of tests in salesforce management.

7. Discuss the importance of training in salesforce management.

8. Explain the steps required of an effective sales training programme.

9. Do you think paying good salaries to the salespersons would make them work effectively? Give your points in the form of arguments.

10. "Top performers will not leave, even for more money, because they like where they are and what they are doing." Examine the reasons for this attitude of top performers. Do top performers need any external push to get them going on the next sale? Give your arguments for your answer in a succinct manner.

11. "Money is a great motivator." Do you agree?

12. Explain the power of motivation in bringing in more sales.

REFERENCES

1. The Myers-Briggs Type Indicator (MBTI) assessment is a personality test designed to measure preferences in how people see the world and make decisions. The MBTI was originally developed in the 1940s by Katharine Cook Briggs and her daughter, Isabel Briggs Myers, who thought that an understanding of personality preferences would help women who were entering the workforce for the first time to identify the sort of war-time jobs which would suit them best. By the early 1960s, the initial questionnaire had become refined into the MBTI.

15

STRATEGIC BRAND MANAGEMENT

After reading this chapter, you will be able to

- ❂ *Understand the meaning of "brand" in marketing,*
- ❂ *Learn how a brand is evolved,*
- ❂ *Recognise the value of brand name,*
- ❂ *Understand the concept of strategic brand management,*
- ❂ *Recognise the need for brand positioning,*
- ❂ *Understand the concept of strategic brand management process, and*
- ❂ *Learn the process of managing brands over time.*

KEY TERMS

- ❂ Brand evolution
- ❂ Strategic brand management
- ❂ Brand hierarchy
- ❂ Brand positioning
- ❂ Quality positioning
- ❂ Value positioning
- ❂ Feature-driven positioning
- ❂ Problem/solution positioning
- ❂ Rivalry-based positioning
- ❂ Brand equity
- ❂ Brand protection
- ❂ Strategic brand management process
- ❂ Customer-oriented strategies
- ❂ Derivative plans
- ❂ Competitor-oriented strategies
- ❂ Brand performance
- ❂ Brand life cycle
- ❂ Introduction stage
- ❂ Growth stage
- ❂ Maturity stage
- ❂ Decline stage

INTRODUCTION

Brand is the identification mark of a product. It tells explicitly or tacitly who the manufacturer is and to whom it belongs. It is an easy way of conveying the vital message to the market. In fact, most people do not know who the manufacturer is; but they buy the product on the basis of the brand name. They want to buy Horlicks; but they do not know the name of the manufacturing company. Brand name is a big weapon in the armoury of the manufacturer. Some products continue to be successful merely because they have strong brand names. Common examples are Coca Cola, Horlicks and the like. When the product is supported by quality, the brand becomes stronger and more valuable. Due to the great importance of the brand for a manufacturer, brands are protected by legal framework. In India, Tata, Reliance, and Birla are the names of the companies which may be considered as equivalent of their brand names.

Brand is a unique and identifiable trade name given to a product or a service. A brand includes a name, logo and visual elements like symbols or images. A consumer who prefers a particular brand basically agrees to select that brand over others based primarily on the brand's reputation. However, there are customers who verify the truth in the claims of the so-called big brands; these customers are rational ones and as the present-day consumers are becoming more and more conscious of essential elements they expect to be present in a product. The customers consider brands as their favourites. They do not give up their brands so easily unless they are convinced that the particular brand does not offer them value for their money. Normally, powerful brands enjoy unconditional support from the customers. Therefore, brand names are the biggest asset to the organisation.

Successful brand becomes the symbol which provides some important functions for customers and increases the product value in their eyes. Brand identifies source or maker of a product and allows customers to assign responsibility to particular manufacturer or distributor. It also allows customers to lower search costs for products.

A brand represents many intangible aspects of a product or service: a collection of feelings and perceptions about quality, image, lifestyle and status. It creates in the mind of customers and prospects the perception that there is no product or service on the market that is quite like yours. In short, a brand offers the customer a guarantee and then delivers on it.

A brand needs to be strengthened in order to sustain the competitive advantage created by the brand. The reasons for brand strengthening, which cause a strategic approach to management, are numerous. Competitive advantage of enterprise, for instance, depends on its reputation and brand strength. Aaker[1] cites the following statements:

1. Enterprises are different, disregarding more similarity in their products and services.
2. Corporate brand could have a programme that contributes to strengthen brands of particular products.
3. Association of brands (including all other brands of enterprise) contributes to make confidence.
4. Brand strengthening covers all products and markets and makes the process of brand management easier and more effective.
5. The brand's meaning for employees has to be supported by mission, goals, values, and culture of enterprise. The enterprise brand often gives a message for customer relationship that is quite different from the product brand.
6. The brand enables a special synergy.

In a dynamic environment, it is imperative to create strong brand[2] which is based on brand loyalty, brand awareness and image, perceived quality, brand associations, and other proprietary assets, such as patents, trademarks, and channel relationships. These assets provide various benefits and value, which results in strong brand extensions and right skills and originality of its creators.

EVOLUTION OF A BRAND

The making of a good brand is not an easy job. It requires careful planning and execution. It also requires enormous resources and hard work. Many brands start in a small way; they reach a spot that is unimaginable in heights within a short span of time. Look at the famous brand of Nirma. It took less than a year to become a popular brand. It is due to its powerful advertisement that evoked positive responses from all quarters. Let us also take Chik shampoo. This product reached Himalayan heights in a similar fashion. CavinKare started selling the product in an unbelievable 50-paise sachet in 1999. This made the product very popular in the rural and semi-urban areas of the country, as it possessed the requisite quality and available in small quantity. In 2003, Chik Shampoo was declared the winner of the best performing brand in 2003 by AAAI, amongst the top ten brands in household availability.

Branding is a cyclic process with three elements. First, there is the brand reality. This consists of the product's identity, its differentiating features, and its niche. This comes in many ways to include the media, advertising, public relations, and training. Second, every communication outlet/forum should consistently communicate the same message about the product. Third, product development follows and considers the future. Product development is built upon year after year and is predicated on brand identity. It is difficult to alter what the public perception of a product is, so changing image can happen only incrementally with smart communications.

Every practice—including the practice of brands—benefits from a clear vision of where it is been, and where it is going. It carries a picture of its own evolution. Creating the right quality product, selecting a suitable brand name, popularising it through the right media, making it carry a message and thus accomplishing the marketing objectives are the important stages in the development of just a name into a brand. Let us now study them at some length.

Creating the Right Quality Product

The basic requirement of a good brand is with the manufacturer, who must create a product that is capable of satisfying the customer needs. One expert defined quality as the extent to which products, services, processes, and relationships are free from defects, constraints, and items which do not add value for customers. Even though there are many definitions for quality, this definition seems to be sensible and meaningful. Such a product is able to deliver the requirements of not only the customer but also the manufacturer. Therefore, the first task of an organisation must be to identify the right quality and clear specifications must be written down. These specifications must be transformed into a tangible product.

Selecting a Suitable Brand Name

The product must necessarily possess a good brand name that will be able to convey the message to the market. A good brand name has its own qualities. Many authors give various qualities required of a brand name. All are correct. You cannot neglect even a single trait of the brand name. However, let us also discuss some of the important ingredients of a good brand name.

i. A good brand name must be first of all very attractive and easy for remembrance.

ii. It must be able to differentiate our product from that of our competitors.

iii. It must be self-propelling. It must be a name that people will talk about. It must be a name that works its way through the world on its own.

iv. It must have some kind of emotional connection. It must exude qualities like confidence, mystery, presence, warmth, and some sense of humour.

v. The name must be in a single word or at the most two short words. The word(s) must be able to tell what the product is about.

vi. It should not have unwanted meanings in different languages. It must be linguistically clean.

vii. The name must be unique within the industry.

viii. The name must tell upon the personality of the organisation.

Exhibit 15.1   Evolution of a Brand

CavinKare, headed by C.K.Ranganathan from Cuddalore, Tamil Nadu, made the pioneering attempt to offer shampoos in small pillow packs. At that time, the market was flooded with 70-odd small shampoo labels with little differentiation. Velvette was aggressively marketed by Godrej. Consumers would ask for a Velvette but walked away happily with whatever label the retailer gave them. Many never knew the difference, for others it did not matter.

In 1983, Chik shampoo was launched by CavinKare. The initial launch was in 10 ml pack. The market was cluttered with low-cost shampoos. "But there was a clear opportunity for a good quality shampoo with appealing perfume at a price to delight the consumer." Chik endeavoured to provide to the masses a significantly superior product than those available at similar price points. Chik shampoo used French perfume to differentiate itself on the plank of superior fragrance.

CavinKare encouraged trial through a consumer scheme, where anyone could take any 4 empty shampoo sachets to a retailer and take home a Chik sachet free. Though more risky, this scheme paid off and more and more people began asking for Chik at their local retail outlet. Later, the scheme was altered this way: the company started giving 1 free Chik Shampoo sachet in lieu of 5 Chik shampoo sachets only. Soon, consumers started asking for Chik sachets only. It was a tremendous success for the company.

Chik became very popular in the southern markets. Chik continued to use popular cinema celebrities and extended endorsements to TV in 1992. In 1992, the brand became the numero uno in South India. At that time, the MNCs sold products in bottles, not in sachets and sold only from fancy stores. They did not look at the small kirana stores, nor at the rural market. This was where CavinKare differed and also succeeded. The company went to rural areas in South India where people hardly used shampoo. They showed them how to use it by doing live demonstration and asked people to have a feel and smell of the shampoo.

They worked backwards, developing the formula and packaging took them a few years. They launched Chik shampoo sachet for just 50 paise in September 1999, the first ever such price point. The result was tremendous. The rural market grew at twice that of the urban sector. Today, Chik is the No.1 Indian rural brand and possesses a rural market share of 65%. Their target is to be a ₹ 1,500 crore (₹ 15 billion) company by 2012.

Popularising the Brand Name through the Right Media

Selection of the right media to publicise the brand name is an important step in the process. It is important for a new as well as an established organisation. The chosen media must convey the message to the target audience. A brand name publicised in the wrong media can harm the marketing efforts of the company. The company must decide a good industrial journal if it is an industrial product. It may be a journal for executives like Business Week or Business Today in the case of a brand for executive suits. It may be a popular medium in the case of all-category brand name. Therefore the company must consider all the relevant factors before deciding the right kind of media.

Making it Convey a Message

The brand name must convey a strong message to the target audience. Whenever the brand name appears in a place or media, it must convey a message. When the customer or the prospect happens to come across the brand name, he/she must be able to look at it positively and also with pride. The customer must feel that, "This is my brand. This brand has no equivalent in the market." When it happens in the minds of the customers, then you have done it! Your brand is becoming popular. But one thing must be kept in mind. There is no end to this process of evolution. A strong brand is constantly evolving, but not changing directions. It cannot take any direction it thinks fit. It is wrong to do so. Changing the direction means changing the policies of the organisation. The brand must keep its words. This is so because many times this may hurt the feelings and expectations of the customers. This may be done by an organisation that is in confusion and has no clear goals.

Accomplishing the Marketing Objectives

One of the marketing objectives is to create a powerful brand name. Once this objective is achieved, the other marketing objectives are not far to achieve. As the brand name becomes more and more familiar and popular among the customers, we can find a proportionate rise in the sales figures of the company. The company needs to evaluate the position the brand has brought for the company. The positioning of the brand must be on planned lines. In such a position, the organisation can achieve its objectives easily and aim for higher levels.

VALUE OF BRAND NAMES

Ascertaining the value of a brand is a gigantic task. It is very difficult to calculate it correctly. Brand is valued in the balance sheet under "Intangible Assets" or "Goodwill". Each company values its brand differently but they all agree that brand name has certain value. Let us take the example of a familiar brand name, namely, Tata. Tata has certainly a very strong brand value not only in India but also throughout the world. Finding out the value of Tata is a task which the company finds a Herculean task.

Finding out the exact value of the brand is a big task. However what we should recognise the fact that brand names bring in most of the sales of the company. Even though brand value is not the immediate concern of the company, the investors are very much concerned about it. However the investors need not worry about the value of the brand of the company in which they propose to invest because the market value of the shares will take care of everything including the brand value.

The total value of a brand in a particular product/service is composed of three parts. One part is due to the physical and readily identifiable (and replicable) features of the brand that delivers specific, tangible benefits to the purchaser, thus impacting purchase choice. We call these the tangible product features. The second part is due to some perceived intrinsic value associated with the brand name due to such things as the image transferred to the purchaser, trust, longevity in the marketplace, social responsibility, consistent performance, and so forth (i.e., the intangibles), impacting purchase choice. We refer to this as the brand's equity. The third component is the price/cost of the product. Thus, the total value (or utility) of a product or service is a function of 1) its physical, tangible, deliverable features, 2) its brand equity, and 3) its price.

A brand value is directly related to customer loyalty. That is, if a particular brand maintains a significantly higher perception of value to a consumer than any other brand in the category, that consumer will consistently purchase that brand and also recommend that brand to others. Conversely, as brands in the category become less differentiated in terms of both tangible and intrinsic features, price becomes the amjor differentiator of value, and thus, there is little loyalty. People tend to trade off price against the combined bundle of tangible product features and brand equity in order to optimise total utility or value.

Now the question is: Will the brand value go down? This is a relevant question. Yes. A brand's value will go down if the company does not sustain the product features and other related aspects like promotion. The company must continually work for its betterment and this continuous effort on the part of the top executives alone will keep the brand value eroded. Otherwise the brand name will lose its sheen as well as its customers. The most important requirement is the untiring efforts of the company to remain in the good books of the customers. Cola Cola, started in 1886, continues to keep its brand value and it is estimated that its value is somewhere around $75 billion.

STRATEGIC BRAND MANAGEMENT

A brand when becomes popular among the customers is the biggest advantage to the organisation. It even offers a unique advantage to the manufacturer. It is difficult to compete with a powerful brand. To compete with a powerful brand, it requires another equally powerful brand. Suzuki is a famous global brand and in India it is the leading car brand. Only brands like Tata and Hyundai can match the popularity of Suzuki. Such a unique advantage of the organisation has to be sustained so that the brand will find an ever increasing popularity among the customers. Strategic management of brands performs this function. Strategic brand management is concerned with the process of making the brand more and more powerful and longer lasting. The brand needs to establish itself in the market in order to position itself in the market. Brand positioning is important for the organisation, as it reflects the extent of customer's recognition of the product.

One must be aware of the fact that brands are not created overnight. It takes a number of years or even decades. The company and its executives struggle hard to find a place in the minds of the customers and ultimately this effort leads to a successful brand. No one thought that BMW would be a successful brand. Bavarian Motor Works (BMW) is known as the "ultimate driving machine." This rallying cry applies to all its products to include automobiles, motorcycles, and sport utility vehicles. BMW's communication strategy and brand equity comes with its message about speed, driving, and handling. Strategic brand management is the philosophy and core behind all business development. The rallying cry defines and makes for both an internal and external image/presence. Constantly refining the rallying cry is part of brand management. Branding is the arena that puts the "big picture" perspective into focus and determines where the company takes and makes its future.

Strategic brand management can do well if it is based on planning brand portfolio. A brand portfolio of enterprise, in partner relationships, often consists of brands of several enterprises. Some authors have developed a model called "molecule of brand", where each brand is described as an atom and its size indicates the role of brand. The greatest atom indicates leading brand, the atom of middle size indicates strategic brand, and the smallest atom indicates supported brands.[3] Strategic brand management is more successful if the brand decisions are based on strategic analysis. It provides the basic information for decision-making. The analysis firstly includes analysis of market, customer, competition, and power of mark. Information received from strategic analysis enable the management to focus on customers. Brand is the instrument which, if used carefully, contributes to creating and maintaining long-term and profitable customer relationship.

The starting point in strategic analysis for the needs of decision-making is brand hierarchy. A brand hierarchy is based on premises that a product can be branded in different ways depending on how many new and existing brand elements are used and how they are combined for any one product. Since certain brand elements are used to make more than one brand, the hierarchy can be constructed to represent how products are nested with other products because of their common brand elements. Keller[4] has differentiated four potential levels in hierarchy:

1. The highest level of hierarchy is a corporate (or company) brand.
2. A family brand is the next-lower level and it is defined as a brand that is used in more than one product category, but is not necessarily the name of the company.
3. The third level is an individual brand. It is the brand that has been restricted to essentially one product category, although it may be used for several different product types within the category.
4. The last level is called a modifier which is a means to designate a specific item or model type or a particular version of configuration of the products.

The most important component of strategic brand management is the right positioning of the brand in the market. Positioning is how a product appears in relation to other products in the market. We can say it the other way also. Positioning is the place enjoyed by a product in the minds of the customers. To position your offering properly, you need to identify the key attributes or benefits that represent the value of your product or service. That will, in turn, create trust in your brand. As you begin to understand the relationship that your customers have with your brand, you will be able to more efficiently meet their needs, wants and desires through your brand.

Measuring brand equity is an important component of strategic brand management. There are qualitative and quantitative research methods that can be used to understand the brand's meaning and value to consumers. Qualitative techniques include brand collages, which allow us to understand how consumers see the brand using pictures and words. Quantitative techniques include financial asset value calculations. Also popular are calculations of the customer's willingness to pay, which answers the question: How much more are customers willing to pay for your brand?

Another important component of strategic brand management is the protection of brands. Traditionally, protection came from legal teams whose work with trademarks remains as an element of protecting the brand but is, by no means, the entire protection needed. Marketers today should institute policies to avoid the dilution of brands.

Brand Positioning

Positioning is the art of creating a brand that can persuade and realistically demonstrate its relevance to a customer's daily life to become his/her regular choice. Positioning is not created by the marketer or the individual brand itself, but by how others perceive it. Today we find almost all products as branded items. In the olden days, milk, bread and many more items were offered without brand names. But today, we find almost all items ranging from wheat flour to salt are branded. This is due to the customer's awareness. Not only that, the manufacturers themselves try to find out new markets and the result is the availability of even common products as branded ones. Salt is branded as Tata salt and Annapoorna salt. What a revolution the marketing has made on the market! When the products are available as branded items, the quality of the product is assured and, therefore, the customers go after it.

Successful brand positioning is a difficult task. Many brands stumble faster than they need to do it. To avoid that, it is necessary to define brand positioning clearly before creating awareness in the minds of customers, to promote those brand attributes that are important from the standpoint of customers, to invest enough in the difference that competitors can easily copy, to answer to competitive actions in accordance with both customer needs and possibilities of enterprise.

When we say positioning, there are many types of it. Let us study them briefly here.

Quality positioning   Perception of quality is probably one of the most important elements for a brand to possess in it. Quality, or the perception of quality, lies in the mind of the buyer. Build a powerful perception of quality, and you will succeed in creating a powerful brand. When marketers are able to narrow down a product's focus, they become a specialist rather than a generalist, and a specialist is perceived to know more, or be of "higher quality" than a generalist. Another way to build the perception of high quality is to simply attach a higher price tag to your brand. A higher price allows the affluent consumer to obtain psychological satisfaction from the public purchase and consumption of a high-end product. A good example for quality positioning is Toyota. Their method of advertising their brand is very unique. They equate Toyota to quality. They do not go for price or advertisement wars.

Value positioning   Although at one time, items that were considered to be a good "value" meant that they were inexpensive, that stigma has fallen by the wayside. Today, brands that are considered a value are rising in popularity amongst consumers. In fact, packaged good brands, especially cereals, experienced a backlash when their prices rose too quickly. Private supermarket labels, as well as smart companies, which introduced a breakfast cereal that aims at undercutting reputed brands have found a strong market.

Feature-driven positioning   More marketers rely on product/service features to differentiate their brands than any other method. The advantage is that the message is clear, and the positioning will be credible if you stick to the facts about the product. Unfortunately, feature-oriented stances are often rendered useless if the competition comes out with a faster or more advanced model.

Problem/solution positioning   As the name implies, problem/solution positioning shows the consumer how a sticky situation can be relieved quickly and easily with the brand or service. What problem/solution campaigns lack in imagination, they usually make up for in directness and credibility. Packaged good brands tend to be the most frequent users of problem/solution prompts. For example, tinned meals cut meal preparation time to minutes. Detergents and cleansers also make good use of these prompts.

Rivalry-based positioning   This type of positioning deals with how one brand is thought of compared to its obvious competitors. Therefore, the idea of a rivalry-based position might seem redundant but many campaigns take this approach. Laundry detergents, for example, are constantly going head-to-head to prove which one has the most power to lift stains. Car manufacturers also come in this category.

The Brand Equity Concept

Brand equity is the value of the brand in the marketplace. A high equity brand has high value in the marketplace. High brand value means that the brand has the ability to create some sort of positive differential response in the marketplace. A brand of high equity is easily recognisable when customers come across an advertisement wherever they are. A person may be travelling in a train or may be making an air travel. The person seated next may be reading a newspaper or a magazine. In this case, the loyal customer must be able to comfortably recognise a favourite brand even at a brief glimpse when the person reading the magazine is turning pages. Such is the power of brands. Another important feature of a brand possessing high brand equity is that the customer is prepared to pay a premium price knowingly well that there are other brands of same calibre in the market. Still the customers are after their brand. What does this mean? It means that the brand is enjoying high reputation and, in turn, high brand equity. Staunch customers go one step further to recommend their brand to others. These manifestations result in positive responses of the customers.

Where do these positive responses come from? These responses are the result of hard labour made by the organisation to which the brand belongs. The advertising strategies, the media selected for showing these advertisements, the advertisement copy, the dedication of all the executives, the unconditional cooperation of the owners to the efforts of the executives, the quality of packaging, the channel chosen to distribute the product, the attitude of the salespersons, and above all the quality of the product make the positive responses of the customers. Once these positive responses are created, they are hard to erase. They become part and parcel of the lives of the customers. They want to live with the brand. When they are unable to reach to their brand, they become emotional and feel lost. This is a kind of mesmerising effect. The brand equity is well-rooted in the minds of the customers. It is hard to erase it.

For creating real loyalty it is necessary to satisfy the following criteria: 1) customers perceive the focal brand as superior related to the preferred competitive brands, 2) level of customer inclination towards focal brand must be higher than inclination towards the other brands, 3) customers intend to buy the focal brand when they have the need for buying. An efficient strategic reaction is directed to retaining current customers and making barriers for brand change by increasing customer satisfaction and loyalty. Managing quality, satisfaction, loyalty, and profitability as strategic instruments contributes to strengthening brand equity and improving business performance.

Depending on the level of brand loyalty, different strategies could be formulated:

i. When a profitable segment is loyal with high rate of using, focus has to be on changing loyalty in favour of enterprise's brand,

ii. Under conditions with enough number of small users of loyal brand, focus on raising their rate of using enterprise's brand is a desirable strategic reaction,

iii. If there are enough number of big users that ask for variety, an efficient reaction is to use a brand name as eminent attribute and create new relative competitive advantage,

iv. In cases when many users ask for variety, and they are small users, it is necessary to react in the way that the brand name has become significant attribute.[5]

Protection of Brands

Companies large and small spend significant proportions of their revenue on branding efforts as well as those things that influence customer perception of brand like product development, support and customer service. Therefore, it is essential for them to take necessary steps to protect the hard earned reputation of their brands.

Large brands like Coca Cola and Colgate are better able to protect their brands. Still spurious items appear in the market. It is an important function for the manufacturers to safeguard its brand from the spurious ones. The cooperation of the customers plays a vital role in this regard. But less reputed brands do not have sufficient resources to see that their brands are protected. Therefore, the bogus makers find it as an easy avenue to do their job easily.

There are a few ways of protecting the brands in the market. In addition to legal channels, many other methods are available for the manufacturer to protect the brand from the manufacturers who make bogus products. A direct line of communication that enables customers to easily feedback their questions and comments can help to identify those manufacturers or dealers who sell bogus items. A simple email and mail address displayed prominently on your website or other marketing material is sufficient in the first instance.

Spurious items manufacturing activity undermines the legitimate distribution channels through which genuine products are distributed and sold. Law-abiding wholesalers and retailers face unfair competition when lower-priced spurious items are introduced into a market through illegal activity. Therefore, the loyal distributors and dealers can help thwart the attempts of the spurious goods manufacturers. The distributors and dealers must be imparted sufficient training to identify bogus products available in the market. This would also earn for them lot of money because circulation of spurious items affect the profitability of genuine dealers. Therefore the cooperation of these wholesalers and dealers must be obtained in order to unearth spurious items in the market.

STRATEGIC BRAND MANAGEMENT PROCESS

Strategic brand management process is important for creating and sustaining brand equity. Developing a strategy that successfully sustains or improves brand awareness strengthens brand associations, and emphasises brand quality. The brand strategy means permanent investment in research and development, publicity, and customer services. The activities of measuring and controlling brand effects are also important.

The strategic brand management process adds value to the company's products and services by creating a unique identity in the marketplace. Brands have impact on the customers and the destiny of the products and services. Brand is more than a product name or packaging but it is a mix of so many things. They include the brand name, symbols, colours, experiences, interests, target market preferences, designs, tagline, slogan, idea, promotional messages, and so on. They together communicate the brand message in the marketplace and position the brand in a unique way. The strategic management process must be a well-defined function within the company and should be managed as an ongoing activity. Therefore, it needs a creative and very well-developed brand management strategy and tactics.

Planning a brand portfolio is suggested as an instrument for more efficient decision-making in brand management process. Since the brand portofolio is the set of all brands and brand lines that an enterprise offers to customers in a particular category, the planning of brand portfolio represents a process that includes the following phases: identifying brands in the brand portfolio, estimating contribution of each brand to business performance, estimating the brand (actual and future) position, differentiating brands in the portfolio, considering their possibilities and abilities of enterprise to exploit them, reinvestigating the portfolio, and developing a strategy of brand reconstruction.[6]

Let us now study the strategic brand management process. Strategy is a concept related to time period. It consists of the right methodology to be used to achieve the objective in the long run. It must help to accomplish the objective progressively in the long run. The process of accomplishment of the objective has to be steady and there should not be any zigzag growth. If we find this type of growth, we may conclude that the strategy is not working as per our plan. There is some deficiency in the system. A perfect strategy would never fail unless any catastrophe happens in the marketplace or in the global economy. Strategy is the base on which the brand management process is built upon. The strategy we choose may vary depending on the organisational objectives. An organisation may pursue vigorous strategy if it wants to accomplish a big objective in a short period of time. The company may go in for slow but steady approach, if it is not in a hurry to accomplish the stated goals. Therefore, it all depends on the organisation's goals. A goal will become achievable only if it is practical and market-oriented. One cannot build castles in the air. But when the environment is ripe for pursuing a suitable objective, then the organisation must not miss the opportunity.

The strategic brand management process consists of the following steps.

1. Identification of suitable market segment for brand positioning,
2. Planning the strategy for the segment,
3. Formulating the brand positioning programmes,
4. Formulation of derivative plans,
5. Execution of the derivative plans,
6. Measuring and interpreting the brand performance, and
7. Sustaining the brand equity.

Let us now study these steps in the strategic brand management process in some detail.

I. Identification of the Market Segment

Segmenting the market is a strategy that involves dividing a market into subsets of consumers who have common needs and applications for the goods and services offered in the market. These subsets of consumers have something in common. They may belong to the same income group. Or, they may belong to the same age group. If they do not belong to the same income/age group, they may have similar wavelength of thoughts. Some of the organisations do not identify particular segments because they are involved in mass marketing. However, most of the organisations go in for the process of selection of their specific segment so that they can work effectively to target the customers. The identification of the right segment and appropriate product positioning has been discussed in Chapter 7 titled *Market Segmentation* and

Product Positioning. Therefore, let us now concentrate on the strategies that can be employed for brand positioning.

2. Planning the Strategy for the Segment

Positioning is vital to the success of a product in the market. Together with branding, it determines whether or not the product succeeds. Positioning refers to the objective characteristics and benefits of a product that will appeal to a specific group of consumers. "A place for everything and everything in its place," claimed Henri Fayol, the Father of Modern Management. Therefore, a brand must also have its right place. Brand positioning starts with a rigorous assessment of the audience. What beliefs pop-up in their mind when they think about a particular brand and its category? What are the good and bad memories coming back to mind? One thing is very clear. Brand positioning strategies can fall between these two: the customer-oriented strategy or competitor-oriented strategy.

The customer-oriented strategies   Peter England always campaigns their product concentrating on the consumer, the user of its product. Louis Philip also concentrates on this kind of campaigns. These strategies give specific features of their products, educate their customers and create a place in the minds of the customers. They focus their strategy to attract the customers by giving reasons for the superiority of their products.

The competitor-oriented strategies   The manufacturers who are facing cut-throat competition use this strategy to outsmart the competitors. They show statistics in favour of their products and try to prove that their product is superior in all respects. Dettol television commercials always concentrate on advertisements, which show that this product would give you more protection, than the others. Tata Motors try to beat Suzuki's Swift Dzire by giving all the plus points which are much superior to Swift Dzire. Onida was positioned against the giants in the television industry through this strategy. ONIDA colour television was launched with the message that all others were clones and only Onida was the leader. "Neighbour's Envy, Owner's Pride".

While it is important to understand what competitors are doing in order to act in a distinctive and powerful way, it is also useful to learn from their mistakes and successes. For instance, the company that became Apple needed to distance itself from the cold, unapproachable, complicated imagery created by the other computer companies at the time that had names like IBM, NEC, DEC, and SAP.

3. Formulating the Brand Positioning Programmes

A programme is a list of activities arranged in a logical sequence to be performed in order to accomplish the intended goals. When the brand positioning strategy is in hand, the next step is to see that the strategy is executed. The first step in this direction is to prepare a schedule of activities to be performed in the marketplace.

Let us take the example of positioning of a particular brand "ABC". The market segment is the officegoers between the age group of 25 and 50. The strategy formulated for the purpose is, for instance, positioning the brand by features. This strategy is a consumer-oriented strategy. All the efforts have to be targeted at them by presenting to them the facts about ABC. The aim of the marketer here is to implant the brand name in the minds of the officegoers of a particular age group. To carry out this task, the following activities may have to be performed.

1. The first task is to formulate the ad copy. The ad copy must be powerful in that it must catch the immediate attention of the customers.
2. The second task is the final evaluation of the ad copy.
3. The next task is the selection of the media in which the advertisement has to be given. While selecting the medium many factors are to be considered. The organisation's budget for promoting the brand, the media, the worthiness of the media, and the like. In selecting the media, the marketer has to be careful in that the media is an effective one. The reach of the advertisement must be given due attention.
4. The frequency of the advertisement has to be decided. This is very much related to the cost aspect of the ad.

It is important that timing of each activity must be considered as it is essential for carrying out the tasks without any overlapping. Sometimes, overlapping may lead to confusion at the time of execution of the tasks.

4. Formulation of Derivative Plans

For each of the activities mentioned above, derivative plans must be drafted. Derivative plans are the step-by-step procedures required to accomplish the proposed tasks. They are important in that they are the on-the-spot activities of the organisation. These on-the-spot activities have to be planned with high precision by collecting necessary information in order to ensure that the derivative plans do not fail on any account.

5. Execution of the Derivative Plans

Derivative plans have to be executed by suitable people. This is an on-the-spot activity. The success of the entire programme depends on the execution of the derivative plans. Therefore, utmost care must be taken to see that things move as per schedule.

6. Measuring and Interpreting Brand Performance

This step is very much a part of marketing research. The marketing research team of the organisation has to make a perfect study of the brand performance in the marketplace at regular intervals. The findings of this study would be very much helpful in formulating future strategies. At the same time, this research can reveal the weak spots in our brand management programmes which can guide the marketer in the right direction. Exercises that are designed to evaluate the performance of a brand closely are generally called Brand Audits. Most commonly these audits involve detailed internal description of how and through what sources is a brand being marketed and a thorough external investigation, through focus groups and other consumer research techniques that indicate exactly what the brand's activities do to consumer perceptions.

The measures of a brand's performance and potential and hence of brand equity are distinct for every stage of the brand's life cycle. This however does not imply that measures for a particular stage becomes irrelevant for other stages. Most measures like brand awareness, market share and profit margins remain critical throughout a brand's lifetime. The point being made therefore is that at each stage there are some parameters that become more relevant at that point of time and hence must be given greater priority.

7. Sustaining Brand Equity

Brand audits prove to be extremely effective when they are periodically conducted frequently. Apart from help in building brand equity, they give managers a clear picture of the products and service on offer, and how they are being marketed and branded. Consumer feedbacks, a part of brand audits, often uncover conflicting beliefs and attributes between the company's perception and consumer's expectations. They often indicate the managers the key areas to work on while building a strong brand image. Brand audits help the organisation to find out the position of the brand in the marketplace. After ascertaining the position, the marketer must take necessary steps to reinforce the brand, if needed.

MANAGING BRANDS OVER TIME

One way of brand management over time is to strengthen brand equity by developing marketing programmes, which express brand knowledge consistently as not to confuse the consumer. For example, Toyota publicises its brand name even without giving the name of the product in their ads. This is a novel way of strengthening their brand. Market leader like Coca-Cola has constantly run marketing programmes even after becoming market leaders. However, this does not imply that the same campaign is running repeatedly, rather they come up with innovative strategies to reinforce brand knowledge.

Innovation is one of the keys in managing brand and ensuring that brand remains ahead of the competition curve. If companies operating in entertainment category or matter of fact insurance do not innovate, then value of their brand is lost as these categories are product-driven. For example, Apple, without its innovation in the form of iPod MP3 player, would have found it difficult facing competition from Sony. If the company's category is not product-driven, marketing campaigns associated with brand image play an important role in sustaining the brand. For example, Pepsi is operating in highly competitive carbonated drinks' category, over the years their marketing campaign is focused on highlighting their brand position as a drink for younger generation.

The product life cycle concept is very much relevant in the management of brands over time. They go hand in hand till the end. The product life cycle shows how unit sales may change over time. It describes how competitive conditions change over time. Let us go along with the product life cycle to understand how a brand can be managed effectively in the lifetime of a product and how a brand can be reinforced.

Introduction Stage

The introduction stage is when a new product or service is being introduced. What the brand strategy must do now is explain to the target customers, the value of the new technology versus the old technology. In the case of a new product, the brand name of the product must be sown deeply in the minds of the customers and prospects. The brand name must possess all the characteristics of a good brand name. Many organisations spend heavily on the promotion of their new brand name. Existing companies also do well in this connection whether their product is in the introduction stage or not. Take the example of Toyota. They advertise their brand name today. They do not give emphasis on their cars. They convey the message through their ads that is "Toyota the synonym of Quality". They emphasise quality of their product in the marketplace spending lot of money. They do not make comparisons with other companies in the industry.

Growth Stage

The main characteristic of this stage is that you now have direct competitors. These are the fast followers who have entered the market soon after your launch. At the same time, customers are starting to become very knowledgeable and demanding, regarding their expectations. It is most likely the marketer will have a major functional—or better, emotional—benefit that is superior to that of the competitors. Now is the time to associate that benefit with the brand which the marketer wanted to own. In this stage, brand name becomes familiar to the customers as well as the prospects. Novel and creative ads can do the job better. Even ads involving humour will pay. But too much of emphasis on the brand name through the ads might lead to a negative response. Therefore, a measured and well-conceived brand management strategy is very essential in this stage.

Maturity Stage

Competitors often consolidate during the maturity stage. Now customers are very knowledgeable about the product or service and may view their purchase decision as routine. Organisations must retain their current customers by reinforcing their brand values but must attract new customers by finding what may be subtle differences versus their competitors. Strong reinforcement of the brands is essential in this stage. This is the stage which gives the company a big chunk of the profit. The reputation of the brand plays a dominant role in the marketplace. Customers ask for the product using its brand name. The product becomes synonym with the brand.

Decline Stage

The reason the competitive life cycle declines is that a new product or service emerges that is more effective than the existing technology at meeting customers' needs. At this point, the brand must be sufficiently stretchable so that the company can move to the new technology. There may be a number of brands that are dominant in a technology but have faced difficulties moving to a new technology in the minds of customers.

The management of brand through its life cycle stages may be a good option to the marketer. However, the basic requirement for a product or organisation is to build a strong brand name which is capable of withstanding any kind of onslaught by the competitors. Only that brand can serve the organisational purpose in a powerful way. Therefore, big organisations follow an aggressive brand development and management strategy in order to make its brand stronger.

SUMMARY

* Brand is the identification mark of a product. It tells tacitly who the manufacturer is and to whom it belongs. It is an easy way of conveying the vital message to the market. In fact, most people do not know who the manufacturer is; but they buy the product on the basis of the brand name.

* The making of a good brand is not an easy job. It requires careful planning and execution. It also requires enormous resources and hard work. Many brands start in a small way; they reach a spot that is unimaginable in heights within a short span of time.

* Creating the right quality product, selecting a suitable brand name, popularising it through the right media, making it carry a message and thus accomplishing the marketing objectives are the important stages in the development of just a name into a brand.

* Ascertaining the value of a brand is a gigantic task; yet it is very difficult to calculate it correctly. Brand is valued in the balance sheet under "Intangible Assets" or 'Goodwill'. Each company values its brand differently but they all agree that brand name has certain value.

* Strategic brand management is concerned with the process of making the brand more and more powerful and long-lasting. The brand needs to establish itself in the market in order to position itself in the market. Brand positioning is important for the organisation, as it reflects the extent of customer's recognition of the product.

* Strategic brand management process is important for creating and sustaining brand equity. Developing a strategy that successfully sustains or improves brand awareness strengthens brand associations, and emphasises brand quality. The brand strategy means permanent investment in research and development, publicity, and customer services.

* The strategic brand management process consists of these steps: 1) identification of suitable market segment for brand positioning, 2) planning the strategy for the segment, 3) formulating the brand positioning programmes, 4) formulation of derivative plans, 5) execution of the derivative plans, 6) measuring and interpreting the brand performance, and 7) sustaining the brand equity.

* One way of brand management over time is to strengthen brand equity by developing marketing programmes, which express brand knowledge consistently as not to confuse the consumer. Innovation is one of the keys in managing brand and ensuring that brand remains ahead of the competition curve.

* The product life cycle concept is very much relevant in the management of brands over time. They go hand in hand till the end. The product life cycle shows how unit sales may change over time. It describes how competitive conditions change over time.

REVIEW QUESTIONS

1. Explain the need for a powerful brand name. Give the views of Aaker regarding the strength of a brand name.

2. "When the product is supported by quality, the brand becomes stronger and more valuable." Discuss the merits and demerits of this statement.

3. "A brand represents many intangible aspects of a product or service." What are the intangible aspects of the product or service? Can a brand exist without these intangible aspects? Probe the truthfulness of the statement.

4. Explain the process of brand evolution.

5. "Many brands start in a small way; they reach a spot that is unimaginable in heights within a short span of time." Give an example of such a brand and explain how the brand developed into a big one.

6. "Branding is a cyclic process with three elements." Explain the three elements involved in the making of a brand.

7. "The product must necessarily possess a good brand name that will be able to convey the message to the market." Explain how far the name of the brand will work for the organisation. Are there any assumptions for the success of the brand? If so, discuss their relevance to the success of the brand.

8. What do you think of a brand name once it has reached high level of prominence? Does it need support of the organisation any more? Discuss the logic in your answer.

9. Write an essay on strategic brand management.

10. Explain the different types of positioning of a product.

11. "Successful brand positioning is a difficult task." Explain why it is a difficult task.

12. Explain the brand equity concept.

13. Explain the strategic brand management process.

14. How do you manage brands over time on the basis of product life cycle concept?

REFERENCES

1. Aaker, A.D. (2004). Leveraging the Corporate Brands, *California Management Review*, Sprint.

2. Michon, Ch. (2002). Réflexion d'inspiration lacanienne sur le développement durable d'une marque forte, *Revue française du marketing*, No. 189/190, 4–5, pp. 37–48.

3. Michon, Ch., (2000). *Le marque, son rôle stratégique au coeur du marketing*, Revue Française du Marketing, No 176, pp. 7–21.

4. Keller, L.K. (2003). *Strategic Brand Management, Building, Measuring, and Managing Brand Equity*, 2nd edn. Prentice Hall International, Inc. NJ.

5. Peter, P.J. and Olsen J.C. (2005). *Consumer Behaviour and Marketing Strategy*, 7th edn. McGraw-Hill/IRWIN, Boston.

6. Hill, S., Ettenson, R. and Tyson, D. (2005). Achieving the Ideal Brand Portfolio, *Sloan Management Review*, Winter, pp. 85–90.

16

CREATION OF COMPETITIVE ADVANTAGES

After reading this chapter, you will be able to

- *learn the basics of a competitive advantage,*
- *recognise the three views of competitive advantages,*
- *recognise the difference between core competencies and competitive advantages,*
- *understand the process of evolution of competitive advantages,*
- *learn about the qualities of a sustainable competitive advantage,*
- *know about the keys to competitive advantages and*
- *learn the process of competitive advantage creation.*

KEY TERMS

- Unique resource
- Sustenance of demand
- Customer loyalty
- Core competencies
- Benchmarking
- Reinforcement
- Hard decisions
- Loyal workforce
- Organisational culture
- Master plan
- Authority delegation
- Progress review

INTRODUCTION

A winning team must possess adequate advantages over its rival. The players defending their territory must be strong enough in order not to allow the ball into their territory. At the same time, the forward player must be a special person who would take the ball into the opponent's territory. Another unique advantage should be the team spirit which every one in the team must possess. Sometimes, a lone player takes the ball into the enemy's area and shoots a goal. This may also lead to the team's success. Therefore, the team must possess strong advantages over its rival which would help it win the game.

A business is not born to get defeated. It must win the game. Its aim is to excel in the field selected by it. To accomplish its objective, the businessperson must select the trump cards to play in order to land in success. These trump cards are the competitive advantages. It is a pity to note that some businesses fail in the market, even though its products are good in quality; it is reasonably priced and it is well-positioned in the market. In these cases the obvious reasons are that the company has failed to confront its competitors with necessary weapons in its arsenal. Such companies might have lacked sufficient unique advantages in the market. It is not only important to create competitive advantages but also necessary to sustain them so that the business can continue to survive in the market.

WHAT IS A COMPETITIVE ADVANTAGE

Competitive advantage management is a set of methods and strategies that work to not only position your company or business but also make it stand out in the market. Understanding the competitive advantage of your company over its rival companies is the key to creating a dominant position in your market.[1] Without it the business plan will be incomplete as well as ineffective.

The first task of competitive advantage management is to create competitive advantages for the organisation. In today's business world, the cry is for sustainable competitive advantages. Competitive advantages are not created overnight. They are built upon the policies and practices of the top management. Therefore, the making of competitive advantages starts with the formulation of the organisation's policies and ends with their execution. To sustain the momentum created by the top management in the process of creation of competitive advantages, the top management must not only continue to guard its competitive advantages but also take necessary steps to reinforce them.

The Three Views of Competitive Advantage

In their research paper *Corporate Advantage Revisited: Considering Competitive, Comparative, and Nonmarket Aspects*, Sebastian Träger and Achim Seisreiner[2] discuss the three views held by authors of repute. The following are the three views.

    i.   Market-based view of competitive advantage.

    ii.   Resource-based view of competitive advantage.

    iii.   Nonmarket-based view of competitive advantage.

Let us study briefly each of these three views of competitive advantage.

Market-based view of competitive advantage   This view is supported by Porter, Cockburn *et al.*, and Teece *et al.* Michael Porter is the main proponent of the market-based view of competitive advantage. The main content of the market-based view of strategic management thinking is that the success of a firm crucially depends on the market or industry attractiveness and is thus largely a function of strategic firm positioning. Accordingly, this approach assumes that firm's performance can be improved if industry conditions are favourable or, even more importantly, if they can be altered in a favourable way. Therefore, the success of the firms depends on either the choice of the "right" market or the ability to transform a market's characteristics in a convenient way. Among those performance-influencing industry characteristics identified by Porter[3] are the bargaining power of suppliers and customers, threats of new entrants and substitutes and the degree of industry rivalry. In order to perform well, a firm must be positioned in such a way that its capabilities provide the best defence against existing and potential strong competitive threats and enable best exploitation possibilities where competitive forces are weak.

According to Williamson,[4] in order to generate supernormal returns which denote a firm's success, the fundamental objective of a firm has to be to build up and eventually exercise some sort of market leadership or market power to lastingly influence the industry-specific competitive landscape. In order to achieve this goal, lowering the firm's costs per unit sold below the levels of its closest competitors or differentiating the product portfolio to market areas with above-average consumer willingness to pay (unique selling proposition) are recognised to be the most promising competitive strategies. Hence, superior differentiation or most efficient cost structures are the two kinds of competitive advantages a firm must strive for in order to outperform the industry—thereby (sustainably) earning supernormal rents.

Resource-based view of competitive advantage   Dierickx/Cool,[5] Barney,[6] Amit/Schoemaker,[7] Peteraf,[8] Collis[9] and some others argue that a firm's success is crucially dependent on industry conditions and derived positioning strategies and that the resource-based view of competitive advantage in today's understanding finds firm performance to be linked to internal (corporate) characteristics such as resource endowment, capabilities, and knowledge. Consequently, superior firm performance can be expected, if the resources at corporate disposal are of unique quality (i.e., valuable, rare, durable, imperfectly mobile, non-imitable, and non-substitutable), if they are uniquely combined and put in productive usage (distinctive, dynamic, or core capabilities), and if they are continuously improved in a unique way (knowledge as intangible and structural capital). If these conditions are met, a firm's activities are likely to be efficient and may thus lead to competitive advantage and, as a result, to superior performance.

According to Barney,[10] three categories of firm-specific resources are available for sustainable competitive advantage: (1) Physical resources are those tangible elements used in a firm's production process, ranging from its plant and equipment to its access to raw materials; (2) Organisational resources include the firm's structure and processes, from strategic planning systems to reward and control processes; and (3) Human resources include the training, experience, judgment, relationships, and insight of individual managers and workers in a firm. According to Rumelt,[11] the success or return of a selected competitive strategy critically depends on the degree of uniqueness of the resources at corporate disposal and not on mere industry characteristics. To put it differently, idiosyncratic characteristics of the resources available to a firm determine the direction of present and future business activities and hence of potential competitive advantages.

Nonmarket-based view of competitive advantage   This view is supported by Baron,[12] Spiller,[13] and others. Unlike the market-based or resource-based view of competitive advantage, the non-market perspective argues that a firm is able to alter the competitive landscape by (additionally) directing activities towards collective-action institutions such as governments or interest groups thereby opening new sources of rent generation. Instead of finding profitable market niches or developing unique resources and capabilities, firms, for example, can influence the legislative decision-making process which may ultimately either increase the costs of its direct competitors (e.g., through environmental regulations) or enables market access and thus competition in formerly protected business areas (e.g., through deregulation or privatisation). Accordingly, a firm will be advantageous in a competitive sense if it is able to shape the business environment in such a way that it is capable to position itself uniquely or to prevent competitors from accessing strategically important resources and markets. This will naturally result in firms having a competitive advantage over their rivals.

Key Aspects of Competitive Advantage

Irrespective of the views expressed by different experts, a competitive advantage may be rightly defined as a unique resource of an organisation which can create and sustain demand for its product in the long-run, which the competitors do not possess and which is capable of creating and nourishing customer loyalty. It is so because all the views ultimately centre around the paths taken to reach competitive advantages of the firm. This definition has three aspects:

   i.   a unique resource,

  ii.   creation and sustenance of demand, and

 iii.   creation of customer loyalty.

Let us study these aspects in more detail.

A unique resource   A competitive advantage needs to be a unique resource. A unique resource is an asset of the organisation. It has been accumulated by the organisation over time. It is a resource which no other seller in the market possesses in equal terms. An organisation can boast of possessing a unique or competitive advantage when it has an edge over the specific resource or advantage possessed by others in the market. The unique advantage must be able to draw the prospects towards the product and keep its existing customers in its fold with more cohesiveness. A unique advantage cannot be called unique if it does not perform these two functions namely, bringing to its fold new customers and keeping in its fold existing customers with greater loyalty.

Another important aspect mentioned is the uniqueness of the resource which no other player in the market possesses in equal terms. It is true that every manufacturer would try to create uniqueness in their product on some line. But a company claiming to possess a unique advantage must possess it as a monopoly. Others may also possess it but with a much lesser level or degree. When they do not possess sufficient power in their unique advantage, there is no meaning in calling it as a competitive advantage.

Creation and sustenance of demand   The second characteristic of a unique advantage is that the competitive advantage said to be possessed by an organisation must be able to create and sustain the demand for its product. A competitive advantage must have the capability to attract the prospects and make them loyal customers of the company. For example, a company has earned a name in the market that the products of the company are unfailing in quality. This is a competitive advantage of that company. This advantage can bring in new customers and also make the new and existing customers feel pride for being customers of that company. This is a strong competitive advantage of the company. But a company can boast itself to be a quality-conscious organisation only when it is able to prove it in the market. One cannot claim to be a quality-oriented organisation in words but it must show it in deeds as well. In general, whatever the nature of claim may be, it must have a strong base. Otherwise the organisation will lose its credibility in the market.

Creation of customer loyalty   A by-product of competitive advantage is customer loyalty. The competitive advantage of the organisation has many benefits for it. One of the important benefits is creation of customer loyalty. The customer becomes attracted towards the company when the product is satisfactory and fulfils the expectations. When the product purchased gives trouble-free service, the customer becomes more tilted towards the organisation. At every opportunity the customer speaks about the product to friends and others. A satisfied customer is the biggest asset of the organisation. It increases the reputation of the company and its brand name and, in turn, leads to goodwill creation. The value of the brand also shoots up. Not only the marketing objectives but also the organisational objectives are accomplished with much ease and comfort.

Core Competencies and Competitive Advantage

A core competency is a factor extant in a company that leads to the competitive advantage of the organisation. There can be a number of core competencies that can lead to advantages to the organisation which a company enjoys over its rivals. These core competencies when reinforced or becomes stronger, they become as the competitive advantages of the company. The following are a few examples of core competencies which can transform into competitive advantages that a company may gain in the course of its work.

- i. Talented manpower
- ii. Unparelleled quality
- iii. Low cost products
- iv. Talented research and development team
- v. Excellent marketing network
- vi. Excellent marketing information system
- vii. Loyal employees
- viii. Forward looking management
- ix. Organisational culture

EVOLUTION OF COMPETITIVE ADVANTAGES

A competitive advantage is an advantage enjoyed by an organisation which its rivals do not possess. Sometimes it evolves naturally. A competitive advantage develops knowingly or unknowingly in an organisation by virtue of its policies that have been practiced right from the days of the inception of the company. Initially the management may not be aware that their policies would lead to competitive advantages of the company; but at a later stage they recognise the presence of a competitive advantage in their organisation.

Hero Cycles had a modest beginning with production of mere 639 bicycles during 1956; but today the company is manufacturing 18,800 cycles per day. With the 48% share of the Indian market, this volume has catapulted Hero in the "Guinness Book of World Records" in 1986 and edge over global players is being maintained since then. Their competitive advantage is their cost leadership. Today the company is the leading manufacturer of two wheelers in the world. Hero Group, besides being the world's largest manufacturers of bicycles, motorcycles and chains to this date, has diversified into newer segments like Information Technology, IT enabled services and financial services. The Hero Group has done business differently, right from its inception and that is what has helped them to achieve break-through in whatever product category they ventured in. The Group's low key, but focused, style of management has earned the reputation among its investors, employees, vendors and dealers, as also worldwide recognition. The company could develop to the present level due to the tireless efforts of the Munjal brothers who could develop competitive advantages for the organisation from their foresight and determination to excel.

Competitive advantages can be created by the organisation by careful planning and its execution. Planning for competitive advantage is a decision to be made by the top management. If the management is desirous of creating this, then the management has to chalk out a big plan which may take a longer time as it may involve changing the total landscape of the organisation. But it is certain that competitive advantages can be created by a smart management. There cannot be two opinions on this point. The management must ride against the tide with hope. The methodology to be used to create competitive advantages will be studied in a separate section of this chapter.

Qualities of Sustainable Competitive Advantages

A sustainable competitive advantage is one which has a prolonged duration of its existence in the market. It is not that a competitive advantage will remain competitive all the time in the market. It has to be nurtured and follow-up actions are necessary to keep it going. Let us now study the qualities required of a sustainable competitive advantage.

Popular but difficult to benchmark   A high quality competitive advantage must be popular among the customers and the competitors as well and everyone else must be aware of it; but no one can easily adopt it. A competitive advantage must be very difficult for the competitors to benchmark. Many organisations believe that benchmarking is an easy task. But it is not so. Even if one knows the secrets of success of an organisation, benchmarking cannot be done in the same way. Methods, procedures, techniques, tools, and above all the organisational culture are involved in creating the quality and reputation of the organisation. Therefore, it requires tenacity and application of mind to successfully benchmark a system.

High degree of customer loyalty   A good competitive advantage can boast so only when it has a sizeable number of loyal customers. A powerful competitive advantage creates a strong customer base. The more powerful the competitive advantage, the more loyal the customers are. Therefore, a sustainable competitive advantage must possess the quality to attract the customers to its fold quickly as well as strongly.

Backed by reinforcement from management   A high quality competitive advantage must be under the surveillance of key executives of the organisation. The management must entrust this task of taking follow-up measures to reinforce the hard earned advantage with a senior executive. The senior executive must carry out studies to ensure that the competitive advantage remains intact and not eroded. Managing the competitive advantage is an unending process. If there is any lenience in this connection, all the organisation's efforts may go in vain. Therefore, a close monitoring of the status of the competitive advantage is very essential.

Valued by customers   A good competitive advantage is valued by the customers very high and they stand tall when they speak of it. A good competitive advantage makes the possession of the product as the pride of the customer. The customers are satisfied with the benefit offered by the product and they are strong in their position that they have received value for their money. Sometimes in their zeal for *their* brand, customers go to the extent of making suggestions to the company for improving the product further.

Keys to Competitive Advantage

An organisation can also develop its competitive advantages by conscious efforts of the top management. Careful planning and its meticulous implementation with an objective in mind can land any organistion in a bundle of competitive advantages. Today, the organisations are working hard to achieve competitive advantages because they very well know that only an organisation with tangible competitive advantages can survive in the long run. But gaining competitive advantage requires:

* hard decisions,
* high-calibre executives,
* full-fledged support of executives and management,
* the determination to do it, and
* a loyal workforce.

These keys when operated correctly will lead to a score of competitive advantages in the organisation. All these together can accomplish it and the company will be in the forefront. This can be put as an equation also.

$$Ca = Hd + Hce + Ms + Dn + Lw$$

where,

Ca—Competitive Advantage

Hd—Hard decisions,

Hce—High-calibre executives

Ms—Management Support

Dn—Determination

Lw—Loyal workforce

Let us study these determinants of competitive advantages in some more detail.

Hard decisions The management must go ahead with decisions which are basic for the creation of a competitive advantage. The decisions are hard because the management will have to confront difficult times due to the implementation of these decisions.In the first place, the organisation must decide to create a suitable organisational culture which is very basic to a sustainable competitive advantage. Of course the company can do this with the existing kind of culture, but an enduring presence of a competitive advantage requires a good organisational climate. The organisation can make an all-out effort to recruit high quality personnel for manning its research and development department hoping that they would deliver results. These R&D executives would deliver it in the short run; but they would fail to sustain the momentum because of the absence of good climate within the organisation. These R&D men soon become familiar to the organisational culture prevalent in the organisation and they too become submerged in the current. The management must start from the scratch. It is well and good if the organisation already possesses a superior climate. In this case, the job of the management would become easier. But in the other case, the first step the management should take is to change its corporate culture. The members of the organisation must be injected a new value system and new blood must be injected into them.

Some of the important decisions to be made in order to develop competitive advantages in an organisation are given here.

1. An unparelleled compensation package for the members of the organisation
2. Being impartial in matters of employee discipline
3. Redefining the organisational culture, if necessary
4. Adoption of modern production processes in place of outdated ones
5. Making key decisions to sustain/improve productivity of the organisation
6. Golden handshake with employees found to be unfit for the organisation

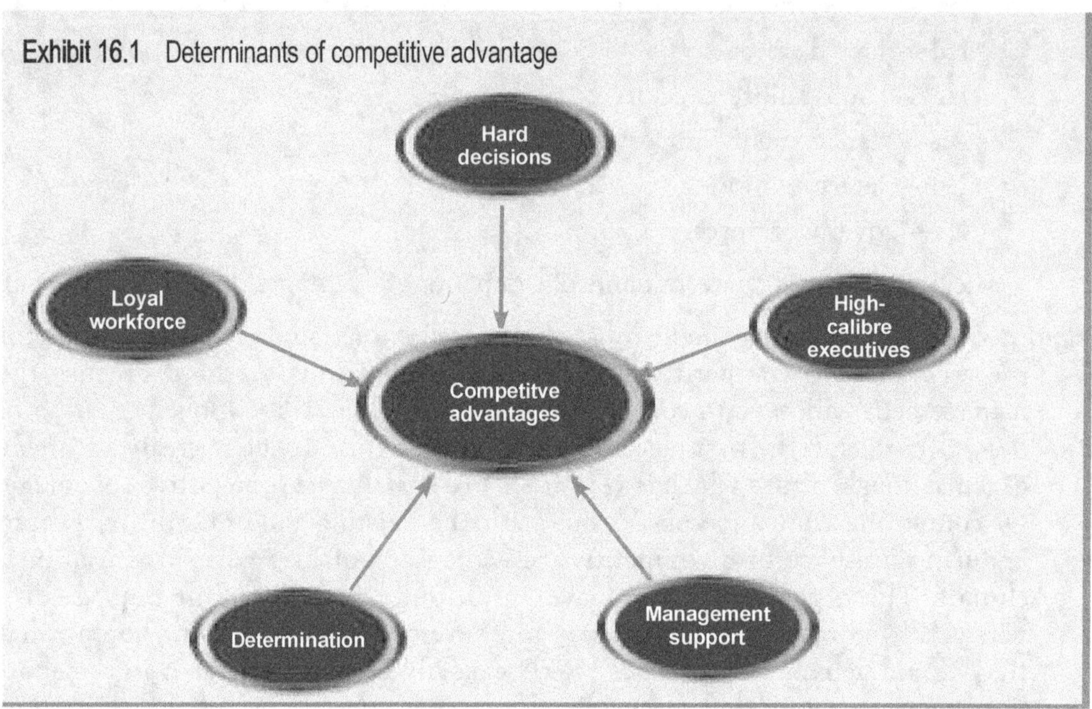

Exhibit 16.1 Determinants of competitive advantage

High-calibre executives The executives must be sensitive to issues, current as well as predicted. They must possess the right kind of creativity and sense of approaching the issues with a practical mindset. They must be dedicated and determined in their mission. These executives can guide the top management in the right direction which is very much required of a growing organisation. An organisation with high-calibre executives can tide over any kind of crises with much ease and comfort. They know very well what to do, when to do, and how to do it in a given situation. The top management's priority must be to manage them with honour and recognition. The executives find it greatly nourishing and satisfactory when their superiors speak high of them in the midst of people. When the executives deserve it, the management should not fail to honour them at the earliest moment available. Because these executives are the keys to the organisation's growth, their services must be remembered by their superiors.

Management support The unconditional and full-fledged support of the executives and management to the efforts of the members of the organisation in accomplishing the given assignment is very basic to the success of their endeavour. Therefore, the management and the senior executives must extend their all-out support to the projects and programmes of the organisation. There should not be any kind of hatred among the cadres of management as well as top management.

Common differences of opinion are found among the line and staff managers. In most of the organisations, the problem of line and staff are found very common. The conflicts between them must not be allowed to develop in the organisation. These conflicts must be resolved as and when they appear and before they take unmanageable proportions. Cordial relationships between them are essential for the welfare of the organisation.

Determination to accomplish given tasks   Be it an operational level executive or a finance officer, they must possess an unstinted determination to do it. They must be able to finish the given assignment with success and least cost of resources. Such must be the culture of the organisation that the members must be trained in these lines. The organisational culture must make them capable of doing any difficult job with necessary degree of application of mind and these employees must not think it to be below their dignity to seek the advices of the experts on the field. After all everyone in the organisation is working for a common cause and this positive attitude must be developed in the members of the organisation. It is the sense of belongingness of the members of the organisation that will motivate the members to act swiftly in order to achieve the target on time.

The determination to accomplish the given tasks can result in creation of competitive advantages for the organisation.

Loyal workforce   Building a loyal workforce is mostly the responsibility of the management. A loyal workforce is the biggest asset of an organisation. The organisation's workforce must be loyal as well as caring for its wellbeing. However, it is difficult to find all the employees as Theory Y people in an organisation. However, the right kind of management can turn them as loyal and sincere to the company. Loyal workforce can solidly help in the process of creating competitive advantages for the organisation. Being in possession of loyal workforce itself is a competitive advantage. Most of the employees would become loyal and dedicated if the following factors are made available to them.

1. Satisfactory compensation package
2. Satisfactory working conditions
3. Recognition of talents
4. Recognition of achievements
5. Right kind of motivation
6. Sense of security of job
7. Reasonable scope for promotion
8. Parental care

Another way of creating loyal employees is that the management too must be loyal to them. It means that management must be responsive to the genuine needs of its employees. The management must avoid taking temporary steps to solve employee problems. An enduring solution will lead to enduring mindset among the employees. It is so because most of the managements do not view seriously thereafter and they forget the fact that what they did was only a temporary remedy.

THE PROCESS OF COMPETITIVE ADVANTAGE CREATION

The keys to competitive advantage studied in the previous section provide the direction which must be taken by the organisation in order to create competitive advantages for it. Competitive advantages can be developed by a new as well as an existing organisation if they decide to do so. A shrewd management which wants to make its journey interesting and effortless must put in hard work and apply first class techniques to develop sustainable competitive advantages in the organisation.

Small as well as big companies must create competitive advantages to make its entry into the business successful. Small companies have their competitors in their class of companies. Therefore, small companies cannot shun the idea of creation of competitive advantage. Let us now study the process of creating competitive advantages for an organisation. It involves several steps as explained below.

1. Decide the Competitive Advantage(s) to be Created

The first step towards creation of competitive advantage in an organisation is to determine what competitive advantage the company wants to create. As pointed out earlier in the chapter, there are several competitive advantages. The management has to choose from among them the most appropriate advantage it wants to create. The company may like to possess a dedicated salesforce or workforce. Or, it may like to have a competitive edge in its price which is called as "price or cost advantage." Sometimes the company may like to differentiate its product from others prominently. This differentiation may be done on several counts. Firstly, it may be quality. Quality differentiation is an important criterion to create the unique advantage. Secondly, the company may want to differentiate its product by choosing a particular channel of distribution. It is common that some products are available only in departmental stores or chain stores as the company follows a price skimming strategy. Thirdly, the company may like to create competitive advantage by creating an excellent research and development team which works faster and which is highly creative in its thoughts that would help an organisation in finding out new products. Fourthly, the company may possess a dedicated lot of executives who make the best use of their talents to lift the company from all spheres. Therefore, the company willing to develop competitive advantage(s) must choose the preferable advantage which in its opinion will help accomplish its objective.

2. Create Suitable Climate in the Organisation

The organisational culture plays a vital role in creating the unique advantage for the organisation. A company with excellent culture can do things of any nature. A new company can build its culture easily compared to that of an existing one. An existing company will find it very difficult to inject a new culture in the employees of the organisation. The reasons are obvious. Switching to a new culture is a tough job in an existing organisation. However, it is possible if the management has the tenacity and determination to do it.

The most appropriate internal environment must be created by the management. Suppose, the company wants to create cost advantage, it must carry out some specific activities. The company must

    i.   find out the best sources of materials and machinery which would be available at a comparatively low cost.

    ii.   use the production techniques which result in higher productivity which would reduce the cost of production.

    iii.   employ superior workforce in the factory who will make the best use of their time inside the factory.

    iv.   install machinery which is free of maintenance for a reasonably longer period of time.

    v.   see that the defectives are much below the normal level so that wastage can be avoided.

    vi.   see that the workers' absenteeism levels are minimum, and

    vii.   minimise the cost of selling and distribution through a good travel schedule.

Similarly for every competitive advantage, the company must carry out specific activities to make the organisation suitable for the competitive advantage. These activities must be found out and suitable steps must be taken to alter the company's internal environment to suit the competitive advantage.

3. Prepare a Master Plan

The Macmillan dictionary defines a master plan as a plan giving all the details of how you intend to succeed in doing something difficult. The management must prepare a master plan/strategy to bring about necessary changes in the organisation. A master plan is a broad outline of programmes, procedures, and directives necessary to bring about the necessary changes in the organisation. In our previous example of the company's decision to create cost advantage, the various steps to be taken to create cost advantage were listed out. Here, the master plan would chalk out a broad outline in order to create the particular advantage. In general, the master plan would include all the points given below.

i. The names of the members of the committee in charge of the master plan
ii. The objectives of the master plan
iii. The timeframe for accomplishing the objectives
iv. The beginning point
v. The sequence of activities to be performed in order to reach the objectives along with the time required to perform each activity
vi. The details of instructions to be given to the executives in charge of execution of the master plan
vii. The details of the executives in charge of specific activities
viii. The details of cost involved in the process
ix. Broad guidelines to the executives as to the methodology to be adopted in their functioning
x. Details of progress reporting procedures
xi. The name of the executive in charge of monitoring progress

The organisation has to act swiftly and as per the master plan. Any deviation from the plan must be brought to the notice of the committee overseeing the operations. Alternative arrangements must be made to minimise the damage done to the process.

4. Chalk Out Sub-plans for the Executives

Formulation of sub-plans is an important step in the process of creating the competitive advantages for the organisation. There can be two ways of approaching this step. One, the sub-plans may be made out by the committee members themselves. Or, it may be finalised during a meeting with the executives in charge of the activities. The latter method is better because it is a kind of managing by objectives. When objectives or any task responsibility is taken up with the people in charge of executing them, naturally it will have a sense of commitment for those executives. Therefore, it is better to determine minute details of their tactics which may be determined through a discussion with the executives.

5. Arranging Meetings with the Executives

The executives-in-charge of implementing the programme must be chosen with utmost care and their willingness must be obtained prior to their assignment. Meetings must be convened with the executives in order to make them knowledgeable and to make them feel at home. The main purposes of these meetings are

    i.   to underline the importance of the process,

    ii.   to clarify any points raised by them about their proposed activities,

    iii.   to issue necessary instructions which are to be taken care in the course of their work,

    iv.   to give them detailed sub-plans to be executed by them,

    v.   to welcome any suggestions from the executives, and if they are found to be worthy, they may be incorporated in the sub-plans, and

    vi.   to make them confident of accomplishing the given assignment.

The meeting must be chaired by the members of the committee-in-charge of the master-plan execution. The chairman of the committee must create a friendly atmosphere during the meeting. Every small point must be discussed and all the doubts, how silly they may look at the outset, must be clarified by the committee members. This will encourage the executives to mingle freely with the committee members.

6. Delegating Authority to the Executives

Obviously the next step is to delegate the necessary authority to the executives involved in the process. While doing so, the rules of delegation must be strictly followed. Authority delegated must be in proportion to the responsibility entrusted. Any excessive authority or any excessive responsibility might harm the process. Once the authority is delegated, the executives may begin their work and report the progress at regular intervals as required by the committee.

7. Review the Progress

The committee-in-charge of competitive advantages must conduct review sessions at regular intervals to monitor the progress made. If any changes or improvement in the strategy are required to be made, steps may be taken to carry out them. Concise reports must be presented by the executives in charge of the competitive advantages creation process. These reports may also contain suggestions of the concerned executive in the process. These suggestions may be discussed by the committee and suitable steps may be decided by the committee.

SUMMARY

- A competitive advantage may be defined as a unique resource of an organisation which can create and sustain demand for its product in the long run, which the competitors do not possess and which is capable of creating and nourishing customer loyalty.

- A core competency is a factor extant in a company that leads to the competitive advantage of the organisation. There can be a number of core competencies that can lead to advantages to the organisation which a company enjoys over its rivals. These core competencies when reinforced or becomes stronger, they become as the competitive advantages of the company.

- A competitive advantage develops knowingly or unknowingly in an organisation by virtue of its policies that have been practiced right from the days of the inception of the company. Initially the management may not be aware that their policies would lead to competitive advantages of the company; but at a later stage they recognise the presence of a competitive advantage in their organisation.

- Competitive advantages can be created by the organisation by careful planning and its execution. Planning for competitive advantage is a decision to be made of the top management. If the management is desirous of creating this, then the management has to chalk out a big plan which may take a longer time as it may involve changing the total landscape of the organisation.

- The qualities required of a sustainable competitive advantage are 1) popular but difficult to benchmark, 2) high degree of customer loyalty, 3) backed by reinforcement from management, 4) valued by customers.

- The keys to gaining competitive advantage are 1) hard decisions, 2) high-calibre executives, 3) full-fledged support of executives and management, 4) the determination to do it, and 5) a loyal workforce.

- A shrewd management which wants to make its journey interesting and effortless must put in hard work and first class techniques to develop sustainable competitive advantages in the organisation. The competitive advantages can be created by following a process that requires careful planning and execution.

REVIEW QUESTIONS

1. Explain the term "competitive advantage".
2. Discuss the three views of competitive advantages.
3. List out the key aspects of competitive advantages.
4. "A competitive advantage develops knowingly or unknowingly in an organisation by virtue of its policies." Do you agree? Give your arguments with real-time examples.
5. Discuss some of the important decisions to be made in order to develop competitive advantages in an organisation.
6. "Loyal workforce can solidly help in the process of creating competitive advantages for the organisation." Explain how a loyal workforce can help to create competitive advantages.
7. Discuss the evolution of competitive advantages.
8. State the qualities of sustainable competitive advantages.
9. Identify the keys to a competitive advantage.
10. Discuss the process of competitive advantage creation.

REFERENCES

1. Greg Roworth owner of http://www.autopilotbusinessplan.com
2. Träger, Sebastian and Seisreiner, Achim *Corporate Advantage Revisited: Considering Competitive, Comparative, and Nonmarket Aspects*, ACCS 2005: Session: Corporate Strategy and Competitive Advantage.
3. Porter, M.E. (1980). *Competitive Strategy: Techniques for Analyzing Industries and Competitors*. Free Press, New York.
4. Williamson, O.E. (1991). "Strategizing, economizing, and economic organization." *Strategic Management Journal*, Winter Special Issue. 12: 75–94.
5. Dierickx, L. and Cool, K. (1989). "Asset stock accumulation and sustainability of competitive advantage." *Management Science*. 35: 1504–1511.
6. Barney, J.S. (1991). "Firm resources and sustained competitive advantage." *Journal of Management*. 17: 99–120; "Looking inside for competitive advantage." *The Academy of Management Executive*.9: 49–61.
7. Amit, R. and Schoemaker, P. (1993). "Strategic assets and organizational rent." *Strategic Management Journal*. 14: 33–46.

8. Peteraf, M. (1993). "The cornerstones of competitive advantage: A resource-based view." *Strategic Management Journal.* 14 (3): 179–191.

9. Collis, D.J. (1994). "How valuable are organizational capabilities?" In: *Strategic Management Journal.* 15: 143–152.

10. Barney, J.S. (1991). "Firm resources and sustained competitive advantage." *Journal of Management.* 17: 99–120.

11. Rumelt, R.P. (1984). "Toward a strategic theory of the firm." In: Lamb, R. (Ed.), *Competitive Strategic Management.* Prentice-Hall, Englewood Cliffs, NJ. pp. 556–570.

12. Baron, D.P. (2001). "Theories of strategic nonmarket participation: Majority-rule and executive institutions." *Journal of Economics and Management Strategy.* 10: 47–89.

13. Spiller, D.F. (2001). Introduction, *Journal of Economics and Management Strategy,* Vol. 10, pp. 3–5.

17

STRATEGIC SERVICES MANAGEMENT

After reading this chapter, you will be able to

- ❂ *recognise the role of the after-sales services in an organisation,*

- ❂ *recognise the need for strategic service management in an organisation,*

- ❂ *understand the important elements of strategic service management, and*

- ❂ *determine the methodology to be followed in the management of these elements.*

KEY TERMS

- ❂ Knowledge management
- ❂ Service cost
- ❂ Profitability
- ❂ Strategic service
- ❂ Optimal investment

- ❂ Rapid payback
- ❂ Price management
- ❂ Right price
- ❂ Internal promotions and transfers

- ❂ Campus recruitment
- ❂ Training
- ❂ Orientation
- ❂ Compensation
- ❂ Authorised service stations

INTRODUCTION

The American Express Customer Service Barometer[1] released in July 2010 its findings on attitudes and preferences toward customer service. It is a survey conducted in India and eleven other countries to find out what the customers have in their mind while making purchases. As per the survey results, 82% of Indian consumers value good customer service the most while making a purchase. Pradeep Kapur VP & GM (World Service India), American Express said, "Customers want and expect high-quality service, especially as they focus on getting good value for their money in a difficult economic environment, and are willing to spend more with those that deliver excellent service—suggesting substantial growth opportunities for businesses that get customer service right." The survey has found that 76% of Indian consumers are ready to pay up to 11% more for excellent customer service.

The survey results just mentioned speak the truth about the significance of after-sales service expected by the Indian customers. Today's customers are conscious of their rights and value of their money. The result is a search for a good manufacturer who offers a quality product along with a good package of service warranty. First, they check for the quality of the product; then they ask for particulars of after-sales service. After the recent economic meltdown across the developed nations, customers have become hard people and the salesmen find them very tough to deal with. They ask for this and that while they visit the showrooms. The sales staff of the outlet has to explain even very small details to them in order to make the sale.

In 1981, Rolls-Royce[2] generated some 20% of its revenues from after-sales services. By declaring the service business a high priority and aligning its strategy accordingly, the company was able to expand its service business impressively from 1981 through 2008. Today, more than 50% of Rolls-Royce's revenues are derived from its service business. The company's success in services has defined its growth story—and boosted its profits significantly. Inspired by the success of Rolls-Royce, many other companies followed suit and succeeded in the strategy. In India too, Hindustan Motors is able to survive because of its service business for its lakhs of already sold Ambassador cars.

A benchmarking study[3] conducted by The Boston Consulting Group of 50 manufacturers of industrial machinery that also provide after-sales services confirmed the attractiveness of service business for industrial goods companies. On an average, the service businesses of the companies in their sample accounted for about 30% of their revenues—and contributed more than 50% of their total operating profits, at a profit margin of 24%. Among the top-quartile companies, services contributed an average 47% of revenues and earned average profit margins of 36%.

BCG's project experience[4] suggests that the success of proactive sales rests on three pillars:

* Offering standardised products
* Tracking the installed base by means of sophisticated tools, including comprehensive service records and technical records for all installations
* Developing a sales-oriented culture

WHAT IS STRATEGIC SERVICES MANAGEMENT

Today's manufacturers have become very well aware of the need for quality in their products. But beyond a level, they are unable to improve the quality of their products substantially because almost all the leading manufacturers have reached the saturation points. Therefore, they have to look for other strategies to woo their customers and the avenues available in this regard are sales promotions, and effective advertisements in leading journals, newspapers, and television channels. While all these methods do well, there is yet another area which has long been neglected by the manufacturers as well as sellers. This area is service after sales. Even though the culture of "use and throw" has picked up in India, this is not the case for big-ticket products like lap-tops and other consumer durables, and even homes.

It is true that sales promotional methods bring to the organisation a good volume of sales. But the fact is that neither the manufacturer nor the customer benefit in a big way by these methods. A good chunk of expenditure goes to the pockets of advertisement media and only a small portion of money spent goes to the customers as offers. But in the case of after-sales service, the story is different. As most of the products made by leading manufacturers offer flawless performance for a reasonable number of years, an extended warranty for the products is able to satisfy the customers with a bigger smile. The money spent on after-sales service is productive in the sense that the service offered to the customers for repairing their equipment makes them satisfied and also that the service done also brings business to the manufacturer. After the warranty period is over, the customer is prepared to spend for the parts that need replacement.

Strategic services management involves a chain of people who are involved in the selling process like distributors, dealers and many others. It has to go beyond the short-term issues of problem diagnosis, replacement part location and delivery, technician scheduling and dispatch, and price optimisation and address the long-term issues of regular part re-orders when inventory reaches threshold levels, appropriate workforce training and staffing, and performance monitoring to ensure that price levels and service quality remain at an optimal level.

Strategic services management focuses on the long-term impact upon the customers by providing them a world class service which makes an indirect appeal to the customers' conscience which becomes satisfied by the way the service is provided.

This kind of strategic service creates a mark in the minds of the customers, creates a feeling that the manufacturer is doing all the best possible to satisfy them, and leaves an impression in the customers about the quality of service offered by the manufacturer. It is true that nobody is going to find fault with the manufacturer if a vehicle is creating problems after running 1,50,000 kilometres on the road. But the customer expects that the manufacturer must come for help to make an additional 50,000 kilometres of trouble-free performance. Here comes strategic services management when the manufacturer obliges the request of the customer, making the customer happy as well as loyal to the manufacturer.

ELEMENTS OF STRATEGIC SERVICES MANAGEMENT

Strategic services management aims at creating greater satisfaction which would reinforce the customer's relationship with the company. The manufacturer's task is not complete when the products get sold in the market. The acid test begins when the customers begin using the product. At this point of time, the customers are happy with the product. This satisfaction level must be maintained by the product performance. In reality, the customers' expectations are very high; but when they begin to use/consume the product, two possibilities are there. One, they use the product with high hopes. Two, they use the product under suspicion; they are afraid whether the product would go the unexpected way. This suspicion is slowly erased from customers mind as they continue to use the product with satisfaction.

One of the most important aspects of the aftermath of selling is the process of offering quality after-sales services to the customer. When we go deeper into the matter, we can ascertain a few important aspects of strategic services management which help the organisation in making this function successful. Let us study these aspects of strategic services management.

Strategic Service Knowledge Management

Knowledge management is a process that begins with acquiring of the basics of the pertinent knowledge and organising the information so acquired in a way that can be effectively delivered to the customers through right people and ends with actual using of knowledge for maximising the satisfaction levels of the customers. Knowledge management can be successfully used in several fields including research and development, manufacturing, and marketing. Knowledge is a diverse stock of information and we must use the right information in the right place. The idea of knowledge management can be applied to strategic services management also successfully.

Possession of adequate knowledge of service related issues is very much essential to the manufacturer. The service personnel of the organisation are the key people who train technicians for carrying out of servicing of products. First of all the service personnel of the company must have a first-hand knowledge about the product. They must be experts in the field with a flair for teaching the knowledge to the technicians. These technicians are actually located at various points in the market. First of all, they need to be taught the role of after-sales service in an organisation. It is important that the technicians must be promised good compensation packages by the manufacturer. They must also be assured merit-based pay hikes. At the same time, they must be cautioned against any inefficiency in their job performance.

Strategic services knowledge management must look into the following considerations in the process of offering after-sales service to the customers.

1. *Lower service cost*   It is important that the manufacturer must offer service at a low cost wherever possible. By making the fullest use of services knowledge management, the company must avoid repeat calls from the customers. When customers do not make a repeat call, it may mean two things. Firstly, the customer is satisfied with the service and the product is doing well. Or, the customer has become irked with the kind of service offered by the dealer. This can be checked by making follow-up calls by the service station manager or his staff.

2. *Improved service*   Services knowledge management also leads to better quality of service. Customers are more likely to receive the right answers faster, with no need to be put on hold or transferred to another agent. And, the value of superior customer service, of course, is enormous. The customer becomes more attached with the company. The product also performs better as it offers flawless service. Such customers make repeat purchases and become loyal to the manufacturer.

3. *Consistency in service*   Without a knowledge management system, it is very difficult for an enterprise to know the responses customers receive from the organisations offering service. This information is greatly useful for the manufacturer in devising a better system in future. The service station manager must ensure that customers with the same kind of grievance receive the same kind of response except the case of emergency services. It is necessary that the waiting customers must be convinced on the position of the manager on the need to attend emergency services regardless of the customer's status.

4. *Better treatment of customers*   The customers visiting the service station must be offered courteous service. It is important that the service executive must have plain talking with the customer. The customer must be explained the real position; there must be transparency in the executive's approach, but with courtesy.

Strategic Service Parts Management

According to Joseph D. Patton,[5] the objective of service parts management is to satisfy customers by providing necessary parts, at the user's location, for a reasonable price, in usable condition, at the proper time. This can be referred to as the five rights of parts: item, place, price, quality and time. Availability of spare parts is an important aspect of strategic services management. If the service station does not possess required number of spares, it cannot offer prompt service to the customers. Even though customers are ready to wait for a couple of days or even a week in order to fix the original parts, they are so because they have no other way out. However, this kind of waiting makes the customers little bit unsatisfactory towards the kind of service.

One of the Korean car manufacturers operating in India has the policy of collecting orders on a particular day only during the week from its service stations. This policy results in undue delay in getting the vehicles serviced; sometimes, the customer has to keep away from their cars for more than ten days. Suppose a key component has to be replaced in the car. The company has the policy of accepting orders only on Tuesdays and in this case, the customer comes with his car on Tuesday. The service station manager takes his own time to prepare the estimate and he places the order for the required spare only on the next Tuesday. About eight days are already lost by the customer in this process. It would take another four or five days for the spare to reach the station. The service engineers take their own time to fix the spare in the car. Therefore, it takes totally a full period of two weeks for the customer to get his car serviced. Is it not too much? Is it the kind of justice meted out to a customer? The manufacturer must think about it and he must consider the inconveniences suffered by the customers.

An effective strategic parts management is the alignment of forecasting, planning, and inventory management in order to ensure satisfaction of the customer by returning the product well-serviced quickly as well as promptly. Delays in shipping, unnecessary wait times and so on must be avoided. Many a times, the manufacturer also suffers financial losses in replacing a costly part in the product. Let me share my own experience in this regard. I purchased a car in July 2009 from a dealer in Madurai. I was very much fond of my car as I believed that the manufacturer was a world class company and their products also would be of high quality. In a few days after buying the car, the car started making a very huge horn-like sound for about five minutes while it was being parked in the garage. The people around the garage did not mind it initially. I conveyed the matter to the dealer from whom I purchased the car and he advised me to bring the car to their service station immediately. I did it. The service engineer fully checked the vehicle and found no fault in the car. Even though I was not fully satisfied with the response of the service engineer, I was left with no other way except to take the car to my house.

The very next day, the same kind of noise came from the vehicle. I was very much disturbed by the incident and took the car again to the service station. I suggested the service executive to keep the vehicle in their custody for a few days and see for himself about the fault in the car. A call came from the service executive informing that the same kind of noise which was very intolerable came from the vehicle in the midnight. He felt very sorry for the way the car disturbed me and my neighbours because he had to come to the service station at midnight from his home to stop the harassing sound reported by the security personnel of the service station. He promised me to replace the entire system in the vehicle which he suspected for the noise, and he did it within a couple of days.

Now that more than one year has passed and the vehicle is performing excellently. I was fully satisfied with the way the service executives of the dealer did their work. Therefore, three points can be taken from the said incident. One, the service executive should be a person having complete knowledge of the product. Two, the service parts must be readily available. Three, the service executive must treat the customers with courtesy which can heal the wounds of the customer suffered from the malfunctioning of the product.

Another important point is that the manufacturer or the service station executive must not take a casual view about the complaints lodged by the customers. They have to take them seriously and act with all seriousness. In India, after-sales services are not taken seriously and the customer is not encouraged by most of the dealers to report any malfunctioning of the product immediately. They say it while the customer visits their showroom for making the purchase. The dealers in India think that their job is over once the product is delivered to the customer. The customers in India have to visit the dealers with suspicion and hesitation in their minds because the dealers do not offer the same kind of courtesy which was extended to them at the time of the customers' first visit to their showrooms.

Important aspects of service parts management The spare parts management of the manufacturer needs an equally efficient team of service executives who can carry out the job to the satisfaction of the customers. Perhaps, this requires more planning and speed of service so that the down time caused by the breakdown of a machine will be the least. Let us now look into some of the important questions involved in the process of spare parts management.

1. *Prompt supply of spare parts* The most important aspect to be looked into is the supply of spare parts on time. The faulty part would have caused an unthinkable degree of damage to the customers and their assets. It may be the least in the case of a customer who purchased a refrigerator or a television. But take the example of an industrial customer. The production line might have been brought to a halt for non-availability of the particular spare part in the city. In such a case, the manufacturer must ensure prompt supply of the spare parts to the customer. The industrial customer

may lose lakhs of rupees for every hour of the stoppage of the production line. In such cases, the manufacturer must act very promptly and may airlift the spare part immediately or send the part through a special vehicle.

2. *Optimal investment in spare parts* In the case of airplanes in need of a critical spare, the loss incurred by the company may run into millions of rupees if the plane is not operated for a few days for want of the spare part. At the same time, the problem is that the manufacturer cannot keep a good stock of the material because the material itself may cost a few lakhs of rupees. Therefore, keeping a heavy stock all the times might need a heavy investment in the stock. But this may strain the financial position of the manufacturer. However, an optimal solution to the problem must be found out to see that both the customer and the manufacturer do not suffer much.

3. *Nature of break downs* Products can break down anywhere in the country, and not necessarily in a location that is near the manufacturer's central warehouse. Therefore, if the manufacturer has multiple storage locations and multiple service locations, they need to optimise the storage location for each part as well as the quantity. If it's a small and relatively inexpensive part and thousands of them needed a year at customer sites all over the country, it is suggested to store a portion of the inventory at each of the company's warehouses.

4. *Quality of spare parts* Even though we manufacture quality components for the regular products, it is necessary that an additional check on the quality of the spare parts is essential. The spare parts must never fail in quality because they are to be used for the product of aggrieved customers. Any let up in this regard might lead to disastrous consequences for the company because the customers may lose all the confidence in the manufacturer's capability to supply quality products.

5. *Rapid payback* It means generation of value by quickly converting customer grievances into organisation's opportunities. The company must cash in on the service requirements of the customers. By offering quality after-sales service, the company can revitalise its reputation which would lead to greater customer loyalty. Service with smile, service with the customer's welfare in mind and service with the organisational objectives in mind can better serve the ultimate goals of the organisation.

Strategic Service Price Management

The next important area of strategic services management is the management of prices for the services rendered to the customers. Formulating the services pricing policy of the organisation is important in the sense that it decides the profitability of the organisation and the nature of customer relationship with the organisation. The manufacturer must note here that profitability must not be the sole criterion for fixing the price for the services being offered. The customers must be in an advantageous position because they must never find the services of the organisation too costly as this will make them switch loyalty.

The principle underlying the pricing policy of services must be maximisation of organisation's profitability by fixing lower prices and entertaining more customers to the fold of the organisation. Many customers complain of very high prices of original spare parts available with the authorised service stations of the manufacturer. This makes the customers switch to counterfeit spares which result in many untoward incidents like accidents. Finally the blame is put on the manufacturer. This cannot happen if the manufacturer supplies the spares for the right price. It is important to note that many of the authorised service centres of the company charge very heavily and they also take lot of time to get the things ready for delivery. Unscrupulous service executives prepare big estimates for undertaking service for the product which drives away the customers from them. They say this and that and the customer becomes restless with the behaviour of the service executives.

Price management requires the ability to employ optimisation-based sophisticated pricing techniques and adaptive business logic. By charging the most, the company can get its market-base restricted, while charging the most competitive price could stretch the organisation too thin. In addition, charging what was the right price yesterday might not be the right thing to do because market conditions constantly shift and it might not be the right price today. The right price is hard to find because it's a function of how many potential customers could, and likely would, buy the product or service at a given price and of the economies of scale the company is able to leverage at a given volume. However, the organisation must find out a right price for its services. The price so fixed must satisfy the organisational objectives as well as the customers' expectations.

The service executive must study the minds of the customers before embarking upon the pricing of the services. The ultimate criterion the customers would consider is the quality of the services offered. Today's customers are quality conscious rather than price conscious. But a very high price for the services will also make them rethink on continuance as a customer of the organisation. At the same time, a lower price will affect the credibility of the organisation. Therefore, the right pricing strategy depends on the following factors.

1.   The overall reputation of the service provider
2.   The organisational objectives
3.   The nature of customer segment
4.   The quality of service rendered
5.   The expectations of the customers

6.   The cost of servicing
7.   The quality of service personnel
8.   The stage in the life cycle of the product

Strategic Service Personnel Management

Managing the personnel in the service department is the responsibility of the service manager. There is no separate service personnel management department even in large organisations. Therefore, the service executive must be a person of high calibre and talent. He needs to be well-trained in all aspects of service personnel management. Let us now study the important aspects of service personnel management.

Recruitment and selection   Selection of service department staff is a tough job. Identifying the people with right qualifications and talents is a challenging job for the organisation. The major sources of service department staff may be 1) internal promotions and transfers, 2) campus recruitment in technical training institutes, and 3) recommendations of the company's service staff. In the case of internal promotion and transfers, the advantages are many. The promoted employee will be a person well-known to the executives of the organisation. The employees suitability to the position can be easily judged. The important point is that the employee must agree to work in the service department. The service department offers lot of challenges to the people working there because each case reported will be a unique one and at times some of the cases may be challenging also. Those people who really love challenging tasks readily accept to take the service job. In the case of transfers, it is important to see that transfers are made with the consent of the employees concerned.

Campus recruitment in the technical training institutions offers a good scope for recruiting suitable hands for the service department. The faculty in these institutions consists of knowledgeable people and they know about the quality of their students very well. This is a reliable source of service staff. The company may also make enquiries with the people whose names have been furnished as references. The third important source of staff is the present employees of the organisation. This can be a reliable source because the recommending employee knows very well about the candidate provided the present employee is honest and trustworthy.

Training and orientation   The training needs of the new employees of the service department must be ascertained by the service executive. It is important to understand the kind of training required by the individual employees so that the right kind of training may be imparted to them. The training programme must be arranged at a suitable place. Sometimes it may be the service department itself. They may give the trainee on-the-job training. The service executive is the right person to determine the nature of training required by the new employees.

Orientation sessions must also be conducted in order to make them familiar to the new environment.

They need to be told in detail their role in the organisation and the avenues available for career growth must be explained to them by the senior employees of the service department who are entrusted with the job of handling the orientation sessions. But it is a pity to note that many organisations do not conduct orientation sessions. Even though management literature tells a lot on the need to hold orientation sessions, these organisations are not serious about them. A company aspiring for a high-class organisational culture must necessarily conduct orientation sessions without fail. Orientation sessions help the new employees to know about their place of work and the role they play in the organisation.

Service personnel compensation Service personnel may be classified as core staff, supporting staff, and helpers. The compensation may be fixed according to their position in the department. Most of the service personnel are employed by the authorised dealers who have their service stations. Usually the showrooms and service stations owned by these dealers are constructed under specific conditions insisted upon by the manufacturer. The layout, the policies to be followed by the dealers, and many other issues are covered in the agreement signed between the manufacturer and the dealer. The agreement also suggests the wage policy to be followed by the dealer in the case of the showrooms and the service stations. However, the requirements in respect of wage policy to be followed are not strictly insisted upon by the manufacturer.

It is essential that the core staff must be paid adequate wages because they are the core staff whose basic responsibility is to identify the part of the vehicle or the machine that requires servicing and to issue detailed instructions to the supporting staff about the work to be carried out in the vehicle or machine. They also prepare estimates for the work to be carried out. The service quality depends on the quality of the core staff. Sufficient supervision needs to be there to see that other staff members also work well in the service stations.

SUMMARY

* The American Express Customer Service Barometer released in July 2010 its findings on attitudes and preferences toward customer service. It is a survey conducted in India and eleven other countries to find out what the customers have in their mind while making purchases. As per the survey results, 82% of Indian consumers value good customer service the most while making a purchase.

* Strategic service management focuses on the long-term impact upon the customers by providing them a world class service which makes an indirect appeal to the customers' conscience which becomes satisfied by the way the service is provided. This kind of strategic service creates a mark in the minds of the customers, creates a feeling that the manufacturer is doing all the best possible to satisfy them, and leaves an impression in the customers about the quality of service offered by the manufacturer.

* The important elements of strategic service management are 1) strategic service knowledge management, 2) strategic service parts management, 3) strategic service price management, and 4) strategic service personnel management.

* Knowledge is a diverse stock of information and we must use the right information in the right place. The idea of knowledge management can be applied to strategic services management also successfully. Possession of adequate knowledge of service related issues is very much essential to the manufacturer.

* According to Joseph D. Patton, the objective of service parts management is to satisfy customers by providing necessary parts, at the user's location, for a reasonable price, in usable condition, at the proper time. This can be referred to as the five rights of parts: item, place, price, quality and time.

* Formulating the services pricing policy of the organisation is important in the sense that it decides the profitability of the organisation and the nature of customer relationship with the organisation.

* Managing the personnel in the service department is the responsibility of the service manager. There is no separate service personnel management department even in large organisations. Therefore, the service executive must be a person of high calibre and talent. The service executive needs to be well-trained in all aspects of service personnel management.

REVIEW QUESTIONS

1. Explain the need for effective services management.

2. What are the elements of strategic services management?

3. "The money spent on after-sales service is productive in the sense that the service offered to the customers for repairing the equipment makes the customer satisfied and also that the service done also brings business to the manufacturer." Do you agree? Give your arguments for agreeing or otherwise of the statement.

4. Discuss the importance of service parts management.

5. "The acid test begins when the customer begins using the product." Why is it called as an acid test? Explain your answer by giving real time examples.

6. Do you think possession of adequate knowledge of service related issues is very much essential to the manufacturer? Give valid reasons for your answer.

7. "The company must cash in on the service requirements of the customers." What do you mean by this statement? Substantiate your answer with greater explanation.

8. "It is essential that the core service staff must be paid adequate wages." Do you agree? Give reasons for your answer.

9. What is strategic service price management? Explain its need for an organisation.

10. Explain the important elements of strategic service personnel management.

REFERENCES

1. http://about.americanexpress.com/news/pr/2010/barometer.aspx

2. An article by The Boston Consulting Group titled *"Achieving excellence in after-sales services."* For more details see the website http://www.bcg.ru/documents/file28873.pdf

3. *Ibid.*

4. *Ibid.*

5. Patton, D. Joseph (1984). *"Service parts management." The International Society of Automation.* Research Triangle Park, North Carolina.

18

CUSTOMER RELATIONSHIP STRATEGIES

After reading this chapter, you will be able to

- *Recognise the need for effective customer relationship,*
- *Recognise the position of customer relationship management in today's business,*
- *Learn customer relationship creation process,*
- *Become knowledgeable about customer relationship strategies, and*
- *Know about customer relationship management software.*

KEY TERMS

- Customer database
- Information file
- Lifetime customer value
- Clickstream analysis
- Targeting
- One-to-one marketing
- Relationship programmes
- Corporate families
- Privacy issues
- Customer service
- Premises
- Strategic capabilities
- Loyalty programmes
- Customer letters
- Free service camps
- Customer feedback assessment
- Special events
- Personal visits
- CRM software
- Gap analysis

INTRODUCTION

"Customer is the Boss."

"Customer is the King."

"Customer is the God."

The tone rises as time changes. These statements are highly exaggerated ones which were the outbursts of people who wanted to give a boost to their employees in their relationship with their customers. They wanted to stress the significance of the customer. Of course the customer is the most significant person for a business organisation. No one can have a second opinion. It is the customer who decides the destiny of an organisation. Customers can work both ways. They can make the organisation's foundation strong enough to withstand several floors. At the same time, the customers have the power to demolish the same in no time. The question is what the customers have in mind. The ultimate task of the organisation is to create an excellent image about it in the minds of the customers. Organisations vie with each other to do this. Not everybody succeeds in this process. Executives with the right mindset and talent succeed in this process.

The story of CavinKare mentioned in Chapter 15 explains what an organisation can do to woo the customers. In fact, every successful organisation has a wonderful history of its own. Take the example of Reliance, TVS, Hero, WalMart, Ford, General Motors or Coca Cola. These people achieved excellence through hard work, the right mindset, and a focused purpose. They remain successful in their own fields of operation. Even though some of these giants had some problems due to some uncontrollable factors, they were able to come out successfully. Again, this is mainly due to their hard work, their mindset, and their focused purposes. All these factors collectively operate in the market and the ultimate result comes through the customer. A successful organisation can take pride for their success, but only privately. Explicit celebrations without due recognition for the customer will bring in negative results.

NEED FOR EFFECTIVE CUSTOMER RELATIONSHIP

The company may be a very large one having very high reputation. It may have billions of assets. It may be looked as the market leader in the industry circles. Or, it may be in possession of high-calibre human resource. All these can come from the consumer acceptance of the product. One may argue that there are many other factors to play in the success of a product. True. But it may not be always so. The recognised formula is that a company can succeed if it produces world class and flawless products, fixes modest prices, adopts effective sales promotional measures, has an excellent distribution network, and has a good after-sales-service network. This is okay. But still many companies which possessed all these claims to their credit failed miserably. The true reasons for the success of an organisation still remain unknown even though researchers ponder over them for decades. They are not able to come to a conclusion on this issue. While the causes of business failures are given specifically, the answer to the question of why and how a business succeeds still eludes many. The failure of AIWA in India is a clear case of its failure in adopting suitable customer strategy. Even though its sales jumped initially, it could not sustain the momentum.

A close relationship with the customer can make a big difference in the organisation's growth, other things being equal. We are living in the age of competition. If we take any industry, barring a few, we find cut-throat competition for capturing the market. Most of the products are in the buyer's market. The quality of most of the products is similar if not identical and they follow similar strategies. In this age of high competition for the customers, the need arises to find out new strategies to woo the customers. Customer relationship strategies can play a useful role in this environment. A satisfied customer is worth hundred prospective customers. The satisfied customer must be retained so that new customers will be introduced by him/her. If the satisfied customer happens to be an influential personality in an area, the task of the company becomes easier. An influential customer can bring in hundred new customers to our fold. If we are able to identify the leading customer in the area, then the job of the marketing executive will be made easy. A good customer relationship strategy can do this job. These influential people are also called as change agents.

CUSTOMER RELATIONSHIP MANAGEMENT TODAY

Few firms today are realising the potential from their often-considerable investments in customer relationship management (CRM). In part, this is because it is uncommon for management and staff to embrace CRM as a vision for how the business could be. Seen only as a means to generate more short-term sales, CRM can be little more than a means to efficiently interact with chosen customers with appropriate value propositions.[1]

CRM has still a long way to go. Companies must realise its importance in the growing competitive environment in the marketplace. Perhaps no company has yet achieved the full potential for CRM. Considering best practices from a number of firms suggest that opportunities remain for all organisations to achieve better results and deeper relationships with CRM.[2] Therefore, organisations must give the due recognition for CRM. When companies realise the importance of the customer, it is intriguing to note that they do not pay the attention and care it deserves. People need to know the link between CRM and their own success or the initiative might be seen as just another programme.

It is important to note that today CRM is gaining the favour from knowledgeable marketing executives the world over and it is expected that it will play the key role in deciding the destiny of the organisations. Organisations which are alive to this line of thought alone will be able to survive unless they possess extraordinary competitive advantages in the industry. The need to better understand customer behaviour and focus on those customers who can deliver long-term profits has changed how marketers view the world. Today, the tone of the conversation has changed from customer acquisition to retention. This requires a different mindset and a different and new set of tools.[3] In fact, customer relationship strategies are creating a revolution in the history of marketing. Indeed, this revolution in customer relationship management has been referred to as the new "mantra" of marketing.

Objectives of Customer Relationship

The objectives of customer relationship are apparent and simple. The ultimate objective of any organisation is to maximise sales. The question is how we do it. We can increase our sales merely by selling the product to people who ask for it. We may not know who is buying and who is not buying. We do not keep track of the buyers. They are just buyers. That's all. This type of sales increase need not sustain for a longer period. Many a times even without knowing or without caring who are buying our products, we may make a good amount of sales. But that type of business will not have sustainability. Such a business may not make customers loyal. In order to have a long-term growth of our business, we have to have customer relationship.

Plainly speaking, the objectives of customer relationship are three in number. Let us list them.

1. To create and sustain new customers
2. To sustain existing customers
3. To attract ex-customers to our fold

Let us have a brief discussion on these points.

Creation and sustenance of new customers   An ambitious businessman must strive hard to create new customers. This is the secret of business growth. The marketer's plan of action must revolve around this aim. Bringing a new man to our fold as a customer is a difficult job in today's competitive business arena. Companies are vying with each other to do this. A business which is successful in carrying out this task becomes successful in achieving its ultimate objectives as well. But the most important principle to be followed in this context is to adopt genuine means to capture the minds of the customers. This alone can help to make the customer loyal. Any message that contains untrue information or claims will boomerang and the company will be in trouble sooner or later. This principled approach helps to retain the customer forever.

The new customers will be happy that they have reached the right destination and will never think of going back. This is the right approach for any business.

Sustenance of existing customers   Nourishing existing customers is not tougher than creating new customers. The marketer must create new strategies acceptable to the existing customers. But, at the same time, it is important that the customers must never get the feeling that they are being cheated by the company through unethical practices. This will hurt the customer's feelings and the customer will never remain loyal any more. The existing customer must continue to remain satisfied with the services and products of the company. The marketer's specific objectives in this regard must be the following.

1.   To keep the customer more satisfied than ever before,
2.   To make genuine offers to the customer,
3.   To continue to offer useful new products,
4.   To maintain contacts with customers even after the sale through product performance enquiries, and
5.   To take steps to make them a member of the corporate family.

Wooing ex-customers   It is the toughest task before the marketer. The ex-customer might have left the corporate family due to some solid reasons. But as time is the best medicine that can cure many ills created by personal judgments, the marketer must take steps to contact ex-customers. These customers, by now, would have experienced a lot about the products available in the market. At some point of time, the customer could have come to the conclusion that the previous dealer had done a better job than many other dealers that the customer came across. This is the turning point for us. Before approaching the ex-customers, a reasonable amount of time must be given to the customer for *testing* the market. Sometimes the customers may come to us on their own. At other times, the marketer may have to take the initiative. In any case, a consumer-oriented organisation would get back all the *lost* customers sooner or later.

THE CUSTOMER RELATIONSHIP CREATION PROCESS

The customer relationship strategies may also be looked as a process consisting of a series of steps involved in making the company's efforts to make the relationship with the customer meaningful. Let us now study these steps in order to understand more fully the relevance of customer relationship in effective marketing.

Creating Customer Database

The first step in finding a good customer relationship strategy is the construction of a customer database or information file.[4] This is the foundation for any customer relationship activity. Complete particulars about the customers must be included in this file. But it is important to see that only relevant information is gathered from the customers because some may suspect the purpose of data collection and will hesitate to reveal information about them. It is also true that some of the customers may not be cooperative at all initially and will need repeated persuation. Ideally, the database should contain information about the following:

1. *Transactions*   This should include a complete purchase history with accompanying details like the place of purchase, the price paid, the offers made by the dealer, the nature of after-sales-service offered by the seller, the frequency of purchase, the mode of delivery of the product and some other points.

2. *Customer contacts*   The customer must be encouraged to provide contact details by the dealer. The customer must be told about the customer contact points so that they would do this job comfortably. The marketing executive must note the fact that these are not mandatory for the customer. In order to attract and encourage the customers to contribute necessary information, they must be ensured that the information will be useful to them as well. Details in this connection must be provided to them. The marketing executive must prove their sincerity by making courtesy calls to the customers' places.

3. *Descriptive information*   The customers must be encouraged to provide information like their family status, their occupation, and the like. Some of the customers may not feel comfortable to reveal their income particulars for personal reasons as some of them may earn very less and others a very high income. In both cases, it may be difficult to elicit information from the customers. This is for segmentation and other data analysis purposes.

4. *Response to marketing stimuli*   The customers must be asked about the kind of stimuli and their influence on them. However, this kind of information must be asked from a cooperating customer. This part of the information file should contain whether or not the customer responded to a direct marketing initiative, a sales contact, or any other direct contact.

Companies have traditionally used a variety of methods to construct their databases. Durable goods manufacturers utilise information from warranty cards for basic descriptive information. Unfortunately, response rates to warranty cards are in the 20–30% range leaving big gaps in the databases. Service businesses are normally in better shape since the nature of the product involves the kind of customer–company interaction that naturally leads to better data collection. For example, banks have been in the forefront of customer relationship activities for a number of years. Telecom industries (long distance, wireless, cable services) similarly have a large amount of customer information.

Companies such as Procter and Gamble and Unilever[5] selling frequently-purchased consumer products have greater problems constructing databases due to lack of systematic information about their millions of customers and the fact that they use intermediaries (i.e., supermarkets, drug stores) that prohibit direct contact. The challenge is to create opportunities for customer interaction and, therefore, data collection. This can be from running contests to encouraging customer visits to websites.

Database Analysis

Analysing the database of the customers is the next step in the process of customer relationship management. It has been the practice the world over to analyse the customer databases with the sole objective of defining the customer segments. A variety of multivariate statistical methods ranging such as cluster and discriminant analysis have been used to group together customers with similar behavioural patterns and descriptive data which are then used to develop different product offerings or direct marketing campaigns. Direct marketers have used such techniques for many years. Their goals are to target the most profitable prospects for catalogue mailings and to tailor the catalogues to different groups.

There is increased attention being paid to understanding each "row" of the database, that is, each customer and what he/she can deliver to the company in terms of profits. As a result, a new term, lifetime customer value (LCV), has been introduced into the lexicon of marketers. The idea is that each row/customer of the database should be analysed in terms of current and future profitability to the firm.[6]

Other kinds of data analyses besides the lifetime customer value are appropriate for customer relationship purposes. Marketing executives are interested in what products are often purchased together, often referred to as market basket analysis. Complementary products can then be displayed on the same physical page in a hard-copy catalogue or a virtual page on a website. A new kind of analysis born from the Internet is *clickstream analysis*. In this kind of data analysis, patterns of mouse "clicks" are examined from cyberstore visits and purchases in order to better understand and predict customer behaviour.[7] The goal is to increase "conversion" rates, the percentage of browsing customers to actual buyers.

Customer Selection

The marketer must select a good sample of customers from the list of customers. It is important to note that not all customers are willing to contribute information to the company. There are many reasons for this. Lethargy, fear of misuse, non-availability of time, and fear of frequent calls from the marketer are some of the reasons for the refusal of a majority of the customers for providing information about them. Therefore, the marketer must decide what category of customers must be selected for analysis. Of course, the main purposes of creating the customer base are to gather necessary information to formulate the marketing strategies of the organisation. One of the objectives is to properly segment the customers which would go a long way in formulating the marketing strategies.

The results from the analysis could be of various types. If segmentation-type analyses are performed on purchasing or related behaviour, the customers in the most sought after segments (e.g., highest purchasing rates, greatest brand loyalty) would normally be selected first. Other segments could also be chosen depending upon additional factors. For example, if the customers in the heaviest purchasing segment already purchase at a rate that implies further purchasing is unlikely, a second tier with more potential would also be attractive.

On what basis should these customer selection decisions be made? One approach would be to take the current profitability based on the above equation. An obvious problem is that by not accounting for a customer's possible growth in purchasing, you could be eliminating a potentially important customer. Customers with high LCV could be chosen; this does a better job incorporating potential purchases. However, these are difficult to predict and you could include a large number of unprofitable customers in the selected group. No matter what criterion is employed, de-selected customers need to be chosen with care. Once driven away or ignored, unhappy customers can spread negative word of mouth quickly, particularly in today's Internet age.

Targeting the Customers

The next step is to target the existing as well as potential customers for creating a favourable image about the product and the organisation. It is also necessary to go back to the old and long-time customers and see that their grievances are found out and suitable remedial measures are taken. Mass marketing approaches such as television, radio, or print advertising are useful for generating awareness and achieving other communications objectives, but they are poorly-suited for customer relationship due to their impersonal nature. More conventional approaches for targeting selected customers include a portfolio of direct marketing methods such as telemarketing, direct mail, and, when the nature of the product is suitable, direct sales. Writers such as Peppers and Rogers[8] have urged companies to begin to dialogue with their customers through these targeted approaches rather than talking *at* customers with mass media.

In particular, the new mantra, "one-to-one" marketing, has come to mean using the Internet to facilitate individual relationship building with customers.[9] An extremely popular form of internet-based direct marketing is the use of personalised e-mails.

When this form of direct marketing first appeared, customers considered it no different than "junk" mail that they receive at home and treated it as such with quick hits on the delete button on the keyboard.

It pays more the organisation when the best customers are selected and targeted in order to see that the marketing efforts of the company are not in vain. Therefore, the marketer would like to concentrate on their best customers for a number of reasons. These reasons include the following.

1. The best customers are more likely to buy our products or services.
2. These customers are more profitable to serve over their lifetime.
3. They are less expensive to acquire in comparison to new customers.
4. In many cases the marketer has already established relationships with them.
5. They are a great channel for new business referrals that close.
6. The marketer's track record has proved that he/she can serve them with success.

Relationship Programmes

The marketers may organise useful customer relationship programmes to motivate them and retain them in their fold. But playing too much of the game would lead to negative results. Therefore, the marketer must exercise utmost care not to over-react to the customer's queries. While customer contact through direct e-mail offerings is a useful component of customer relationship, it is more of a technique for implementing the strategy than a programme itself. Relationships are not built and sustained with direct e-mails themselves but rather through the types of programmes that are available for which e-mail may be a delivery mechanism.

The overall goal of relationship programmes is to deliver a higher level of customer satisfaction than competing firms deliver. There has been a large volume of research in this area.[10] From this research, managers today realise that customers match realisations and expectations of product performance, and that it is critical for them to deliver such products which would offer them a high level of satisfaction. In addition, research has shown that there is a strong, positive relationship between customer satisfaction and profits.[11]

Corporate Families

One of the major uses of the web for both online and offline businesses is to build a network of customers for exchanging product-related information and to create relationships between the customers and the company or brand. These networks and relationships are called *families*. The goal is to take a prospective relationship with a product and turn it into something more personal. In this way, the manager can build an environment which makes it more difficult for the customer to leave the "family" of other people who also purchase from the company. The marketer can take the initiative to build corporate families in which the customers of a particular company can become members. It is not that this corporate family must exchange information about our company's product alone. The members of a family are free to exchange information on any product with which they are concerned. This would help to tighten the bond with the customers.

Privacy Issues

It is necessary that the customers must be given a total assurance that their information will never be misused. Many organisations sell the information to other organisations which is a total breach of trust. Revealing the information to other companies is an unforgivable act. Therefore, it is the duty of the companies to keep up the promise made to the customers at the time of collecting information from them.

The customer relationship system depends upon a database of customer information and analysis of that data for more effective targeting of marketing communications and relationship-building activities. There is an obvious trade-off between the ability of companies to better deliver customised products and services and the amount of information necessary to enable this delivery. Particularly with the popularity of the internet, many consumers and advocacy groups are concerned about the amount of personal information that is contained in databases and how it is being used.

Customer Service

Customer service is vital in making a customer become the company's loyal customer. There are two types of customer service. The first is the reactive service. It is a service where the customer has a problem with the product like product failure, and product exchange. The second is the proactive service. Proactive service is required in a situation where the manager has decided not to wait for customers to contact the firm but to rather be aggressive in establishing a dialogue with customers prior to complaining or other behaviour sparking a reactive solution. If a customer has purchased the product after a great amount of argument and suspicion and does so only because of the assurance given by the marketer, proactive service can play a good role. For important customers, the company can make enquiries about the performance of the product at regular intervals. The topic of service management has been discussed in Chapter 17.

CUSTOMER RELATIONSHIP STRATEGIES

A strategy is one which is used to accomplish a given goal. It contains a clear set of activities to be performed in order to achieve these goals. It is an action plan. Therefore, strategies are vital for the success of the marketing and other efforts of an organisation. Strategies are formulated by experts who are very familiar to the specific situation in which the problem exists. But good strategies never fail. If they fail, the reason may be beyond the control of the marketer or the organisation. Strategies must be formulated after a great amount of application of mind in the right direction with specific goal. It is a must to frame a set of probabilities that may appear as we begin to execute the strategies. These may also be called as premises. Premises are the assumptions which are expected to operate in the environment. Therefore, we have to formulate our strategy taking into account these premises.

According to Ian Gordon,[12] there are four main customer relationship strategic capabilities:

i. *Technology*   The technology that supports customer relationship.

ii. *People*   The skills, abilities and attitudes of the people who manage customers.

iii. *Process*   The processes companies use to access and interact with their customers in the pursuit of new value and mutual satisfaction.

iv. *Knowledge and insight*   The approaches the company uses to add value to customer data so that they acquire the knowledge and insight needed to deepen the relationships that matter.

These strategic capabilities are to be used in its right perspective and while doing so, they will give an edge for the organisation in meeting customer requirements perfectly.

Loyalty Programmes

Loyalty programmes provide rewards to customers for repeat purchase. A recent McKinsey study[11] found that about half of the ten largest retailers in the US in each of the top seven sectors (category killers, department stores, drug stores, gasoline, grocery, mass merchandisers, specialty apparel) have such programmes with similar findings in the UK. The study also identified the three leading problems with these programmes: they are expensive, mistakes can be difficult to correct as customers see the company as taking away benefits, and, perhaps most importantly, there are large questions about whether they work to increase loyalty or average spending behaviour. A problem that can be added to this list is that due to the ubiquity of these programmes, it is increasingly difficult to gain competitive advantage.

While the goals and design of each programme can differ widely, James Cigliano, Margaret Georgiadis, Susan Whalley and Darren Pleasance[14] believe retailers can take four steps so their loyalty programs deliver value to the bottom line:

Step 1   Set realistic and focused programmer goals

Step 2   Make rigorous program design trade-offs to achieve goals

Step 3   Leverage distinctive assets to make the economics work

Step 4   Execute skillfully and persistently to sustain participation and impact.

Let us now discuss important tools that may be used to enhance customer loyalty.

Customer letters   Customer letters to the organisation is a strategy to keep alive the contacts with the customers. As all the letters can carry a small gift to the customers who participate in the programme. Letters which are special may be given special rewards, when they carry useful points for the organisation.

Free service camps   Companies are organising free service camps at selected locations to assist the customers by repairing their equipment and here a special discount may be granted to the spares that may have to be used in the equipment. This will draw a large number of customers because customers are longing for such an opportunity which they consider as golden.

Customer feedback assessment   The customer feedbacks received can guide the marketer to the right way of improving the customer relationship. This would help to ascertain the gap between the organisation and the customers. This may be called as *gap analysis*. The opinions of the customers supply necessary information to the marketer who can act upon them after a thorough study.

Organising special events   Organising special mega events exclusively for the customers at concessional prices can work well for improving the customer relationship which would, in turn, lead to greater customer loyalty.

Personal visits   Top marketing executives must develop a habit of visiting key customers and interacting with them. This would make them happy and the bond will be strengthened. The marketer may also invite the customers to the organisation so that the customers would see for themselves the working of the organisation. The customer will come to know of the organisational culture prevalent there and will get an opportunity to exchange opinions with the marketer.

Direct web page contacts   It is important to provide custom web pages for important customers, sharing information in both directions on pricing, order status and tracking, quality, returned goods, product design, end-user feedback, etc. Customers must be satisfied fully with minimal direct contact by field salespersons or customer-service people.

CUSTOMER RELATIONSHIP MANAGEMENT SOFTWARE

Nowadays, CRM software has become very common. Many software companies are having their software and if needed, they make customised software for specific requirements. Managing contacts with the customers via outlook or other email and calendar equipped tool can certainly help the business, but it will most likely do nothing to personalise the organisation's communication with every client or keep track of the services or products the company offers. To maintain cohesive records of all client interactions for business one may have to consider customer relationship management software.

For any business trying to market products or services, good CRM software can be a critical element in increasing sales. The relationship of a business to its customers is something that must be maintained and monitored continuously and CRM software provides the means to do that. In fact, complete CRM software consists of many systems that are expensive and complicated to install, but most companies don't need anything that complicated. Most businesses can go with a less-complete system of CRM software that provides most of the same functions at less expense. A CRM software system can maximise sales and it can also help to monitor customers and their information. A CRM software system can be complicated and expensive, but you can find a system that is not only cost-effective, but also easy to use and implement into your company.

CRM software spans the enterprise with salesforce automation, marketing automation, help desk, customer service, knowledge management, order processing, defect tracking, project management and more. It can carry out the following tasks.

- Increase revenue and sales productivity
- Improve marketing efficiency and targeting
- Provide world-class customer service
- Provide CRM portals for self-service, chat, forums
- Manage sales orders, help desk, and engineering

SUMMARY

- A close relationship with the customer can make a big difference in the organisation's growth, other things being equal. We are living in the age of competition. If we take any industry, barring a few, we find cut-throat competition for capturing the market.

- Most of the products today are in the buyer's market. The quality of most of the products is similar if not identical and they follow similar strategies. In this age of high competition for the customers, the need arises to find out new strategies to woo the customers. Customer relationship strategies can play a useful role in this environment.

* Today, CRM is gaining the favour from knowledgeable marketing executives the world over and it is expected that it will play the key role in deciding the destiny of the organisations. Organisations which are alive to this line of thought alone will be able to survive unless they possess extraordinary competitive advantages in the industry.

* The objectives of customer relationship are three in number. They are 1) to create and sustain new customers, 2) to sustain existing customers, and 3) to attract ex-customers to our fold.

* The customer relationship strategies may also be looked as a process consisting of a series of steps involved in making the company's efforts to make the relationship with the customer meaningful. The steps in the process include creating customer database, database analysis, customer selection, targeting the customers, organising relationship programmes, creating corporate families, and customer service.

* Many customer relationship strategies are available. One of them is loyalty programmes. Some of the tools to enhance customer loyalty are customer letters, free service camps, customer feedback assessment, organising special events, personal visits, and direct webpage contacts.

REVIEW QUESTIONS

1. "While the causes of business failures are given specifically, the answer to the question of why and how a business succeeds still eludes many." Do you agree? Give reasons for your viewpoint.

2. Explain the need for effective customer relationship.

3. Explain the status of customer relationship management today.

4. Make a probe into the objectives of customer relationship. Explain how each objective is related to it.

5. Explain the process of creating an excellent customer relationship.

6. Discuss the various types of customer relationship programmes and strategies that may be used to promote customer relationship.

7. What is customer relationship management software? What kinds of tasks it can undertake?

8. Explain the effectiveness of customer service camps. Are these camps worthy in attaining their obiectives?

9. What is gap analysis? How will you undertake a gap analysis? Explain the steps.

REFERENCES

1. Gordon, Ian. (2002). "Best practices: Customer relationship management." *Ivey Business Journal*. p. 5.

2. *Ibid.*

3. Winer, Russell S. of Haas School of Business, University of California at Berkeley in a paper titled Customer *Relationship Management: A Framework, Research Directions, and the Future.* April 2001.

4. See, for example, Rashi Glazer, "Winning in smart markets." *Sloan Management Review*, Summer, 1999, pp.59–69.

5. Winer, Russell S. of Haas School of Business, University of California at Berkeley in a paper titled *Customer Relationship Management: A Framework, Research Directions, and the Future.* April 2001.

6. Winer, Russell S. of Haas School of Business, University of California at Berkeley in a paper titled *Customer Relationship Management: A Framework, Research Directions, and the Future.* April 2001. p. 8.

7. Wendy, W. Moe and Peter, S. Fader describe clickstream analysis more completely in their paper, "Uncovering Patterns in Cybershopping," published in *California Management Review*, Summer 2001.

8. Don Peppers and Martha Rogers, *The One-to-One Future*, (New York: Doubleday, 1993), Ch. 4.

9. There is some disagreement about how successful one-to-one on the Internet has been. For a perspective on the negative side, see Susan Kuchinskas, "One-to-(N)one?" *Business* 2.0, September 12, 2000, pp.141–8.

10. Richard L. Oliver, *Satisfaction: A Behavioral Perspective on the Consumer*, (Boston, MA: Irwin McGraw-Hill, 1997), and Valarie A. Zeithaml and Mary Jo Bitner, *Services Marketing*, (Boston, MA: Irwin McGraw-Hill, 2000) are good examples.

11. Eugene, W. Anderson, Claes Fornell and Donald, R. Lehmann. "Customer satisfaction, market share, and profitability." *Journal of Marketing.* pp. 53–66.

12. Gordon, Ian.(2002). "Best practices: Customer relationship management." *Ivey Business Journal.* p. 2.

13. James Cigliano, Margaret Georgiadis, Susan Whalley and Darren. (2002). *The Price of Loyalty. McKinsey Quarterly.* No. 4.

14. *Ibid.*

INDEX